Mastering VMware Horizon 7

Second Edition

Learn advanced desktop virtualization techniques and strategies and dive deeper into VMware Horizon 7, take responsibility for optimizing your end user experience

Peter von Oven

Barry Coombs

BIRMINGHAM - MUMBAI

Mastering VMware Horizon 7

Second Edition

First published: March 2015

Second edition: October 2016

Production reference: 2061016

Published by Packt Publishing Ltd.

Livery Place

35 Livery Street

Birmingham B3 2PB, UK.

ISBN 978-1-78646-639-6

www.packtpub.com

Credits

Authors

Peter von Oven
Barry Coombs

Reviewer

Mario Russo

Commissioning Editor

Kartikey Pandey

Acquisition Editor

Namrata Patil

Content Development Editor

Onkar Wani

Technical Editor

Shivani Mistry

Copy Editor

Safis Editing

Project Coordinator

Ulhas Kambali

Proofreader

Safis Editing

Indexer

Aishwarya Gangawane

Production Coordinator

Nilesh Mohite

Cover Work

Nilesh Mohite

Foreword

For the better part of two decades modern IT administrators benefited from a fairly predictable progression of more powerful, yet cheaper technology at their disposal to provision to users to keep them happy and productive in their daily jobs.

While powerful and responsible for where we are today - one facet lingers today as a penalty we all must contend with. This is the issue of "scale". Scale should be thought of as the RATIO of users, devices, applications per admin - not simply the sheer size of any deployment. For therein lies the problem we all continue to try to solve: How to take this remnant of the power of Moore's Law and the proliferation of cheap, powerful Windows Workspaces and reign it back in.

Virtualization ushers in a completely new way to think about both the process and architecture of deploying Windows Workspaces to end users. No longer do we need to think of a workspace as a static stack of hardware, OS, software, and user environment. Furthermore - we don't necessarily need to continue to have a one to one relationship with every one of them.

Instead we use the power of virtualization, centralization, and abstraction to allow us to assemble workspaces on demand - combing new OS's, applications, security policies, and many more as needed, where needed, and how they are needed.

Solutions like VMware Horizon, Citrix XenDesktop, or Amazon Workspaces should be considered for any organization looking to get scale to begin to work for them, instead of against them. And much like the foundational platforms of the past such as Compaq, HP, Dell, and others - an ecosystem has emerged to cater to a host of operational, security, and application lifecycle management requirements.

In this book you will begin or perfect your journey to a new way to think about the provisioning, deployment, and management of next-generation Windows Workspaces.

J. Tyler Rohrer

Co-Founder Liquidware Labs

About the Authors

Peter von Oven is an experienced technical consultant and has spent the past 20 years of his IT career working with customers and partners in designing technology solutions aimed at delivering true business value. During his career, Peter has been involved in numerous large-scale enterprise projects and deployments and has presented at key IT events, such as VMworld, IP EXPO, and various VMUGs and CCUG events across the UK. He has also worked in senior presales roles and presales management roles for some of the giants of IT, such as Fujitsu, HP, Citrix, and VMware, and has been awarded VMware vExpert for 2015 and 2016.

Over the past 12 years and more, Peter has focused his skills and experience by specializing in the desktop and application virtualization market and today works as toe UK Pre Sales Director for the market-leading desktop transformation specialists, Liquidware Labs.

Peter got his first taste for writing when assisting with some of the chapters in the book Building End-User Computing Solutions with VMware View, which then lead to five other Packt titles, VMware Horizon Mirage Essentials, VMware Horizon Workspace Essentials, co-written with Peter Bjork and Joel Lindberg, VMware Horizon View Essentials, Mastering VMware Horizon 6, co-written with Barry Coombs, and Learning VMware App Volumes.

There are a few people I want to thank for the continued and ongoing support they have given me during the writing of this book. First, and most importantly, I would like to thank my wife and daughters for putting up with me while I spend many weekends and evenings writing – I couldn't do it without their support.

This book wouldn't have happened if I hadn't had the support from some of the key vendors in the EUC space. Firstly, I would like to thank the team at Tintri (Mark Young and Claire Randall) for the loan of the Tintri T820 storage array that enabled me to not only build out the example labs, but to also really understand how storage impacts a VDI solution.

I would also like to thank friend and ex-colleague Steve Horne for his expertise and knowledge in helping with how to define and approach any desktop or VDI transformation project, and of course thanks to my co-author Barry Coombs for helping with the original content.

Finally, a big thank you to the Packt Publishing team again, for giving me the opportunity to write this book.

Barry Coombs is the Operations and Pre Sales Director for ComputerWorld by day and an avid Blogger following everything to do with the virtualisation, storage and cloud industries.

Barry's responsibilities range from identifying new technologies and architecting solutions for customers to speaking and hosting customer focused events surrounding virtualisation, end user computing, storage and cloud computing. Barry blogs at VirtualisedReality.com and DefineTomorrow.co.uk and is co-host of the EUCPodcast.com podcast.

Outside of work Barry is a proud father and husband who enjoys spending time with his family, cycling (Although needs to find more time), photography and yet again more tech!

Barry enjoys talking about technology and sharing his findings with others in the community. Barry was awarded VMware's vExpert award for contributions to the VMware Community in 2010 through to 2016 Barry can usually be found on twitter (@VirtualisedReal) chatting about virtualisation and technology in general.

This is Barry's third book on end-user computing technologies, after previously being a co-author for *Building End-User Computing Solutions with VMware View* in 2012, and *Mastering VMware Horizon 6* in 2015.

> *I would like to thank Peter for his hard work updating this book to the latest version and to my wife Laura and daughter Olivia who support me in everything I do.*

About the Reviewer

Mario Russo has worked as an IT Architect, a Senior Technical VMware Trainer, and in the pre-sales department. He has also worked on VMware Technology since 2004.

In 2005, he worked for IBM on the First Large Project Consolidation for Telecom Italia on the Virtual VMware Esx 2.5.1 platform in Italy with Physical to Virtual (P2V) tool.

In 2007, he conducted a drafting course and training for BancoPosta, Italy; and project disaster and recovery (DR Open) for IBM and EMC.

In 2008, he worked for the Project Speed Up Consolidation BNP and the migration P2V on VI3 infrastructure at BNP Cardif Insurance.

In 2014 Customize Dashboard and Tuning Smart Alert vCOPs 5.7 POSTECOM Italy Rm

He is a VCI Certified Instructor 2s Level of VMware and is certified VCAP5-DCA , VCP3-4 , VCP5-DV VCP5-DT ,VCP-Cloud – NPP Nutanix – ZCP Zerto – Veeam VTSP – VCE Certified Converged Infrastructure Associate (VCE-CIA) – AWS Solutions Architect Associate Badge – MCSE Security – MCSA Messaging – NSX Network Virtualization Expert.

He is the owner of Business to Virtual, which specializes in virtualization solutions.

He was also the technical reviewer of the book, *Implementing VMware Horizon View 5.2*, *Implementing Implementing VMware vCenter Server, Troubleshooting vSphere Storage, VMware Horizon View 5.3 Design Patterns and Best Practices* at Packt Publishing, and *Instant Getting Started with VMware Fusion , Implementing VMware vCenter Server , VMware vSphere Security Cookbook , Mastering vRealize Operations Manager , Getting Started with VMware Virtual SAN , Implementing VMware Horizon 7 - Second Edition*.

I would like to thank my wife Lina and my daughter Gaia. They're my strength.

www.PacktPub.com

For support files and downloads related to your book, please visit `www.PacktPub.com`.

Did you know that Packt offers eBook versions of every book published, with PDF and ePub files available? You can upgrade to the eBook version at `www.PacktPub.com` and as a print book customer, you are entitled to a discount on the eBook copy. Get in touch with us at `service@packtpub.com` for more details.

At `www.PacktPub.com`, you can also read a collection of free technical articles, sign up for a range of free newsletters and receive exclusive discounts and offers on Packt books and eBooks.

`https://www.packtpub.com/mapt`

Get the most in-demand software skills with Mapt. Mapt gives you full access to all Packt books and video courses, as well as industry-leading tools to help you plan your personal development and advance your career.

Why subscribe?

- Fully searchable across every book published by Packt
- Copy and paste, print, and bookmark content
- On demand and accessible via a web browser

Table of Contents

Preface

VMware Horizon View is the platform to deliver centralized, virtual desktop machines hosted on a server running a hypervisor, and located in a data center. The end user then connects remotely to their virtual desktop machine from their endpoint device such as a Windows laptop, Apple Mac, or tablet device.

This technology was first introduced by VMware in 2002, and has developed and matured to become the mainstream technology that we know today as Virtual Desktop Infrastructure (VDI).

VDI provides users the freedom to work in a way that suits them, by freeing them from the restrictions of not having to be in the office, but also allowing them the choice of device they use making them more productive, and ultimately your business more agile.

From an IT administrator's perspective, it allows you to centrally manage your desktop environment, from being able to manage desktop images, to the ease of adding and removing user entitlements, all controlled from a single management console.

VMware Horizon 7 and Horizon View version 7.0.2 is VMware's latest virtual desktop solution, designed to centralize and virtualize your desktop environment using the market leading virtualization features and technology within VMware's Software Defined Data Center (SDDC) portfolio.

Horizon View 7 builds upon this technology platform, and today goes far beyond just VDI in delivering a rich user experience, enabling BYOD, flexible working, enhanced security, application delivery, and end-to-end management.

Delivering an end user experience requires a different approach from other infrastructure-based initiatives, and getting this right is the key for a project to have a successful outcome, and this book will show you how to succeed.

What this book covers

Chapter 1, *Introduction to VDI and VMware Horizon 7*, this chapter covers an introduction to VDI, explaining what it is, and how it compares with other VDI type technologies. We will then cover a brief history of the VMware VDI story, followed by an overview of the latest solution.

Chapter 2, *An Overview of Horizon View Architecture and Components*, will introduce you to the architectural components that make up the core VMware Horizon solution, concentrating on the virtual desktop elements of Horizon View Standard and the functionality of brokering virtual desktop machines.

Chapter 3, *Design and Deployment Considerations*, will introduce you to design and deployment techniques to take into consideration when undertaking your VMware Horizon project. We will discuss techniques to prove the technology and understanding how it will work inside your business, methods to assess your user's existing workload and how to use this information to help design your VMware Horizon Solution.

Chapter 4, *Installing and Configuring Horizon View*, will cover the installation process of the core Horizon View components, such as the Connection Server, Security Server, Replica Server, Enrollment Server, as well as the Cloud Pod Architecture feature. Following the installation, we will start to configure the base elements of a Horizon View installation.

Chapter 5, *Securing Horizon View with SSL Certificates and True SSO*, covers the aspect of VMware Horizon View, and in particular, how we deliver secure communication to the end user client, and also the different infrastructure components within the data center. The first half of this chapter will start with an overview of what an SSL certificate is, and then how to create and issue a certificate before configuring Horizon View to use it. In the second half of the chapter we will look at configuring the VMware True SSO feature.

Chapter 6, *Building and Optimizing the Virtual Desktop OS*, covers how to create and configure the virtual desktop machines after building the Horizon View infrastructure and its components, and then build the desktop operating system on them, configuring it so that it is running at its optimum performance level to run in a virtual environment.

Chapter 7, *Managing and Configuring Desktop Pools*, covers how Horizon View uses the concept of desktop pools to create a collection of virtual desktop machines for specific use cases, which in turn are allocated to the end users. In this chapter, we will look at the process to configure the different types of desktop pools.

Chapter 8, *Delivering Remote Applications with View Hosted Apps*, dives deeper into the key feature of Horizon Advanced Edition, and looks at how Horizon View publishes an application directly into the Horizon View Client, without the need of having to launch a full virtual desktop machine. We will walk through the installation and configuration process to get our first set of Horizon View published applications available to the end users.

Chapter 9, *Delivering Session-Based Desktops with Horizon View*, covers the other half of View's remoting capabilities and looks at how Horizon View can deliver session-based desktops from a Microsoft RDSH infrastructure.

`Chapter 10`, *Horizon View Client Options*, covers how the View Client is used to receive and display the virtual desktops and applications on the end user's device. In this chapter, we will look at the options for the View Client, both hardware and software, and discuss the various options and why you would choose one method over another.

`Chapter 11`, *Upgrading to a New Version of Horizon View*, covers all the things you need to consider before upgrading and will then take you through the upgrade process. This chapter is designed for those that are currently running a previous version of Horizon View and are looking to upgrade to the latest version.

`Chapter 12`, *Troubleshooting Tips*, covers some troubleshooting techniques and methods for use within Horizon View rather than going through a list of problems and issues.

`Online Chapter`, *Fine-Tuning the End-User Experience*, available at `https://www.packtpub.c om/sites/default/files/downloads/5657_FineTuningtheEndUserExperience.pdf`, covers one of the key tasks in building the best user experience possible, which is to start fine-tuning the performance and experience for the end user's session with their virtual desktop machine. In this chapter, we will look at the tuning techniques and the pre-built Group Policy objects that can be applied to create that experience.

`Online Chapter`, *Managing User Environments in Virtual Desktop Infrastructure*, available at `https://www.packtpub.com/sites/default/files/downloads/5657_ManagingUserEnvir onmentsinVirtualDesktopInfrastructure.pdf`, introduces you to Horizon View Persona Management, what it is, and why you would want to deploy it. We will then examine how it is driven by Standard Active Directory Group Policy finishing with an in depth look at the policies available. The second part of this chapter introduces you to VMware UEM and how to get up and running.

What you need for this book

To get the most out of this book, you should have some experience of working as a desktop administrator with skills and knowledge around building and designing Microsoft Windows-based desktop environments. You should also be familiar with the VMware vSphere platform (ESXi and vCenter Server) and be comfortable with building and configuring virtual machines as well as configuring storage and networking for use in a virtual infrastructure. Throughout this book, you have the opportunity to follow step-by-step practical guides in deploying Horizon View in an example lab environment. If you want to work through the practical examples, you will need the following software:

- VMware Horizon View Version 7, 7.0.1, or 7.0.2
- vSphere for Desktop (ESXi and vCenter Server 6)

You can download a trial copy of Horizon View 7 from the following link:

```
https://my.vmware.com/web/vmware/info/slug/desktop_end_user_computing/vmware
_horizon/7_
```

You will also need the following software to build virtual machines and deploy applications:

- Microsoft Windows Server 2012 R2 64-bit
- Microsoft Windows 7 Professional 32-bit or 64-bit
- Microsoft Windows 10
- Microsoft SQL Express 2012
- Microsoft Office 2016

Who this book is for

If you are a desktop administrator or part of a project team looking at deploying a virtual desktop and/or application delivery solution, or take advantage of some of the latest features, then this book is perfect for you and your ideal companion in helping to deploy a solution to centrally manage and virtualize your desktop estate using Horizon View 7.

You will need to have some experience in desktop management using the Microsoft Windows desktop and server operating systems, and general Windows applications, as well as be familiar with the Active Directory, SQL, and VMware vSphere infrastructure (ESXi and vCenter Server) technology.

Conventions

In this book, you will find a number of text styles that distinguish between different kinds of information. Here are some examples of these styles and an explanation of their meaning.

Code words in text, database table names, folder names, filenames, file extensions, pathnames, dummy URLs, user input, and Twitter handles are shown as follows: "We can include other contexts through the use of the include directive."

Any command-line input or output is written as follows:

```
certutil -setreg DBFlags +DBFLAGS_ENABLEVOLATILEREQUESTS
```

New terms and **important words** are shown in bold. Words that you see on the screen, for example, in menus or dialog boxes, appear in the text like this: "Click the **OK** button when you are ready to create the snapshot"

 Warnings or important notes appear in a box like this.

 Tips and tricks appear like this.

Reader feedback

Feedback from our readers is always welcome. Let us know what you think about this book—what you liked or disliked. Reader feedback is important for us as it helps us develop titles that you will really get the most out of.

To send us general feedback, simply e-mail feedback@packtpub.com, and mention the book's title in the subject of your message.

If there is a topic that you have expertise in and you are interested in either writing or contributing to a book, see our author guide at www.packtpub.com/authors.

Customer support

Now that you are the proud owner of a Packt book, we have a number of things to help you to get the most from your purchase.

Downloading the color images of this book

We also provide you with a PDF file that has color images of the screenshots/diagrams used in this book. The color images will help you better understand the changes in the output. You can download this file from `https://www.packtpub.com/sites/default/files/down loads/MasteringVMwareHorizon7SecondEdition_ColorImages.pdf`.

Errata

Although we have taken every care to ensure the accuracy of our content, mistakes do happen. If you find a mistake in one of our books—maybe a mistake in the text or the code—we would be grateful if you could report this to us. By doing so, you can save other readers from frustration and help us improve subsequent versions of this book. If you find any errata, please report them by visiting `http://www.packtpub.com/submit-errata`, selecting your book, clicking on the **Errata Submission Form** link, and entering the details of your errata. Once your errata are verified, your submission will be accepted and the errata will be uploaded to our website or added to any list of existing errata under the Errata section of that title.

To view the previously submitted errata, go to `https://www.packtpub.com/books/conten t/support` and enter the name of the book in the search field. The required information will appear under the **Errata** section.

Piracy

Piracy of copyrighted material on the Internet is an ongoing problem across all media. At Packt, we take the protection of our copyright and licenses very seriously. If you come across any illegal copies of our works in any form on the Internet, please provide us with the location address or website name immediately so that we can pursue a remedy.

Please contact us at `copyright@packtpub.com` with a link to the suspected pirated material.

We appreciate your help in protecting our authors and our ability to bring you valuable content.

Questions

If you have a problem with any aspect of this book, you can contact us at `questions@packtpub.com`, and we will do our best to address the problem.

1
Introduction to VDI and VMware Horizon 7

In this first chapter, we are going to discuss the subject of what VDI actually is, and then discuss the specifics of how that relates to **VMware Horizon 7**.

VMware Horizon 7 is the latest release, and the foundation of VMware's **End User Computing** (EUC) solution for desktops. VMware first entered the VDI market around 14 years ago, when they showed the concept of virtualizing a desktop operating system, as the market for server virtualization was becoming more mature and a more prevalent technology.

By taking the same principles that were used in server virtualization and applying them to a desktop operating system, they were able to create a centrally-managed and deployed virtual desktop solution that would potentially lower the cost of desktop computing.

Before we get into discussing product specifics, let's define what we mean when we talk about **Virtual Desktop Infrastructure** (VDI), and then take a brief stroll down memory lane and look at where and how it all started.

What is VDI?

When we talk about **Virtual Desktop Infrastructure**, (**VDI**) as it's more commonly referred to, we are typically describing a solution whereby the desktop operating system is hosted as a virtual machine running on a **hypervisor**, which in turn is hosted on a server that is part of the data center server infrastructure.

This type of desktop virtualization is also sometimes referred to as a **Hosted Virtual Desktop (HVD)**.

The following diagram shows a high-level view of a typical virtual desktop infrastructure:

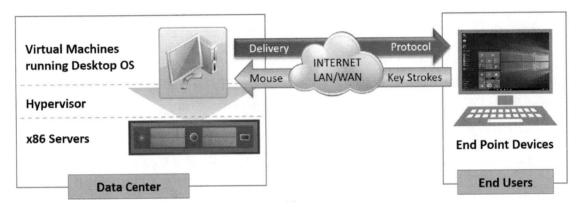

How does it work? A user connects remotely from their end-point device (a PC, thin client terminal, or mobile device) to a connection broker. The connection broker manages the available resources and connects the user to an appropriate virtual desktop. In the first VDI solutions that came to the market, there was no concept of a connection broker, and a user would connect directly to a virtual desktop machine.

Once connected, the screenshots of the virtual desktop machine are sent over the network to the endpoint device using an optimized delivery protocol, and the mouse movements and keystrokes are sent back to the virtual desktop machine via the same protocol.

No data leaves the data center, but instead, screenshot updates (pixel changes) are sent over the network. It's like watching a smart TV with the pictures broadcast on your television from the television studios, rather than the actors performing the show in your lounge, and you interact with the TV via the remote control.

From an architectural perspective, the virtual desktop typically gets built on demand, bringing together the different components that make up a full desktop. The operating system, user profile, desktop policies, and applications are all treated as separate, individual components, abstracted from the underlying machine, and then delivered back together to create a user's desktop experience.

This is often referred to as a composite desktop and is shown in the following diagram:

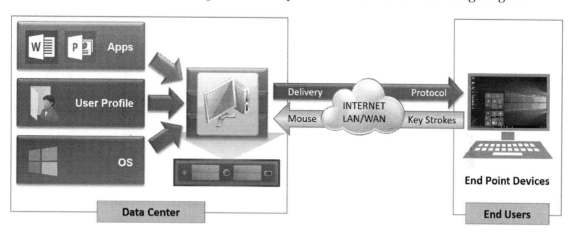

You should remember that virtual desktop machines need to be treated differently to physical desktops, and to reap all the benefits of virtual desktop machines, they should be built from the ground up and managed as virtual machines, using some of the components that have been specifically designed for the management of virtual desktop infrastructure, which we will discuss in the next chapter.

VDI sometimes get confused with **Server Based Computing (SBC)** or **Remote Desktop Services (RDS)**. So what are the differences between these technologies and VDI (if any)?

Let's take SBC/RDS first, as this is the technology that has probably been around the longest. In fact, you could probably trace it back as far as the 1950s, with the introduction of mainframe technology that was designed to deliver centralized computer power to run a set of applications, with users connecting to the applications using a green-screen-type terminal, which was more or less just a screen with a keyboard. This is shown in the following diagram:

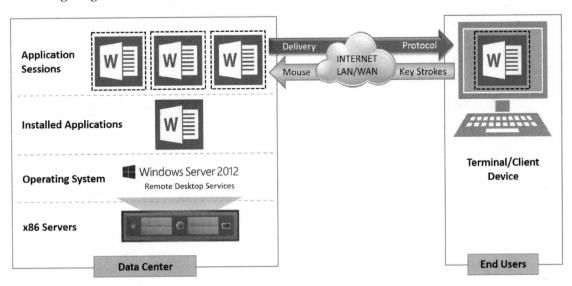

SBC or RDS is seemingly not that different to VDI in the way that it works. You are remotely connecting to an application that is running on server infrastructure hosted in a data center. But that's where the similarities end.

Let's take delivering applications first. The difference is that the applications are installed and run on the actual servers themselves, and are using a multi-user version of that application to create the individual user sessions.

A user would then connect to their own individual, separate, and protected session of that application, instead of connecting to an instance of the operating system containing the applications. As everything is running in the data center, users would connect to the session via a terminal or thin client. In fact, SBC is sometimes referred to as thin-client computing.

Using this same model, you can also deliver hosted desktop sessions in the same way. Instead of connecting to a separated, protected individual application session, the user now connects to a separated, protected individual session of the server's operating system. The one thing to note here is that the user is essentially running a server-based operating system session such as Windows Server 2012, rather than a Windows 10 desktop session.

The benefits of deploying VDI

By virtualizing your end-user desktop estate into a centrally-managed service, you can deliver benefits not only to the IT administrators but also to the users. Some of these are detailed as follows:

- **Security and compliance**: No data actually leaves the data center unless the IT department has specifically configured a policy to allow it, such as the ability to connect a USB pen drive. All that gets transmitted to the client devices are the screenshots of the virtual desktop, with keyboard and mouse interactions being sent back to the virtual desktop. It's a bit like having a remote control for your desktop.

- **Centralized and simplified management**: Centralized desktops equal centralized management. Now that the desktops are virtualized and hosted in the data center, it is much easier to perform tasks such as updating and patching an operating system or installing new applications. The virtual desktops are all created from a single gold image that is maintained and updated centrally, so you don't have to visit every physical machine. You can simply update the image, recreate the virtual desktops with a few mouse clicks, and hey presto, all users get the new updated version. You can also troubleshoot the environment more easily, without the need for a desk visit.

- **Flexibility and agility**: Having desktops hosted on a virtual platform allows you to scale up and scale down much more easily, without the need to necessarily purchase more physical desktops. You could use thin-client devices, or allow users to connect their own devices, as resources are now moved to the datacenter server infrastructure and accessed remotely. Environments can be spun up quickly and taken down just as easily, to accommodate seasonal workers or contractors working on specific projects. Users now have access to their virtual desktops wherever they are and no longer need to be in the office, at a desk, or have a PC to access their corporate desktop. They can continue to be productive even with inclement weather, traffic, or other events preventing them from getting to the office.

- **Mobile and BYOD from anywhere**: Virtual desktop clients enable mobile devices, tablets, and non-corporate-owned devices to connect securely to corporate desktops. Following the flexible working theme, users can now choose a device that suits them to access their corporate desktop. Whether it be a tablet, smartphone, or a non-Windows platform, users can still access their corporate desktop securely from remote locations.

- **Operational cost savings**: Implementing a virtual desktop environment and adopting operational best practices around image, patch, and profile management with centralized application deployment will result in saving **operational expenditure (OPEX)**, compared to traditional desktop management. **Capital expenditures (CAPEX)** are still required to support the virtual desktop environment. One of the things I hear all the time is that deploying VDI will reduce costs. The thing to point out is that yes, it will reduce OPEX, but typically, the CAPEX at the beginning of a VDI project will be higher as you deploy the infrastructure. Overall, though, the costs will reduce through savings in the management of the solution, and you will not be caught in the typical three-year PC refresh cycle trap.

A complete history of VMware and VDI

The concept of virtualizing Windows desktops has been around since as early as 2002, when VMware customers started virtualizing desktop workloads and hosting them on a VMware server and **ESX** servers in the data center. As there was no concept of a connection broker at that time, and neither was the phrase VDI really used, customers simply connected using the RDP protocol directly to a dedicated desktop virtual machine running Windows XP.

It wasn't until 2005 that VMware first showed the idea of having the concept of a connection broker. By demonstrating a prototype at VMworld, VDI entered the limelight, raising the profile of the technology. It was also at the same event that companies such as Propero showed their version of a connection broker. Propero would later become the Horizon View connection server.

In early 2006, VMware launched the VDI alliances program, with a number of technology vendors such as Citrix, HP, IBM, Sun, and Wyse Technology joining this program.

By 2007, the prototype connection broker was introduced to customers to help with development before it was given to the VMware product organization to productize it and turn it into a real product. The released product was called **Virtual Desktop Manager 1.0 (VDM)**. The year 2007 was a busy year, and it also saw VMware acquire Propero for $25 million, in order to accelerate their connection broker development, leading to the VMworld announcement and release of VDM 2.0 in January 2008.

After the release of VDM 2.0 in early 2008, a second release came at the end 2008, along with a new name: VMware View 3.0. This was also the year that Citrix entered the VDI market, releasing XenDesktop 2.0, following the acquisition of XenSource.

VMware View 4.0 was released in 2009 and was the first version to include the **PCoIP** protocol from Teradici. PCoIP delivered a much richer user experience than RDP.

In 2010, VMware View 4.5 was released with new features such as local mode (offline desktops), PCoIP enhancements, Windows 7 support, and the ability to tier storage. This was also the year that VMware talked publicly about the biggest VDI reference case to date with Bank of Tokyo Mitsubishi, who deployed 50,000 virtual desktop machines. You can read the case study at `http://tinyurl.com/oua28bh`.

The following year, 2011, VMware View 4.6 was released with two notable new features. First was the iPad client, which allows a user to connect to their virtual desktop session on an iPad, using the PCoIP protocol. The second new feature was the PCoIP Secure Gateway function for the View Security Server, which allows users to connect to their virtual desktop without needing a VPN connection.

Later the same year, View 5.0 was released with more new features, aimed at improving the end-user experience, the key one being the introduction of Persona Management which allowed a user's profile to be independent from the virtual desktop. When a user logs in via the same profile to any virtual desktop, their profile is delivered on demand. View 5.0 also introduced 3D graphic support using the latest vSphere 5.0 platform, as well as some major enhancements to the PCoIP protocol.

Although only a point release in May 2012, View 5.1 had a number of significant enhancements, especially around storage, with the introduction of the View Storage Accelerator, View Composer Array Integration, and the ability to scale the hosting infrastructure up to a 32-node cluster when using NFS storage. This version also added Radius two-factor authentication, improved USB device support, a standalone View Composer, and the ability to support profile migration from XP to Windows 7, as well as from physical desktops to virtual desktops, with Persona Management.

In March 2013, VMware View 5.2 was released, and to bring it in line with VMware's launch of the brand launch of Horizon (launched at the same time), it was renamed to Horizon View 5.2. In this release, there were a number of new features based on end-user experiences, such as support for unified communications with Microsoft Lync 2013, hardware-accelerated graphics with **Virtual Shared Graphics Acceleration** (**vSGA**), and Windows 8 support. One of the biggest updates came in the form of a feature pack that allowed a user to access their desktop in an HTML 5 browser using the VMware Blast protocol.

A second release, later in 2013, Horizon View 5.3, saw the introduction of **Virtual Dedicated Graphics Acceleration** (**vDGA**) which allowed a virtual desktop to have dedicated access to a GPU in the host. It is also the first release to support Windows Server 2008 R2 as the virtual desktop machine, meaning you can *skin* the operating system to look like a desktop. The main reason for this was that there is no **Service Provider License Agreement** (**SPLA**) for Windows 7, so the license agreement doesn't allow you to deploy Windows 7 as a virtual desktop until you purchase a Microsoft **Virtual Desktop Access** (**VDA**) license. In this model, you do not require a VDA license per user. The other advantage is that Windows Server 2008 Datacenter Edition allows you to have unlimited virtual machines. It's licensed on a per-CPU model. It's worth noting that we are running the Windows Server operating system as a replacement for the desktop operating system and not as a desktop session.

The final 5.x release arrived in March 2014, with Horizon View 5.3.1, which added support for **Virtual SAN** (**VSAN**).

Horizon 6.0 with View was released in June 2014, and the core feature of this version was the addition of View hosted applications, the first time VMware supported hosting applications and desktops using RDS. View 6.0 also introduced the Cloud Pod Architecture, the ability to span the View infrastructure across multiple data centers.

Also of note in the View 6.0 release was the removal of View Local Mode, which allowed users to download their virtual desktop to their local device. VMware suggested using Mirage to provide this functionality, although this ultimately became a product in its own right with Horizon FLEX.

As part of the 6.0 release, there were a couple of updates. The first was 6.0.1, which was release in September 2014 and added USB 3.0 support, extended printing, HTML access for Windows 8.x, and system tray redirection for hosted applications.

The final 6.0 release, 6.0.2, was released in December 2014. In this release, there was no update to the View infrastructure components such as the connection server, but it was instead billed as a new feature pack. It added new versions of the View Agent, HTML access, MMR redirection, and scanner redirection, to name but a few.

Support for NVIDIA GRID vGPU was the biggest of the new features in View 6.1, which was released in March 2015. Also in this release, VMware added support for IPV6, Virtual SAN 6.0, Virtual Volumes, and Windows Server 2012 R2 running as desktops.

In June 2015, the final 6.1 release, 6.1.1, was launched, adding features such as client drive redirection, support for Linux desktops, MMR for RDS desktops, and HTML support for hosted applications.

That now brings us up to the previous version of Horizon View, 6.2. Launched in September 2015, View 6.2 added support for Windows 10 desktops, Access Point integration, AMD vDGA, 4K monitors, and Virtual SAN 6.1, along with a number of enhancements to the Cloud Pod Architecture, admin console, and Linux desktops.

Following on from View 6.2, VMware also launched two maintenance releases; 6.2.1 was released in December 2015, and 6.2.2 was released in February 2016.

The timeline is shown pictorially in the following diagram:

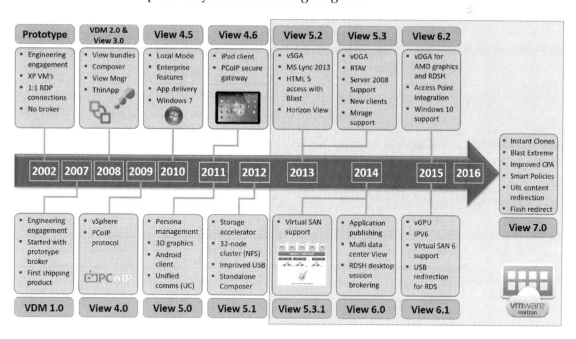

That brings us right up to date and to the latest version, VMware Horizon 7, with a few more enhancements being added with the 7.0.1 release on June 16 2016, and then version 7.0.2 being released on September 15 2016. In the next section, we will start to explore VMware Horizon 7 in more detail.

VMware Horizon 7

VMware Horizon 7 is the next generation of VMware's EUC vision and strategy to deliver desktop computing environments and publishing applications. In the previous sections, we have discussed some of the differences between VDI and SBC/RDS, and the advantages of the two solutions. However, with Horizon 7 you have the ability to deliver VDI desktops, published applications, and session-based desktops, all from one platform.

VMware Horizon 7 was released on March 22, 2016 and is available in four different editions. In the next section, we will cover these different product editions for Horizon 7.

The VMware Horizon 7 product editions

There are four different editions within the Horizon 7 portfolio, each with a different theme, which adds additional functionality and features.

The themes can be categorized as the following:

- Virtual Desktop Infrastructure Components (Standard)
- Application Delivery and Management (Advanced + Enterprise)
- Operations Management (Enterprise)
- Infrastructure and Hosting Components (All editions)

The four different editions are described in the following sections.

Horizon for Linux

As the name implies, Horizon for Linux allows you to centralize Linux-based virtual desktop machines, and deliver them with Horizon View. The big advantage of Linux desktops is that you can move away from other, costlier, operating systems, further reducing the cost of deployment.

Horizon for Linux supports a number of Linux distributions, including Ubuntu, RHEL, and CentOS, as well as taking advantage of some of the other features that View has to offer, such as NVIDIA graphics solutions.

Horizon Standard Edition

With **Horizon Standard Edition**, you have the core VDI solution and all of its features, as well as the ability to deliver session-based desktops. Included in this edition is the licensing for the hosting infrastructure: vSphere and vCenter for desktop. Also included is ThinApp, VMware's application virtualization/packaging solution, which allows you to extract applications from the underlying OS and deliver them back independently.

Horizon Advanced Edition

With **Horizon Advanced Edition**, the theme is all about application delivery and management. This is the first edition that includes application publishing as part of the View solution, allowing an application running on a Microsoft RDSH backend to be published via the View client using the PCoIP protocol, HTML, or VMware Blast. This feature means that a user can now just have an individual application delivered to their client device rather than on a full-blown desktop.

Also included in the Advanced Edition is a unified workspace solution that provides an application catalog with a brokering functionality. The catalog allows users to select applications from a catalog of entitled applications, which then brokers ThinApp packages, SaaS-based applications, XenApp published applications, and Microsoft Office 365.

The Advanced Edition also includes VMware Mirage, to deliver centralized image management for physical desktops. For a detailed overview of VMware Mirage, you can read *VMware Horizon Mirage Essentials, Peter von Oven, Packt*.

Horizon Enterprise Edition

Horizon Enterprise Edition builds on the previous two versions and adds features to deliver operations management using vRealize Operations for Horizon. This gives IT admins the ability to monitor the health and performance of the solution, as well as capacity planning capabilities for ensuring the optimum configuration as you scale.

One of the biggest additions to the Enterprise edition is App Volumes, which gives you the ability to deliver just-in-time applications to a virtual desktop. For a detailed overview of VMware App Volumes, you can read *Learning VMware App Volumes, Peter von Oven, Packt*.

The table in the following screenshot details the features available in each edition:

	Horizon For Linux	Horizon Standard	Horizon Advanced	Horizon Enterprise
Desktop Infrastructure				
Windows Virtual Desktops (View)		☑	☑	☑
Windows Session-based Desktops (View)		☑	☑	☑
Linux-based Virtual Desktops (View)	☑			☑
Blast Delivery Protocol	☑	☑	☑	☑
Instant Clone Just-in-time Desktops				☑
User Environnent Management (VMware UEM)				☑
Application Delivery & Management				
Unified Workspace – XenApp, RDSH, SaaS, ThinApp			☑	☑
Application Remoting (RDSH)			☑	☑
Application Packaging (ThinApp)		☑	☑	☑
Physical Desktop Image Management (Mirage)			☑	☑
Application Layering (App Volumes)				☑
Operations Management (vRealize for Horizon)				
Operations Dashboard - Health Monitoring & Performance				☑
Capacity Management - Planning & Optimization				☑
Infrastructure Components (Hosting)				
VMware vSphere for Desktop	☑	☑	☑	☑
VMware vCenter Server for Desktop	☑	☑	☑	☑
Virtual SAN Advanced for Desktop			☑	☑

In this book, we will be covering all of the Horizon 7 editions in some shape or form; however, we will concentrate on the virtual desktop elements of the solution.

Summary

In this chapter, we have taken a look at what VDI is and covered the history of where it all began for VMware, demonstrating that VMware was, and still is, at the forefront of virtual desktop and application delivery.

We then went on to discuss the latest release, VMware Horizon 7, and the different editions that are available, namely, Horizon for Linux, Horizon Standard, Horizon Advanced, and Horizon Enterprise.

In the next chapter, we will take a deep dive into the technology of Horizon View and start taking a look at the architecture components.

2

An Overview of Horizon View Architecture and Components

In this chapter, we will introduce you to the architecture and infrastructure components that make up the core VMware Horizon solution, concentrating on the virtual desktop elements of Horizon with Horizon Standard edition, plus the Instant Clone technology that is available in the Horizon Enterprise edition.

We are going to concentrate on the core Horizon View functionality of brokering virtual desktop machines that are hosted on a VMware vSphere platform. Hosted applications will be covered in Chapter 8, *Delivering Remote Applications with View Hosted Apps*, and session-based desktops will be covered in Chapter 9, *Delivering Session-Based Desktops with Horizon View*.

Throughout the sections of this chapter, we will discuss the role of each of the Horizon View components, explaining how they fit into the overall infrastructure, their role, and the benefits they bring. Once we have explained the high-level concept, we will then take a deeper dive into how that particular component works. As we work through the sections, we will also highlight some of the best practices, as well as some useful hints and tips along the way.

We will also cover some of the third-party technologies that integrate and complement Horizon View, such as antivirus solutions, storage acceleration technologies, and high-end graphics solutions that help deliver a complete end-to-end solution.

After reading this chapter, you will be able to describe each of the components and what part they play within the solution, and why you would use them.

Introducing the key Horizon components

To start with, we are going to introduce, at a high level, the core infrastructure components and the architecture that make up the Horizon View product. We will start with the high-level architecture, as shown in the following diagram, before going on to drill down into each part in greater detail:

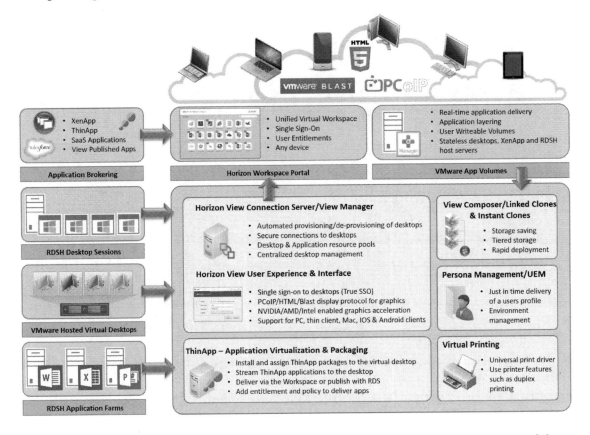

All of the VMware Horizon components described in the image are included as part of the licensed product, and the features that are available to you depend on whether you have the Standard Edition, the Advanced Edition, or the Enterprise Edition.

It's also worth remembering that Horizon licensing also includes ESXi and vCenter licensing, to support the ability to deploy the core hosting infrastructure. You can deploy as many ESXi hosts and vCenter servers as you require to host the desktop infrastructure.

High-level architectural overview

In this section, we will cover the core Horizon View features and functionality for brokering virtual desktop machines that are hosted on the VMware vSphere platform.

The Horizon View architecture is pretty straightforward to understand, as its foundations lie in the standard VMware vSphere products (ESXi and vCenter). So, if you have the necessary skills and experience of working with this platform, then you are already nearly halfway there.

Horizon View builds on the vSphere infrastructure, taking advantage of some of the features of the ESXi hypervisor and vCenter Server. Horizon View requires adding a number of virtual machines to perform the various View roles and functions.

An overview of the View architecture for delivering virtual desktops is shown in the following diagram:

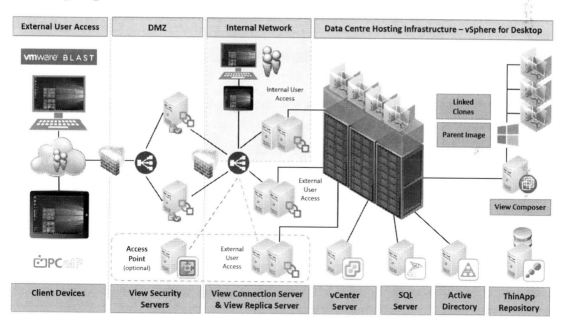

View components run as applications that are installed on the Microsoft Windows Server operating system, with the exception of the **Access Point**, which is a hardened Linux appliance, so it could actually run on physical hardware as well. However, there are a great number of benefits available when you run them as virtual machines, such as delivering HA and DR, as well as the typical cost savings that can be achieved through virtualization.

The following sections will cover each of these roles/components of the View architecture in greater detail, starting with the Horizon View Connection Server.

Horizon View Connection Server

The **Horizon View Connection Server**, sometimes referred to as **Connection Broker** or **View Manager**, is the central component of the View infrastructure. Its primary role is to connect a user to their virtual desktop by means of performing user authentication, and then delivering the appropriate desktop resources based on the user's profile and user entitlement. When logging on to your virtual desktop, it is the connection server that you are communicating with.

How does the Connection Server work?

A user will typically connect to their virtual desktop machine from their end-point device by launching the View client, but equally, they could use browser-based access. We will cover the View client and other access methods in Chapter 8, *Horizon View Client Options*.

So how does the login process work? Once the View client has launched (shown as **1** in the next diagram), the user enters the address details of the View Connection Server, which in turn responds (**2**) by asking them to provide their network login details (their **Active Directory (AD)** domain username and password).

It's worth noting that Horizon View now supports the following different AD Domain functional levels:

- Windows Server 2003
- Windows Server 2008 and 2008 R2
- Windows Server 2012 and 2012 R2

Based on the user's entitlements, these credentials are authenticated with AD (**3**) and, if successful, the user is able to continue the logon process. Depending on what they are entitled to, the user could see a launch screen that displays a number of different virtual desktop machine icons that are available for them to log in to. These desktop icons represent the desktop pools that the user has been entitled to use.

A pool is basically a collection of similar virtual desktop machines; for example, it could be a pool for the marketing department where the virtual desktop machines contain specific applications/software for that department. We will discuss desktop pools in greater detail in Chapter 7, *Managing and Configuring Desktop Pools*.

Once authenticated, the View Manager or Connection Server makes a call to the vCenter Server (**4**) to create a virtual desktop machine, and then vCenter makes a call (**5**) to either **View Composer** (if you are using Linked Clones) or will create an **Instant Clone** using the VM Fork feature of vSphere to start the build process of the virtual desktop if there is not one already available for the user to log in to.

When the build process has completed and the virtual desktop machine is available to the end user, it is displayed/delivered within the View Client window (**6**) using the chosen display protocol (PCoIP, Blast, or RDP).

This process is described pictorially in the following diagram:

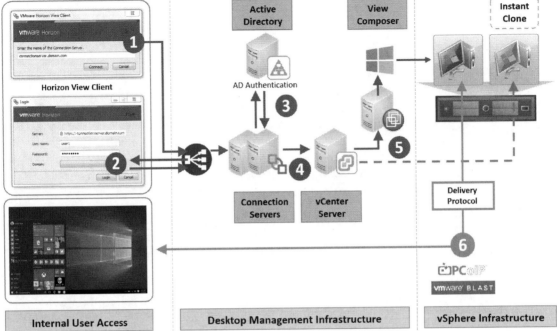

There are other ways to deploy VDI solutions that do not require a connection broker, although you could argue that strictly speaking, this is not a true VDI solution. This is actually what the first VDI solutions looked like, and just allowed a user to connect directly to their own virtual desktop via RDP. If you think about it, there are actually some specific use cases for doing just this.

For example, if you have a large number of remote branches or offices, you could deploy local infrastructure allowing users to continue working in the event of a WAN outage or poor network communication between the branch and head office. The infrastructure required would be a subset of what you deploy centrally in order to keep costs minimal.

It just so happens that VMware have also thought of this use case and have a solution that's referred to as a **Brokerless View**, which uses the VMware Horizon View Agent Direct-Connection plugin to connect directly to a virtual desktop machine without needing the Connection Server. However, don't forget that in a Horizon View environment, the View Connection Server provides greater functionality and does much more than just connecting users to desktops, as we will see later in this chapter.

As we previously touched on, the Horizon View Connection Server runs as an application on a Windows server, which could be either a physical or a virtual machine. Running as a virtual machine has many advantages; for example, it means that you can easily add high-availability features, which are critical in this environment, as you could potentially have hundreds or maybe even thousands of virtual desktop machines running on a single host server.

Along with brokering the connections between the users and virtual desktop machines, the Connection Server also works with vCenter Server to manage the virtual desktop machines. For example, when using Linked Clones or Instant Clones and powering on virtual desktops, these tasks are initiated by the Connection Server, but they are executed at the vCenter Server level.

Now that we have covered what the Connection Server is and how it works, in the next section, we are going to look at the requirements you need for it to run.

Minimum requirements for the Connection Server

To install the View Connection Server, you need to meet the following minimum requirements to run on physical or virtual machines:

- **Hardware requirements**: The following table shows the hardware required:

Hardware Requirements

	Required	Recommended
Processor	Pentium IV 2.0 GHz or higher	4 CPUs
Networking	One or more 10/100 Mbps NICs	1 Gbps NIC
Memory	4 GB or higher	10 GB for 50 or more desktops

- **Supported operating systems**: The View Connection Server must be installed on one of the operating systems listed in the following table:

Operating System

	Version	Edition
Windows Server 2008 R2 SP1	64-bit	Standard & Enterprise
Windows Server 2012 R2	64-bit	Standard & Enterprise

In the next section, we are going to look at the Horizon View Security Server.

The Horizon View Security Server

The Horizon View Security Server is another component in the architecture and is essentially another version of the View Connection Server, but this time, it sits within your DMZ so that you can allow end users to securely connect to their virtual desktop machine from an external network or the Internet. As you will see in Chapter 4, *Installing and Configuring Horizon View*, the installation process is pretty much the same as installing the View Connection Server, but instead, you select the Security Server role from the drop-down menu at the start of the installation.

You cannot install the View Security Server on the same machine that is already running as a Connection Server or any of the other Horizon View components.

How does the Security Server work?

To start with, the user login process at the beginning is the same as when connecting to a View Connection Server, essentially because the Security Server is just another version of the Connection Server running a subset of the features, with the exclusion of the ADAM database. The difference is that you connect to the address of the Security Server. The Security Server sits inside your DMZ and communicates with a Connection Server sitting on the internal network that it is paired with. So, now we have added an extra security layer as the internal Connection Server is not exposed externally, with the idea being that users can now access their virtual desktop machines externally without needing to first connect to a VPN on the network first.

The Security Server should not be joined to the Domain.

This process is described pictorially in the following diagram:

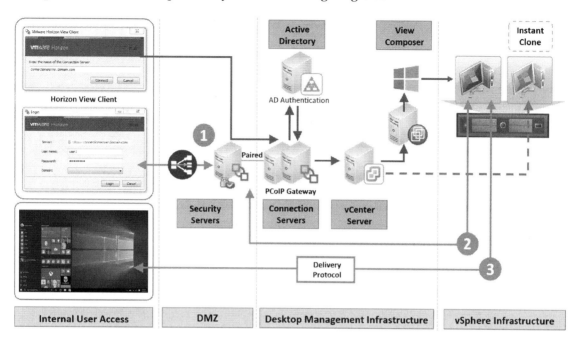

We mentioned previously that the Security Server is paired with a Connection Server. The pairing is configured by the use of a one-time password during installation. It's a bit like pairing your smartphone with the hands-free kit in your car using Bluetooth.

We will cover this in the *Installing of the Security Server* section in `Chapter 4`, *Installing and Configuring Horizon View*.

When the user logs in from the View Client, they now use the external URL of the Security Server to access the Connection Server, which in turn authenticates the user against AD. If the Connection Server is configured as a PCoIP gateway, then it will pass the connection and addressing information to the View Client. This connection information will allow the View Client to connect to the Security Server using PCoIP. This is shown in the diagram by the green arrow (**1**). The Security Server will then forward the PCoIP connection to the virtual desktop machine (**2**), creating the connection for the user. The virtual desktop machine is displayed/delivered within the View Client window (**3**) using the chosen display protocol (PCoIP, Blast, or RDP).

The Horizon View Replica Server

The **Horizon View Replica Server**, as the name suggests, is a replica or copy of a View Connection Server and serves two key purposes.

The first is that it is used to enable high availability to your Horizon View environment. Having a replica of your View Connection Server means that, if the Connection Server fails, users are still able to connect to their virtual desktop machines.

Secondly, adding Replica Servers allows you to scale up the number of users and virtual desktop connections. An individual instance of a Connection Server can support 2000 connections, so adding additional Connection Servers allows you to add another 2000 users at a time, up to the maximum of five connection servers and 10,000 users per Horizon View Pod. We will discuss the Pod and Block architecture in `Chapter 3`, *Design and Deployment Considerations*.

When deploying a Replica Server, you will need to change the IP address or update the DNS record to match this server if you are not using a load balancer.

As with the Security Server, you will see, in `Chapter 4`, *Installing and Configuring Horizon View*, that the installation process is again almost the same as the Connection Server, but this time, you select the Replica Server role from the drop-down menu with the different role options.

How does the Replica Server work?

So, the first question is, what actually gets replicated? The Connection Broker stores all its information relating to the end users, desktop pools, virtual desktop machines, and other View-related objects, in an **Active Directory Application Mode** (**ADAM**) database. Then, using the **Lightweight Directory Access Protocol** (**LDAP**) (it uses a method similar to the one AD uses for replication), this View information gets copied from the original Connection Server to the Replica Server.

As both the Connection Server and the Replica Server are now identical to each other, if your Connection Server fails, then you essentially have a backup that steps in and takes over, so that end users can continue to connect to their virtual desktop machines.

Just like with the other components, you cannot install the Replica Server role on the same machine that is running as a Connection Server or any of the other Horizon View components.

The Horizon View Enrollment Server and True SSO

The Horizon View Enrollment Server is the final component that is part of the Horizon View Connection Server installation options, and is selected from the drop-down menu from the installation options screen. So, what does the Enrollment Server do?

Horizon 7 sees the introduction of a new feature, called **True SSO**. True SSO is a solution that allows a user to authenticate to a Microsoft Windows environment without them having to enter their AD credentials. It integrates into another VMware product, VMware Identity Manager, which forms part of both Horizon 7 Advanced and Enterprise editions.

Its job is to sit between the Connection Server and the Microsoft Certificate Authority and to request temporary certificates from the certificate store.

This process is described pictorially in the following diagram:

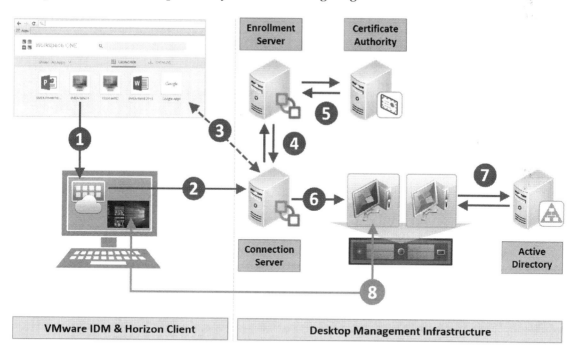

A user first logs in to VMware Identity Manager, either using their credentials or other authentication methods such as the following:

- RSA SecurID
- Kerberos
- RADIUS authentication
- RSA Adaptive Authentication
- Standards-based third-party identity providers

Once successfully authenticated, the user will be presented with the virtual desktop machines or hosted applications that they are entitled to use. They can launch any of these by simply double-clicking, which will launch the Horizon View Client, as shown by the red arrow (**1**) in the previous diagram. The user's credentials will then be passed to the Connection Server (**2**), which in turn will verify them by sending a **Security Assertion Markup Language** (**SAML**) assertion back to the Identity Manager (**3**).

If the user's credentials are verified, then the Connection Server passes them on to the Enrollment Server (**4**). The Enrollment Server then makes a request to the Microsoft Certificate Authority (CA) to generate a short-lived, temporary certificate for that user to use (**5**).

With the certificate now generated, the Connection Server presents it to the operating system of the virtual desktop machine (**6**), which in turn validates with Active Directory as to whether or not the certificate is authentic (**7**).

When the certificate has been authenticated, then the user is logged on to their virtual desktop machine, which will be displayed/delivered to the View Client using the chosen display protocol (**8**).

 True SSO is supported with all Horizon 7 supported desktop operating systems for desktops, as well as Windows Server 2008 R2 and Windows Server 2012 R2. It also supports PCoIP, HTML, and Blast Extreme delivery protocols.

VMware Access Point

VMware Access Point performs exactly the same functionality as the View Security Server, as shown in the following diagram, with one key difference. Instead of being a Windows application and another role of the Connection Server, the Access Point is a separate virtual appliance that runs a hardened, locked-down Linux operating system:

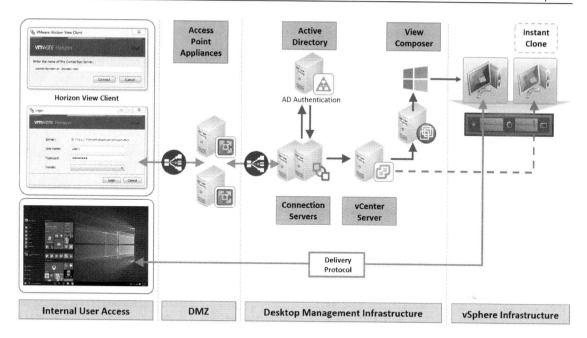

| Internal User Access | DMZ | Desktop Management Infrastructure | vSphere Infrastructure |

Although the **Access Point Appliances** deliver pretty much the same functionality as the Security Server, it does not yet completely replace it, especially if you already have a production deployment that uses the Security Server for external access. You can continue to use this architecture.

> If you are using the secure tunnel function, PCoIP Secure Gateway, or the Blast Secure Gateway features of the Connection Server, then these features will need to be disabled on the Connection Server if you are using the Access Point. They are all enabled by default on the **Access Point Appliances**.

A key difference between the **Access Point Appliances** and the Security Server is in the way it scales. Before, you had to pair a Security Server with a Connection Server, which was a limitation, but this is no longer the case. As such, you can now scale to as many Access Point appliances as you need for your environment, with the maximum limit being around 2000 sessions for a single appliance. Adding additional appliances is simply a case of deploying the appliance, as appliances don't depend on other appliances and do not communicate with them. They communicate directly with the Connection Servers.

Persistent or non-persistent desktops

In this section, we are going to talk about the different types of desktop assignments and the way a virtual desktop machine is delivered to an end user. This is an important design consideration, as the chosen method could potentially impact on the storage requirements (covered in the next section), the hosting infrastructure, and also which technology or solution is used to provision the desktop to the end users.

One of the questions that always get asked is whether you should deploy a dedicated (persistent) assignment, or a floating desktop (non-persistent) assignment. Desktops can either be individual virtual machines, which are dedicated to a user on a 1:1 basis (as we have in a physical desktop deployment, where each user effectively owns their own desktop), or a user has a new, vanilla desktop that gets provisioned, built, personalized, and then assigned at the time of login. The virtual desktop machine is chosen at random from a pool of available desktops that the end user is entitled to use.

If you remember, back in Chapter 1, *Introduction to VDI and VMware Horizon 7*, we talked about building the composite desktop. This is the model that is used to build the user's desktop.

The two options are described in more detail as follows:

- **Persistent desktop**: Users are allocated a desktop that retains all of their documents, applications, and settings between sessions. The desktop is statically assigned the first time that the user connects, and is then used for all subsequent sessions. No other user is permitted access to the desktop.
- **Non-persistent desktop**: Users might be connected to different desktops from the pool each time that they connect. Environmental applications, or user data does not persist between sessions and is instead delivered as the user logs on to their desktop. The desktop is refreshed or reset when the user logs off.

In most use cases, a non-persistent configuration is the best option; the key reason is that, in this model, you don't need to build all the desktops upfront for each user. You only need to power on a virtual desktop as and when it's required. All users start with the same basic desktop, which then gets personalized before delivery. This helps with concurrency rates. For example, you might have 5,000 people in your organization, but only 2,000 ever log in at the same time; therefore, you only need to have 2,000 virtual desktops available. Otherwise, you would have to build a desktop for each one of the 5,000 users that might ever log in, resulting in more server infrastructure and certainly a lot more storage capacity. We will talk about storage in the next section.

The one thing that used to be a bit of a showstopper for non-persistent desktops was around how to deliver the applications to the virtual desktop machine. Now that application layering solutions such as VMware App Volumes are becoming a more mainstream technology, the applications can be delivered on demand as the desktop is built and the user logs in.

Another thing that we often see some confusion over is the difference between dedicated and floating desktops, and how Linked Clones fit in. Just to make it clear, Linked Clones, Full clones, and Instant Clones are not what we are talking about when we refer to dedicated and floating desktops. Cloning operations refers to how a desktop is built and provisioned, whereas the terms persistent and non-persistent refer to how a desktop is assigned to an end user.

Dedicated and floating desktops are purely about user assignment and whether a user has a dedicated desktop or one allocated from a pool on demand. Linked Clones and Full Clones are features of Horizon View, which uses View Composer to create the desktop image for each user from a master or parent image. This means that, regardless of having a floating or dedicated desktop assignment, the virtual desktop machine could still be a linked or full clone.

So, here's a summary of the benefits:

- It is operationally efficient. All users start from a single or smaller number of desktop images. Organizations reduce the amount of image and patch management.
- It is efficient storage-wise. The amount of storage required to host the non-persistent desktop images will be smaller than keeping separate instances of unique user desktop images.

In the next sections, we are going to cover an in-depth overview of the cloning technologies available in Horizon 7, starting with Horizon View Composer and Linked Clones, and the advantages the technology delivers.

Horizon View Composer and Linked Clones

One of the main reasons a virtual desktop project fails to deliver, or doesn't even get out of the starting blocks, is down to the heavy infrastructure and storage requirements. The storage requirements in particular are often seen as a huge cost burden, which can be attributed to the fact that people are approaching a VDI project in the same way they would approach a physical desktop environment's requirements. This would mean that each user gets their own dedicated virtual desktop and the hard disk space that comes with it, albeit a virtual disk; this then gets scaled out for the entire user population, so each user is allocated a virtual desktop with some storage.

Let's take an example. If you had 1,000 users and allocated 250 GB per user's desktop, you would need *1,000 * 250 GB = 250 TB* for the virtual desktop environment. That's a lot of storage just for desktops and could result in significant infrastructure costs, which could possibly mean that the cost to deploy this amount of storage in the data center would render the project cost-ineffective compared to physical desktop deployments.

A new approach to deploying storage for a virtual desktop environment is needed, and this is where linked clone technology comes into play. In a nutshell, Linked Clones are designed to reduce the amount of disk space required, and to simplify the deployment and management of images to multiple virtual desktop machines, making it a centralized, and much easier, process.

Linked Clone technology

Starting at a high level, a clone is a copy of an existing or parent virtual machine. This parent **virtual machine** (**VM**) is typically your gold build, from which you want to create new virtual desktop machines. When a clone is created, it becomes a separate, new virtual desktop machine with its own unique identity. This process is not unique to Horizon View; it's actually a function of vSphere and vCenter, and in the case of Horizon View, we add in another component, View Composer, to manage the desktop images. There are two types of clone that we can deploy, a full clone or a linked clone. We will explain the difference in the next sections.

Full Clones

As the name implies, a full clone disk is an exact, full-sized copy of the parent machine. Once the clone has been created, the virtual desktop machine is unique, with its own identity, and has no links back to the parent virtual machine from which it was cloned. It can operate as a fully independent virtual desktop in its own right and is not reliant on its parent virtual machine.

However, as it is a full-sized copy, be aware that it will take up the same amount of storage as its parent virtual machine, which leads back to our discussion earlier in this chapter about storage capacity requirements. Using a full clone will require larger amounts of storage capacity and will possibly lead to higher infrastructure costs.

Before you completely dismiss the idea of using full clone virtual desktop machines, there are some use cases that rely on this model. For example, if you use VMware Mirage to deliver the operating system as a base layer, it only works today with Full Clones and dedicated Horizon View virtual desktop machines.

If you have software developers, then they probably need to install specialist tools and a trust code onto a desktop, and therefore, need to *own* their desktop. Or, perhaps, the applications that you run in your environment need a dedicated desktop due to the way the applications are licensed.

Linked Clones

Having now discussed Full Clones, we are going to talk about deploying virtual desktop machines with Linked Clones.

In a linked clone deployment, a delta disk is created and then used by the virtual desktop machine to store the data differences between its own operating system and the operating system of its parent virtual desktop machine. Unlike the full clone method, the linked clone is not a full copy of the virtual disk. The term linked clone refers to the fact that the linked clone will always look to its parent in order to operate, as it continues to read from the replica disk. Basically, the replica is a copy of a snapshot of the parent virtual desktop machine.

The linked clone itself could potentially grow to the same size as the replica disk if you allow it to. However, you can set limits on how big it can grow, and should it start to get too big, then you can refresh the virtual desktops that are linked to it. This essentially starts the cloning process again from the initial snapshot.

Immediately after a linked clone virtual desktop is deployed, the difference between the parent virtual machine and the newly-created virtual desktop machine is extremely small, and therefore reduces the storage capacity requirements compared to that of a full clone. This is how Linked Clones are more space-efficient than their full clone brothers.

The underlying technology behind Linked Clones is more like a snapshot than a clone, but with one key difference: View Composer. With View Composer, you can have more than one active snapshot linked to the parent virtual machine disk. This allows you to create multiple virtual desktop images from just one parent.

Best practice would be to deploy an environment with Linked Clones in order to reduce the storage requirements. However, as we previously mentioned, there are some use cases where you will need to use Full Clones.

One thing to be aware of, which still relates to the storage, is that, rather than capacity, we are now talking about performance. All linked clone virtual desktops are going to be reading from one replica and will therefore drive a high number of **Input /Output Operations Per Second (IOPS)** on the storage where the replica lives. Depending on your desktop pool design, you are fairly likely to have more than one replica, as you would typically have more than one data store. This in turn depends on the number of users who will drive the design of the solution. We will cover this in detail in Chapter 3, *Design and Deployment Considerations*.

In Horizon View, you are able to choose the location where the replica lives. One of the recommendations is that the replica should sit in fast storage, such as a local SSD.

Alternative solutions would be to deploy some form of storage acceleration technology to drive the IOPS. Horizon View also has its own integrated solution, called **View Storage Accelerator (VSA)** or **Content Based Read Cache (CBRC)**. This feature allows you to allocate up to 2 GB of memory from the underlying ESXi host server, which can be used as a cache for the most commonly read blocks. As we are talking about booting up desktop operating systems, the same blocks are required; as these can be retrieved from memory, the process is accelerated.

View Storage Accelerator is enabled by default when using Instant Clones and cannot be configured.

Another solution is **View Composer Array Integration** (**VCAI**), which allows the process of building Linked Clones to be offloaded to the storage array and its native snapshot mechanism rather than taking CPU cycles from the host server.

There are also a number of other third-party solutions that resolve the storage performance bottleneck, such as Atlantis Computing and their ILIO product, or using an all-flash array such as Tintri.

In the next section, we will take a deeper look at how Linked Clones work.

How do Linked Clones work?

The first step is to create your master virtual desktop machine image, which should contain not only the operating system, core applications, and settings, but also the Horizon View Agent components. This virtual desktop machine will become your parent VM, or your gold image. We will cover the build process in `Chapter 6`, *Building and Optimizing the Virtual Desktop OS*.

This image can now be used as a template to create any new subsequent virtual desktop machines.

 The gold image or parent image cannot be a VM template.

An overview of the linked clone creation process is shown in the following diagram:

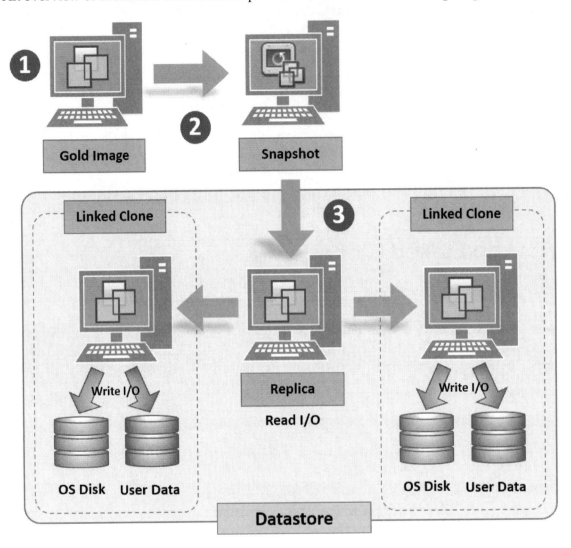

Once you have created the parent virtual desktop or **Gold Image** (1), you then take a **Snapshot** (2). When you create your desktop pool, this snapshot is selected and will become the **Replica** (3) and will be set to be read-only. Each virtual desktop is linked back to this replica; hence the term **Linked Clone**. When you start creating your virtual desktops, you create Linked Clones that are unique copies for each user.

Try not to create too many snapshots for your parent VM. I would recommend having just a handful, otherwise this could impact the performance of your desktops and make it a little harder to know which snapshot is which.

What does View Composer build?

During the image building process, and once the replica disk has been created, **View Composer** creates a number of other virtual disks, including the linked clone (operating system disk) itself. These are described in the following sections.

Linked Clone disk

Not wanting to state the obvious, the main disk that gets created is the Linked Clone disk itself. This Linked Clone disk is basically an empty virtual disk container that is attached to the virtual desktop machine as the user logs in and the desktop starts up.

This disk will start off small in size, but will grow over time depending on the block changes that are requested from the replica disk by the virtual desktop machine's operating system. These block changes are stored in the linked clone disk, and this disk is sometimes referred to as the delta disk, or differential disk, due to the fact that it stores all the delta changes that the desktop operating system requests from the parent VM. As mentioned before, the linked clone disk can grow to the maximum size, equal to the parent VM but, following best practice, you would never let this happen. Typically, you can expect the linked clone disk to only increase to a few hundred MBs. We will cover this in the *Linked Clone processes* section later.

The replica disk is set as read-only and is used as the primary disk. Any writes and/or block changes that are requested by the virtual desktop are written/read directly from the linked clone disk.

It is a recommended best practice to allocate tier-1 storage, such as local SSD drives, to host the replica, as all virtual desktops in the cluster will be referencing this single read-only VMDK file as their base image. Keeping it high in the stack improves performance, by reducing the overall storage IOPS required in a VDI workload. As we mentioned at the start of this section, storage costs are seen as being expensive for VDI. Linked Clones reduce the burden of storage capacity, but they do drive the requirement to derive a huge amount of IOPS from a single LUN.

Persistent disk or user data disk

The **persistent disk** feature of View Composer allows you to configure a separate disk that contains just the user data and user settings, and not the operating system. This allows any user data to be preserved when you update or make changes to the operating system disk, such as a recompose action.

 It's worth noting that the persistent disk is referenced by the VM name and not username, so bear this in mind if you want to attach the disk to another VM.

This disk is also used to store the user's profile. With this in mind, you need to size it accordingly, ensuring that it is large enough to store any user profile type data such as Virtual Desktop Assessments. This is another reason why it's a good idea to run a desktop assessment, as we will cover in Chapter 3, *Design and Deployment Considerations*, so that you can build up a picture of what your user desktop profiles and user data requirements look like.

Disposable disk

With the **disposable disk** option, Horizon View creates what is effectively a temporary disk that gets deleted every time the user powers off their virtual desktop machine.

If you think about how the Windows desktop operating system operates and the files it creates, there are several files that are used on a temporary basis. Files such as temporary Internet files or the Windows page file are two such examples. As these are only temporary files, why would you want to keep them? With Horizon View, these type of files are redirected to the disposable disk and then deleted when the VM is powered off.

Horizon View provides the option to have a disposable disk for each virtual desktop. This disposable disk is used to contain temporary files that will get deleted when the virtual desktop is powered off. These are files that you don't want to store on the main operating system disk as they would consume unnecessary disk space. For example, files on the disposable disk are things such as the pagefile, Windows system temporary files, and VMware log files.

Note that here, we are talking about temporary system files and not user files. A user's temporary files are still stored on the user data disk so that they can be preserved. Many applications use the Windows temp folder to store installation CAB files, which can be referenced post-installation. Having said that, you might want to delete the temporary user data to reduce the desktop image size, in which case you could ensure that the user's temporary files are directed to the disposable disk.

Internal disk

Finally, we have the internal disk. The **internal disk** is used to store important configuration information, such as the computer account password, which would be needed to join the virtual desktop machine back to the domain if you refreshed the Linked Clones. It is also used to store **Sysprep** and **Quickprep** configuration details. We will cover Quickprep in Chapter 6, *Building and Optimizing the Desktop Operating System*.

In terms of disk space, the internal disk is relatively small, averaging around 20 MB. By default, the user will not see this disk from their Windows Explorer, as it contains important configuration information that you wouldn't want them to delete.

The following diagram shows you an outline of the different disk types created:

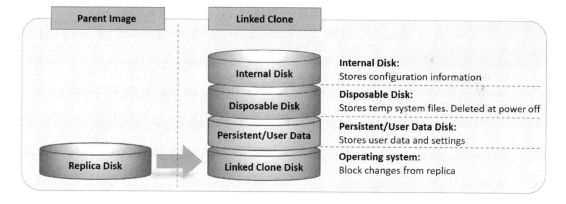

Understanding how the linked clone process works

There are several complex steps performed by View Composer and View Manager and that occur when a user launches a virtual desktop session. So, what's the process to build a linked clone desktop, and what goes on behind the scenes? When a user logs into Horizon View and requests a desktop, View Manager, using vCenter and View Composer, will create a virtual desktop machine. This process is described in the following sections.

Creating and provisioning a new desktop

first step in the process is to create and provision the virtual desktop machine following the steps described here:

> The first step in the process is to create and provision the virtual desktop machine following the steps described here: An entry for the virtual desktop machine is created in the Active Directory Application Mode (ADAM) database before it is put into provisioning mode.
>
> 1. The linked clone virtual desktop machine is created by View Composer.
> 2. A machine account is created in AD with a randomly generated password.
> 3. View Composer checks for a replica disk and creates one if one does not already exist.
> 4. A linked clone is created by the vCenter Server API call from View Composer.
> 5. An internal disk is created to store the configuration information and machine account password.

The virtual desktop machine has now been created and the next step is to customize it.

Customizing the desktop

Now that you have a newly created, linked clone virtual desktop machine, the next phase is to customize it.

The customization steps are as follows:

1. The virtual desktop machine is switched to customization mode.
2. The virtual desktop machine is customized by vCenter Server using the `customizeVM_Task` command and is joined to the domain with the information you entered in the View Manager console.
3. The linked clone virtual desktop is powered on.
4. The View Composer Agent on the linked clone virtual desktop machine starts up for the first time and joins the machine to the domain, using the `NetJoinDomain` command and the machine account password that was created on the internal disk.
5. The linked clone virtual desktop machine is now Sysprep'd. Once complete, View Composer tells View Agent that customization has finished, and View Agent tells View Manager that the customization process has finished.
6. The linked clone virtual desktop machine is powered off and a snapshot is taken.
7. The linked clone virtual desktop machine is marked as provisioned and is now available for use.

When a linked clone virtual desktop machine is powered on with the View Composer agent running, the agent tracks any changes that are made to the machine account password. Any changes will be updated and stored on the internal disk.

In many AD environments, the machine account password is changed periodically. If the View Composer Agent detects a password change, it updates the machine account password on the internal disk that was created with the linked clone.

This is important, as the linked clone virtual desktop machine is reverted to the snapshot taken after the customization during a refresh operation. For example, the agent will be able to reset the machine account password to the latest one.

The linked clone process is depicted in the following diagram:

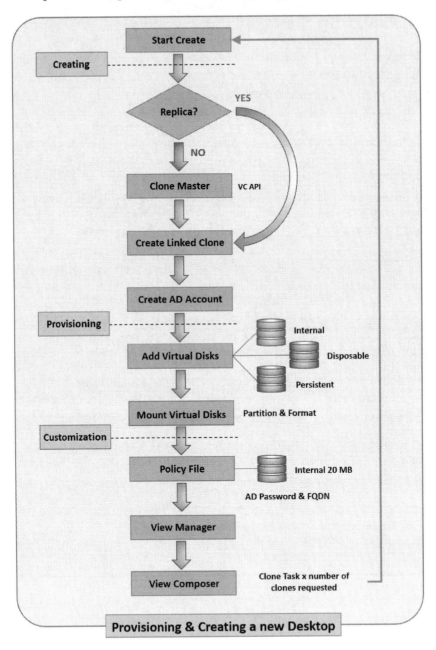

Additional features and functions of Linked Clones

There are a number of other management functions that you can perform on a linked clone disk from View Composer; these are outlined in this section and are needed in order to deliver the ongoing management of the virtual desktop machines.

Recomposing a linked clone

Recomposing a linked clone virtual desktop machine or desktop pool allows you to perform updates to the operating system disk, such as updating the image with the latest patches, or software updates. You can only perform updates on the same version of an operating system, so you cannot use the recompose feature to migrate from one operating system to another, such as going from Windows 8.1 to Windows 10.

As we've covered in the *What does View Composer Build?* section, we have separate disks for items such as a user's data. These disks are not affected during a recompose operation, so all user-specific data on them is preserved.

When you initiate the recompose operation, View Composer essentially starts the linked clone building process over again; thus, a new operating system disk is created, which then gets customized, and a snapshot, such as the ones shown in the preceding sections, is taken.

 During the recompose operation, the MAC addresses of the network interface and the Windows SID are not preserved. There are some management tools and security-type solutions that might not work due to this change. However, the UUID will remain the same.

The recompose process is described in the following steps:

1. View Manager puts the linked clone into maintenance mode.
2. View Manager calls the View Composer resync API for the Linked Clones being recomposed, directing View Composer to use the new base image and the snapshot.
3. If there isn't a replica for the base image and snapshot yet, in the target datastore for the linked clone, View Composer creates the replica in the target datastore (unless a separate datastore is being used for replicas, in which case, a replica is created in the replica datastore).

4. View Composer destroys the current OS disk for the linked clone and creates a new OS disk linked to the new replica.

5. The rest of the recompose cycle is identical to the customization phase of the provisioning and customization cycles.

The following diagram shows a graphical representation of the recompose process. Before the process begins, the first thing you need to do is update your **Gold Image** (1) with the patch updates or new applications you want to deploy as the virtual desktops.

As described in the preceding steps, the snapshot is then taken (2) to create the new replica, **Replica V2** (3). The existing OS disk is destroyed, but the **User Data** disk (4) is maintained during the recompose process:

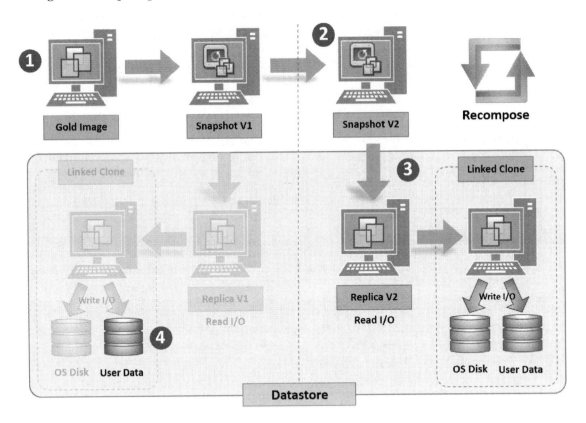

Refreshing a linked clone

By carrying out a refresh of the linked clone virtual desktop, you are effectively reverting it to its initial state, when its original snapshot was taken after it had completed the customization phase. This process only applies to the operating system disk and no other disks are affected.

An example use case for refresh operations would be recomposing a non-persistent desktop two hours after logoff, to return it to its original state and make it available for the next user.

The refresh process performs the following tasks:

1. The linked clone virtual desktop is switched into maintenance mode.
2. View Manager reverts the linked clone virtual desktop to the snapshot taken after customization was completed: – `vdm-initial-checkpoint`.
3. The linked clone virtual desktop starts up, and View Composer Agent detects weather the machine account password needs to be updated. If not, and the password on the internal disk is newer than the one in the registry, the agent will update the machine account password using the one on the internal disk.

One of the reasons why you would perform a refresh operation is if the linked clone OS disk starts to become bloated. As we previously discussed, the OS-linked clone disk could grow to the full size of its parent image. This means it would be taking up more disk space than is really necessary, which kind of defeats the objective of Linked Clones. The refresh operation effectively resets the linked clone to a small delta between it and its parent image.

The following diagram shows a representation of the refresh operation:

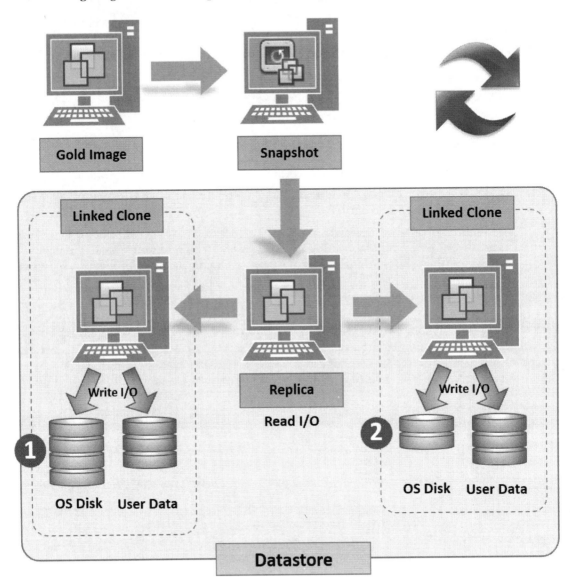

The linked clone on the left-hand side of the diagram (**1**) has started to grow in size. Refreshing reverts it back to the snapshot as if it were a new virtual desktop, as shown on the right-hand side of the diagram (**2**).

Rebalancing operations with View Composer

The **rebalance operation** in View Composer is used to evenly distribute the linked clone virtual desktop machines across multiple datastores in your environment. You would perform this task in the event that one of your datastores was becoming full while others have ample free space. It might also help with the performance of that particular datastore. For example, if you had 10 virtual desktop machines in one datastore and only two in another, then running a rebalance operation would potentially even this out and leave you with six virtual desktop machines per datastore.

 You must use the View Administrator console to initiate the rebalance operation in View Composer. If you simply try to vMotion any of your virtual desktop machines, then View Composer will not be able to keep track of them.

On the other hand, if you have six virtual desktop machines on one datastore and seven on another, then it is highly likely that initiating a rebalance operation will have no effect, and no virtual desktop machines will be moved, as doing so has no benefit. A virtual desktop machine will only be moved to another datastore if the target datastore has significantly more spare capacity than the source.

The rebalance process is described in the following steps:

1. The linked clone is switched to maintenance mode.
2. Virtual machines to be moved are identified based on the free space in the available datastores.
3. The operating system disk and persistent disk are disconnected from the virtual desktop machine.
4. The detached operating system disk and persistent disk are moved to the target datastore.
5. The virtual desktop machine is moved to the target datastore.
6. The operating system disk and persistent disk are reconnected to the linked clone virtual desktop machine.
7. View Composer resynchronizes the linked clone virtual desktop machines.
8. View Composer checks for the replica disk in the datastore and creates one if one does not already exist, as per the provisioning steps covered earlier in this chapter.
9. As per the recompose operation, the operating system disk for the linked clone gets deleted and a new one is created and then customized.

The following diagram shows the rebalance operation:

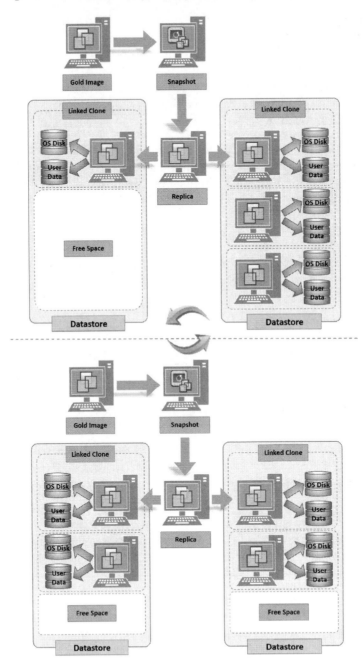

In the next section, we are going to look at the method for creating virtual desktop machines with the Instant Clone feature.

Instant Clones

The Instant Clones feature is actually a functionality built into the vSphere platform rather than a specific Horizon feature, and was made available from the vSphere 6.0 U1 release, but is only now becoming a supported feature as part of Horizon 7.

It uses the VMware VM Fork technology to very quickly provision virtual desktop machines. An instant clone is created from an already powered on and running virtual desktop machine, called the **Parent VM**, which is quiesced before the Instant Clone is created. This is what makes Instant Clones quicker to provision than Linked Clones with View Composer.

The Instant Clone shares its memory and its disk with the parent VM for read operations, and is created immediately, and in an already powered-on state, unlike with View Composer-based Linked Clones that have to power-on as part of the creation process. As well as sharing the memory and disk with the parent VM, the Instant Clone has its own unique memory and delta disk file.

The following diagram shows the Instant Clone architecture:

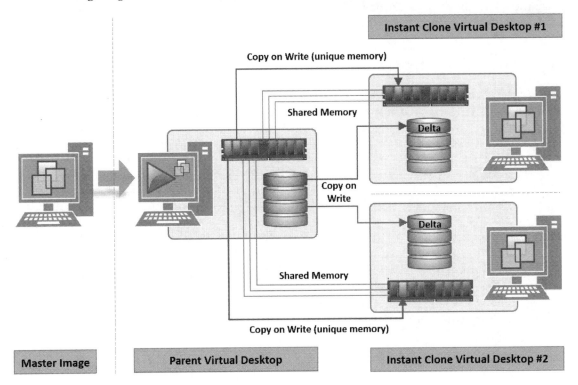

When the end user logs off the Instant Clone virtual desktop machine, it is destroyed, and when the user logs on again they will have a new Instant Clone created. If they need any data to persist then they would use the Writeable Volume feature of App Volumes to deliver that functionality and UEM to manage their personalization settings.

 To take advantage of Instant Clones, the virtual desktop machines will need to be running virtual machine hardware version 11 or higher.

There are a number of benefits to using Instant Clones when compared with Linked Clones:

- Instant Clones provision in seconds compared to minutes for Linked Clones
- Boot Storms are eliminated as the parent desktop is powered on, and all Instant Clones are created in an already powered-on state
- No requirement to perform refresh or recompose operations as desktops have a short lifecycle
- Patching the operating system requires you to just update the parent VM, rather than running a recompose operation, resulting in an end user receiving the updated virtual desktop machine on their next log on automatically

- Lessens the load on the vCenter server
- No requirement for SE Spare Disk or CBRC

Given that Instant Clones is still a relatively new technology, there are a couple of limitations that you should be aware of:

- RDSH servers are not currently supportedâ☺☺use Linked Clones instead.
- Only supports Windows 7 and Windows 10.
- Only supports floating desktop pools. No support for dedicated pools.
- Maximum of 2000 desktops.
- Only supports a single vCenter and single vLAN.
- No support for vGPU or vDGA, but limited support for vSGA.
- VSAN or VMFS datastores only. No support for NFS.

View Persona Management

Let's start with a little bit about the background and history behind View Persona Management. **View Persona Management** was originally a technology product called **Virtual Profiles** and was acquired by VMware from RTO Software in 2010. It was first introduced with View 5.0, and it allows you to configure user profiles so that they dynamically synchronize with a remote profile repository that is located on a file server in the data center. Its purpose is to manage user profiles within a virtualized desktop environment.

More information about the acquisition can be found at `http://www.vmware.com/files/pdf/VMware-RTO-acquisition-FAQ.pdf`.

VMware View Persona Management was first introduced with View 5.0, and it allows you to configure user profiles that dynamically synchronize with a remote profile repository located on a file server in the data center.

Why do we need to manage user profiles differently in VDI?

In a VDI solution, one of the key benefits is the way the virtual desktop is either built on demand or delivered from a pool of prebuilt, floating desktops and then delivered back to the user. The typical deployment model is the floating model, which basically means that the user doesn't actually own their own desktop.

When they log in, they could have any desktop delivered to them from a pool of available virtual desktop machines. This means that the virtual desktop that is delivered would not be personalized to that particular user. It would just be a standard vanilla build of the operating system and applications.

This is where View Persona Management comes into play and delivers the user's profile to the floating virtual desktop they have been assigned, effectively making it theirs.

When we talk about the desktop being built on demand, we are referring to how a desktop is put together from several different components. The desktop can be broken down into three components: the operating system, applications, and the user's personalization or profile, essentially the bit that makes the desktop yours. As a user logs on, all these pieces come together to deliver the end user desktop experience. In this particular example, we are talking about the user's profile.

This is shown in the following diagram:

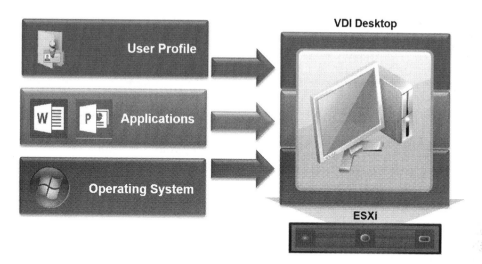

In this section, we will have a detailed look at View Persona Management to manage the user profile element and the key benefits it delivers. A deep dive into a technical overview and details on how to configure View Persona Management can be found in `Online Chapter`, *Managing User Profiles in Virtual Desktop Infrastructure, available at* `https://www.pa cktpub.com/sites/default/files/downloads/5657_ManagingUserEnvironmentsinVirt ualDesktopInfrastructure.pdf`.

The benefits of Persona Management

At high levels, View Persona Management provides the following features:

- Fast loading of user personalization settings, with just-in-time retrieval of user profile data
- Little or no infrastructure required-just a file share or the use of an existing folder redirection structure
- Profile consistency maintains personalization between sessions
- Efficient architecture with no dependency on Windows roaming user profiles
- Multiplatform support for Windows XP, Windows Vista, Windows 7, Windows 8.x, and Windows 10

In addition to the listed features, View Persona Management also helps reduce virtual desktop TCO by enabling the move to a stateless virtual desktop environment. In some deployments, users were placed in dedicated pools solely to retain their profile settings, which added to the cost and complexity in management. On the subject of cost, as Persona Management is an integrated part of Horizon View, you don't necessarily need to purchase additional third-party products, unless you need additional functionality above and beyond the basics.

While on the subject of management, there are no additional components to set up or install, as everything is driven by Active Directory Group Policy; in terms of scalability, again, as there are no infrastructure overheads such as databases, scalability does not cause any problems.

VMware User Environment Manager (UEM)

The **VMware UEM** product is a new edition to the Horizon portfolio and was added when VMware acquired the Dutch company Immidio back in February 2015. Immidio was a software company that created products that were aimed at helping their consultants out in the field, with the core product being called **Flex+**.

UEM adds additional functionality above the standard Persona Management solution, also providing a central management console, and delivers personalization of the end user's virtual desktop machine as well as the ability to dynamically configure policies. It works across a number of environments such as virtual desktop machines and physical PCs, as well as cloud-based Windows desktop environments.

 To manage a virtual desktop machine with UEM, you will need to install the **FlexEngine** components onto the virtual desktop machine. Make sure you include this as part of your master image or parent VM.

There are five key use cases that UEM can be used with:

- **Application Configuration Management**: Allows you to configure an application's initial settings rather than deploying the application's own default settings. You can configure predefined settings as one-time defaults, fully enforced (application starts with the user's personalized settings every time), or partially enforced (application starts as configured but allows the user to perform limited personalization), using the VMware UEM Application Profiler to capture predefined settings for an application.

- **User Environment Settings**: Allows you to centrally manage User Environment settings such as the following:
    - Application blocking
    - Application shortcuts and file type associations
    - Drive and printer mappings
    - Environment variables
    - Files, folders, and registry settings
    - Folder redirection
- **Personalization**: Abstracts user-specific desktop and application settings from the underlying OS and then makes these settings available across multiple devices, Windows versions, and applications. It also supports operating system migration such as Windows 7 or Windows 8.1.
- **Application Migration**: Allows an end user to effectively have roaming application and personalization settings that they can move between different operating system versions, such as Windows 7 to Windows 8.1.
- **Dynamic Configuration**: Using condition sets allow you to combine conditions based on variables such as user, location, and device, to deliver dynamic delivery of content and appearance. For example, delivering access to a network printer based on an end user's location, or create particular drive mapping that is based on the user's identity.

SmartPolicies

SmartPolicies is a feature of Horizon 7, and uses UEM 9.0 to deliver a set of policies that are specific to Horizon View virtual desktop machines.

 To use SmartPolicies, you need to make sure that the virtual desktop machines are running Horizon Agent 7.0 or later and VMware User Environment Manager 9.0.

With SmartPolicies, you can configure the following:

- USB redirection
- Printing
- Clipboard behavior
- Client drive redirection
- PCoIP profile

UEM or Persona Management?

So, the question is, which solution should you use? UEM is available as part of Horizon Enterprise Edition or as a standalone product, so that means higher or additional cost, unless of course you planned on purchasing Enterprise Edition in the first place.

UEM delivers a far greater set of configuration variables and features, as well as having a central management console that makes it far easier to manage and deploy. However, you may already have a more comprehensive UEM solution in place. If you are using a lesser edition of Horizon, then Persona Management may well deliver your requirements, and if not, then maybe it's worth considering a third-party product such as Liquidware Labs ProfileUnity or AppSense.

Printing from a Virtual Desktop Machine

A question that often comes up when deploying a VDI solution is, how do you manage printing? As your virtual desktop is now effectively running on a server in the data center, does that mean that, when you hit the print button, your print job comes out there? What about printer drivers? Typically, your desktop has the driver installed for the printer that is nearest to you, or it might be a locally-attached printer. Does that mean you need to install every possible printer driver onto your virtual desktop machines? Luckily, the answer to these questions is no, and in this section, we will briefly cover how VMware Horizon View manages printing.

Bundled within Horizon View is an OEM virtual printing solution, **ThinPrint**, for which a company called Cortado is the OEM. ThinPrint allows your end users to print either to a network-based printer or to a local printer that is attached from the user's endpoint device to their virtual desktop machine via USB redirection. We will cover USB device management in the next section.

To answer the question about the printer drivers that must be installed, ThinPrint uses a single, virtual print driver that replaces all other print drivers. You can still install a specific print driver, if necessary, for use cases where your printer has some additional features or functionalities. However, the virtual print driver provides support for most multifunctional printers, supporting features such as double-sided printing.

The other question is centered around location; where your print job actually prints is also addressed with ThinPrint, which provides a location-based printing feature that allows you to map to a printer that is nearest to your endpoint device.

Installing the virtual printing components

There are two key components to the virtual printing solution that gets installed as part of the Horizon View installation process; they are as follows:

- **.print Engine**: This gets installed as part of the Horizon View Agent installation on the virtual desktop machine. It includes the virtual print driver.
- **.print Client**: This gets installed as part of the Horizon View Client on the endpoint device and provides information on available printers. It also receives print jobs from the engine component.

Managing USB devices

We are all used to plugging USB devices into our laptops and desktop machines. If you are working in a VMware Horizon View environment, you might want to continue using your USB devices within that virtualized desktop. USB device redirection is a functionality, built into Horizon View, that allows the USB device to be physically connected to the endpoint device while working as if it's connected to the virtualized desktop.

On the flip side, you might want to prevent users from plugging devices into their virtual desktop machines, to ensure you have a secure environment. After all, deploying a VDI environment is one reason companies use to create a secure environment and protect data.

USB device support in Horizon View

There isn't a list that details every single device that works within Horizon View, as that would be one very long list and it would be impractical to test everything out there, given the number of USB devices on the market.

Generally speaking, most USB devices should work in a Horizon View environment, as all it essentially does is redirect the USB traffic from the View Client running on the endpoint device to the View Agent running on the virtual desktop machine. A complete list of *validated* devices does not exist; if there are any questions about the functionality of a particular device, you should contact the USB device's manufacturer.

There might be some devices that will not work, purely dtue to he nature and the behavior of the device itselfâ⊚⊚for example, some security devices that check the physical properties of the machine or device they are plugged into. We used to classify USB webcams as unsupported devices. However, with the introduction of **Real Time Audio Video (RTAV)**, these devices are now supported. We will cover this later on in this chapter.

In the next section, we will talk about how you can select which USB devices get redirected by using USB filtering.

Filtering supported USB devices

In some circumstances, you might not want to allow users to have the ability to plug in external USB devices and redirect them to their virtual desktop machine. The question is do you allow users to plug USB devices into their physical desktops?

Horizon View has a feature that can prevent USB devices from being redirected to the user's virtual desktop machine. You can apply this by using a policy on the endpoint device, the virtual desktop, or by means of an Active Directory Group Policy. For example, your organization might want to prevent USB memory sticks from being used as this would give the user the ability to copy data from the virtual desktop machine (one of the reasons for the deployment of VDI is so that data is centralized and doesn't leave the data center).

You can create specific filters to include devices (by manufacturer or by type) that you want to allow, but block all others. So, if you have a corporate, standard-type device, it will be allowed. You could even go to the next level and choose a particular model of device, while blocking any other devices, even though they are from the same vendor.

Managing multifunction USB devices

In your environment, you might have some USB devices that each have several different functions while still using a single USB connection. For example, a multimedia keyboard could have a touchpad mouse, speakers, a fingerprint reader, and the keyboard itself.

Horizon View supports a function known as device splitting. This allows you to just redirect certain components of that device rather than the entire device. With our multimedia example, you might want to leave the mouse as a local device on the end point while redirecting the fingerprint reader to allow secure login to the virtual desktop.

ThinApp application virtualization

ThinApp is an agentless application virtualization or application packaging solution that decouples applications from their underlying operating systems. It's designed to eliminate application conflict, streamline application delivery, and improve management. ThinApp licenses are included with the Horizon View license and can be used on both physical and virtual desktops, therefore providing a mechanism to deliver applications across all of your desktop modelsâ••your entire end-user estate.

How does application virtualization work?

ThinApp encapsulates applications into a package consisting of a single .exe or .msi file and abstracts them from the following:

- The host operating system
- Any traditionally installed applications already running on the system
- All other virtual applications running on the system

Applications then run in their own isolated virtual environment, with minimal or zero impact on the underlying operating system, virtual file system, or virtual registry.

When you create a ThinApp package, you are basically capturing all the application files, registry settings, and file system changes that an application requires for it to run. It also captures its own agent as part of the process, so the end-point device requires nothing to be installed, unless you deliver your ThinApp packages using the Workspace Portal.

Once packaged, the application can be deployed (either streamed or installed) onto the virtual desktop machine or even a physical desktop. The only requirement ThinApp packages have in order to run is an underlining Windows operating system, either physical or virtual. When running, it's important to note that the package makes no changes to the operating system of the machine it's running on.

There are no requirements for additional backend infrastructure components, as all your ThinApp-packaged applications are stored in a file share on a file server. This means that you can centrally manage and easily update your packages so that all users will receive the updates the next time they launch the application.

To summarize, ThinApp does the following:

- Allows Windows applications to be packaged, distributed, and executed as single .exe or .msi files on either physical or virtual machines

- Builds process links, a **Virtual Operating System** (**VOS**) with a compressed embedded file system, and registry into a single file
- Requires no pre-installed software on the end-user machine (unless using the Workspace Portal for entitlements)
- Provides a zero footprint on the underlying OS
- Necessitates no traditional installation or changes to the local OS registry or file system
- Requires no backend server infrastructure, other than a file share to store your ThinApp packages

For more details on how to use ThinApp in your environment, you can read *VMware ThinApp 4.7 Essentials, Peter Bjork, Packt.*

Antivirus software for virtual desktops

In a traditional desktop model, an antivirus scanning model agent is installed, runs on every desktop, and is responsible for the performance of antivirus detection scans, while maintaining and updating the definition files containing information about the latest malware.

This model works well in the physical desktop world, but presents some challenges when running in a virtual desktop environment. When a detection scan starts, every virtual desktop's resource usage will increase significantly. This will result in end-user performance degradation, and the desktop host server will become resource-bound. That's fine on a physical desktop, but now in VDI, it's the server hosting the desktops that is going to become resource-bound. When recomposing desktops or building them on demand, the desktops will have to download the definitions file each time, taking up network bandwidth and storage capacity. One last thing you need to take into consideration is the memory footprint of the typical desktop AV software that gets installed on each virtual desktop. You will need to allocate more memory to run the agents and scanning process.

Let's say you have a vSphere host server running maybe 100 virtual desktops or so; what if, at 12:00 noon on Thursday, they all kick off a virus scan? That host is likely to become 100% utilized very quickly, both for CPU and storage I/Os, with the result being unresponsive desktops. Instead of affecting one user's desktop, you have now affected 100 users' desktops. You could schedule the scans so that they don't all happen at once, but ideally, you need to look at alternative methods that are designed to work more specifically with a virtual desktop infrastructure.

Secondly, if we are recomposing desktops or building them on demand, we have to download the definitions file every time, which not only takes up network bandwidth, but also unnecessary storage capacity.

So, what is required is a new approach to antivirus protection, specifically designed for virtual desktop infrastructure.

With VMware vSphere 5.5, VMware introduced a product called **vShield Endpoint** that addresses the problems inherent in antivirus scanning in large-scale virtual desktop implementations. In a Horizon View deployment, vShield Endpoint consolidates and offloads all antivirus operations into one centralized **security virtual appliance (SVA)**.

VMware has partnered with antivirus software vendors to provide this bundled solution to antivirus problems in a VDI environment. VMware partners supply the dedicated SVA, which integrates with the vShield Endpoint programmable interfaces to protect VMware virtual desktops against viruses and other malware. Instead of installing the antivirus agents on each individual virtual desktop, you connect one virtual appliance to each virtual machine host.

VMware works with the following partners, who have integrated their antivirus solutions with vShield Endpoint:

- Bitdefender
- Kaspersky
- McAfee
- Sourcefire
- Symantec
- Trend Micro

VMware vShield Endpoint delivers the following features:

- Improved virtual desktop performance by not creating antivirus storms.
- Scanning and defining file updates are centralized using a virtual appliance.
- Free up resources by eliminating the need for AV agents on the virtual desktop.
- No agent to install or update on the virtual desktop machines. The driver is contained within the VMware Tools installation.
- Always-on protection. Antivirus signature updates are processed by SVA. Desktops receive the latest protection as soon as they are powered on.
- Any changes to the antivirus software are configured only in the SVA, not on each desktop. You can change the configurations for antivirus in the SVA without reconfiguring the desktop driver. All changes are made to the SVA instead.

- Simple substitution of antivirus vendors. You can add or change partner solutions by adding or removing the virtual appliances. No need to reconfigure the desktop driver.

VMware vShield Endpoint architecture

There are two main components to **vShield Endpoint**: the SVA and the driver.

As we previously discussed, instead of installing the antivirus software on each virtual desktop machine, you install a SVA and the vShield Endpoint driver on the virtual desktop machines. You will need one SVA per ESXi host server.

The vShield Endpoint driver is then installed on the master or parent desktop image. The vShield Endpoint driver is part of the VMware Tools installation:

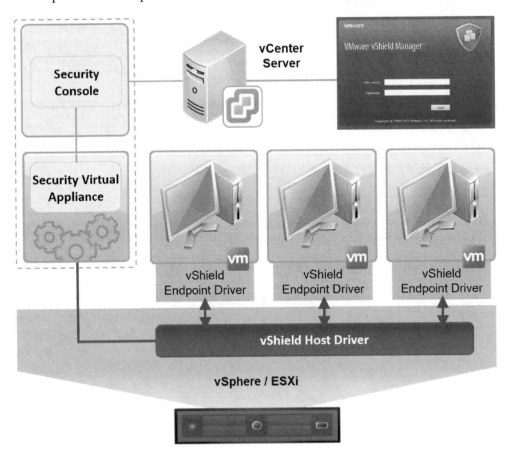

IT administrators can centrally manage VMware vShield Endpoint through the included **VMware vShield Manager** console, which in turn is integrated with VMware **vCenter** Server. Isolating the antivirus scanning engine on a virtual appliance makes it easier to protect the scanning engine than if it were placed on every virtual machine. In addition, detailed logging of activity from the antivirus or anti-malware service satisfies auditor compliance requirements.

PCoIP – delivering the desktop experience

One of the most important elements of a virtual desktop solution is how you get the screen contents of the virtual desktop machine running in the data center delivered to the user's end-point device, which they are connecting from. To do this, VMware Horizon View uses the **PC-over Internet Protocol (PCoIP)**. In this section, we are going to cover what the PCoIP protocol is and how it works in delivering the end-user experience.

Introducing PCoIP

PCoIP is a high-performance display protocol designed and developed by Teradici (`http://www.teradici.com/`). It has been purpose-built to deliver virtual desktops over the LAN or WAN and to provide end users with the best, feature-rich desktop experience.

With PCoIP, the entire screen content is compressed, encrypted, and encoded in the data center before transmitting only the pixels across a standard IP network to PCoIP-enabled endpoint devices (such as zero clients) that use the hardware-based Teradici Terra 1 or Terra 2 chipset, or to Windows, Mac, or tablet devices running the software-based View Client. The key is that no data ever leaves the data center.

PCoIP supports high-resolution, full-frame rates, 3D graphics, HD media, multiple displays (up to four, depending on the endpoint device), and high-definition audio. As we discussed earlier in this chapter, PCoIP also supports USB peripheral redirection.

Unlike some legacy display protocols that were built just to deliver applications, PCoIP was designed and built from the ground up, specifically to deliver a full desktop experience, taking advantage of Teradici-based zero clients with an integrated graphics acceleration technology built into the silicon on these devices, or software-based clients.

PCoIP ensures the best user experience, regardless of the end-user location, whether that is on the LAN or even across a WAN. It dynamically adapts based on the network conditions and user policy.

In the next sections, we are going to cover how PCoIP renders images and how it adapts dynamically to the network environment.

PCoIP host rendering

So, let's start by taking a look at how the different rendering models work. With a desktop PC, the applications, operating system, and graphics drivers work together locally to deliver the best performance on that PC. This is local client rendering.

If we move to a client rendering model, we now introduce a network between the components. Images are now sent across the network to the endpoint device, where they are processed locally using the resources of that endpoint device. Using this model introduces degradation of the application performance as it travels across the network from the host server to the client, and you would still need a fairly powerful Windows-based endpoint device.

So what about host rendering? In a host rendering scenario, the desktop PC environment that we previously described is pretty much the same. However, the PC is now running as a virtual desktop machine. This means that applications will work as they normally would on a physical desktop PC and the rendering is done at the host end. PCoIP then works by encrypting just the pixels on the virtual desktop machine running the View Agent, and then sends them to the endpoint device running the View Client or to a zero client device running Teradici hardware, where the decoding takes place.

Using this model, you can easily deploy lower-powered, non-Windows devices such as zero clients, as the applications have no dependencies on the endpoint on which they run.

Multi-codec support with PCoIP

If you look at how an image is built up and how the content is rendered, some of the components of the image might require the use of different codecs to display the image, depending on what type of image it is. For example, you would use a different codec to display text from one that you would use to display videos.

PCoIP has the ability to analyze these different media image components and apply the appropriate codec for each pixel before compressing, encrypting, and sending the pixels to the endpoint device for decoding. Working in this way allows PCoIP to transmit the pixels more efficiently, which ultimately means less bandwidth and better performance. It also means that you can control the image content quality that is being delivered. We will talk about it in the next section.

Controlling the image quality

The quality of the image that PCoIP delivers can be controlled through the AD Group Policy or SmartPolicies to deliver the appropriate image quality, depending on the use case. The image is built progressively from what is termed a perceptually lossless image to a lossless image, with the latter delivering a high-fidelity, pixel-perfect image. For example, would you really need to build a pixel-perfect image if you were just running Microsoft Word?

The important thing to remember is that the quality of the image will have an impact on the bandwidth required to deliver it. We will cover these controls in more detail in `Online Chapter`, *Fine-Tuning the End-User Experience* available at `https://www.packtpub.com/sites/default/files/downloads/5657_FineTuningtheEndUserExperience.pdf`.

Dynamic networking capabilities

To manage bandwidth use, PCoIP's adaptive encoders automatically adjust image quality on congested networks, based on the limits you set in the policy, and then resume maximum image quality when the network is no longer congested. As PCoIP doesn't transfer any data and just the pixels, it makes sense to use a real-time **User Datagram Protocol (UDP)**, rather than a TCP protocol (the same protocol as **Voice over IP (VoIP)**, to ensure a responsive and interactive remote-user experience. This reduces the overall bandwidth requirement and delivers the best interactive user experience, based on the network bandwidth available at the time.

UDP does not employ error-checking or correction, and therefore removes any overheads in processing the checking and correcting. The lack of retransmission delays that you would find with a TCP protocol means that it is ideal for streaming media. For the end user experience, these delays translate to jerky movements, most commonly experienced when watching video content.

Other display protocols

There are a couple of other mainstream desktop protocols. The main protocols available today are Microsoft **Remote Desktop Protocol (RDP)** and Citrix **Independent Computing Architecture (ICA)**. These are described in more detail in the following sections.

Remote Desktop Protocol (RDP)

The RDP protocol was developed for Microsoft and is used primarily to connect to a remote machine, server, desktop, or virtual machine using TCP IP. RDP is now more commonly known as **Remote Desktop Connection**. You probably use it on a daily basis to connect remotely to your server infrastructure.

When you connect to the remote desktop or machine, you are essentially connecting to a terminal service component, which then relays the screen content back to the client, along with key strokes and mouse movements.

Independent Computing Architecture (ICA) protocol

ICA is another display protocol that is used by Citrix in its products XenDesktop and XenApp. It is similar in design to other protocols, in that it is used to deliver screen content and keyboard strokes to a client device over a TCP IP network connection.

You connect using an ICA client, such as Citrix Receiver, installed on your endpoint device. This loads an ICA file containing the details of the remote system you are connecting to and any properties to apply to that session.

What about HDX? HDX is not actually a protocol or a technology, but rather a marketing brand for **High Definition Experience** (**HDX**). HDX encompasses a number of Citrix technologies that describe the entire user experience rather than concentrating on just the protocol element. You will also see some sub-brands fall under HDX, such as HDX MediaStream, HDX RealTime, and HDX 3D.

PCoIP offloading with the Teradici Apex 2800

In addition to the software solutions discussed in the previous sections, Teradici also offer a server offload card called the Apex 2800. This PCI card is installed into the servers that are hosting the virtual desktops.

The first thing to say about this card is that it is not a **Graphics Processing Unit (GPU)** card. I often hear some confusion around this, and users assume that, by adding an Apex card, you would get the OpenGL and DirectX capabilities, but this is not the case. You might well improve the overall experience and performance, but you will not be adding additional GPU features and functionalities.

The objective of this card is purely to take the load from the CPU in the host when processing image encoding operations. Offloading image encoding to a hardware encoding card reduces peaks in CPU utilization, ensuring a consistent user experience across all users, regardless of task and activity level. In cases where the CPU is being starved of cycles, the offload function enables applications to run more smoothly. If you compare it to something such as **TCP Offload Engine** or the **TOE** card used in the IP storage world for iSCSI, it's much better to use hardware-based cards than it is to use software initiators.

Freeing up CPU cycles and the overall load on the servers' CPU will potentially result in better consolidation ratios of the virtual desktops, that is, more virtual desktops per host server. Typically, you will see an increase of 1.2 times.

Teradici host card for physical PCs

Teradici also has a solution for physical workstations to leverage the PCoIP protocol, the PCoIP Remote Workstation card. This card is not actually for virtual desktop sessions; instead, it allows you to add a Teradici host card into a physical workstation, connect to your workstation, and send remote graphics, audio, and USB from the workstation to a PCoIP-enabled endpoint device, such as a zero client. Think of it as picking up your desktop PC and putting it in the data center, and then running a very long video, mouse, and keyboard cable to it. This use case is typically deployed for high-powered rack mount workstations or PCs.

In reality, the pixels are sent over the network, so where does that fit in with Horizon View? Quite simply, the connection to the physical desktop is managed using Horizon View and the Connection Server to broker the session in the same way you would connect to a virtual desktop machine.

Blast Extreme

Blast Extreme is a new VMware developed protocol that uses the H.264 video codec as an option if you have the appropriate GPU acceleration resource available, allowing it to deliver the user experience to H.264-enabled client devices. H.264 (MPEG-4 Part 10) is an Advanced Video Coding (MPEG-4 AVC) that is a block-oriented motion-compensation-based video compression standard. It's one of the most commonly used video formats and is used for the recording, compression, and distribution of video content such as DVD content.

Blast as a VMware protocol has actually been around for a while, and was first seen in Horizon 5.2 a few years ago, where it was used to deliver HTML5 access to virtual desktop machines. However, now it's not just limited to delivering HTML5 access; it can also deliver the user experience to the latest client devices using standard HTTPS ports.

The Blast Extreme delivery method is also on feature parity with PCoIP, and also supports similar functionality, such as client drive redirection, USB, unified communications, and local printing. Where they start to differ is in resource consumption, with Blast using far fewer CPU cycles, and delivery protocols, with Blast being more flexible.

Like PCoIP, Blast Extreme can compensate for an increase in latency or a reduction in bandwidth and dynamically adjust; however, it can also leverage both TCP and UDP, whereas PCoIP is UDP only.

You can also connect multiple monitors. Depending on the endpoint device, up to four monitors are supported, each one running at 2560 x 1600. Or, you can run three 4K monitors running at 3840 x 2160 for Windows 7 remote desktops with Aero disabled.

Some of the other features of Blast Extreme are detailed in the following list:

- **Blast Adaptive UX**: Delivers end-user access to Horizon View virtual desktop machines and hosted applications via the Horizon View Client or browser-based clients, using either Blast Extreme, PCoIP, or RDP. Automatically adapts to network conditions, delivering the best experience possible, through either.
- **Blast Multimedia**: Delivers rich video playback for Flash, HTML5, QuickTime, Microsoft Silverlight and Windows Media.
- **Blast 3D Services**: Built on the broadest virtualized graphics capabilities in the industry, including hardware-accelerated graphics with NVIDIA GRID vGPU technology. With Blast 3D enabled, Horizon View supports either up to two monitors running up to 1920 x 1200, or a single 4K monitor running at 3840 x 2160.

- **Blast Live Communications**: Delivers full access to communications tools such as headsets and webcams, for rich audio and video. Supports applications such as Skype, Google Hangouts, and Cisco WebEx.
- **Blast Unity Touch**: Delivers a more intuitive interface, allowing you to use Windows desktops, applications, and files from a mobile device.
- **Blast Local Access**: Supports connecting peripheral devices such as USB flash drives, printers, smart card devices, and smartphones to your virtual desktop machine.
- **Blast Horizon Clients**: Blast-enabled clients for delivering a high-end user experience to end-point devices.

Which Protocol – Blast Extreme, PCoIP, or RDP?

Now that we have a good understanding of PCoIP, Blast Extreme, and RDP, which one would you choose?

The most compelling reason to go with PCoIP is the fact that it uses the UDP protocol, which is much better suited to streaming media, and therefore lends itself perfectly to the characteristics of virtual desktop delivery, but as discussed, Blast can also use UDP as the delivery protocol. Just to highlight again, UDP is not concerned with how the data ends up on the endpoint device; it's only concerned with the speed of delivery and how quickly it gets there.

On the other hand, RDP uses TCP as its protocol, which is widely used across the Internet. The key difference with TCP is that it is concerned with how the data is being received. TCP requests an acknowledgment from the endpoint device as to whether or not it has received all of the packets successfully. If the endpoint device does not receive what it was expecting, then it replies, asking TCP to either stop sending packets or to narrow the amount that it receives. UDP just keeps sending and is much speedier, simply because there is no acknowledgment packet back from the endpoint device.

This is where Blast Extreme would come in, as it can use either TCP or UDP as the delivery protocol and is able to determine what network capacity it has available to it and adjust accordingly.

Blast Extreme will also use fewer resources on the endpoint device, especially if you offload the decoding using the NVIDIA GRID technology. However, the only point to be aware of is that when using TCP as the delivery protocol, it could potentially consume more bandwidth as it compensates for packet loss.

There are some cases where PCoIP won't be the appropriate protocol and Blast Extreme or RDP would need to be used. The one we see most often is when the required network ports are being blocked by corporate policy, or from remote locations that lock down Internet connections.

When your desktop is displayed back to you, PCoIP uses UDP port 4172 to send the pixels. This port is sometimes blocked, as it's not typically used. The result of this port being blocked is that, even though you will be able to log on to your virtual desktop via the View Client and everything looks OK, you will just receive a black screen. The black screen is due to the pixels being blocked as they are sent. In this example, the workaround is to access the desktop from an HTML5-enabled browser using Blast Extreme, which uses standard HTTPS ports. We will cover this in `Online Chapter`, *Fine-Tuning the End User Experience* available at `https://www.packtpub.com/sites/default/files/downloads/5657_FineTu ningtheEndUserExperience.pdf`.

The key takeaway here is to engage with your networking and security teams when planning how users connect to their virtual desktop machines and also look at how the users are working and from what locations. It may well be that you don't need external access, and therefore, WAN limitations are no longer a consideration.

Hardware-accelerated graphics for Horizon View

Early versions of virtual desktop technology faced challenges when it came to delivering high-end graphical content, as the host servers were not designed to render and deliver the size and quality of images required for such applications.

Let's start with a brief history and background. Technology to support high-end graphics was released in several phases, with the first support for 3D graphics released in vSphere 5, with View 5.0 using software-based rendering. This gave us the ability to support things such as the Windows Aero feature, but it was still not powerful enough for some of the really high-end use cases due to this being a software feature.

The next phase was to provide a hardware-based GPU virtualization solution that came with vSphere 5.1 and allowed virtual machines to share a physical GPU by allowing virtual machines to pass through the hypervisor layer to take advantage of a physical graphics card installed in the host server.

If we had this conversation a couple of years ago and you had a use case that required high-end graphics capabilities, then virtual desktops would not have been a viable solution. As we just discussed, in a VDI environment, graphics will be delivered using a virtualized, software-based graphics driver as part of the hypervisor.

Also, don't forget that, as we are now using servers to host the virtual desktops, we are using the power of the graphics card in the server, and servers aren't renowned for their high-end graphics capabilities and have limited GPU power, as typically all a server needs to do is display a management console.

That has all changed now. With the release of View 5.2 back in 2013, the ability to deliver hardware-accelerated graphics became a standard product feature with the introduction of **Virtual Shared Graphics Acceleration** (**vSGA**), which was then followed with the launch of **Virtual Dedicated Graphics Acceleration** (**vDGA**).

We will discuss these two technologies in the next sections of this chapter. We will also discuss the latest installment of graphics capabilities in Horizon View, with **Virtual Graphics Processing Unit** (**vGPU**).

Virtual Shared Graphics Acceleration (vSGA)

The vSGA implementation allows for multiple virtual desktop machines to share a physical GPU card, which is installed into the ESXi host server that is hosting those virtual desktop machines.

In this model, the virtual desktop machines do not have direct access to a dedicated physical GPU card. Instead, the standard VMware SVGA 3D graphics driver that is part of VMware Tools is installed on the virtual desktop's operating system. The SVGA driver is a VMware driver that provides support for DirectX 9.0c and OpenGL 2.1.

the GPU in the ESXi server. In this configuration, the driver supplied by the graphics card manufacturer (VIB) is installed on the ESXi hypervisor rather than the virtual desktop machine's own operating system.

Graphics commands from user sessions are intercepted by this driver and sent to the hypervisor, which controls the GPU in the ESXi server. In this configuration, the driver supplied by the graphics card manufacturer (VIB) is installed on the ESXi hypervisor rather than the virtual desktop machine's own operating system. Delivery to the user's endpoint works in exactly the same way, where DevTAP encodes the user experience to PCoIP or Blast Extreme, and delivers it to the end user's device, either in an HTML5 browser or Horizon Client.

The following diagram shows an overview of vSGA architecture:

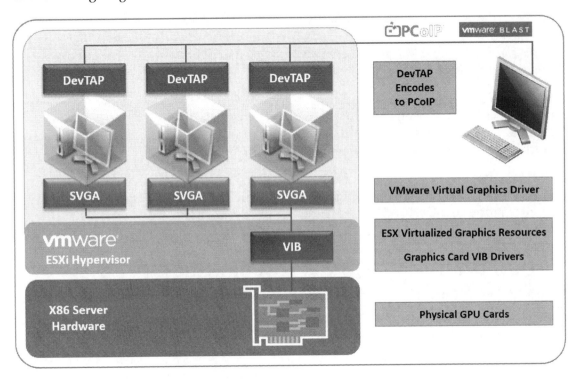

There are a number of configuration and support options to consider, which we will cover in the next sections.

vSGA supported configurations

vSGA will support OpenGL 2.1- and DirectX 9-based applications running either on Windows 7 or 8 virtual desktop machines, virtualized on VMware vSphere 5.1 and greater, using one of the following manufacturers' GPU cards:

- Intel HD Graphics P4700
- Tesla M6 and M60
- Grid K1 and K2
- AMD FirePro S4000X, S7000, S9000, S9050, and W7000

For the latest compatibility guide, see the following link:
`http://www.vmware.com/resources/compatibility/search.php?deviceCategory=vsga.`

How many virtual desktops are supported with vSGA?

This is a question that gets asked when talking about delivering hardware-based graphics within a Horizon View environment, so let's spend some time understanding this. Within Horizon View, you can create different desktop pools depending on the use case, as we will cover in `Chapter 7`, *Managing and Configuring Desktop Pools*, where one of the desktop pools will be configured to use high-end graphics. Typically, you would not want to give all users access to a hardware-based GPU, hence the reason you would create a desktop pool for this particular use case.

So, to answer the question, the number of virtual desktops you can allocate to a GPU is dependent on the amount of **video memory (VRAM)** that you allocate to each virtual desktop. The thing to bear in mind is that the resources are shared, and therefore, normal VMware virtualization rules apply. The first thing to note is how memory is shared.

 Half of the video memory allocated to a virtual desktop machine is allocated from the GPU card's memory and the other half is from the host server's memory. When sizing your host servers, you need to ensure that you have enough memory configured in the server to allocate this as video memory.

Based on this, and with the number of virtual desktops supported being based on the amount of allocated VRAM, let's look at how that works out.

So, the default amount of VRAM allocated to a virtual desktop machine is 128 MB. So, in this example, 64 MB will come from the GPU and the other 64 MB from the host server. If you then take a GPU card that has 4 GB of VRAM on board, you will be able to support 64 virtual desktops (4 GB or 4096 MB divided by 64 MB from the GPU = 64 virtual desktop machines).

Within Horizon View, you can allocate a maximum of 512 MB of VRAM per virtual desktop machine. If you apply this to the preceding example using the same 4 GB GPU card, you now reduce the number of supported virtual desktops down to 16 (4 GB or 4096 MB divided by 256 MB from the GPU = 16 virtual desktop machines).

With the AMD solutions, the maximum number of supported desktops is 15 per GPU.

We stated previously that normal VMware virtualization rules apply, so let's explain exactly what that means. Basically, what happens when you can't fulfil a virtual desktop machine's specification and there are insufficient resources? It won't boot or power on, right? It's the same for GPU configuration. If you configure a desktop pool with more virtual desktop machines than you can support on that GPU, then they will not boot.

If you do happen to configure more virtual desktop machines in a pool where you probably cannot guarantee the GPU resources to be available, set the **Hardware 3D** setting in the **View Administrator** console to **Automatic**. Doing this allows Horizon View to revert to the software-based 3D rendering in order to deliver the virtual desktop machines.

Virtual Dedicated Graphics Acceleration (vDGA)

While vSGA works on a shared basis, vDGA allows for an individual virtual desktop machine to have its own dedicated access to a physical GPU card installed in the ESXi host server. This allows the virtual desktop machine to have a higher level of graphic performance, making it perfect for such use cases as CAD/CAM applications, as it supports DirectX (9, 10, and 11), OpenGL 4.4, and NVIDIA CUDA.

The following diagram shows the architecture for vDGA:

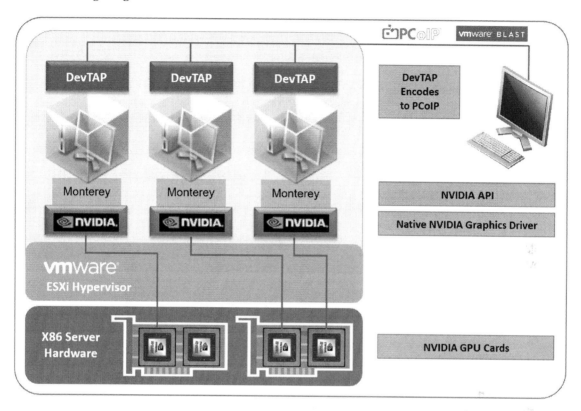

The vDGA solution makes use of a feature called **VMDirectPath I/O pass-through**, sometimes referred to as PCI pass-through, which allows the virtual desktop machine to pass through the hypervisor layer and directly access the hardware in the host server. In this case, the hardware in question is the NVIDIA GPU cards.

 As a virtual desktop machine is mapped directly to a GPU on a one-to-one basis, you cannot use vSphere features such as HA, DRS, or vMotion.

How many virtual desktops are supported with vDGA?

Unlike vSGA, which is limited by the amount of memory on the GPU card, vDGA is limited purely by the number of GPUs or GRID cards you can physically fit into the host server. This is dependent on your server vendor and what they support.

 Server vendors offer NVIDIA GRID-enabled servers that are prebuilt, and therefore, this technology is only available from the OEM channel. The primary reason is that servers require additional power and cooling components to drive the GRID cards.

For example, an NVIDIA GRID K2 GPU card has two GPUs on board, which would mean that you can allocate four virtual desktop machines to this card. Depending on your server hardware platform, you could install more than one card, therefore increasing the number of users that have access to a hardware-enabled GPU in their virtual desktop.

The vDGA-supported configurations

The following GPU cards are supported with vDGA:

- GRID K1 and K2
- Tesla M60 and M60
- Quadro 1000M, 3000M, and 5000M
- Quadro K2000, K2200, K3100M, K4000, K4200, K5000, K5200, and K6000
- AMD FirePro S7150

For the latest compatibility guide, see the following link: `http://www.vmware.com/resources/compatibility/search.php?deviceCategory=vdga`

Virtual GPU (vGPU)

In the previous sections, we have talked about two different models for delivering high-end graphics. However, there are a couple of limitations with each of those solutions.

With vSGA, you get the scalability in terms of the number of users that can use the GPU card; however, because it does not use the native driver provided by the GPU vendor, then some of the ISV's will not certify their applications running on this solution. They would need to certify the VMware SVGA driver, as that's the driver that's used.

So, the answer to tackle the ISV support issue is to use vDGA, which does use the native GPU vendor's graphics driver, but now you are limited in terms of scalability and the high cost. Having a virtual desktop machine dedicated to a GPU, with only a handful of GPUs available in each host server, would make for quite an expensive solution. Having said that, there may be a use case where that would be the correct solution.

So, what we need is a solution that takes the best of both worldsâ©©a solution that takes the shared GPU approach for scalability, yet uses the native graphics drivers.

That solution is called **Virtual GPU** (**vGPU**), and was launched as part of the Horizon 6 Version 6.1 release.

The following diagram shows the architecture for vGPU:

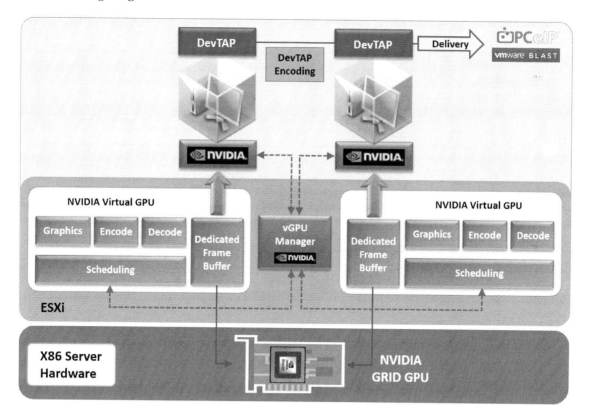

In this model, we have the native **NVIDIA** driver installed in the virtual desktop machines, which then has direct access to the **NVIDIA GRID** card in the host servers. The **GPU** is then effectively virtualized and time-sliced, with each virtual desktop machine having a slice of that time.

> vGPU is only available with VMware vSphere 6 and Horizon View 6.1 and later.

How many virtual desktops are supported with vGPU?

With vGPU, the number of supported users/virtual desktop machines is based on different profiles. These profiles are detailed in the following diagram, and give you the number of users, number of supported monitors, and so on:

Configurations

	vGPU Profile	Video Memory	Max. Monitors	Max. Resolution	Max Users
NVIDIA GRID K2	K280Q	4 GB	4	2560 x 1600	2
	K260Q	2 GB	4	2560 x 1600	4
	K240Q	1 GB	2	2560 x 1600	8
	K220Q	512 MB	2	2560 x 1600	16
NVIDIA GRID K1	K180Q	4 GB	4	2560 x 1600	4
	K160Q	2 GB	4	2560 x 1600	8
	K140Q	1 GB	2	2560 x 1600	16
	K120Q	512 MB	2	2560 x 1600	32

As with the vDGA and vSGA solutions, you need to check that you have the correct supported hardware. In addition, you should also check that your applications are supported in these configurations. You can find the current list of supported applications by following the link to the NVIDIA website:

`http://www.nvidia.com/object/grid-isv-tested-applications.html`

Unified communications support

Like high-end graphics, if we had a conversation about running a unified communications solution or VoIP session on a VDI desktop a couple of years ago, I would have described it as Kryptonite for VDI! Although it technically works, the first call might have an acceptable performance, but adding more users would ultimately bring the servers to their knees with the amount of traffic generated and resources required to conduct the calls. Eventually, the experience would have become completely unusable. **Unified comms** was not a good use case for VDI.

However, this has all changed and you can now happily use a unified communications solution with your virtual desktop. There was always a great use case to deploy Unified comms with VDI; it just never workedâ©©for example, within a call center environment with the ability to provide a DR solution or allow users to work from home during a snow day.

So, why didn't it work? Quite simply, it was because, when you placed a VoIP call from your virtual desktop, the call would go over the PCoIP protocol, causing bandwidth issues and making your desktop perform slowly, and also putting additional load on the servers in the data center in having to process the call. This is detailed in the following diagram, which shows how it was before and the result afterwards:

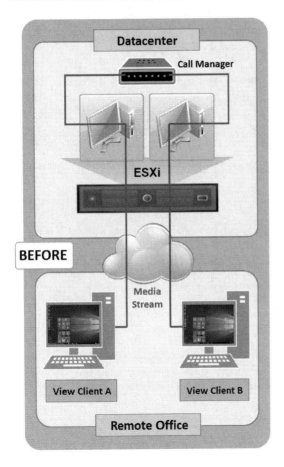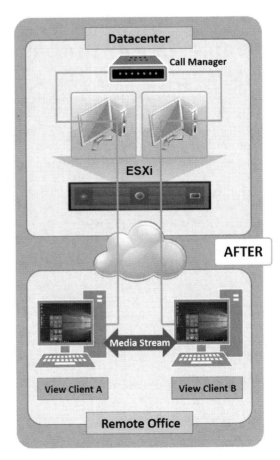

To solve these issues and to enable a working solution, VMware concentrated on three key areas and delivered the following new features/enhancements:

- Offloading media processing to the client device by removing the load that was placed on the server in the data center
- Optimized point-to-point media delivery, eliminating the hairpin effect
- High-quality UC VoIP and video with QoS

How do unified communications work now?

A Remote Procedure Call utilizes a virtual channel to allow the different components of a softphone, running on a virtual desktop machine, to communicate and pass voice and video data to other softphone components in the client device. This is out-of-band communication.

The call control stack (an SIP stack if using SIP signaling) communicates with the call control server or call manager to register or establish the call.

A media engine on the client device performs the encoding and decoding of voice and video streams into native voice and video codecs and then streams the VoIP/video stream directly to the other endpoint (as directed by the call manager server), therefore setting up a peer-to-peer call and not going through the data center. This now eliminates the hairpin effect.

Currently, VMware supports solutions from Cisco, Mittal, Avaya, and Microsoft Lync 2013. We will cover the Microsoft Skype (Lync) solution in the next section.

Support for Microsoft Lync 2013 (Skype for Business)

Horizon View provides certified support for Microsoft Lync 2013, or Skype for Business as it is now called. This includes full support for VoIP and video. The following diagram shows the process of how the client works:

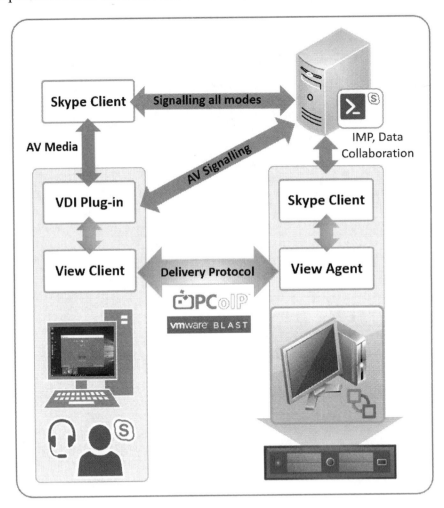

To enable Skype, you need to ensure that the VDI plugin is installed on the endpoint device along with the View client and Microsoft Skype client. VMware has implemented Microsoft's **Dynamic Virtual Channels (DVC)** inside the PCoIP protocol to enable this feature. DVC provides the communication path between the virtual desktop machine and the client endpoint.

There are some limitations to the solution that should be mentioned:

- The Audio Device and Video Device tuning pages are not available
- Multi-view video is not supported
- Recording of conversations is not supported
- The Call Delegation and Response Group Agent Anonymization features are not supported
- Joining meetings anonymously is not supported
- Using the Skype for Business (Lync) VDI plugin along with a Skype for Business (Lync) Phone Edition device is not supported

Real-Time Audio Video (RTAV)

Following on from the unified communications support, the next question we hear concerns support for plugging in a USB webcam and using it with a virtual desktop.

The issue

Like unified communications and VoIP, using a webcam or using audio in and audio out on a virtual desktop machine was not initially supported due to the high bandwidth requirements these types of device require, therefore resulting in poor performance. Any redirection of these types of devices was previously handled with the USB redirection feature of the PCoIP protocol.

This is how audio in worked, but audio in using a 3.5 mm jack socket did not work at all. Audio out did work using the PCoIP audio redirection feature, which was much better than using a USB redirection.

The problem is that you can't split a USB audio device such that the audio out functionality remains local to the client and audio in is redirected. So, using a USB headset in a VoIP-type application required the entire headset to be forwarded to the guest.

How does RTAV fix this issue?

Real-Time Audio Video (RTAV) does not forward audio and webcam devices using USB. Instead, the devices are left local to the client, and audio/images are pulled from the local devices. The audio/images are then encoded and delivered to the guest virtual machine, and then decoded. A virtual webcam and a virtual microphone are installed in the guest virtual machine, which then plays the received audio/video. You will see entries for **VMware Virtual Microphone** and **VMware Virtual Webcam** in the device manager of your virtual desktop machine.

RTAV can support the following:

- Webcams and audio in at the same timeâ◎◎for example, VoIP video-conference-type applications such as Google Talk and Skype
- Audio-in only (without video)â◎◎for example, VoIP applications
- A webcam on its ownâ◎◎for example, webcam-monitoring-type applications and user photo-taking

The RTAV feature only works when using the PCoIP protocol. It does not work with RDP.

URL Content Redirection

The **URL Content Redirection** feature allows you to configure a URL to either open on a local browser on the endpoint device, or open on the virtual desktop machine. Which content opens in which is configured by use of a GPO.

The use case for doing this is to separate internal browsing from internal browsing. It may be that if you want to look at secure content, then you would use the browser on the virtual desktop machine, as the data doesn't leave the data center and any other browsing can happen locally. Another case may be that you want to limit bandwidth usage into the data center and if users are browsing heavy content they can use their local Internet connection.

There are two types of URL that you can configure for redirection:

- URLs that a user enters into the address bar of Internet Explorer
- Links in an application such as Outlook or Word that users can click

View Clients

In this section, we are going to quickly touch on the Horizon View Client, as it is an important component of the solution and the way you receive your virtual desktop machine's screenshots remotely.

The View Client is basically where your virtual desktop machine's screen is decoded and displayed on an endpoint device. There are two distinct types of View Clients, a software-based version, which is installed on the user's endpoint device, and a hardware-based version, which uses zero clients.

We will cover the View Client options in more detail in `Chapter 10`, *Horizon View Client Options*.

Summary

In this chapter, we discussed the Horizon View architecture and the different components that make up the complete solution. We covered the key technologies, such as how Linked Clones and Instant Clones work to optimize storage, and then introduced some of the features that go toward delivering a great end-user experience, such as delivering high-end graphics, unified communications, profile management, and how the protocols deliver the desktop to the end user. Now that you understand these features and components, how they work, and how they fit into the overall solution, in the upcoming chapters, we will be taking a deeper look at how to configure them.

3
Design and Deployment Considerations

Having given you a comprehensive overview of the different components of VMware Horizon in the first couple of chapters, in this chapter, we are going to start looking at how to put those components to use by introducing you to some of the design and deployment techniques that you need to consider when undertaking your VMware Horizon project.

We are going to discuss these techniques in order for you to prove the technology and understand how it needs to work inside your business, starting with issues such as assessing the current environment and how to use this information to design a successful VMware Horizon deployment in your own environment.

Once you fully understand what it is you need to achieve for the business, you can dive deeper into the design considerations for your Horizon View solution, including, but not limited to, ESXi host design, memory and CPU allocations for virtual desktops, storage considerations, thin clients, and other dos and don'ts.

As we may have alluded to, we are going to look at both the business and technical elements to a project, and walk you through this process. To make this easier, we will break these down into three distinct project phases, as shown in the following diagram:

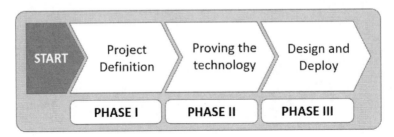

The three phases can be explained as follows:

- **Phase I – Project Definition** is where we look at the business elements of the project, identifying both business and use cases
- **Phase II – Proving the technology** provides the opportunity to test the solution in your environment
- **Phase III – Design and Deploy** for production takes the output and findings from the previous two phases and allows you to design and deploy the solution in production

In the following sections, we are going to discuss the three phases in a little more detail.

Phase I – Project Definition

In this first section, we are going to look at how you approach the project. This is broken down into four steps, as shown in the following diagram:

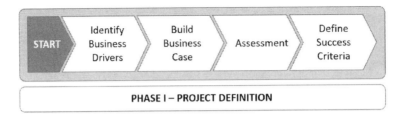

Let's start by looking at the business drivers and understanding what your business requirements look like.

Identifying business drivers – understanding your needs and requirements

Before you jump headlong into your Horizon project, take a step back and ensure that you document what you are actually trying to achieve. More often than not, it can be very easy to get carried away with all the new shiny technological aspects of the solution, such as the installation and configuration of new hardware and software, that the end goal is either lost, or is not relevant to the business.

It may be an obvious point to make, but the key to identifying the business drivers is to really understand what you want to evaluate. By this, we mean is it a strategic decision based on the need to transform your organization with new working initiatives, or is there a more compelling event, such as the end of life of an operating system or application? It may even simply be the need to reduce costs. Whatever the case, you need to get that nailed down, written up, and documented on day one, so the project has meaning and direction, and even more importantly, provide a baseline to refer back to when it comes to review time, to gauge whether or not the project has been successful.

Start by writing a document of requirements that lists the business needs, the current problems you need to solve, the vision, and any compromises and assumptions. As you progress through your project, you should regularly refer back to this document to keep yourself focused on the end goal.

Build business case

Once you have defined the drivers behind an initiative or the compelling event that's kicked off the project, and understood the high-level objectives, the next stage is to start building the business case around these. This requires you to go to the next level of detail and to start drilling into the specific areas the solution needs to address. To do this, you need firstly to understand the business strategy and then identify the key stakeholders for the project. You can then start to define the high-level requirements of each of the areas identified as drivers and also start to define user segmentation. For example, you can look at what different user types you have, how they work today, and what they need going forward. At the end of the day, it will be the end users that decide whether or not the project is a success, not you! This leads us into the next section, the assessment phase.

Desktop assessments

Once you have built your business case and validated it against your strategy, and identified that there is a requirement for a new way of delivering a desktop environment, then the next stage is to run an assessment.

So, what do we mean by an assessment, and what's involved? It comes down to several things that we are looking for. This includes examining your current desktop landscape by means of some form of desktop assessment, so you can understand what is currently being delivered, to whom it is being delivered, and more importantly, how resource-intensive it is. The assessment is designed to build up a picture of what the current environment actually looks like. Some of the key metrics we are looking for include the following:

- Which users are using which applications and the application usage
- Resource consumption (CPU, memory, disk, and network are key)
- Unsuitable applications/use cases
- Which client operating systems are being used?
- Current delivery methods (RDSH, XenApp, VDI, physical PCs, and so on)

What you are ultimately looking to achieve is to create a baseline of what your environment looks like today. Then, as you move into defining the success criteria and proving the technology, you have a baseline as a reference point to demonstrate how you have improved current functionality and delivered on the business case and strategy.

If you have deployed a VDI solution already then you should have most of this data, but even so, if this was a while ago, then it's worth re-running the assessment so you have up-to-date data, especially around the applications in your environment.

Assessment tools

There are a number of different third-party products on the market that you can use to conduct a desktop assessment, and you are often able to use the services of a partner to assist with this process, to help you understand the information from the assessment.

One of the most popular tools for assessment is *Liquidware Labs'* Stratusphere FIT. **Stratusphere FIT** will give you a detailed breakdown of the current environment, as well as detailing the user login process, something that it is key to understand, as a potential reason for deploying VDI is to speed up and manage login times:

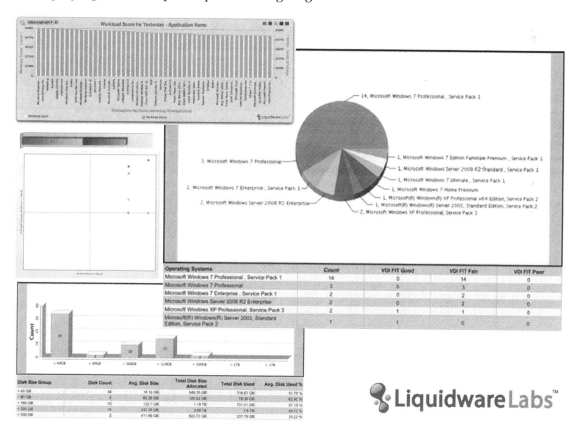

One thing to ensure is that the assessment solution is designed specifically for desktop assessments and not for server virtualization. The two technologies, although both virtualization technologies, are completely different, and while you could probably use desktop assessment software to plan your server virtualization project, it simply would not work the other way around.

As well as the actual collecting of the assessment data, there are a number of other points that you should take into consideration and look at. This will help you understand what some of the raw assessment data is telling you. For example, it might tell you that a particular user is unsuitable to have a virtual desktop due to the amount of resources they consume; however, when you speak to them, you may find that whatever they are doing isn't going to be relevant in VDI.

What do your users actually do?

While working in an IT department, you often have a good level of understanding of the tasks that users undertake and the software that they use to achieve these tasks on a daily basis. However, this can usually be a lot more complex than it might first appear.

By undertaking a desktop assessment, you gather a granular level of understanding about the processes, applications, and experience our users are getting from their existing desktops. This will likely include the applications they use, and those that they don't use, including the installed versions and capacity and performance requirements, as well as user experience metrics, such as login times and application load times.

Applications

Understanding the applications in use is going to be a key element moving forward. This will have an impact in many areas, including the number of pools, pool design, application virtualization, and, potentially, whether the desktop that gets assigned to the user can be non-persistent or you need to allocate a persistent desktop.

With the metrics gathered from the assessment, you will be able to fully understand the current situation of your desktop estate. It's not uncommon to find many disparate versions of software, meaning potential security risks and in other cases, key applications actually crashing on a regular basis. This information will help you build a business case for change and to help you prioritize your rollout to the users with the biggest security holes or the worst user experience.

Performance

If you don't undertake a desktop assessment, it is likely that your desktops might be sized in one of two ways. The first would be by sizing your desktops based on the manufacturer's minimum recommendations, and you will size based on the specifications of a physical desktop PC, which will potentially be the most cost effective, but is likely to cause you the most amount of problems. The flipside would be to base your desktops on the software manufacturer's recommended specifications. While your users might end up happy with this solution, it is likely that this is going to cost you the most and potentially mean that you will fail to get a sign off for your project.

By undertaking a desktop assessment, you can actually understand what the performance curves look like throughout the working day; you are likely to see many dips and spikes throughout the day, such as login storms, AV scans, logoff storms, and other metrics, such as increased Internet usage during lunch breaks. If you work in an education environment, you might see many login and logoff storms during the day. It is important to understand this, as you will need to ensure your solution is designed to meet these requirements. This information can be used to help guide you when sizing the relevant desktop pools, but bear in mind that potentially, you are going to be making changes to the desktops between the assessment phase and deploying VDI desktops. This may be something such as migrating from Windows 7 to Windows 10, or moving to a desktop that has been heavily optimized in comparison to an OEM installation of Windows. The assessment will have been performed on the previous version of the operating system and therefore may not give you 100% accurate information on the resources required.

User experience

Above all else, what matters is user experience, which is the measurement of how good or how poor the user's experience of using their desktop actually is. When you undertake a server virtualization project, if done correctly, the users will probably not even realize it has happened. With a desktop virtualization, or any EUC-type project, it is more likely that they will realize a change has happened and you need to ensure that this is a positive experience for the project to be a success. The measurements of user experience will be wide and varied, but these will include elements such as boot time, application load time, login time, page load time, and application failures.

As you are progressing through the proof of concept, pilot, and tuning processes, you need to ensure that the user experience is constantly improving; failing to take user experience into consideration will result in a definite failure of the project.

Floor walks, interviews, and department champions

While the desktop assessment process is an important part of any EUC project, it should not replace the need to interact with your users. The benefit of human involvement is that you are able to pick up elements that simply would not be possible with software alone.

Start by simply walking through your office, noting what the users are doing, what applications they are using, what accessories, how many screens, if they are using laptops or PCs, and so on.

Once you have this high level of understanding, consider booking meetings with key business leaders in each department to understand their needs, requirements, and the problems they have with their desktops today. You should also start considering who your department champions are going to be!

What are department champions?

If you are going to make a short list of takeaway considerations from this book, department champions should be high on your list. A department champion is a user who is going to be the go-to person within the department for everything to do with their department's desktop, design, testing, and support. They don't need to be IT experts, but should have a desire to help you improve their overall desktop experience. You will work with these champions to help you with the design of their desktops, as they will be your first port of call for testing, and then testing again after you have listened to, and implemented any of the feedback given.

By working with a department champion, you will have a sponsor within the department. They will have a sense of pride over what is being rolled out and will be there to help you sculpt the desktop and be the user on your side to help explain why certain decisions have been made.

Defining the success criteria

The key objective in defining the success criteria is to document what a *good* solution should look like for the project to succeed and become production-ready.

You need to clearly define the elements that need to function correctly in order to move from proof of concept to proof of technology and then into a pilot phase, before finally deploying into production. You need to fully document what these elements are and get the end users or other project stakeholders to sign up to them. It's almost like creating a statement of work with a clearly defined list of tasks.

Another important factor is to ensure that during this phase of the project, the criteria don't start to grow beyond the original scope. That means that any other additional elements should not get added to the success criteria, or at least not without discussing it first. It may well transpire that something key was missed; however, if you have conducted your assessment thoroughly, this shouldn't happen.

Another thing that works well at this stage is to again involve the end users. Set up a steering committee or advisory panel by selecting people from different departments to act as sponsors within their area of business. Actively involve them in the testing phases, but get them on board early to get their input in shaping the solution from the outset.

Too many projects fail when an end user tries something that didn't work. However, the thing that they tried is not actually a relevant use case or something that is used by the business as a critical line of business application, and therefore shouldn't derail the project.

I once saw a VDI project fail due to the unresponsiveness of Microsoft Paint, which knocked the project way off course while the issue was investigated. The upshot was that Paint was not used by anyone, and so was totally irrelevant to the business or use case, but it still burned precious cycles while trying to enhance the performance.

If we have a set of success criteria defined up front that the end users have signed up to, anything outside that criteria is not in scope. If it's not defined in the document, it should be disregarded as not being part of what success should look like.

Phase II – Proving the Technology

In this section, we are going to discuss the approach to proving the technology is fit for purpose. This is another very important piece of work that needs to be successfully completed once you have completed *Phase I*, and is somewhat different to how you would typically approach an IT project. This is the same approach you should take for any end user computing type of project:

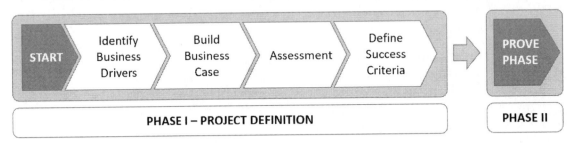

As previously discussed, the starting point is to focus on the end users rather than the IT department. After all, these are the people that will be using the applications on a daily basis and know what they need in order to get their jobs done. Rather than giving them what you think they need, why not ask them what they *actually* need and then, within reason, deliver their requirements. It's that old saying of don't try and fit a square peg into a round hole, as no matter how hard you try, it's just never going to fit.

First and foremost, you need to design the solution around the requirements of the end user rather than spending time and money on building an infrastructure only to find that at the end of the project it doesn't deliver what the users require.

Once the previous steps have been discussed and documented, you should be able to build a picture around what's driving the project. You will understand what you are trying to achieve/deliver and, based upon hard and fast facts from the assessment phase, be able to work on what success should look like. From there, you can then move into testing some form of the technology.

There are three distinct roads we can take within the testing cycle, and it might be the case that you don't need all of them. In actual fact, it is usually best to jump straight to the last one if you can, and look at deploying a pilot to save time and cost, and actually get the end users engaged early.

The three stages we are talking about are as follows:

- Proof of concept (POC)
- Proof of technology (POT)
- Pilot

In the next sections, we are briefly going to cover what each of these stages means and why you might or might not need them.

Proof of concept (POC)

A POC typically refers to a partial solution, often built on any old hardware kicking about, which involves a relatively small number of users, usually within the confines of the IT department, acting in business roles to establish whether the system satisfies some aspect of the purpose it was designed for. Once proven, one of two things tends to happen. Firstly, nothing happens as it's just the IT department playing with technology and there wasn't a real business driver in the first place. This is usually down to the previous steps and not having a defined business case. In a similar way, by not having any success criteria, it will also fail, as you don't know exactly what you are setting out to prove. The second outcome is that the project moves into a pilot phase, which we will discuss in a later section. You could consider moving directly into this phase and bypassing the POC altogether. Maybe a demonstration of the technology would suffice, and using a demo environment over a longer period would show you enough of how the technology works.

Proof of technology (POT)

In contrast to the POC, the objective of a proof of technology is to determine whether or not the proposed solution or technology will integrate into your existing environment and therefore demonstrate compatibility. The objective is to highlight any technical problems specific to your environment, such as how your bespoke systems might integrate. As with the POC, a POT is typically run by the IT department and no business users would be involved. A POT is purely a technical validation exercise.

Pilot

A pilot refers to what is almost a small-scale rollout of the solution, in a production-style environment, to real users, which would show a limited scope of the intended final solution. The scope may be limited by the number of users who can access the pilot system, the business processes affected, or the business partners involved. The purpose of a pilot is to test, in a production-like environment, whether the system is working, as it was designed to, while limiting business exposure and risk. It should also touch real users so as to gauge the feedback from what might ultimately become a live, production solution. This is a critical step in achieving success, as the users are the people that have to interact with the system on a daily basis, and the reason why you should set up some form of working group to gather their feedback. That would also mitigate project failure, as the solution may deliver everything the IT department could ever wish for, but when it goes live and the first user logs on and reports a bad experience or performance, you may as well have not bothered. The pilot should be carefully scoped, sized, and implemented, which breaks down nicely into the following four steps of a successful pilot, as shown in the following workflow diagram:

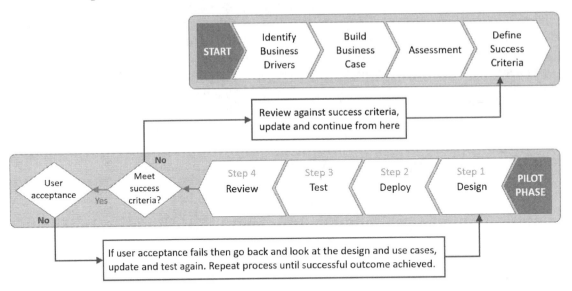

Let's have a look at the steps in a bit more detail.

Step 1 – pilot design

The pilot infrastructure should be designed on the same hardware platforms that the production solution is going to be deployed on, for example, the same servers and storage. This takes into account any anomalies between platforms and configuration differences that could affect things such as scalability, or more importantly, performance.

Even at the pilot stage, the design is absolutely key, and you should make sure you take into account the production design even at this stage. Why? Basically, because many pilot solutions end up going straight into production and more and more users get added above and beyond those scoped for the pilot.

It's great going live with the solution and not having to go back and rebuild it, but when you start to scale by adding more users and applications, you might have some issues due to the pilot sizing. It may sound obvious, but often with a successful pilot, the users just keep on using it and additional users get added. If it's only ever going to be a pilot, that's fine, but keep this in mind and bare this in mine: if you are planning on taking the pilot straight into production, design it for production right at the very start.

It is always useful to work from a prerequisite document to understand the different elements that need consideration in the design. Design elements include:

- Hardware sizing (servers – CPU, memory, and consolidation ratios)
- Pool design (based on user segmentation)
- Storage design (local SSD, SAN, and acceleration technologies)
- Image creation (rebuild from scratch and optimize for VDI)
- Network design (load balancing and external access)
- Antivirus considerations
- Application delivery (delivering virtually versus installing in core image)
- User profile management
- Floating or dedicated desktop assignments
- Persistent or non-persistent desktop builds (linked clone or full clone)

Once you have all this information, you can start to deploy the pilot environment.

Step 2 – deploy the pilot

In the deployment phase of the pilot, you are going to start building out the infrastructure, deploying the test users, building the OS images, and then start testing.

Step 3 – test the pilot

During the testing phase, you need to work closely with the end users and your sponsors, showing them the solution and how it works, closely monitoring the users, and assessing the solution as it's being used. This allows you to keep in contact with the users and give them the opportunity to continually provide real-time feedback. This in turn allows you to answer questions and make adjustments and enhancements on the fly rather than waiting until the end of the project only to be told it didn't work or they just simply didn't understand something.

This then leads us onto the last section, the review.

Step 4 – review the pilot

This final stage sometimes tends to get forgotten. You have deployed the solution, the users have been testing it, and then it ends there for whatever reason. However, there is one very important last thing to do to enable you to move into production.

You need to measure the user experience and the IT department's experience against the success criteria that you set out at the start of this process. You need to get customer sign-off and agreement that you have successfully met all the objectives and requirements. If this is not the case, you need to understand the reasons why. Have you missed something in the use case, have the user requirements changed, or is it simply a perception issue?

Whatever the case, you need to cycle around the process again. Go back to the use case, understand and reevaluate the user requirements (what it is that is seemingly failing or not behaving as expected), and then tweak the design or make the required changes and get the users to test the solution again.

You need to continue this process until you get acceptance and sign-off, otherwise you will not get to the final solution deployment phase:

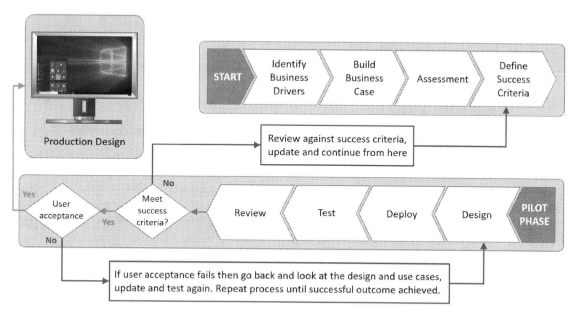

When the project has been signed off after a successful pilot test, there is no reason why you cannot deploy the technology in production. However, it is useful to come back and revisit this every once in a while, to make sure nothing has changed.

Now that we have talked about how to prove the technology and successfully demonstrated that it delivers against both your business case and your user requirements, in the next sections, we are going to start looking at the design for the production environment.

Phase III – designing a production environment

Now that you have proved that the solution works within your environment, you can take all the findings from both the assessment and the pilot phases, and start to build out a design for production. In this section, we are going to cover the main considerations for a successful design, and discuss the general rules of thumb and best practices, before moving on to the specifics of sizing the storage requirement, scalability, availability, and also how to architect the solution.

Before we do, we are going to look at a few different example scenarios that could have been highlighted during the assessment and pilot phases, and look at which technology you should consider deploying.

Technology choices

With VMware Horizon, there is no one-product-fits-all solution to your users' needs, so it is important to consider the use cases and match the different use cases to the different technologies within the VMware Horizon portfolio. Once you have collected the key information from the methods mentioned earlier, it is important to come to a conclusion on which technology is going to meet the users' needs the best. You have several different technologies available to deliver the desktops to the end users—technologies such as Horizon View, Horizon Mirage, ThinApp, and App Volumes.

In the following sections, we will discuss some sample scenarios and the decisions we could make based upon these scenarios.

Example scenario 1

In this example, there are a number of users based in a call center utilizing a Windows desktop to access a customer relationship database. They are also using a web browser to access an intranet page. These users work set hours in a shift pattern across the call center, and they work in a hot desk fashion, utilizing whichever device is available.

Recommendation

This would seem to be the ideal scenario for a Horizon View VDI desktop. With such a simple use case, you might actually decide to deliver these users' desktops through Horizon View and the hosted applications feature, using Microsoft RDS to allow greater levels of consolidation and potential cost savings. Due to the specifics of the use case, you could limit access to the pool using tags configured on the desktop pool and the View Connection Servers. The CRM client could be installed onto the base image or RDS server, or alternatively, could be delivered by ThinApp or App Volumes.

Scenario 2

There are a number of engineering users who need access to a desktop, both online and offline. When offline, they will be utilizing bespoke software to program machinery; often, this work is carried out in areas of poor mobile signal. They rarely come into the office, but do work from home, where they have good Internet access, once or twice a week. They also need access to a job allocation system when they have access to the Internet. At present, this is accessed via connecting to a work VPN and running a Windows client application on their laptops. They would like to be able to adopt iPads to access the job allocation system but are restricted by the need to use the Windows client.

Recommendation

This scenario highlights the exact type of user that does not suit a VDI desktop alone. Previously, if you had tried to make VDI work in this scenario, it would not have led to a good user experience. With the diversity now available in the Horizon Suite, you are able to use the individual components to deliver a solution that can be seamless to the user and offer them a genuine productivity advantage.

In this scenario, you would be looking to centralize and manage the desktops using VMware Mirage. This would allow you to not only store a copy of the devices locally in case of failure or loss, but it would also allow you to update and deliver new software when a connection to the Mirage server is available over the Internet.

However, there is a key requirement to access an online application in the form of the job allocation system; you could, of course, deliver this in the same way as it is delivered today, but you could also consider delivering this through Horizon View and a published application. This would give the advantage of this application being accessible through a variety of devices, without the complexity of a second desktop that VDI would bring. You could also consider AirWatch by VMware to manage the iPad devices.

Scenario 3

In this scenario, you have a marketing department with 10 users, all using desktop PCs with dual screens running Windows XP. Across these desktops are a number of matching applications, but each desktop also has a few individual applications that have been installed by IT for users over the years. They are now looking to start making use of a number of SaaS applications and services such as WebEx, and would also like to have the ability to work from home.

Recommendation

With the end of support for XP, you are going to want to move these users to Windows 8 or Windows 10. As such, you are going to want to check the compatibility of their applications with the new operating system version, and where possible, try and standardize the applications as much as possible without affecting the user. Where there are applications that don't support the latest operating system, you could see weather VMware ThinApp would allow us to virtualize the application on their current Windows XP desktop for us to then subsequently run on the new operating system. As the user has no offline requirements, this would seem a good fit for VDI, and as there is a large commonality across the desktops, you should try and see how a non-persistent linked clone pool would work for these users.

You could deliver the common applications by installing them in the base image and deliver the individual applications where possible via ThinApp and/or App Volumes.

Scenario 4

There is a small CAD department with 10 users utilizing Autodesk AutoCAD 2014. They last purchased five workstations with new high-end graphics cards a year ago for half the users. The users must have access to install their own software and keep a lot of data locally while they are working on designs.

Recommendation

There are a number of options in this scenario. With Horizon 7 and NVidia GRID graphics cards, it is likely that you would be able to offer these users a good experience on a correctly configured virtual desktop. With AutoCAD 2014, it is likely the users will need access to the GPU in a dedicated mode, meaning that with a single K1 card, you could have four entry-level users, or with a K2 card, you could have two high-end users.

As half the workstations have recently been refreshed, you would likely recommend these be kept in use until they are due to be replaced, but use Horizon Mirage for data protection and to manage updates and software rollout. For the remaining users, you should consider dedicated, full-clone desktops inside View, along with a K1 or K2 card.

These desktops would be managed with VMware Mirage the same as the physical machine, but as they are VDI desktops, they would offer the ability for thin clients to be deployed on the office floor rather than expensive workstations. It might also offer extended options for remote working in the future if required. It is recommended that this scenario is heavily tested during the proof of concept (POC) and pilot stages to fully understand the type of graphics card required, along with the CPU and memory resources.

Conclusions

The scenarios described demonstrate that there is no one-size-fits-all solution that can be deployed over diverse businesses requirements. If you were to try and shoehorn some of these scenarios into a single solution, it would result in a poor user experience. With the Horizon Suite, not only are you able to have commonality across the solutions for the users and administrators, but you are also able to offer a diverse range of solutions to meet the differing and diverse requirements of the end users.

Preparing for production

You now have all the information about the current environment, business requirements and goals, and have considered different scenarios to meet the needs of the end users; you can now consider what the production environment will look like. This is where things start to get really serious; you have tested your solution, proved the concept, piloted with a subset of your users, built a business case, and signed off on it. Now is the time to start rolling out to your agreed user base.

This will happen in a number of ways, but initially, it's worth starting this slowly and gathering momentum over time. By gathering momentum in this way, you are able to guarantee success, and less tuning is required along the way. The big bang approach will end in a world of pain, both for the users and for you, when you have so many things to consider when looking at issues.

In the next section, we are going to look at designing for the production deployment.

Horizon View Pod and Block Architecture

We are going to start by discussing the core concept of a Horizon View design: the **Pod and Block Reference Architecture**. This provides the underpinnings to all Horizon View deployments.

The Horizon View pod and block architecture provides you with a reference architecture that can support up to 10,000 users. This is achieved by taking a modular approach to the infrastructure deployment by creating separate Horizon View blocks that are designed to support up to 2,000 users each and contain all the infrastructure components required to support and run those 2,000 virtual desktop machines.

The management components are also deployed as a module called the management block, and hosts components such as the Connection Servers and Security Servers.

The blocks then scale up in multiples of 2,000 until you reach the 10,000 limit (five blocks). This configuration of five blocks is called a pod and gives you one large, unified virtual desktop environment to manage.

If you were to then introduce the Cloud Pod Architecture into the mix, you could scale even further, up to 50,000 users in total.

Now, you might be reading this thinking, "I only have 500 desktops to create in my environment, so this pod and block architecture does not matter to me," but I would urge you to carry on and understand the design principle; it's core to understanding how to deploy Horizon View.

If you are creating a VDI solution for 500 desktops, you will still be utilizing the concepts within the pod and block architecture, but on a smaller scale as you will only be creating one pod which contains a single block.

The following diagram depicts an individual Horizon View block:

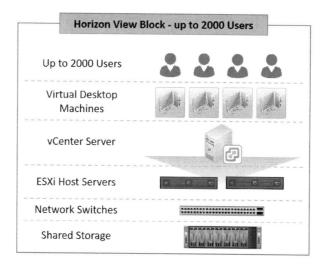

As previously mentioned, the management block contains all the Horizon View infrastructure components, such as the Connection Servers and Security Servers that support the desktop blocks. This is depicted in the following diagram:

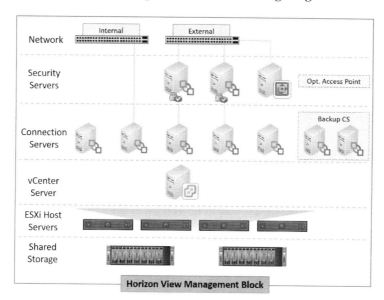

If you are starting out with one block in your pod, you will want to ensure that you still have at least two View Connection Servers for resilience.

VMware does not support the configuration of blocks across a WAN link as the JMS utilized for communication is very susceptible to network latency. However, from Horizon 6 onwards, VMware added support for the Cloud Pod Architecture, which allows you to further scale out and provide high availability across multiple sites.

Within each desktop block, as well as having a number of ESXi hosts of sufficient capacity to be able to accommodate the number of virtual desktop machines, there is also a vCenter server to manage the virtual desktop machines. In addition, there are a couple of other components that are not depicted.

You will also require a View Composer server instance for deploying linked clone virtual desktop machines, along with a supporting SQL database that will host the View Composer database, and the View events database. This should be highly available, as well as being backed up as the Composer database keeps track of all the virtual desktop machines built. The final requirement is a shared storage platform that can either be exclusive to the block or shared across multiple blocks.

It's worth pointing out that as of VMware View 5.2, it is possible to scale a block up to 10,000 users when there are multiple Connection Servers used to overcome the 2,000 connection limit of View Connection Servers. However, this would result in a large single point of failure in the vCenter server itself. You should consider this risk to your business and design your architecture accordingly to mitigate any failures. Would you really want to bring down 10,000 users all at once?

It would be recommended by VMware that, where possible, you limit your pods to 2,000 users to limit the risk of failure.

With a single vCenter Server, you will also be limited in the amount of concurrent operations that you are able to undertake. This will be of major significance, for example, when powering up a large number of desktops or recomposing a large number of pools. If you have multiple vCenter Servers in this scenario, you will be able to further increase the amount of parallel operations that could happen across the vCenter Servers, rather than the serial nature of a single vCenter Server.

Inside the pod, the Horizon View Connection Servers are configured in a cluster, and replicate their data using Microsoft's lightweight directory services and the **Java Message Service (JMS)**. VMware recommends a limit of seven View Connection Servers in a single pod. These are installed as one per block plus two additional, for availability and/or external connectivity.

The following diagram shows the high-level overview of the Horizon View block and pod architecture, complete with the management block. When implemented in a production environment, the users would connect to the View Connection Servers, Security Servers or Access Point appliance via third-party load balancers:

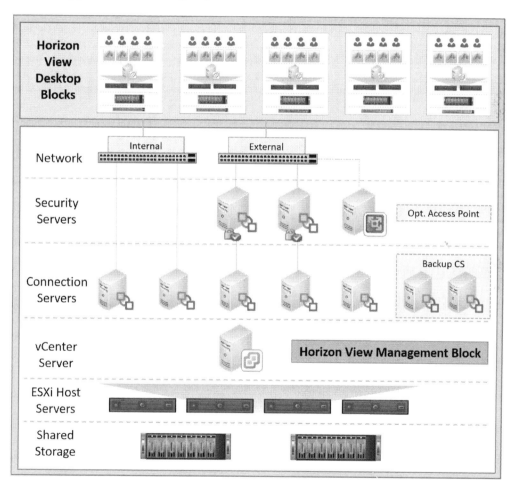

In the following section, we are going to look at how you can extend pods over multiple sites to allow for disaster recovery scenarios, and also how to scale beyond the 10,000 user limit, by configuring your environment with the Cloud Pod Architecture.

Cloud Pod Architecture

The Cloud Pod Architecture in Horizon 7 extends the scalability and feature set from the previous version. You can now federate up to 25 pods across 5 sites, allowing you to deliver a single desktop solution for up to 50,000 users.

When connecting multiple pods in this manner, it will give you the ability to entitle users across pools on both pods and sites. So, if you currently have scaled past a single pod, either for scale on one site or to deliver a view environment on multiple sites, it will now allow you to administer users through a global user entitlement layer. You can now also deliver DR to your virtual desktops, in the event of failure, through the global user entitlement layer.

You can also configure the scope to set whether View shows a user's resources based only locally to them, on the same site but across pods, or in all pods across both sites:

The following diagram depicts the Cloud Pod Architecture:

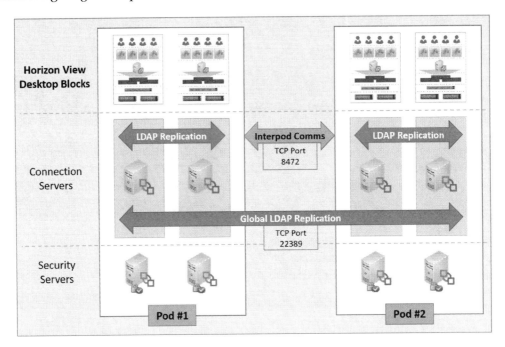

Microsoft Active Directory Lightweight Service and the new **View Interpod API (VIPA)** are used for interpod communications. VIPA is enabled when you enable the Cloud Pod Architecture from the command line on the View Connection Servers and is used when virtual desktops are launched to send health information and to find existing desktops.

By default, when a user connects to Horizon View, and they have a global entitlement, there will be a preference applied by the global entitlement to utilize virtual desktops at the local site rather than across a secondary site where possible. However, this is fully customizable by the administrator when creating the global entitlement.

With the scope configuration options, you can specify where the View Connection Server looks for virtual desktops or hosted applications to satisfy a request from the global entitlement. You can configure the following:

- **All sites**: View will look for virtual desktops or hosted applications on any pod within the federation
- **Within site**: View will look for virtual desktops or hosted applications only on pods in the same site as the pod that the user is connected to
- **Within pod**: View will look for virtual desktops or hosted applications only in the pod that the user is connected to

In addition to the scopes described above, you can also configure an option called home site. This allows you to configure a site that acts as the user's default site and when the user logs in, the View Connection Server will look for virtual desktops in that user's home site.

Along with configuring the Cloud Pod Architecture, you will need to utilize third-party load balancing technologies to allow the benefits of this technology to be seamless to the end users. But this now gives us a way of unifying our multiple View deployments that previously would have been separate entities. We will look at how this is configured in later chapters.

vSphere design for Horizon View

Having now looked at some of the reference architectures, it's time to turn our attention to some of the components that are part of that architecture, namely our vSphere virtualization platform and look at some of the high-level considerations for your design.

vSphere design

In this book, we aren't going into the intricacies of how to install and configure your ESXi hosts. However, we will briefly discuss the recommendations on how you should configure vCenter Server, as well as the hosts and clusters within your Horizon View environment.

It is technically possible to run your Horizon View and virtual server environments from one set of infrastructure, with one vCenter Server, and one or more ESXi clusters. By doing this, you could create a number of points of contention and a lot of difficulty during the time of upgrades.

As we have previously discussed, there are two infrastructure areas when it comes to Horizon View, the management block that runs the vCenter Server, View Composers, and View Connection Servers, and so on, and the second one, which runs the virtual desktops themselves. The recommendation is that these two components be separated physically onto different ESXi hosts and clusters, minimizing any risk of there being performance issues with the server components during heavy use periods or large desktop provisioning processes. From a licensing perspective, this is covered, as it is included with Horizon is the vSphere for desktop entitlement, which basically allows you to deploy as many ESXi hosts and vCenter Servers as you need to support you environment.

You should also run the Horizon View components on a different vCenter Server from your production vSphere environment. Separating the Horizon View components onto a separate vCenter Server will mean fewer clashes of priorities and prerequisites when it comes to upgrading either environment.

The following diagram shows an example of how your virtual environments could be designed:

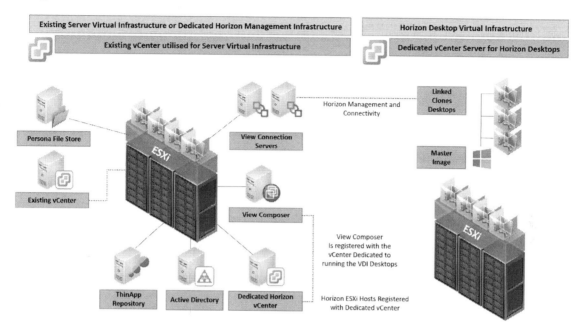

In the following section, we are going to look at the maximum values that can be configured.

Configuration maximums

When building any VDI infrastructure, you very quickly and easily hit the configuration maximums that have been set by the product vendors. When it comes to vSphere and vCenter Server, there are a number of maximums that you should be aware of.

To check the latest configuration maximums for VMware vSphere 6, see the following link: `https://www.vmware.com/pdf/vsphere6/r60/vsphere-60-configuration-maximums.pdf`.

You should also keep in mind that the Horizon View specific maximums. We will discuss those later in this chapter. Don't forget that these maximums are not goals to try and hit, but maximum limits. When designing your architecture, you should also keep in mind what the risk of losing an individual component such as a vCenter Server or a View Connection Server is.

ESXi host servers

In this section, we are going to cover some recommendations on the sizing and quantities of host servers that might be required to host and support your infrastructure.

As with any virtual infrastructure, you need to ensure that redundancy is built in as standard. This means ensuring that your chosen servers have redundant power supplies, RAID hard disks or mirrored SD cards for ESXi, and multiple network cards for network failovers in the case of a card or switch failure.

You also need to look at how many hosts are likely to be required to support your environment, and then add the relative amount of hosts to allow for the N+ capacity that you require. In most environments, this will be N+1, meaning you will have the number of hosts you require to run your virtual desktops plus one additional host to allow for a host failure, thereby ensuring that any outage does not impact your end users.

 Remember that you are effectively going to be sizing for two different environment profiles; one will host the management block infrastructure and the other will host the virtual desktop machines.

In the following section, we are going to cover some of the generic points to consider for your design.

CPU and memory

The next thing to look at is the CPU and memory configurations and recommendations.

Overcommitting CPU and memory resources

As a rule of thumb, never overcommit memory in a VDI environment. This can have many negative knock-on effects if memory is not granted when required, which will ultimately affect user experience.

 Never overcommit the memory for virtual desktop machines. Set the memory reservation to 100 percent. This stops the swap file from being created, saves storage capacity, and helps performance.

When it comes to CPUs, while it would be nice to also not to have an over-commitment, this would simply not be affordable. CPU overcommitment, if done carefully and not pushed too far, can usually be allowed with little to no effect on the end users. However, how far is not too far; that is the question. This will generally depend on the type of workload you are running within your environment. If you look at various resources on the Internet, you will find different answers to this question, with some claiming figures of more than 10 virtual CPUs (vCPUs) per physical core. The only true way to find out what is going to be acceptable in your environment is to review the CPU Ready figure; you can review this metric via vCenter, ESXTOP, or similar tools. When reviewing the CPU Ready figures, you should initially be looking to ensure that you are keeping CPU Ready below 5% per vCPU for the desktops in your environment. Your environment might be able to accept CPU Ready higher than 5%, but this should only be after testing during your POC and pilot stages. Generally, if CPU Ready is as high as 10% per vCPU, the environment is going to struggle enough to affect the user experience considerably.

CPU and memory sizing

The number of hosts required for your Horizon View infrastructure is usually dictated by the number of desktops required, the amount of CPU and RAM these desktops require, what overcommit ratio you can allow for the CPU within your infrastructure, and how much CPU and memory you can physically fit into your chosen host servers.

When taking all of that into consideration, you are looking to include the amount of memory and CPU cores across the infrastructure that allows you to balance these in a cost-effective way without too much wastage.

When selecting your host server platform, you should also consider what effect it would have on the business if that one host were to fail. As such, sometimes, you might consider hosts with two physical CPUs to be a better design decision than having four physical CPUs, especially as the number of cores per CPU continues to increase.

This may well become a financial consideration as well a technical one, and introduces the scale up or scale out argument of whether you should have fewer, larger servers, or spread the load across more, lower-spec servers.

Ensure within your calculations that you are considering the overheads that the ESXi hypervisor requires to be able to run your virtual machines, as well as memory to be dedicated as graphics memory to virtual machines if required.

The following screenshot lists typical values of overheads (in MB) required per VM:

Memory	1 vCPU	2 vCPU's	3 vCPU's	4 vCPU's
256 MB	20.29	24.28	32.33	48.16
1,024 MB	25.9	29.91	37.86	53.82
4,096 MB	48.64	52.72	60.67	76.68
16,384 MB	139.62	143.98	151.93	168.6

Network

There are generally two considerations for the networking in your ESXi hosts, 1 GB or 10 GB. No matter what, you will always want to ensure you have at least two multiport network cards to separate your traffic to allow the resilient network design that you require. As to whether you require 1 GB or 10 GB for the VM LAN traffic within your infrastructure, well, that completely depends on your use case. If you are streaming a lot of HD media into your VDI desktops, then 10 GB might well be required. Whatever the case, make sure you really understand the network requirements, as getting it wrong will definitely result in a poor end user experience.

Graphics

A lot of information has already been covered regarding the hardware and software graphics offload and accelerating options in Chapter 2, *An Overview of Horizon View Architecture and Components*.

The requirements for graphics in your environment should be carefully considered and tested during the POC and pilot stages of your project. You should consider all of the elements mentioned in Chapter 2, *An Overview of Horizon View Architecture and Components*, and then decide what is required with regard to PCI cards in your ESXi hosts. The requirement for PCI cards for graphics acceleration or offloading will affect the hardware you choose for your ESXi hosts, due to the limitations of some of these cards with regard to power and cooling, along with the number of PCIe slots available.

NVidia has a list of supported servers, with the numbers of cards these servers might house, listed at `http://www.nvidia.com/object/grid-partners.html`.

Storage

We could probably write a whole book on storage considerations, designs, and options with regard to your VDI environment. Along with the network, storage is probably among the most important areas to get right. The first, most obvious reason, is that you don't want to end up with insufficient storage for your planned rollout, and the second reason is that failure to specify a storage solution that is going to meet your performance requirements will leave you with unhappy users and a failed project. This is particularly key when deploying linked clone desktops, as we will now discuss.

When it comes to storage, we need to look at two aspects: performance and capacity.

Capacity

Your first consideration will be how much storage space you need for your Horizon View environment. You will need to consider where the relative elements of your virtual infrastructure are to be located. The first and easy bit is going to be totaling the required space for any server components. Often, the server components will live on the same storage device as the rest of your virtual infrastructure, and the desktops will live on a dedicated storage device. However, this is not compulsory and will depend on the type of storage you are utilizing and the levels of separation you desire. You will then need to understand the required storage for your desktops based upon the technologies being used to deploy the desktops, such as linked clones, linked clones with persistent disks, or full clones.

With linked clones, you need to have an understanding of the growth of the linked clone between the refresh and recompose operations. The following figure gives an example of some areas for consideration with regard to storage for a typical desktop pool utilizing linked clones and persistent disks:

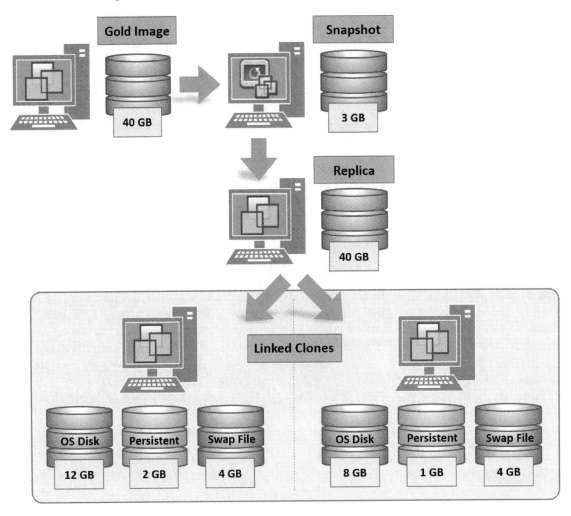

The replica from which a linked clone originates needs to be located on fast storage, either local to the host server or via a SAN. To enable this in Horizon View, you are able to choose the location of where the replica should live, and one of the recommendations is that the replica sits on fast storage, such as local SSD, for example. In the example lab, which we will introduce in the next chapter, we have deployed a Tintri T820 storage array to provide the performance required.

The recommendation is that during your POC and pilot stages, you collect this type of storage usage information. Once you have this information, you will be able to use a spreadsheet to create a model to predict the storage utilization and you can grow your environment. The following screenshot depicts a sample Excel spreadsheet outlining the storage requirement across three desktop pools:

Desktop Pool	Gold Image Size	Linked Clone or Full Clone	Replica Size	Swap File	Persistent Disk per Desktop	No. of Desktops	Space per Desktop	Total Space (GB)
Administration	40 GB	Linked Clone	40 GB	2 GB		200	12 GB	2880
Managers	60 GB	Full Clone		4 GB		20	40 GB	940
Marketing	40 GB	Linked Clone	40 GB	4 GB	10 GB	30	20 GB	1100

During the proof of concept, we have been able to understand the capacity required per desktop for the linked clones. This is a key component to understanding the overall capacity required for the solution moving forward.

This now leads into the other part of the storage story, performance.

Performance

Once you are aware of how much capacity you require for your Horizon View environment, you are able to start considering your performance needs. As always, it is recommended that you understand your performance requirements during the POC and pilot stages and use this to size your storage. When examining your virtual environment, you are looking to keep the read and write latency as low as possible to guarantee a good user experience. The amount of latency acceptable will depend greatly on the workload of your users and the tolerances of the applications they are using. However, keeping average latency as low as 25 ms will often deliver a good user experience for your users.

The question is, how do you ensure you can deliver this type of performance? The first thing to look at would be to deploy some form of storage acceleration technology to drive the IOPS requirements. Horizon View also has its own integrated solution, called **View Storage Accelerator (VSA)** or **Content Based Read Cache (CBRC)**. This feature allows you to allocate up to 2 GB of memory from the underlying ESXi host server that can be used as a cache for the most commonly read blocks. As we are talking about booting up desktop operating systems, the same blocks are required, and as these can be retrieved from memory, the process is accelerated.

Remember CBRC is not required when using Instant Clones.

Another solution is the **View Composer Array Integration (VCAI)**, which allows the process of building linked clones to be offloaded to the storage array and its native snapshot mechanism, rather than taking CPU cycles from the host server.

VCAI is not supported with Instant Clones.

There are also a number of other third-party solutions that resolve the storage performance bottleneck, such as Atlantis Computing and their ILIO products, or an all-flash array such as Tintri. So the question is, how many IOPS do you need?

As with the question of how many virtual desktop machines you can configure per core, the answer to the IOPS question is also, *it depends!* If you read some of the guides and white papers on the subject, you will probably see something like Windows 7 needing 20 to 25 IOPS. That might be correct for steady state, but what about for peak disk activity? The only way you will know the answer to how many IOPS you need is from analyzing your assessment report data.

The following graph depicts a sample storage environment depicting a sample workload as the desktops are booted. Users log in and then continue to use the desktops. On the vertical axis, you can see the IOPS, and on the horizontal axis, you can see time. As you can see, the boot storm is heavily read-intensive, with the login storm and steady state being heavily write-intensive. You need to size accordingly, based on your assessment data:

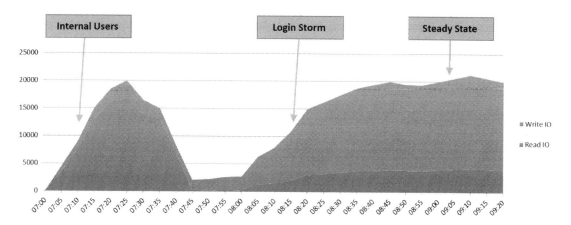

While the desktop may well drive 25 IOPS, what about any applications running on that desktop? How many IOPS will the application require? You don't want to find out the answer to this after you have deployed your solution.

There is also the debate around the split of IOPS between read and write. It is often quoted that the split is 80:20, with 80 writes and 20 reads, but this again will be dependent on your environment and the actual answer will be in your assessment data. It may well transpire that you have 70:30 or even 60:40.

As the IOPS requirements are a key part to the sizing exercise and can have a hit on the virtual desktop machine's performance, you need to get this right, so let's take a closer look at some actual sizing calculations.

One thing that gets forgotten when sizing is the RAID penalty or IOPS penalty when writing to the disks. This means that, for every read operation, there will be multiple write operations occurring, depending on the RAID level being used.

For our example, let's take RAID 5, which has a write penalty of 4, and you need to deliver 200 IOPS with a 60:40 read/write ratio. To calculate this, you can use the following formula:

(Total Workload IOPS * Percentage of read operations)

+

(Total Workload IOPS * Percentage of read operations) * RAID IO Penalty))

Going back to the example, the calculation would look something like the following:

$$\frac{(200\ IOPS * 60\%\ read\ operations)}{+} \qquad = 600\ IOPS$$
$$(200\ IOPS * 60\%\ read\ operations) * 4))$$

So, in this example, you would need to configure a RAID 5 array that could deliver the 600 IOPS that are required.

Once you understand what performance and capacity you require for your VDI environment, you are able to browse the market to understand what solution will work for you.

Horizon View design specifics

Now that we have looked at some of the more general elements of your infrastructure, and the vSphere platform that is going to support your environment, it's now time to turn your attention to the Horizon View-specific components of the infrastructure.

Let's start by looking at the requirements of those components, before looking at sizing the actual virtual desktop machines themselves.

The View Connection Server

The **View Connection Server** is a Windows Server with Horizon View installed as an application. This Server would be hosted as a virtual machine on the management block, and have a recommended configuration as shown in the following table:

Horizon View Connection Server	
Supported operating systems	Windows Server 2008 R2 64-bit
	Windows Server 2012 R2 64-bit
Memory	10 GB
Virtual CPUs	4 vCPU
Hard disk space required	70 GB

As we have touched on previously, if this is purely for a POC or pilot with a limited number of users, you can lower the specification to maybe two vCPUs and 4 GB of memory. You can't resize this afterwards, hence the reason why you should size appropriately should you want to move straight into production without reinstalling.

The View replica server

The **View replica server** is essentially the same as the View Connection Server, as it acts as a backup to the main Connection Server. As such, it should be sized in exactly the same way as the Connection Server.

The View security server

As with the replica server, the security server is just another role of the Connection Server, meaning that it should be sized the same as these components.

The View enrollment server

Again, the enrollment server is another role of the Connection Server, meaning that it should be sized the same as these components.

The View Composer

The View Composer is slightly different from the Connection Server roles. It can either be installed on the same server as vCenter Server is running on or as a standalone server. You would typically install it as standalone for performance or if you are using the vCenter Server Appliance. The configuration recommendations for View Composer are detailed in the following screenshot:

Horizon View Composer	2,000 Users	10,000 Users
Supported operating systems	Windows Server 2008 R2 SP1 64-bit	Windows Server 2008 R2 SP1 64-bit
	Windows Server 2012 R2 64-bit	Windows Server 2012 R2 64-bit
Memory	4 GB	10 GB
Virtual CPUs	2 vCPU	4 vCPU
Hard disk space required	40 GB	60 GB
Maximum desktop pool size	1,000	2,000

vCenter Servers

With the latest version of Horizon View, you have the ability to manage all 10,000 users with a single vCenter Server; however, that is probably not the best way of doing it, as you have no failover should your vCenter Server fail. The configuration recommendation for vCenter Server is detailed in the following screenshot:

vCenter Server	2,000 Users	10,000 Users
Supported operating systems	Windows Server 2008 R2 SP1 64-bit	Windows Server 2008 R2 SP1 64-bit
	Windows Server 2012 R2 64-bit	Windows Server 2012 R2 64-bit
Memory	48 GB	10 - 24 GB
Virtual CPUs	16 vCPU	2 - 8 vCPU
Hard disk space required	180 GB	40 GB
Maximum provisioning operations	20	20
Maximumpower operations	50	50

VMware Access Point

VMware Access Point is a Linux-based appliance and not a Windows application. It therefore gets deployed via the vCenter Server.

As an appliance the configuration is fixed and the recommendation is not to change it. You will need enough free resources to host it, as detailed in the following table:

Access Point	
Memory	4 GB
Virtual CPUs	2 vCPU
Hard disk space required	20 GB

In the next section, we will look at the configuration maximums for the View components.

Configuration maximums

Alongside the **configuration maximums** listed earlier in this chapter for vSphere, you need to be aware of the specific configuration maximums for Horizon View. We have listed some of the more important ones to consider in the following screenshot:

Item	Maximum
Maximum number of connections for a single connection server (PCoIP or RDS)	2,000
Maximum number of connection for 7 connection servers (PCoIP or RDS)	10,000
Blast Secure Gateway connections to remote desktops using HTML Access	2,000
Maximum number of desktops in a cloud pod	50,000
Maximum number of pods in a cloud pod architecture	25
Maximum number of sites in a cloud pod architecture	5
Maximum View Connection Servers in a cloud pod architecture	125
Clusters per desktop pool	1
Hosts per cluster	32
Maximum monitors with PCoIP	4
Maximum monitors with 3D Rendering enabled	2
Maximum monitors with RDP 7	16
Maximum 4K monitors with	3

In the following sections, we'll look at the other supporting infrastructure that is required to host the virtual desktop machines.

Networking

Network optimization is important for giving the users a great experience, as this is how their virtual desktop machine is going to be delivered and you need to consider a couple of different factors when sizing the network.

Firstly, you need to look back at your different use cases, paying close attention to where your end users will be connecting from, and whether they are connecting over a LAN, WAN, or the Internet. Although there is nothing you can do from a network perspective for Internet users, you can configure policies that limit some of the features and capabilities that could potentially consume more bandwidth.

On the subject of bandwidth, let's take a closer look at the things you need to think about.

Bandwidth considerations

When it comes to bandwidth, the question of how much bandwidth is required often pops up in conversation, and again the answer depends on what your end users are doing, which in turn will determine how much they would consume. This is something that the assessment data will tell you, however. VMware has published some guideline figures, as shown in the following screenshot:

Average Bandwidth User Requirements

	Typical Tasks	Average Bandwidth
Light user	Basic office productivity, no video or high-end graphics	50 - 150 Kbps
Medium user	Office productivity optimized for Horizon View	250 Kbps - 1 Mbps
Heavy user	Advanced office user with 3D graphics, Aero	400 Kbps - 2 Mbps
Power user	High-end user running video and CAD applications	2 Mbps +

The figures in the previous table refer to the bandwidth requirements overall, but depending on the bandwidth that's available, this will also dictate the audio bandwidth and ultimately, the audio quality. This is outlined in the following screenshot:

Audio Bandwidth Requirements

	Available Network Bandwidth	Audio Usage
CD quality audio	Up to 8 Mbps	1,500 Kbps
Stereo audio	Between 2 and 8 Mbps	400 Kbps
Mono audio	Between 700 Kbps and 2 Mbps	90 Kbps
Compressed mono audio	Between 125 Kbps and 700 Kbps	60 Kbps

It's worth noting that if you cannot provide at least the minimum bandwidth requirements for audio, then audio will be disabled for that particular session.

You can, however, make configuration changes to enhance the end-user experience. The PCoIP protocol is completely configurable using the Windows group policy so that you can tune the user experience accordingly. We will cover more on how to tune and optimize the virtual desktop machines in `Online Chapter`, *Fine Tuning the End-User Experience* available at `https://www.packtpub.com/sites/default/files/downloads/5657_FineTuningtheE ndUserExperience.pdf`.

There are two other considerations when looking at the networking aspects of your View deployment; the first is the latency of the connection.

We previously discussed bandwidth and what is required for the different use cases, but latency can also have a big impact on the end-user experience. Typically, the maximum tolerance is anything between 250 milliseconds and 300 milliseconds for acceptable performance. Anything above this may well work but could result in a degraded user experience, however, this would depend on the use case. For example, a basic office worker may work fine when compared with a heavy user. This is again information you would determine from your pilot with the end users.

Load balancing

Another requirement for Horizon View is the need to use load balancers between View Connection Servers, both for internal and external connections. This not only allows you to scale your solution, but also offers high availability should there be a failure.

It should be noted that there is no load balancer functionality included within Horizon View. As such, you will require third-party load balancers. It is possible to make use of **Microsoft Network Load Balancing (NLB)** on small-scale and proof-of-concept deployments, but as your solution starts moving on from POC to pilot stage, you should consider the need for dedicated physical or virtual load balancers.

When selecting a load balancer, you need to ensure it is able to offer session persistence. This ensures the connected user is already directed to the same View Connection Server or View Security Server during their session. You should also ensure that the load balancing solution that is implemented is highly available.

The following diagram shows how a typical load balancing solution for Horizon View would be configured:

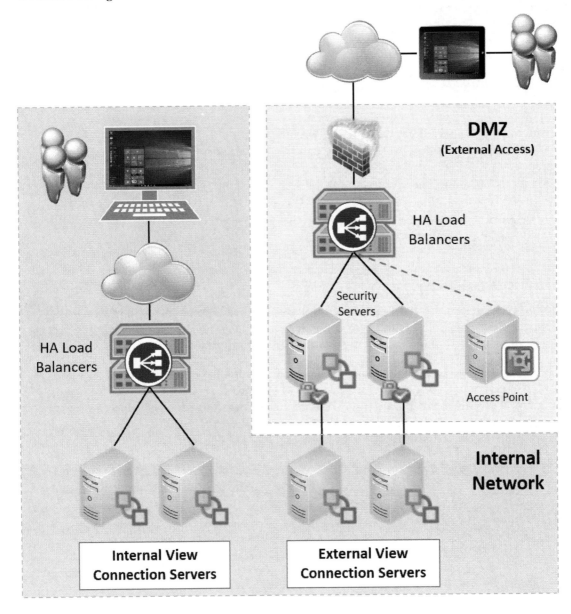

As you can see, there are multiple VMware Horizon Connection Servers configured for internal and external connections. The internal Connection Servers are load balanced behind an HA pair of load balancers. Externally, there are also two View Connection Servers, each paired with a dedicated View Security Server. The View Security Servers are then load balanced using a dedicated HA pair of load balancers. Also shown is the optional Access Point that you could deploy in place of the View Security Servers.

Remote Desktop Session Server Design considerations

Since Horizon View 6, VMware has supported Microsoft RDS as a means of delivering hosted desktop sessions rather than full virtual desktop machines desktops. Hosted desktops have full support for PCoIP, whereas previously, while session-based desktops had been supported, they were only supported using RDP as the delivery protocol.

Along with the support for RDS as a desktop source, you also use RDS servers to present published applications to your users. This is referred to as Horizon View Hosted Applications. We will cover hosted desktop sessions and hosted applications later on in this book, in Chapter 8, *Delivering Remote Applications with View Hosted Apps* and Chapter 9, *Delivering Session-Based Desktops with Horizon View*. In those chapters, we will look at installing and configuring those features, but for now let's concentrate on the design considerations for RDS-based environments.

Horizon View uses the concept of farms to place together hosts that provide a common set of applications or desktops for users. When you are creating applications or desktop pools, you will point them at the specific farms that you have created. A farm might contain anywhere between 1 and 200 RDS hosts.

With Horizon View, the RDS servers are able to be either physical or virtual. An important point to consider when designing your RDS servers in a virtual environment is to ensure you do not over-commit virtual CPUs to the underlying physical CPUs. In the following diagram, we will try and illustrate why:

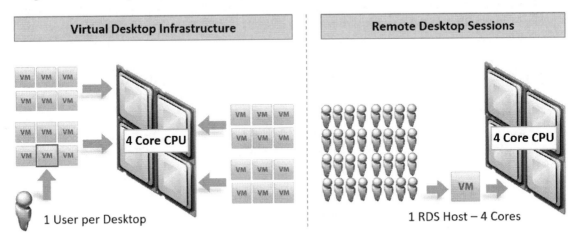

With VDI, you are able to achieve good levels of consolidation by over-allocating virtual CPUs to physical cores. With RDS, you can achieve good levels of consolidation by over-allocating users to physical or virtual cores. If you over-allocate virtual CPUs to physical CPUs, it will ultimately result in poor performance for your end users. As ever, you don't want to design memory over allocation into the design as standard.

If you are utilizing RDS for published applications, you need to consider the design with regard to application deployment. Will all of your applications be deployed on one server farm or are there going to be separate server farms for different applications? You need to consider the resources such as CPU, memory, and disk that are required for each of your RDS servers, depending on their workload.

Consideration should also be made on how many PCoIP connections are required based on your application and desktop design. In the following diagram, you can see that the end user has a View virtual desktop as well as running an application from **Server Farm A** and another application from **Server Farm B**. In total, this user will be utilizing three PCoIP connections, one for the View virtual desktop, one for the application from **Server Farm A**, and one for the application from **Server Farm B**. As a result, you will need to be sure that you understand the maximum connections for one View Connection Server and decide how you are going to scale the solution to meet your design needs:

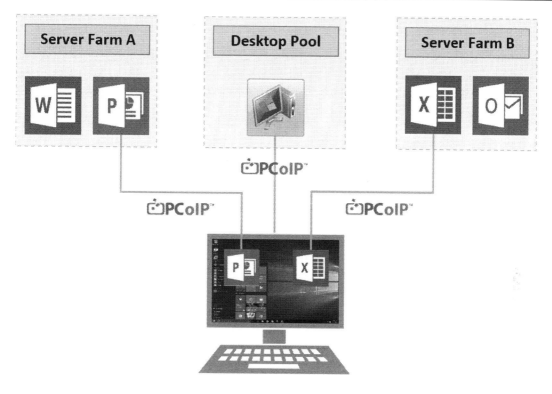

With RDS, the View Connection Server can support a maximum of 150 sessions, based on a configuration of 4 vCPUs and 64 GB of memory.

As a point to note, you can also use Horizon Workspace ONE to deliver published applications to virtual or physical desktops. So, your VDI or RDS desktops could be in a completely separate View environment to that of your hosted applications.

Supporting infrastructure design

Outside of the virtual infrastructure components, there are a number of other components that you will have to consider when it comes to designing a Horizon View solution. We would recommend you use migration to a new desktop solution as an opportunity to review all components associated with delivering the end users' desktop experience. There are also a number of third-party services that Horizon View is reliant on, which we will discuss in the coming sections.

Database requirements

Microsoft SQL Server or Oracle are key components for View Composer and the View events database. Without the View Composer database being available, View is unable to undertake any provisioning or recompose operations. As such, you might wish to consider the availability of the database server and split the environment up as per the block architecture, to use multiple database servers at one per block. You should also ensure you have regular and up-to-date backups of the View Composer database in the case of loss or corruption.

Horizon View supports the following databases:

Database Type and Version	Service Pack Level	Edition
Microsoft SQL Server 2014	SP1 and no Service Pack	Standard
		Enterprise
Microsoft SQL Server 2012	SP2	Express
		Standard
		Enterprise
Microsoft SQL Server 2008 R2	SP2 and SP3	Express
		Standard
		Enterprise
		Datacenter
Oracle 12c	Release 1 (any release up to 12.1.0.2)	Standard One
		Standard
		Enterprise

File servers

File servers are often overlooked when it comes to creating a Horizon View environment, but often play a critical role in the overall functionality of the VDI environment.

For example, they will be storing things like ThinApp packages or user profiles.

First of all, let's size your file server for performance, ensure that your file server has sufficient RAM and CPU to meet user demands, particularly at peak times, and then continue to monitor utilization, and ensure you add extra capacity as and when it is required. It's not just CPU and memory—the performance of the disks associated with your file server will also be critical.

With your applications and Personas being saved on the file servers, we need to consider the effect of these resources being unavailable when the users are trying to use their desktops. In the case of the streamed applications, ThinApp will not be loaded or might fail midway through using an application if the file server goes offline. With the Persona on the file server, this could have a severe impact on the users accessing their data, or there may be unconsidered effects, such as the application data being unable to load or reduced performance of the desktop.

As such, the availability of file servers needs to be a serious consideration if you plan on using a shared storage device that supports CIFS shares. You could consider storing these files on this device; otherwise, a clustered file server or a DFS share should probably be considered to ensure the availability. Of course, these decisions need to be taken alongside the business needs. If your View environment is going to be small initially, and your file server is stored on a virtual environment, the built-in HA functionality might be enough for your requirements.

IP addressing

Often overlooked in a VDI rollout are IP addressing, subnets, and DHCP requirements. Quite often, in a large company, you are going to use multiple subnets across the business as you separate areas with VLANs. When you slowly start scaling your deployment, it can sometimes be easy to forget that your subnets or DHCP scopes won't be large enough, until it is too late and you run out of addresses. You should consider how you are going to configure your VDI desktops with regard to IP schemes. By default, through the View Administrator, it is only possible to assign each pool with a single network tag. As such, when the desktops are rolled out, they will use the same network tag that the golden image is configured to use. However, it is possible to configure multiple network tags to pools via the View PowerCLI, which we will discuss in Chapter 7, *Managing and Configuring Desktop Pools*.

Horizon 7 supports IPv6, but be aware that when you configure the Horizon View infrastructure components, such as the Connection Server, you must also use either IPv4 or IPv6 and not a mixed mode, as that is not supported.

Antivirus

Antivirus can often be the nemesis of a good VDI design. If the antivirus solution is not configured in a way that is understanding of the shared nature of the VDI solution, it can often be the cause of large performance issues across the environment.

The first consideration with any optimized desktop solution is to ensure that you optimize your antivirus solution to be considerate to the use cases of the users and the applications that they are using. With a VDI solution, you often want to deliver just the right amount of resources to ensure that it meets the users' needs while not over-delivering resources that can have a knock-on effect to the overall cost of the solution. We have personally seen in VDI environments with misconfigured antivirus, that double the CPU, RAM, and disk resources are required. Clearly, this could have a massive effect on the cost of the overall solution and, ultimately, your ability to deliver the project on budget.

Secondly, full desktop scans need to be considered. You need to consider whether full scans are required at all on the desktops if they are being refreshed on a daily basis. If full AV scans are a defined requirement, ensure that they are run out of hours and staggered across the desktops. Simultaneously starting scans across all the desktops will affect the RAM, CPU, and the IOPS being consumed, and potentially cause knock-on effects across the environment.

Group policy

As ever, group policy can have a major effect on your desktops, irrespective of whether they are physical or virtual. When designing any EUC solution, there are three main areas you should consider when designing your group policies, namely, functionality, lockdown, and performance.

Functionality

Group policy can be your best friend, particularly when implementing non-persistent desktops. Correctly configured, you should be looking to use group policy to configure first-use settings for your desktops and Microsoft applications, alongside the obvious login scripts and mapped drives.

Lockdown

Using group policy to lock down desktops can offer an advantage in a VDI environment, again, particularly for non-persistent desktops where you don't want users saving documents in areas that won't be redirected, or customizations that probably won't be saved. Our advice would be, in a new VDI environment, try not to use the implementation of your new VDI infrastructure as an opportunity to introduce new strict lockdowns while implementing VDI itself. Often, when these kinds of stringent lockdowns are implemented at the same time as VDI, the VDI solution will be blamed for any disruptions or reduction in user experience caused by the new lockdowns. Our advice would be, if a new stringent lockdown policy is required, either try to implement it on the physical desktops prior to the migration to VDI, or implement the VDI solution first, before introducing the new lockdowns.

You will also find that it can be difficult to troubleshoot where a problem may reside by introducing too many changes at once.

Performance and management

We aren't going to use this book to write about the A to Z of group policy configuration for optimal performance. There are already a number of resources on the Internet and multiple topics on this subject. However, we would recommend that you keep on top of your group policies, ensuring old unnecessary policies are removed wherever possible. Use a functional design, where you group together GPOs into functional groups but don't take them to the nth degree by creating a GPO per setting. This will ensure ease of management and will reduce the performance effect when changes are made.

Key Management Server

To ensure seamless license activation between recompose operations of Windows and Office, a **Microsoft Key Management Server (KMS)** is imperative to your VDI design. Your desktop will find the KMS via DNS or via manual assignment, which you can preconfigure into the base image and will then be assigned the relevant keys to gain activation.

If you wish to activate Microsoft Office products using the KMS server, you also need to install the Microsoft Office 2013 Volume License Pack on your KMS server. This can be downloaded from the Microsoft Download Center.

Microsoft KMS is quickly and easily configured as a role within Windows 2012 and earlier versions of Windows. As part of the configuration, you will need your KMS license key from Microsoft. This key will be input during configuration, and your KMS will need to be activated by Microsoft over the Web or via the phone. Once the role is configured, you are ready to start rolling out and activating your desktops with KMS. However, you should be aware that there is a threshold for activations prior to KMS going live of 25 client machines. So, if you want to give this a try, ensure your first pool is larger than 25 machines. Once the threshold has been reached, you will be able to activate single machines one at a time, if required. If you wish to activate Microsoft Office products using the KMS server, you also need to install the Microsoft Office 2013 Volume License Pack on your KMS server. This can be downloaded from the Microsoft Download Center. Printing

Printing is often a black art, and working with any VDI or RDS, this can often be complicated further. Included with Horizon View is the ThinPrint technology that allows a number of configurations when it comes to printing from your desktop pools. We covered ThinPrint in some detail in `Chapter 2`, *An Overview of Horizon View Architecture and Components*.

However, often the simplest solution across the board is to implement a *follow me* printing solution. With a solution such as **PaperCut**, users print to a virtual follow-me printer. They are then able to release the document to the printer from a localized **Release Station** or compatible printer, which has been explained in the following diagram:

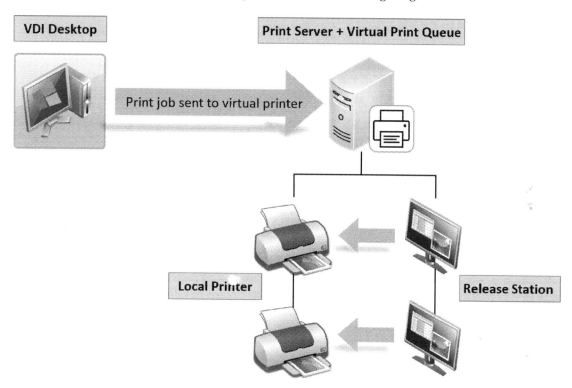

Thin clients

We are going to talk in great detail about thin clients in `Chapter 10`, *Horizon View Client Options* . However, it is important to understand that not all thin clients are built the same way. You need to ensure that for each specific use case, you have considered the thin client requirements and selected the appropriate thin client. It is also important to consider how you are going to manage the thin clients.

Desktop design considerations

You might think that once you have spent your time considering and designing all the elements mentioned earlier, that the hard work is over. Realistically, it has only just begun. Your VDI solution, without the desktops, is just a virtual infrastructure, and the design and functionality of the desktops is critical to a successful implementation. There are a great number of choices we need to make around the design for the desktops within Horizon View. This will be affected by the way the users need to use the desktops and is likely to have a knock-on effect on the way you are going to manage the desktops and the resources the desktops require.

Pool design

You will want to design your desktop pools based on the similarities between the desktops that will allow you to group desktops together. You should use the information collected by the desktop assessment and other sources to start designing how your desktop pools are going to look. While analyzing this data, you are going to look for similarities between the applications and use cases, and make decisions based on the following information on how you will design these pools. You are going to look wherever possible to have the smallest number of pools to ease the ability to maintain the environment, but you will also not want to take this to the nth degree, as trying to recompose ridiculously large pools could be difficult and might affect performance. As you can see, this is going to be a very careful balancing act to get the pool design correct.

Desktop sizing

The following is a list of some recommendations for base desktop sizing collected from a number of different VMware documents. Obviously, the resource required for the desktops will be greatly affected by the applications being used within the desktops as well:

Operating System	Recommended Initial RAM Size	Recommended Initial CPU
Windows XP 32-bit	1 GB	1 vCPU
Windows 7 32-bit	1 GB	1 vCPU
Windows 7 64-bit	2 GB	2 vCPU
Windows 8	2 GB	2 vCPU
Windows 10	2 GB	2 vCPU

In this chapter, we have already covered some of the high level host server considerations, but now you have an idea of what desktop resources you need to deploy, you can go to the next level of detail and look at the clock speeds of the CPUs and determine how many hosts you will need, along with the RAM requirements.

Sizing the desktop host servers

One of the most asked questions when sizing the servers that are hosting the virtual desktop machines is, how many can I fit on each host server, or how many virtual desktops per core? Well the answer is *it depends!*

Firstly, it depends on the CPU resources that your desktops are going to consume, and the answer to that question will only come from your assessment data.

Secondly, and more obviously, it will depend on the CPU you configure in the host servers. This is usually chosen on price/performance, as there is usually a CPU that makes more financial sense and the best cost-per-desktop model.

For this section, as we don't have any actual assessment data to work from, we will use some assumptions on the types of users and CPU requirements for each type of user just to give you an example to work with. The users are then grouped into light usage, medium usage, and heavy usage. We will base our calculations on an industry-standard, rack-mount server configured with two Intel Xeon E5-2660 v3 CPUs that run at 2.6 GHz and have 10 cores per CPU, giving us a total of 20 cores per host server.

In the example calculations, you will also notice that we have subtracted two of the cores from the total available cores on the host server. The reason for this is that the hypervisor layer (ESXi) also needs CPU resources in order to run.

The following sections classify the typical user profile and then give an indication of the per-core ratio and how we arrived at that figure.

Light user

Typical utilization is around 300 MHz of CPU resource. It's also worth adding some additional resources to cover any peaks in workload, and also other tasks, such as sounds and USB devices. For this example, we will add 10 percent to the 300 MHz.

The profile of this user type would be somebody working in a call center, an administrator, or the basic web-browser-type user. These desktops might be suspended for long periods of time and have very low utilization, running just one or two light applications. We can work out the CPU requirements with the following quick calculation:

(CPU Speed in MHz x (Number of Cores – 2) ÷ CPU requirements of each virtual desktop

(2600 MHz x 18 Cores) ÷ 330 MHz = 141.81 (141 desktops)

In this user scenario, using the standard sever described previously, you could host approximately 141 virtual desktop machines, which gives you approximately 17 users per core.

Medium user

Typical utilization is around 500 MHz of CPU resource, plus 10 percent. This type of user would be something like data entry personnel, doctors, students, Microsoft Office users, or a help desk operator. These desktops will mainly be used during business/office hours and are not heavily utilized. We can work out the CPU requirements with the following quick calculation:

(CPU Speed in MHz x (Number of Cores – 2) ÷ CPU requirements of each virtual desktop

(2600 MHz x 18 Cores) ÷ 550 MHz = 85.09 (85 desktops)

In this user scenario, using the standard server described previously, you can host approximately 85 virtual desktop machines, giving you five users per core.

Heavy user

Typical utilization is around 750 MHz of CPU resource, plus 10 percent. This type of user would be something like a developer, system administrator, IT worker, database administrator, or engineer. These desktops will more than likely be heavily utilized throughout the day and also after normal business hours. They may also be running more graphically-intensive or Java-based applications that increase the utilization of the desktop. We can work out the CPU requirements with the following quick calculation:

(CPU Speed in MHz x (Number of Cores – 2) ÷ CPU requirements of each virtual desktop

(2600 MHz x 18 Cores) ÷ 825 MHz = 56.72 (56 desktops)

In this user scenario, using the standard server described previously, you can host approximately 65 virtual desktop machines, giving you three users per core.

What we have highlighted in the previous user scenarios is based on assumptions and example use cases. This is where your assessment data becomes critical, as it will tell you the actual resource requirement figures for you own environment.

Memory sizing considerations

Sizing the memory for the servers hosting the virtual desktop machine is somewhat easier than the CPU, although you might need to play a balancing act with the chosen server. The reason is that, just because it can accommodate the number of desktops from a CPU perspective, it might not have the memory capacity to serve that number.

If you take a virtual desktop that requires 2 GB of memory and look at the light user scenario from the previous section as an example, you would be hosting 141 virtual desktop machines. That means that the host server will need 282 GB of memory just to host the virtual desktop machine, plus enough memory to run the hypervisor too.

Depending on your choice of server hardware, you might not be able to configure this amount of memory, or it might be too expensive, in which case you might end up deploying more, but lower-configuration servers.

 Don't forget, when sizing and configuring memory for the virtual desktop machines, never over-commit the memory, and set the memory reservation to 100 percent. This stops the swap file from being created, saves storage capacity, and helps performance.

Linked clone versus full clone

As we have already discussed in Chapter 2, *An Overview of Horizon View Architecture and Components*, there are two types of desktop images that we can use, linked clones or full clones. To recap briefly, linked clones are created by replicating a golden image into a thin provisioned replica VM. This VM will be the same size as the used space within the golden image; all reads come from this VM and no matter how many desktops we have within the pool within limits, each desktop will have a delta disk for writes that will continue to grow until the linked clone is recomposed, refreshed, or deleted. With a full clone, it does exactly what it says on the tin and will represent a copy of the golden image itself and consume the same amount of space.

As such, to save space on our storage device where possible, we will want to utilize linked clones. However, there are a few important use cases where using linked clones will simply not make sense, such as:

- VMware Mirage integration
- Desktops where regular refresh or recompose is not possible

As you can see, while linked clones are possibly the most attractive from the outside and should be able to be widely used, they are not always going to be possible or the right design choice. When your design utilizes full clone desktops, you should be considering your storage design carefully in line with this design choice. There are many storage manufacturers that offer re-duplication, compression, and single instance storage that allows you to minimize the storage impact of this type of desktop.

Persistent versus non-persistent

Along with deciding whether you are going to use linked clones or full clones, you will also need to decide whether you are going to use persistent or non-persistent desktops. With persistent desktops, the user is allocated a desktop, either manually or automatically, and will always be directed to that desktop when connecting to their desktop pool. With non-persistent desktops, the users will be directed to any desktop in the given pool. In a lot of designs, linked clone desktops will be configured as non-persistent and full clone desktops as persistent; but this is not always the case and will come down to your own specific use case.

The recommendation would be, wherever possible, to utilize non-persistent desktops that are built on demand using linked clones or instant clones. The user's profile would be delivered in association with View Persona Management/UEM, group policy to configure the desktops, and App Volumes to deliver. If your design allows this, it will offer you the easiest way to maintain and refresh the desktops with minimal effect to the users. If your design does not allow this, consider your use case carefully, if you do have to configure persistent desktops due to some value of data or a configuration held within the desktop, consider whether a full clone persistent desktop managed by Horizon Mirage for protection and maintenance might be a better approach.

Offline desktops

An offline desktop is a desktop that will be used when there is no network connection, either LAN- or WAN-based. Previous versions of View had the ability to utilize the transfer server to download a copy of your View desktop to run directly in the View client in offline mode. When connectivity is restored, you are able to synchronize the desktop changes back to the virtual environment. The process of doing this is not overly complicated, but it is very time consuming for the user to wait for the download and upload operations to complete.

As such, while often investigated and implemented during POC, offline mode very rarely made it into production and when it did, it was realistically used only in a small number of use cases.

For offline desktops, VMware now has a product called Horizon FLEX. Horizon FLEX utilizes VMware Mirage to deliver the virtual desktop container, and either VMware Workstation (Windows), or VMware Fusion (Mac) to run the virtual desktop machine.

Building a composite desktop

The key to a flexible desktop design is being able to build and customize the desktops in layers. Layers, in this context, is delivering the individual component parts of the desktop, such OS, persona, as well as applications.

By achieving this, the desktops can not only be more flexible to allow one base image to be used for many more users or pools, but also allow you to configure more linked-clone or instant-clone desktop pools. The following diagram depicts a user's desktop and where all the key elements are being controlled and managed:

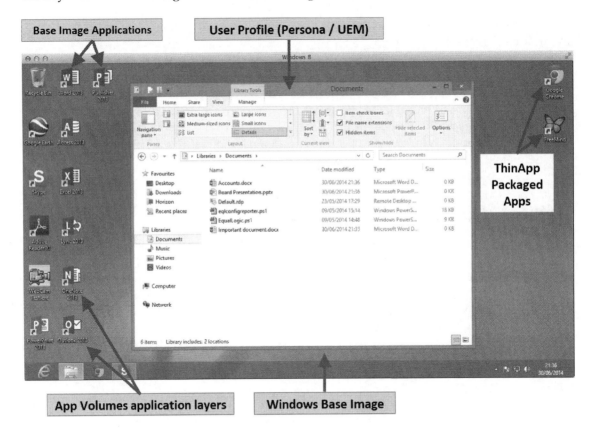

Base layer

Your base layer will consist of an optimized operating system configured to the needs of your business. Agents such as the View agent and AV will be installed into the base image along with any applications. You will need to make a decision as to what applications should be installed into the base image and which ones are going to be delivered by other means. Often, the applications that will get installed into the base image will be applications that are used across the organization or a complete pool, such as the Microsoft Office suite. You will also want to consider the nature of the application; if the application is unable to be virtualized with ThinApp, as it contains drivers, or integrate with the shell, these applications will also need to be installed in your base image.

 You need to get the base image correct as if you are using linked clones or instant clones, then you could end up creating hundreds of desktops very quickly, and you can't afford for them to be wrong.

Applications

You need to have also built an application delivery strategy. This would detail how each application is going to be delivered to the end user. Some applications will be delivered as part of the base operating system, whereas others may be packaged using ThinApp, or layered in using App Volumes.

There is also the option of Workspace ONE, which would deliver a web-based portal containing additional application delivery methods such as Citrix XenApp or SaaS-based applications.

User profiles and environment management

Finally, let's look at delivering the Persona, or user's profile, on top of the desktop. Think of the Persona as everything that makes the desktop personal; for example, application settings, the contents of any documents, and icons on the desktop. There are a number of ways to achieve this, including redirected profiles, group policy, View Persona Management, VMware UEM, and other third-party products such as Liquidware Labs' ProfileUnity. Wherever possible, keeping the solution as simple as possible and not having to combine third-party products is often the easiest way to reduce the management overheads. However, depending on the levels of customization for your users, you might need to introduce some of the products mentioned to achieve this level of customization.

With View Persona Management, the users' profiles are redirected by a set of group policies to a dedicated file server. When a user logs in to their VDI desktop, elements of the profile are downloaded from the file server to the VDI desktop as they are required. As such, once a file has been called from the profile, it is cached on the local VDI desktop for future use. Any changes to the profile are stored locally on the VDI desktop, but periodically uploaded back to the file server.

We are going to cover View Persona Management and UEM in `Online Chapter`, *Managing User Environments in Virtual Desktop Infrastructure* available at `https://www.packtpub.com/sites/default/files/downloads/5657_ManagingUserEnvironmentsinVirtualDesktopI nfrastructure.pdf`.

Disaster recovery and backup

As with any solution, fully understanding the backup and disaster recovery options is highly important. With Horizon View, there are multiple areas where you should understand the backup and recovery options, as well as the options available to you if a DR event should occur.

Backup and recovery options

There are a number of elements that you need to ensure are backed up when it comes to a Horizon View solution; they are summarized as follows:

- View Connection Servers
- View Security Servers
- Microsoft Lightweight Directory Service
- View Composer Database
- vCenter Database
- vCenter
- File servers containing ThinApp and View Persona Data
- Golden images
- Full clone and persistent desktop images

As you can see, there are a number of areas that you need to ensure are protected on a daily basis, if not more often.

Through the Horizon View Administrator, you are able to configure the scheduled backup of the LDAP repository and the View Composer Database. These will be backed up to the following location on your View Connection Servers: `C:\Program data\VMWare\VDM\backups`.

You should ensure that these backup files are regularly backed up to an external backup solution. We will look into the configuration and restoration of the View LDAP repository and View Composer Database in `Chapter 4`, *Installing and Configuring Horizon View*.

It is highly recommended that all server components are protected by some form of backup software solution, such as Veeam Backup and Replication, or VMware Data Protection. As previously mentioned, you could consider protecting and maintaining your full clones using Horizon Mirage.

Disaster recovery options

Due to the integration of Horizon View with View Composer and vCenter Server, it is not recommended or supported to replicate View environments from production to a DR site. Likewise, Horizon View is not supported for use with VMware SRM. You need to ensure that you design a DR strategy for your Horizon View environment in a different manner. There are a number of ways you could consider offering DR for View, but let's just cover one of those for now.

First, we need to think of the components that are important to our View environment; usually, these are as follows:

- Users' Personas
- ThinApp applications
- Golden images
- Full clone desktops

If you have these components available at DR, then you can start recovering your View environment at the DR site with relative ease. The DR site will be configured with a dedicated View environment, preconfigured with all the required components such as vCenter Server, View Connection Servers, and View Security Servers. You then need to understand what you need to do to roll out the VDI solution customized for your business needs during a DR event.

As the users' Personas, ThinApp applications, and App Volumes AppStacks are all located on a file server, you can consider using technology such as **Microsoft Distributed File System Replication (DFSR)** or similar technology. This allows you to have a copy of this data at both the production and disaster recovery sites.

Once you have your ThinApp packages, AppStacks, and Persona at the DR site, you need to understand how you are going to deliver the desktops. As the desktops will be rolled out from the golden images, you should consider replicating the golden image from production to DR utilizing replication integrated into the storage device. You could even do something as primitive as exporting the golden image as an **Open Virtualization Format (OVF)** and moving it to the DR site. You are then able to recompose the desktop pools from this golden image at the DR site.

With regard to full clone desktops, as these are just standard VMs, you could simply consider replicating these directly from the SAN and utilizing SRM to mount them online at the DR site ready to be added back into Horizon View.

Finally, you should think about how users are going to connect to your DR site in the event of a failure. This could be something as simple as getting the users to connect their client device to a different address, or you could make use of global load balancing technology to redirect the regular URL to the DR site.

As you can see, there isn't a simple solution to build a DR site for your Horizon View solution, but if you break it down to its component level, you can easily configure a solution that will work to deliver the desktops and relevant files for our users, should the need arise. You could also consider utilizing the Cloud Pod Architecture to help enable the cross-site management of users between production and DR, deploy a global namespace, and allow View to direct the user to the appropriate virtual desktop resource.

VMware is also able to deliver desktops as a service as part of their Horizon Air Cloud-Hosted Desktops and Apps service. You could consider utilizing this technology in some way to offer DR for your on-premises Horizon View environment.

Example solution scenario

To finish up this chapter, we wanted to give you an example of a real-life scenario to give you the opportunity to put all of the elements covered in this chapter into action and see how they would all fit together. You will see that we have put together a mock scenario. Read through it and make some notes about the elements that you would be configuring and how you would design the architecture for a production environment.

As we said, we are going to build an example design; this design is based on a fictitious company called PVO Engineering Inc. and their requirements for deploying a VDI solution. This is shown in the following topology diagram of their current network environment and locations:

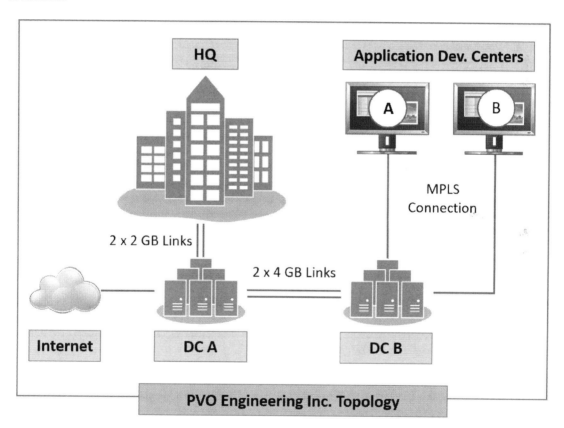

The company has three office locations: an **HQ** office and two remote sites for the application development teams. To serve these, they have two data centers that are running active/active. Data center **A** supports the mobile and **HQ** workers, while data center **B** supports the application development teams. Each data center can support the entire environment in the event of a data center failure.

End-user requirements

In this example, we have conducted an assessment to gather information on the current user installation base of 5,750 users, and we have built up a picture of the types of users and their requirements, along with their location. This is detailed in the following screenshot:

User Type/Requirements	No. of Users	Location	What do they do/need?
Application Developers	125	App Dev Site A	Local admin rights to install software
	125	App Dev Site B	Local admin rights to install software
Office Workers	2,000	HQ	Standard Office applications
	1,500	HQ	Standard Office + Visio + Project
Contractors	250	HQ	BYOD + Local admin rights
Engineering	150	HQ	Require CAD with high-end graphics
	100	HQ	Require 3D and video
Sales	1,500	Remote/Internet	Secure remote access

We now have the information on the different types of user and their requirements. We can now start to consider how we are going to deliver what they need.

Application developers

In the example scenario, there are two remote development sites, but from the network topology you can see that they are WAN-based and connect to data center **B**. They will only use their desktops from within the office and so do not require external access.

They do, however, need the ability to install software on their desktops. To deliver this, in this example scenario we configured a dedicated pool with persistent desktops. The other option would be to configure floating, non-persistent desktops and use App Volumes to deliver Writeable Volumes for the users to install their applications onto.

Whichever option you choose, the virtual desktops themselves need to be of a high specification in terms of memory and CPU.

Office workers

These end users are your basic task workers, and require a fairly basic desktop configuration (2 CPU and 2 GB memory). They are also perfect candidates for floating, non-persistent virtual desktops. The core Office applications would be installed as part of the base image, with any of the additional applications being delivered via View-hosted applications or App Volumes AppStacks.

Contractors

With contractors, it might be difficult to understand what they are coming into the business to work on, and so as one size doesn't fit all, it's probably best to err on the side of caution when it comes to the configuration, and we will size for the most intensive role they could perform. In the example scenario, this would be the application development role. That being the case, they will have the same configuration as the internal applications developers; however, they will need external access.

Engineering

There are two teams in the engineering department. Team one are heavy CAD users and design products, and team two create the engineering training material. Team one therefore requires a high-end graphics solution to run the CAD software, whereas team two doesn't need quite so much graphics resource; however, they still need substantially more than a standard user would need. The solution for engineering would include NVIDIA accelerated graphics technology, which requires dedicated desktops.

Sales

The sales department follows a similar work pattern to the standard office workers, and therefore would use a floating, non-persistent desktop pool. The key difference is that the sales teams would need external access from the Internet.

Now that we have the user requirements, we can start to look at creating a pool design based on delivering these use cases.

The pool design

The pool design reflects the use cases, and any similar desktops will be included into a single pool. Based on the information gathered, we can start building the pool design, which will start to look like the following screenshot:

Desktop Pools

	DC	Pod	Pool Description	No. of Desktops
Application Developers	B	2	Dedicated global pool	250
Office Workers + Sales	A	1	Floating pool	5,000
Engineering - CAD	A	1	Dedicated pool with GPU	150
Engineering - Video	A	1	Dedicated pool with 3D	100
Contractors	A	1	Dedicated pool	250

All of the office workers in the design are part of the same desktop pool, along with sales, even though they have different application requirements. We will look at delivering these applications outside of the core virtual desktop machine image using either ThinApp, the View hosted application feature of Horizon, or App Volumes.

Using the pod and block architecture, we are going to deploy two View pods, one in datacenter **A** and the other in datacenter **B**. The reason being that it makes more sense from the network perspective to have these desktops nearer to the users; however, we will take advantage of the Cloud Pod Architecture, as the developers travel between sites, and will configure a global pool for these users. Although in this example we have decided to configure a dedicated pool for the developers, we could deploy floating desktops and use App Volumes to deliver the ability for the developers to install their own software using the Writeable Volumes feature.

Now that we have an idea of the pools, we can start to shape the pod design and size the management blocks and the desktop hosting blocks. Let's start with the desktop blocks.

Sizing the desktop blocks

In data center **A** with Pod **1**, we have 5,500 virtual desktop machines. As there are 2,000 virtual desktop machines supported per block, we would need to configure three blocks with approximately 1,800 virtual desktop machines per block.

In datacenter **B**, we have **250** virtual desktop machines, so we only need one block.

The next question is how many servers do we need to host the virtual desktop machines? For this example, we will use the users-per-core figures previously discussed in this chapter to cover light users for the office and sales workers, and very heavy users for the developers and engineering users. That means that, for office users, we can configure 98 virtual desktop machines per host and, for the very heavy users, we can configure 50 virtual desktop machines per host.

We also need to remember that we have some distinct differences in the host server requirements, as the engineering users require access to hardware-based GPU. This would result in deploying a cluster for each. The number of hosts required for Pod **1** could look something like the following screenshot. Note that users per core ratios in these examples are based on servers with two 3 GHz, 10-core CPUs and user profiles of 300 MHz for light users, and 1.1 GHz for power users:

	No. of Users	Desktops per Server	No. of Hosts	Cluster
Office + Sales	5,000	98	52 + 1 for DR	A
Contractors	250	50	5 + 1 DR	A
GPU - based CAD (K180Q)	150	8	19	B
GPU - based Video (K140Q)	100	16	7	B
Application Developers	250	50	5 + 1 DR	A
TOTAL			**86**	

For the GPU-based virtual desktop machines, two configuration options have been used, both using NVIDIA GRID K1 graphics cards and vGPU. The CAD users will use a K180Q profile, and the video users will use a K140Q profile.

There is no DR option for the GRID-enabled servers due to the high cost of the hardware. In the event of a failure, users can continue to work, but with lower graphics capabilities.

Pod **2** in datacenter **B** contains just the virtual desktop machines for the application development users and would look something like the following:

	No. of Users	Desktops per Server	No. of Hosts
Application Developers	250	50	5 + 1 for DR
TOTAL			**6**

With Pod **1**, we have exceeded the number of hosts we can support in a cluster, the limit being **32**. Therefore, we would deploy two clusters per desktop block with the number of host servers divided across the clusters, while a separate cluster will support the graphics-enabled users.

The design is now starting to look like the following diagram:

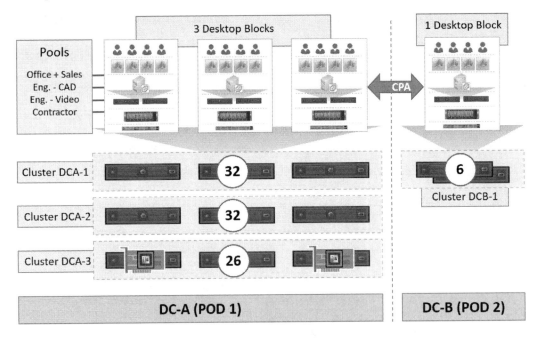

* Host servers based on 3 GHz 10-Core CPUs

Sizing the storage requirements

Using the calculations detailed previously, you can work out the IOPS requirements you need to deliver. In this example scenario, we will base the calculation on a requirement of 30 IOPS per virtual desktop machine, a 30/70 read/write ratio, a RAID 5 array, and a 10 GB disk capacity. Given those variables, we can work out what the storage requirements are, as shown in the following screenshot:

Storage Requirements

	No. of Users	IOPS Required	Capacity
Pod 1	5,500	412,500	55 TB
Pod 2	250	18,750	2.5 TB

These storage requirements are for hosting the desktops only. If you are using components such as App Volumes, or ThinApp for delivering applications, you will need to think about the capacity and performance requirements to support those environments.

Sizing the management blocks

Once we have configured the desktop blocks and know the pool configuration, we can look at sizing the management blocks to provide the supporting infrastructure.

This infrastructure component configuration will look something like the following table:

View Component

	Quantity in Pod 1	Quantity in Pod 2
Connection Server	6 (2 per block)	2 (2 per block)
Security Server	2 (external access)	0 (no external access)
View Composer	3 (1 per block)	1 (1 per block)
vCenter Servers	3 (1 per block)	1 (1 per block)

The final element to look at is the network. You need to assess whether or not the current network configuration will support the users. If not, then you may need to look at some form of network upgrade.

The network requirements

Now that we have our pool design, management and desktop blocks, and the storage requirements, we can look at the network requirements, as shown in the following screenshot:

Network Requirements

	Pod No.	No. of Desktops	Bandwidth per Desktop	Total Bandwidth
Office + Sales	1	5,250	150 Kbps	787.5 Mbps
GPU-based Users	1	250	500 Kbps	125 Mbps
Application Developers	2	250	500 Kbps	125 Mbps

Summary

In this chapter, we have covered some of the essential tasks in designing and building out our Horizon View infrastructure.

We started at a high level, discussing the approach to a VDI project and the different phases to work through in order to plan and test an environment. The most important of these phases is the assessment phase.

Once we worked through these, we looked at the pod and block reference architecture, before examining the sizing of the key Horizon View components, such as the View Connection Server, View Security Server, and View Composer.

Following on from the management architecture, we looked at some of the considerations for sizing and configuring the virtual desktop machines and the user assignments, before finally putting this all together in a high-level example design.

You should now have a methodology for approaching a project, coupled with the knowledge to be able to start sizing your environment specifically to your end-user requirements.

In the next chapter, we will discuss how to install all the components that make up the Horizon View solution. We will take a deep dive into installation and follow the process using step-by-step screenshots; by the end of the chapter, we will have a fully functional View infrastructure up and running.

4
Installing and Configuring Horizon View

In this chapter, we will cover the installation process of the core Horizon View components, such as the Connection Server, Security Server, and Replica Server, and build out the management block to support the infrastructure.

Once the installation is complete, we will then move on to the configuration tasks, and get the Horizon View environment up and running and ready to deliver to the end users.

To help with the installation, we are going to use an example lab, which will guide you through the whole process, step by step. So let's start there and introduce you to the lab.

Welcome to the lab environment

Throughout the practical stages of this book, you have the opportunity to follow the tasks and steps that are being described using the example lab environment. If you prefer, you can use these guides to set up your own environment, whether that's for a proof of concept, pilot, or production deployment.

What you need for the example lab

We are going to start with the management block infrastructure. The example lab management block consists of the following infrastructure components:

- 2 x ESXi host servers running vSphere 6.0 U1
- Tintri T820 VMaware hybrid storage array
- 11 x Windows Server 2012 R2 Enterprise Edition virtual machines for the following roles, which we will configure throughout this chapter:
    - Domain controller (dc.pvolab.com)
    - Connection Server (hzn7-cs1.pvolab.com)
    - Security Server (hzn7-ss1.pvolab.com)
    - Replica Server (hzn7-cs2.pvolab.com)
    - Connection Server for second site CPA (hzn7-cs1b)
    - View Composer (hzn7-cmp.pvolab.com)
    - Enrollment Server (hzn7-enroll.pvolab.com)
    - Certificate of authority server (hzn7-certs.pvolab.com)
    - RDSH Server for hosting desktop sessions (rdsh-desktops)
    - RDSH Server for hosting applications (rdsh-apps)
    - SQL Express 2012 instance with 2 x databases (one for View Composer and one for the events database installed on the Composer Server hzn7-cmp.pvolab.com)
    - 2 x vCenter Servers for the management block (vcs1.pvolab.com), and one for the desktop block (vcs2.pvolab.com)

All machines should be **domain-joined**, with the exception of the Security Server. The lab should look something like the following diagram:

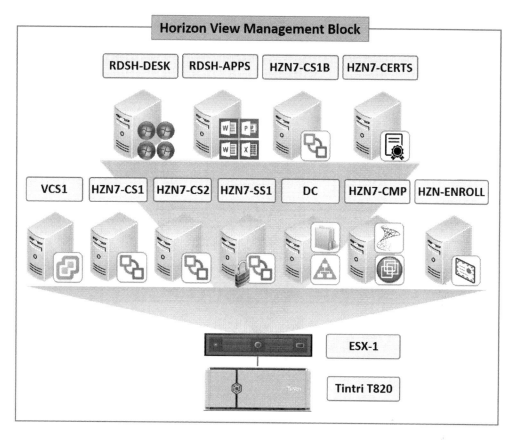

Before we get started, there are a few prerequisites that need to be in place, regardless of whether you are following the example lab or not. For this example, we will assume that you already have in place the virtual infrastructure components such as the ESXi host servers, the vCenter Servers, active directory/domain controller, and SQL Server, and have created the virtual servers ready to have their Horizon View roles installed on them.

It's probably worth also building the infrastructure for the desktop block and having the ESXi host server and vCenter Server already built.

There is no need to build the virtual desktops yet, as we will be covering the build of the virtual desktops in Chapter 6, *Building and Optimizing the Virtual Desktop OS.*

The following diagram shows the desktop block configuration for the example lab:

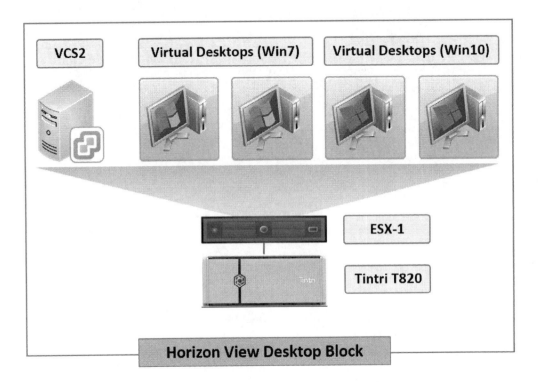

One final thing is to download the Horizon 7 software. For the example lab, all the software components and installation files were saved on a shared folder on the domain controller. You can download Horizon 7 from here: http://tinyurl.com/gubm9bx.

With the lab infrastructure now in place, you can start the installation and configuration.

Preparing Active Directory

Horizon View requires **Active Directory (AD)** for authentication of users and desktops, as well as making use of group policy to control and tune many aspects of your end users' desktops. This will be covered in later chapters.

Horizon View is compatible with the following AD-functional domain levels:

- Windows 2008 and Windows 2008 R2
- Windows 2012 and Windows 2012 R2

When deploying your View Connection Servers, they either need to be in the same domain as the desktops that you are going to deploy, or in a domain with a two-way transitive trust to the domain where your desktops will be located.

Active Directory user accounts

We recommend that you also take this opportunity to create a number of user accounts that will be needed across your installation.

These accounts will include service accounts for your View Connection Server Services and Composer Services. You need an AD account to be used by View to log in and manage components within your vCenter, and a user for View Composer to manage the creation of computer accounts in AD.

vCenter user account

You will need an AD user to allow View to connect to your vCenter Server. This account should also be added as a local admin on the vCenter Server, as we will be using View Composer to create linked-clone desktops. Once you have created your user within AD, you will need to give this user permission in your vCenter Server.

The following screenshot lists the permissions required by this user:

Required Group	Privilege Required (1)	Privilege Required (2)
Folder	Create Folder	
	Delete Folder	
Datastore	Allocate Space	
	Browse Datastore	
	Low Level File Operation	
Virtual Machine	Configuration	All
	Inventory	All
	Snapshot Management	All
	Interaction	Power Off
		Power On
		Reset
		Suspend
	Provisioning	Customize
		Deploy Template
		Read Customization Specifications
		Clone Virtual Machine
		Allow Disk Access
Resource	Assign Virtual Machine to Resource Pool	
	Migrate Powered off Virtual Machine	
Global	Act as vCenter Server	
	Enable Methods	
	Disable Methods	
	System Tag	
Host	Configuration	Advanced Settings
Network	All	

Let's now add the user to the vCenter Server, by first creating a new role specifically for the View vCenter User, as follows:

1. Log in to the vCenter Server using the VMware vSphere web client dialog box. Once logged in, from the **Home** screen, click on the **Roles** icon (**1**), as shown in the following screenshot:

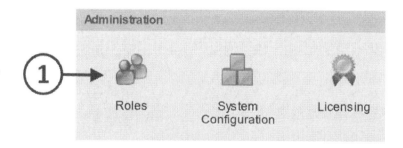

2. Next, create a new role by clicking the green + (**2**) symbol in the top left, and then type in a role name in the **Role name** box (**3**). In the example, the role name is entered as **View vCenter User**.

3. In the **Privilege** box, expand the **Host** and **Configuration** sections. Check the boxes to select the relevant privileges to match the required privileges that we covered previously, as shown in the following screenshot:

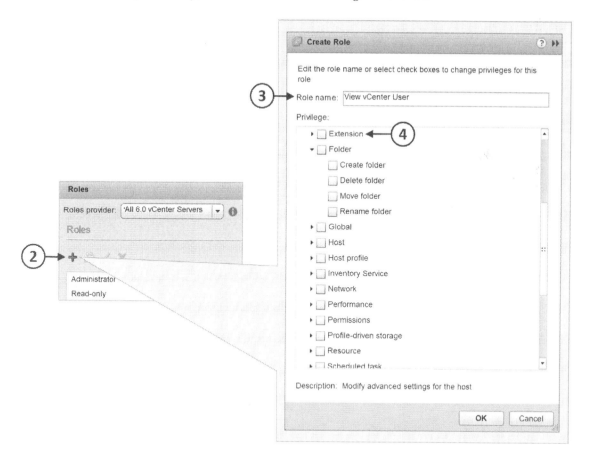

4. Next you need to add the permissions.

5. From the VMware vSphere Web Client Home screen, under the **Inventories** section at the top of the home tab page, click on the **vCenter Inventory Lists** icon (**5**).

6. Now click on the entry for **vCenter Servers** (**6**), as shown in the following screenshot:

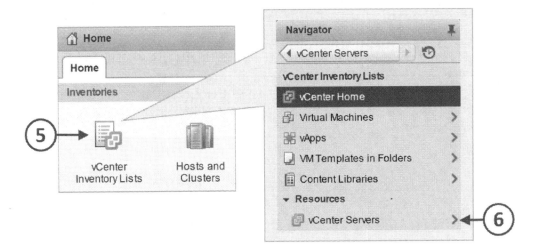

7. You will now see the **vCenter Inventory List**, which will show the vCenter Server used for the management block in the example lab, as shown in the following screenshot:

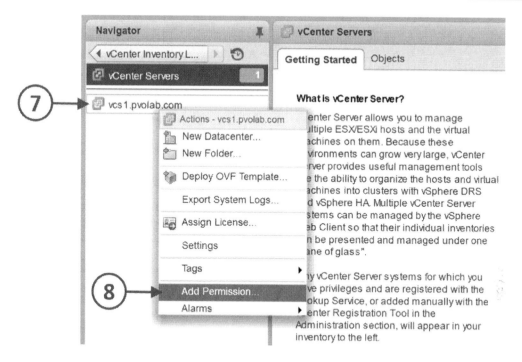

8. Click to highlight the vCenter Server **vcs1.pvolab.com** (7), then right-click, and then from the contextual menu, click the option for **Add Permission...** (8).

9. You will now see the **Add Permission** dialog box.

10. From the **Assigned Role** box, click the arrow for the drop-down menu (**9**), and select the user **ViewVCUser**, and then click the **Add...** button (**10**). This is shown in the following screenshot:

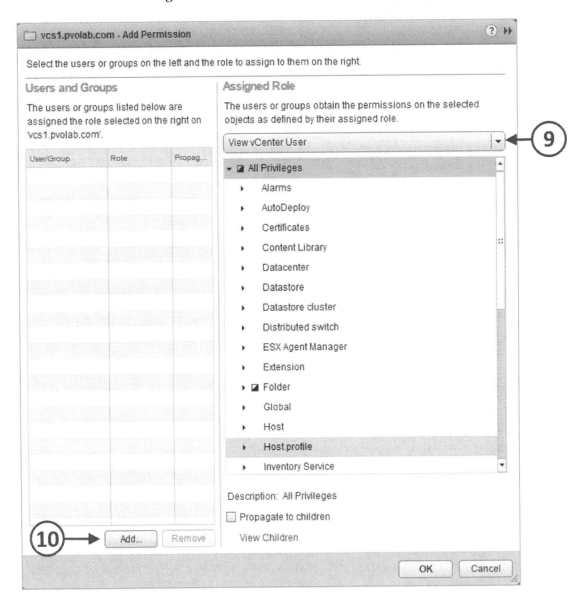

11. You will now see the **Select Users/Groups** box, as shown in the following screenshot:

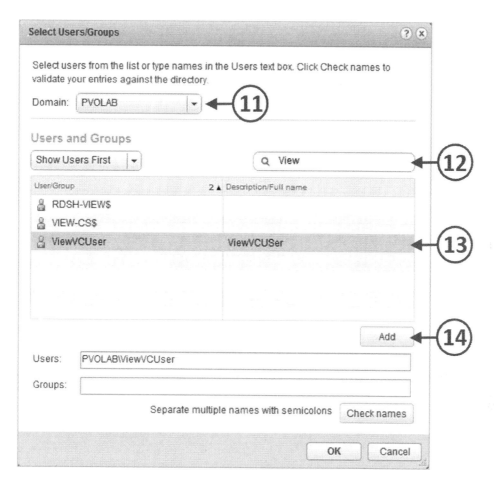

12. From the **Domain** box, click the arrow for the drop-down menu (**11**), and select the domain that contains the user account that was set up previously.

13. In the search box (**12**), enter the first part of the username and click the magnifying glass icon. The results will be displayed below. Click on the **ViewVCUser** (**13**) to select it, and then click the **Add** button (14). The username should now appear in the **Users** box.

14. Click the **OK** button when you have completed the configuration.

View Composer user account

You will also require an AD user for your View Composer account, as this account will be responsible for the addition and deletion of computer accounts for your clones linked to the domain. The following are the required AD permissions this user should have:

- List contents
- Read all properties
- Write all properties
- Read permissions
- Reset password
- Create computer objects
- Delete computer objects

The permissions for this account need to apply at the root domain level for the AD container and all child objects of the container. You will also need to ensure that you have advanced features selected when creating this user. This account will be used later to configure the View Administrator for the View Composer connection.

View Desktop Organizational Units (OUs)

Although you are more than likely to have OUs already in place to support your current desktop environment, now is the time that you should start considering what that looks like and whether it will work for your new virtual environment. You should think about having dedicated OUs that easily allow you to configure specific group policies based on the requirements of the virtual desktop pool being created.

If you are planning to still have an element of physical desktops in your environment, then you will need to create new OUs for the new virtual desktops. It's not a good idea to mix and match in case you add policies that would not suit one of the environments. For example, you wouldn't want to apply a physical desktop policy to a virtual desktop.

IP addressing and DNS requirements

For your Horizon View installation, there are going to be a number of requirements for IP addresses and DNS names used by the different View components.

The typical requirements for IP addresses and DNS names are summarized for each of the components in the following screenshot:

View Component	Internal IP Address	Internal DNS Name	External IP Address	External DNS Name	Network
vCenter Server	✓	✓	✗	✗	Production
View Composer Server	✓	✓	✗	✗	Production
SQL Server	✓	✓	✗	✗	Production
View Connection Server	✓	✓	✗	✗	Production
Interal Load Balancer	✓	✓	✗	✗	Production
View Connection Server (External)	✓	✓	✗	✗	Production
View Secutiry Server	✓	✓	✗	✗	DMZ
VMware Access Point	✓	✓	✗	✗	DMZ
External Load Balancer	✓	✓	✓	✓	DMZ

As you can see from the screenshot, the suggestion is that load balancers are utilized to load balance connections between the internal View Connection Servers, as well as between the external View Security Servers. In a smaller environment, you might decide to go with only one View Security Server, in which case you would require the external DNS name rather than the load balancer.

In the next section, we are going to start installing the Horizon View components.

Installing View Composer

View Composer can either be installed directly onto a Windows server running vCenter Server, or alternatively, it can be installed on a standalone Windows Server. The following screenshot lists the requirements for creating a server for View Composer:

Component	Recommended Supported Configuration
Operating Systems	Windows Server 2008 R2 SP1 64-bit (Std, Ent, DC Editions)
	Windows Server 2012 R2 64-bit (Std & Ent Editions)
Processor	2GHz or faster and 4 CPUs
Networking	1Gbps NICs
Memory	8GB RAM or higher for deployments of 50 or more
Disk Space	60 GB
Database Options	Microsoft SQL Server 2014 32-bit & 64-bit, no SP & SP1, Std & Ent
	Microsoft SQL Server 2012 32-bit & 64-bit, SP2, Express, Std & Ent
	Microsoft SQL Server 2008 R2 32-bit & 64-bit, SP2 & SP3, Express, Std, Ent & DC
	Oracle 12c Release 1 (up to 12.1.0.2) Standard One, Std & Ent

Now you know what you need for View Composer, you can start the installation.

It may seem a little odd to install View Composer before the first Connection Server is installed, but the reason it's done in this order is because during the initial configuration of the first Connection Server, when you configure a vCenter Server, you will need to enter the details of the View Composer server, if used, so that the View Connection server can connect to it.

In the example lab, View Composer is going to be installed on a standalone server; however, you could install it directly onto the vCenter Server if the vCenter Sever is Windows-based. The standalone **Composer** is used for scalability and when you have deployed the **vCenter Server Appliance**. As the vCenter Server Appliance is Linux-based and the Composer software is Windows-based, then obviously it cannot be installed on the vCenter Server Appliance.

Before we start the installation, there is just one more thing to do, and that's set up a SQL database for the View Composer database.

Configuring SQL for View Composer

Steps for configuring SQL for View Composer are as follows:

1. Open a console to the virtual machine running SQL Server and launch the **Microsoft SQL Server Management Studio** application. In the example lab, the SQL Server is installed on the same server as we are going to install View Composer onto, so the server name is **hzn7-cmp.pvolab.com**. You will see the login box, as shown in the following screenshot:

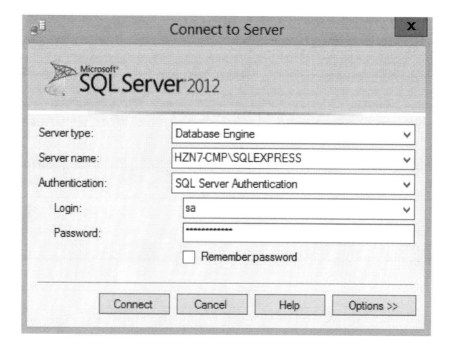

2. Log in in using the SA account credentials and then click the **Connect** button.

3. You will now see the **SQL Server Management Studio** screen. From the **Object Explorer**, expand the **Security** folder and select **Logins(1)**. Right-click and select the option for **New Login...(2)**, as shown in the following screenshot:

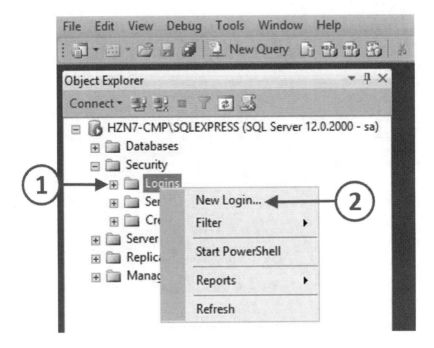

4. You will then see the **Login – New** screen, as shown in the following screenshot:

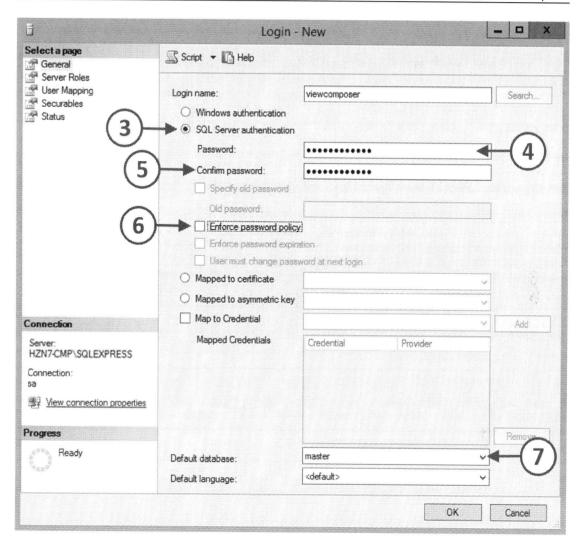

5. In the **Login name** box (**1**), enter the new login name. In the example lab, the new login is going to be called **viewcomposer**. Click the radio button for **SQL Server authentication** (**3**), and then in the **Password** box (**4**), enter a new password. Type the new password again in the **Confirm password** box (**5**).

6. Next, uncheck the **Enforce password policy** box (**6**). Finally, in the **Default database** drop-down box (**7**), select the option for **master**. We will update this to reflect the correct database for View Composer once we create it in the next step.

7. Click **OK** once you have configured this screen. You will return to the **Object Explorer**.

8. Now that you have created the login account, you need to create a new database for View Composer. From the **Object Explorer**, select the **Databases** folder (**8**), right-click, and select **New Database...(9)**, as shown in the following screenshot:

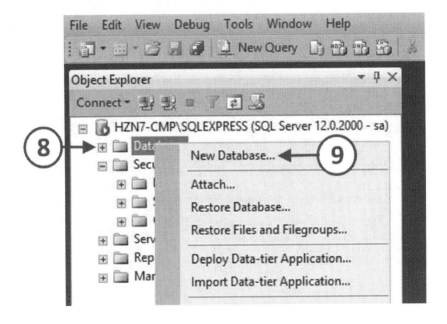

9. You will see the **New Database** screen, as shown in the following screenshot:

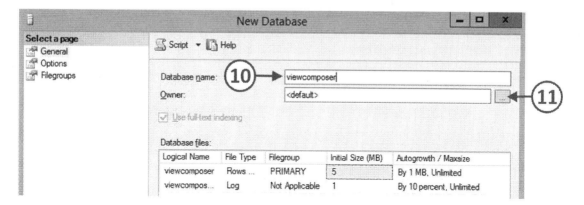

10. In the **Database name** box (**10**), type in a name for this database. In the example lab, the database is called **viewcomposer**.

11. In the **Owner** box, click the **...** box (**11**). You will now see the **Select Database Owner** screen, as shown in the following screenshot:

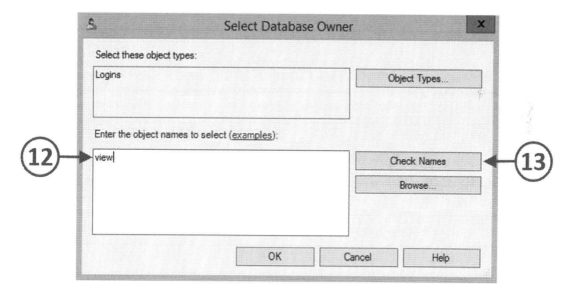

12. Type **view** into the **Enter the object names** box (**12**), and then click the **Check Names** box (**13**). This will search for any entries that contain the work view.

13. You will now see the **Multiple Objects Found** box, as shown in the following screenshot:

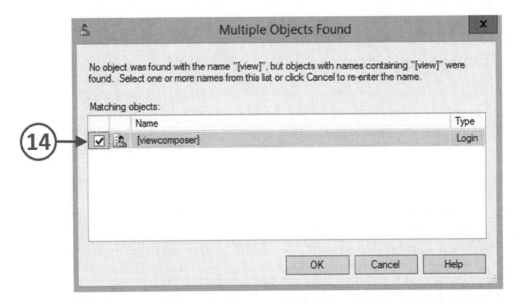

14. Check the box for **viewcomposer (14)**. This is the login we created previously.
15. Now click the **OK** button, and you will return to the **Select Database Owner** box, which will now show the **viewcomposer** user entered.
16. In the **Select Database Owner** box, click **OK** to accept the database owner.
17. You will now return to the **New Database** screen, which will show both the database name and the database owner, as shown in the following screenshot:

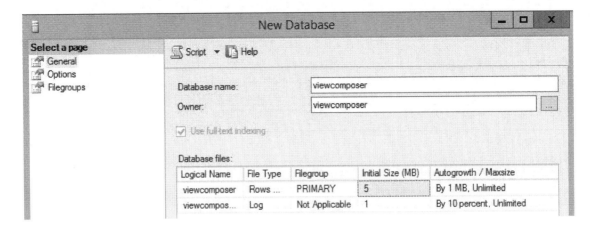

18. Click **OK** to complete the process and close the **New Database** screen.

19. The final configuration task is to go back and edit the **viewcomposer** user login and enter the **viewcomposer** database details.

20. From the **Object Explorer**, expand the entry for **Logins (15)** and then select the option for **viewcomposer (16)**. Right-click and then from the contextual menu, select the option for **Properties (17)**. In the **Default database** box, click the drop-down menu (**18**) and select the option for **viewcomposer**, as shown in the following screenshot:

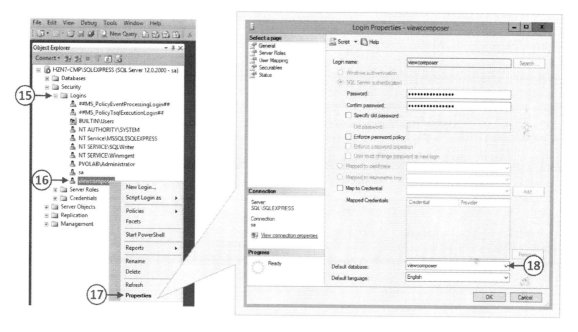

21. Click the **OK** button to complete the configuration changes.

22. Before you close the **SQL Server Management Studio**, there is one other database to create, so repeat the entire process as previously described and create a database and database owner for the View Events database. In the example lab, both the owner and database have been called **viewevents**. We will use this later in the chapter.

With the database configuration now complete, we can go ahead and install the View Composer software.

View Composer installation process

1. Open a console to the **HZN7-CMP** virtual machine, ensure you have .NET 3.5 SP 1 installed, and then locate the Horizon View installation software, as shown in the following screenshot:

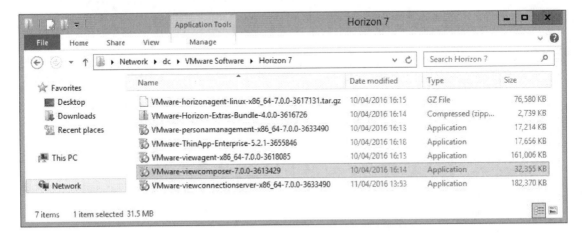

2. Launch the `VMware-viewcomposer-7.0.0-3613429` file to start the installation.

3. If you see the **Open File – Security Warning message**, click the **Run** button.

4. You will now see the **Welcome to the Installation Wizard for VMware Horizon 7 Composer** screen, as shown in the following screenshot:

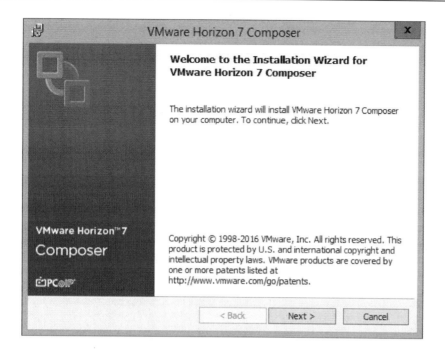

5. Click the **Next >** button to start the installation. You will now see the **License Agreement** screen, as shown in the following screenshot:

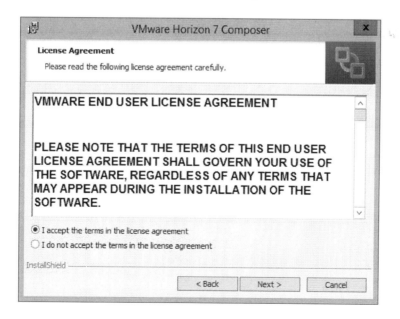

6. Click the radio button for **I accept the terms in the license agreement**, and then click the **Next >** button. You will then see the **Destination Folder** screen, as shown in the following screenshot:

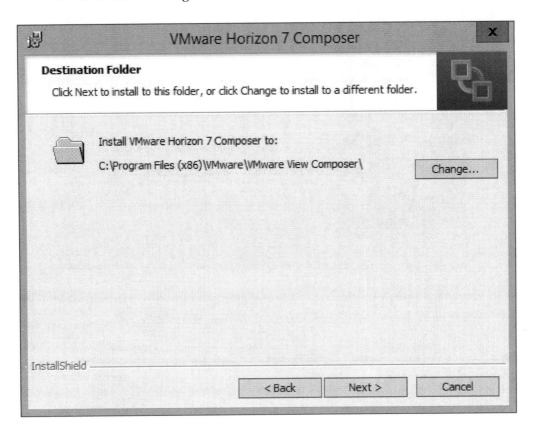

7. Leave the folder as the default and then click the **Next >** button to continue. You will now see the **Database Information** screen, as shown in the following screenshot:

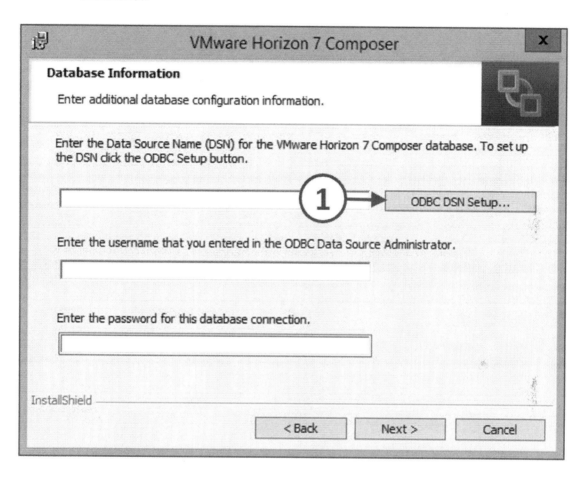

8. The first thing you need to do is to create an ODBC DSN to connect to the View Composer database.

9. Click the **ODBC DSN Setup...** button (**1**). You will now see the **ODBC Data Source Administrator(64-bit)** box, as shown in the following screenshot:

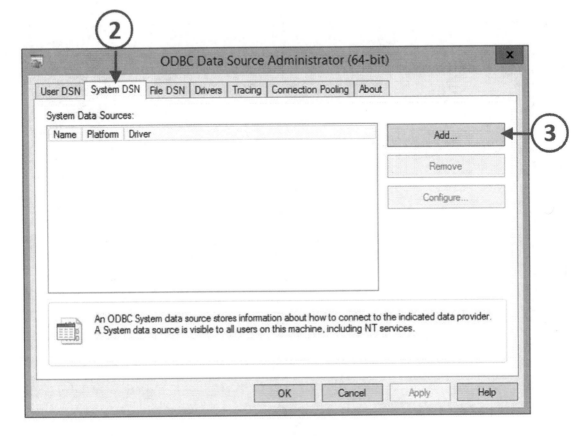

10. Click the tab for **System DSN** (**2**), and then click the **Add...** button (**3**).

11. In the **Create New Data Source** box that you now see, click the option for **SQL Server Native Client** (4), and click the **Finish** button, as shown in the following screenshot:

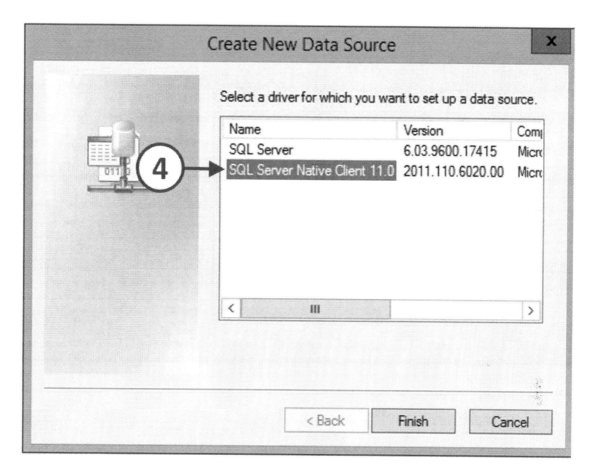

12. You will now see the **Create a New Data Source to SQL Server** box, as shown in the following screenshot:

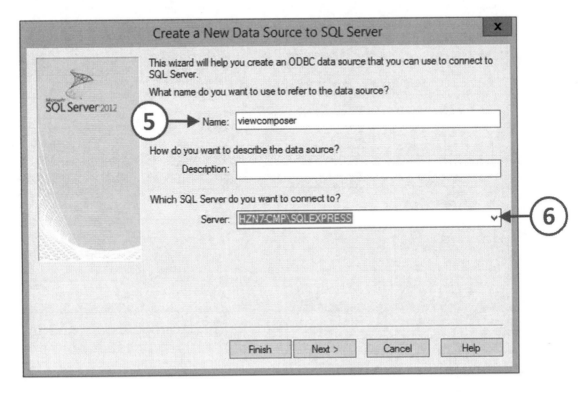

13. In the **Name** box (**5**), type in a name for this data source. In the example lab, this is called **viewcomposer**.
14. In the **Server** box, click the drop-down arrow (**6**) and select the SQL Server that you want to connect to. In the example lab, this is **HZN7-CMP\SQLEXPRESS**.
15. Click the **Next >** button to continue.
16. Next, you need to enter the authentication details.

17. Click the radio button for **With SQL Server authentication** (7), and then in the **Login ID** box (8), enter the user login details. In the example lab, we are going to use the SA account. Finally, in the **Password** box (9), type in the password for the SA account, as shown in the following screenshot:

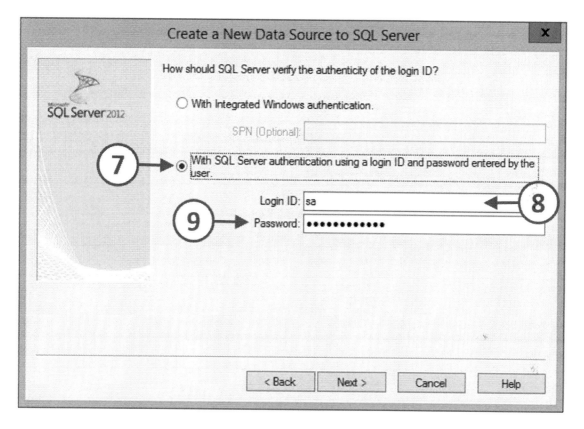

18. Click the **Next >** button to continue.
19. In the next configuration box, you need to change the default database details to reflect the database for the View Composer.

20. Check the **Change the default database to** box (**10**), and then in the box below it, click the drop-down arrow (**11**) and select the **viewcomposer** option, as shown in the following screenshot:

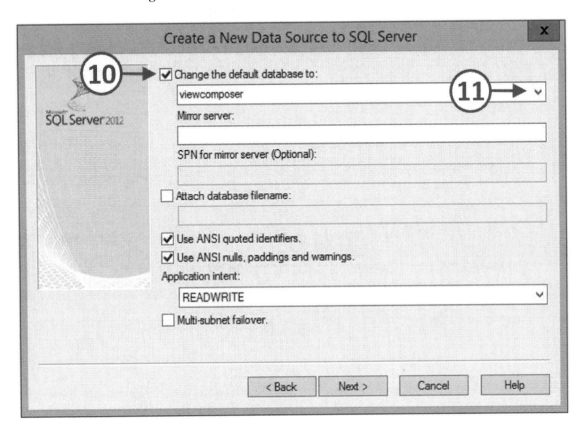

21. Click the **Next >** button to continue.

You will see the final configuration box, as shown in the following screenshot:

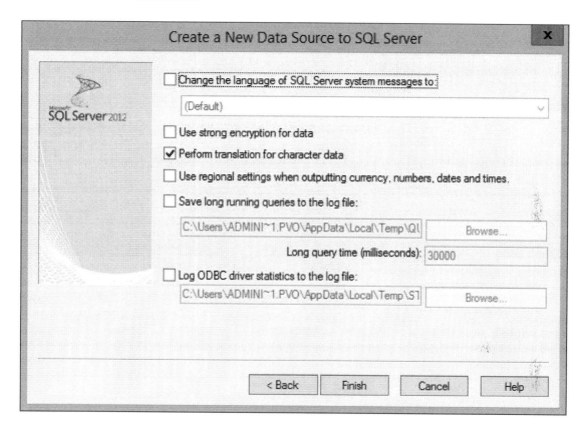

22. Click the **Finish** button to complete the configuration.
23. The final thing to do is to test the newly created connection.
24. Click the **Test Data Source...** button (**12**).

25. You should see the test results box showing the message **TESTS COMPLETED SUCCESSFULLY!**, as shown in the following screenshot:

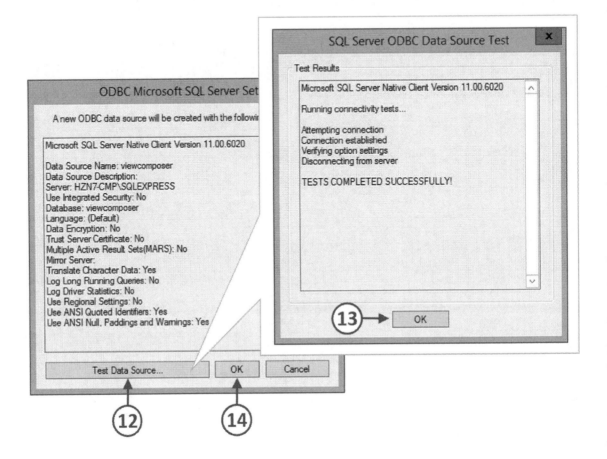

26. Click the **OK** button (**13**) to complete the tests and close the **Test Results** box.
27. Next, click **OK** to close the **ODBC Microsoft SQL Server Setup** box (**14**).
28. You will now return to the **ODBC Data Source Administrator** screen, which will show you the newly created System DSN connection to the viewcomposer database.

29. Click the **OK** button to close the **ODBC Data Source Administrator** screen and return to the View Composer installation screen and the **Database Information** configuration box.

30. You can now enter **viewcomposer** in the **DSN** box (**15**), and in the username box (**16**), type **SA**, followed by the password for the **SA** account in **the Enter a password for this database connection** box (**17**). This is shown in the following screenshot:

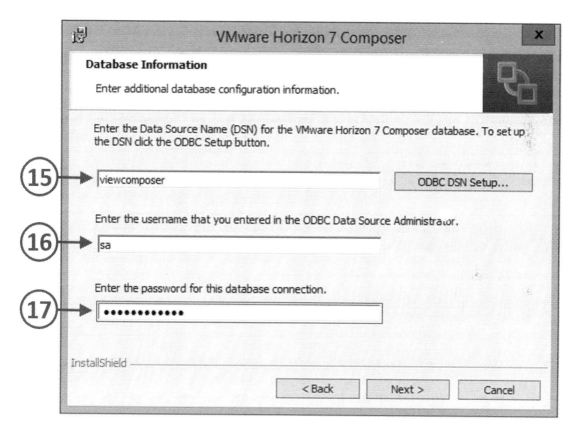

31. Click the **Next >** button to continue.

32. On the **VMware Horizon 7 Composer Port Settings** screen, leave the **SOAP Port** setting as default, as shown in the following screenshot:

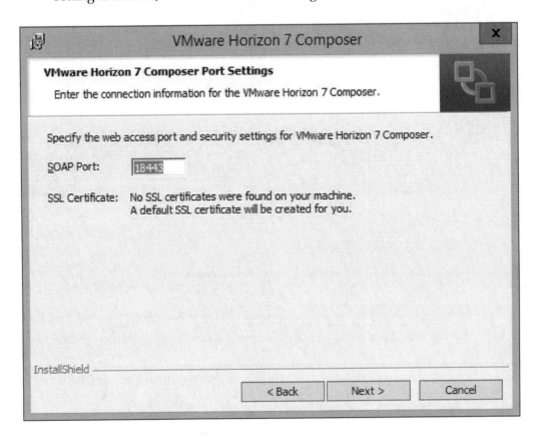

33. The **Simple Object Access Protocol (SOAP)** port is used by View to communicate with Composer in an XML format. The recommendation would be to leave this setting as is unless there is a specific reason to change it. Click the **Next >** button to continue.

34. You will now see the **Ready to Install the Program** screen, as shown in the following screenshot:

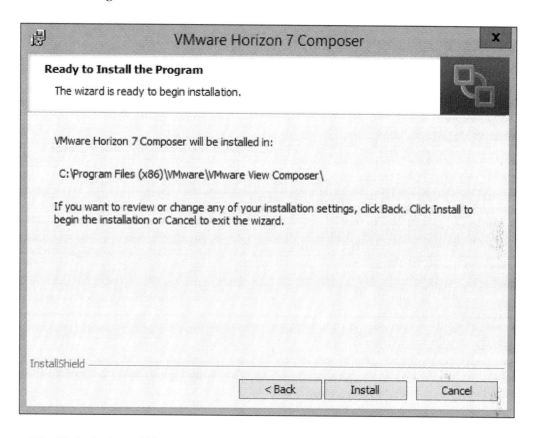

35. Click the **Install** button to start the installation.

36. Once the installation has completed, you will see the **Installer Completed** screen:

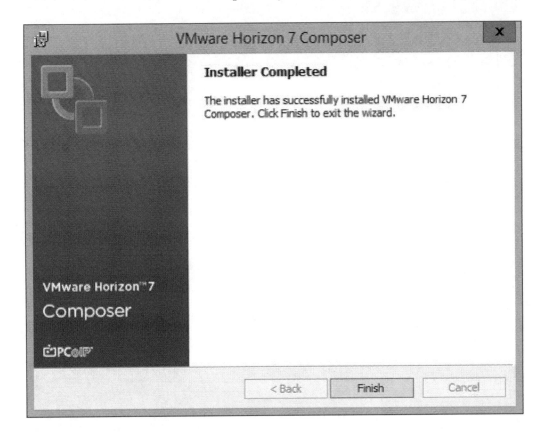

37. Click the **Finish** button to close the installer.

If, for any reason, the installation of View Composer fails, installation logs are held on the View Composer in the following folder: `%TEMP%\vminst.log_date_timestamp`. Additionally, MSI logs are also created and can be found in the following folder: `%TEMP%\vmmsi.log_date_timestamp`.

1. You will then be prompted to restart the virtual machine. Click the **Yes** button to reboot the View Composer virtual machine:

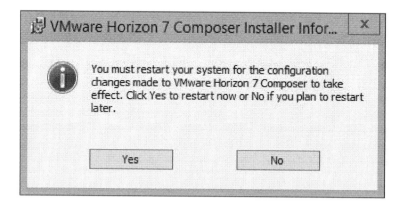

2. When the View Composer virtual machine has restarted, log in and then check that the View Composer service is running. To do this, press the Windows key and *R* to open a **Run** dialog box. In the box, type `services.msc`. You will now see the **Services** screen, as shown in the following screenshot:

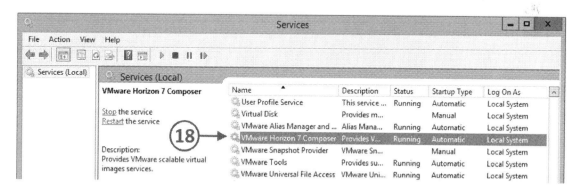

3. Scroll down and check that **VMware Horizon 7 Composer** (18) is running. When you are happy it's running, close the **Services** screen.

You have now successfully installed the View Composer.

Installing the View Connection Server

The View Connection Server and its others roles (Security Server, Replica Server, and so on) are installed on a dedicated Windows Server. The following screenshot lists the requirements to be aware of when creating Connection Server-based roles:

Component	Recommended Supported Configuration
Operating Systems	Windows Server 2008 R2 SP1 64-bit (Std, Ent, DC Editions)
	Windows Server 2012 R2 64-bit (Std & Ent Editions)
Processor	4 CPUs
Networking	1Gbps NICs
Memory	10 GB RAM or higher for deployments of 50 or more
Disk Space	60 GB

The next step in setting up the example lab is to deploy the first of the View Connection Servers. This first instance of the Connection Server is going to be installed on the virtual machine with the hostname **HZN7-CS1** that was built at the start of this chapter, and will need a static IP address assigned to it and to be joined to the domain:

1. Open a console to the HZN7-CS1 virtual machine, and then locate the Horizon View installation software. In the example lab, this was saved to a shared folder on the Domain Controller and is shown in the following screenshot:

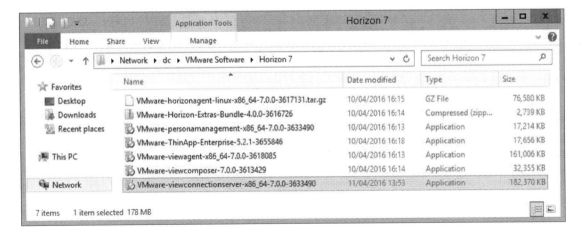

2. Launch the `VMware-viewconnectionserver-x86_64-7.0.0-3633490` file to start the installation.

3. If you see the **Open File – Security Warning message**, click the **Run** button.

4. You will now see the **Welcome to the Installation Wizard for VMware Horizon 7 Connection Server** screen, as shown in the following screenshot:

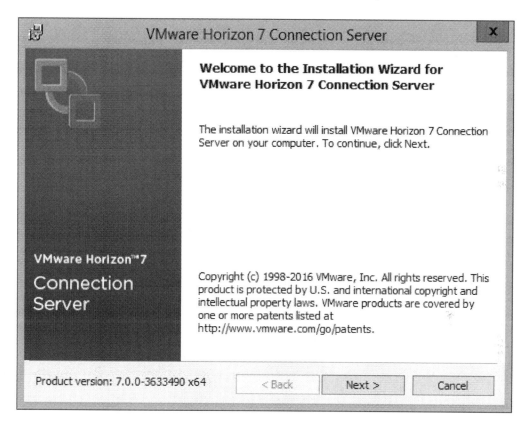

5. Click the **Next >** button to start the installation. You will now see the **License Agreement** screen, as shown in the following screenshot:

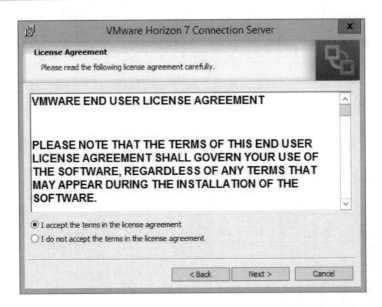

6. Click the radio button for **I accept the terms in the license agreement**, and then click the **Next >** button. You will then see the **Destination Folder** screen, as shown in the following screenshot:

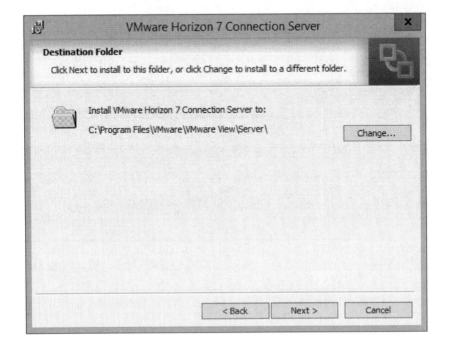

7. Leave the folder as the default and then click the **Next >** button to continue. You will now see the **Installation Options** screen, as shown in the following screenshot:

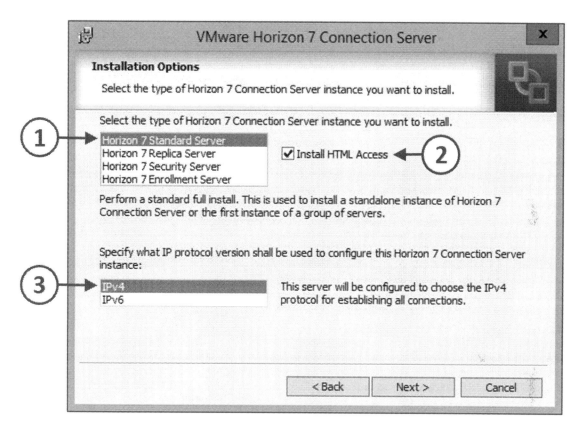

8. As this is the first View Connection Server, from the list of Horizon 7 Connection Server roles, select the option for **Horizon 7 Standard Server** from the list (**1**).

9. We are also going to install HTML access, so check the box for **Install HTML Access** (**2**). This will allow users to access their desktops using the Blast Protocol from an HTML 5 web browser. The final option on this screen is to select which IP protocol to use, either IPv4 or IPv6. For the example lab, select the **IPv4** option (**3**).

 Remember that you cannot mix and match IPv4 and IPv6 in the same environment, so for the example lab, IPv4 is going to be used for all components.

10. Once you have completed the options selection, click the **Next >** button to continue.

11. You will now see the **Data Recovery** screen.

12. On the **Data Recovery** screen, you need to enter a password that will be used for the backups of the View Connection Server. In the **Enter data recovery password** box, type in the password you want to use, and then type it again in the **Re-enter password** box. Finally, enter a password prompt in the **Enter password reminder (optional)** box. This is shown in the following screenshot:

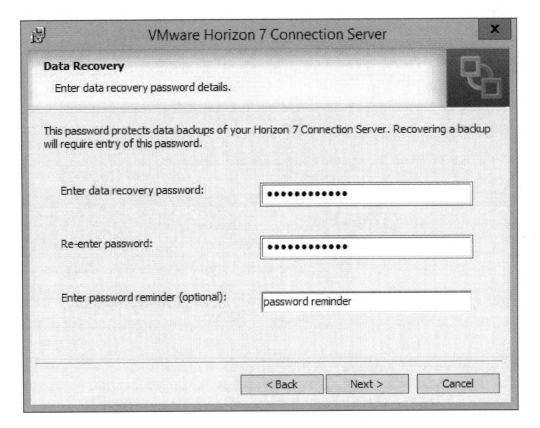

13. Click the **Next >** button to continue.

14. You will now see the **Firewall Configuration** screen, as shown in the following screenshot:

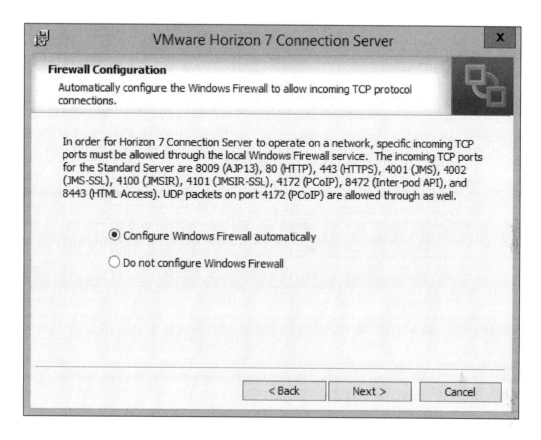

15. Click the radio button for **Configure Windows Firewall automatically**, and then click the **Next >** button to continue.

Windows Firewall is a requirement for Horizon View, specifically for Security Server to Connection Server communications. Under no circumstance should you disable the Windows Firewall service on your View servers. The recommendation is to allow Windows Firewall to be configured automatically, and note down the required ports where needed.

16. You will now see the **Initial Horizon 7 Administrators** screen, as shown in the following screenshot:

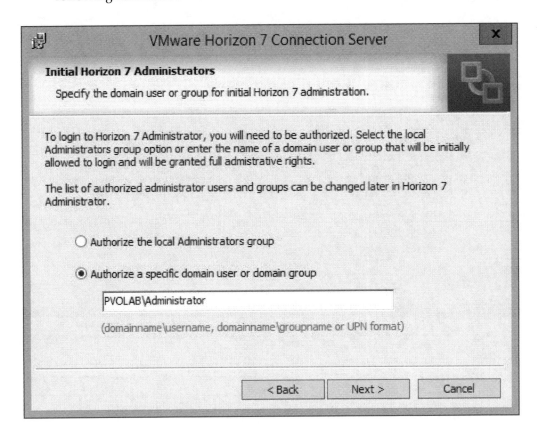

17. On this screen, you need to configure which users on your domain, or on the local server, are going to be configured as your first View Administrators.

18. In the example lab, we are just going to use the standard Administrator account; however, it is recommended that you create a specific user and/or group of users who will have admin access to View.

19. Click the radio button for the **Authorize a specific domain user or group**, and then, in the box, enter the domain name followed by the username. In the example lab, you would type in `pvolab\Administrator`.

20. Click the **Next >** button to continue. You will now see the **User Experience Improvement Program** screen.

21. The **User Experience Improvement Program** is an optional program that anonymously sends product stats to VMware. It's not a licensing check! For the example lab, ensure that the box is unchecked (**4**), as shown in the following screenshot:

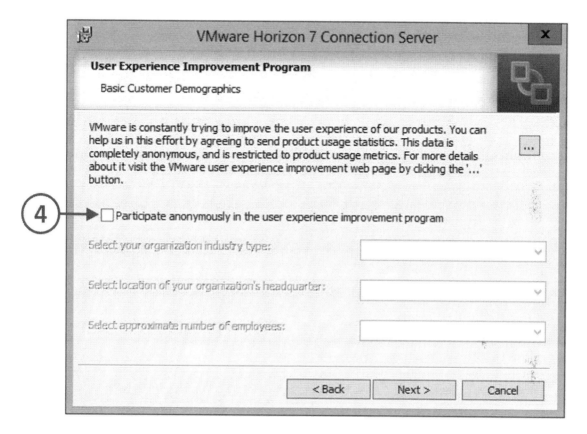

22. Click the **Next >** button to continue.

23. You will now see the **Ready to Install the Program** screen, as shown in the following screenshot:

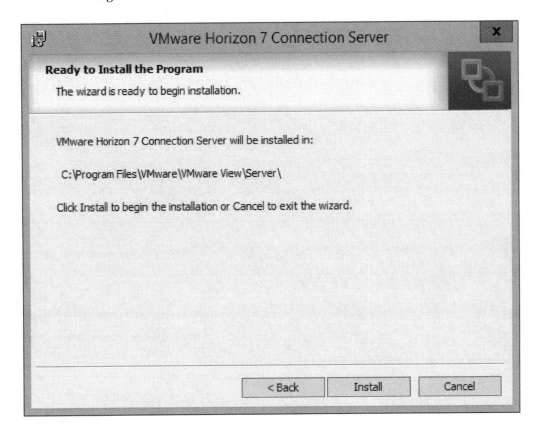

24. Click the **Install** button to start the process.

25. Once the Connection Server has been installed, you will see the **Installer Completed** screen, as shown in the following screenshot:

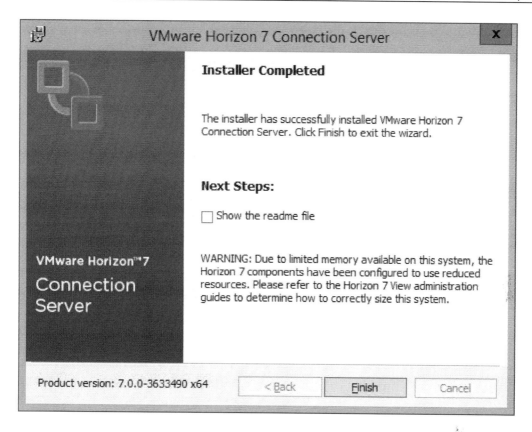

 If the installation fails for any reason, the installation logs are held in the Connection Server at `%TEMP%\vminst.log_date_timestamp`. Additionally, there are MSI logs created, which can be found at `%TEMP%\vmmsi.log_date_timestamp`.

26. You have the option to check the **Show the readme file** box on this screen before you close it. Its recommended that you review this document, as it discusses the importance of valid SSL certificates in the Horizon View installation, which we will cover in more detail in `Chapter 5`, *Securing Horizon View with SSL Certificates and True SSO*.

27. Finally, click the **Finish** button to complete the installation and close the installer.

You will now see that an icon for the **Horizon 7 Administrator Console** has been placed on the desktop:

In the following section, we are going to log in to the View Administrator and complete the initial configuration tasks.

Initial configuration of the View Connection Server

With the View Connection Server now installed, you can connect to the management console, called the **View Administrator**, and start the configuration tasks.

From a workstation, with Adobe Flash 10.1 or higher installed, open a browser and enter the address details of the View Connection Server. In the example lab, the address to enter would be `https://hzn7-cs1.pvolab.com/admin`.

 As SSL certificates have yet to be configured, you need to create a security exception to allow you to browse to the HTTPS page with an unsecured certificate. We will cover SSL certificates in `Chapter 5`, *Securing Horizon View with SSL Certificates and True SSO*.

You will now see the **View Administrator** login screen, as shown in the following screenshot:

Log in to the View Administrator using the Administrator account and password, ensure that the domain is set to match your domain, and then click the **Log In** button. You should now be logged in to the View Administrator for the first time.

The first component to be configured is the product licensing.

Configuring licensing

1. On the left-hand side of the screen, you will see that on the **Inventory** menu, the option for **Product Licensing and Usage** is already highlighted. Next, click the **Edit License...** box (**1**), as shown in the following screenshot:

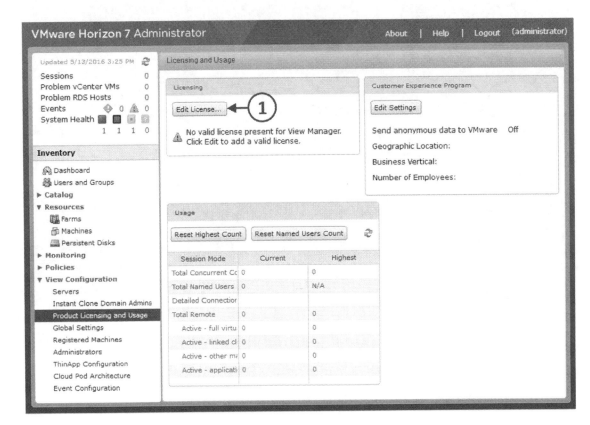

2. You will now see the **Edit License** box, as shown in the following screenshot:

3. In the **License serial number** box, enter your license key and then click the **OK** button. In the preceding example, the license key has been shown as **xxxxx** to hide the actual license key.

4. Once completed, you will see that in the **Licensing** box, the detailed information relating to the license key you input is now shown. In the example lab, an evaluation license key has been used, and for this reason, an expiration date is shown. It also shows you what features are enabled under the specific license key and also the usage model. In this case, the environment is licensed using a named user license model.

 Horizon View can be purchased in a concurrent or named user-licensing model.

The following screenshot shows the **Licensing** information for the example lab:

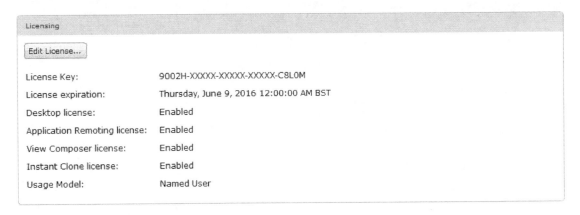

While you are on this screen, you can check your current usage, as shown in the following screenshot:

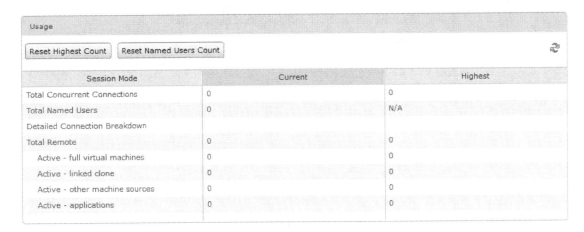

This allows you to ensure you are within the remit of your purchased licenses and also allows you to have visibility of the usage so that you can preempt an upgrade before reaching the limits.

Chapter 4

Adding the vCenter Server to View Administrator

The next task is to configure the connection between the View Administrator and the vCenter Server:

1. From the View Administrator main screen, expand the option for **View Configuration** (1), and then select **Servers** (2). Next, from the Servers screen, ensure that the tab for **vCenter Servers** is selected (3), and then click the **Add...** button (4). This is shown in the following screenshot:

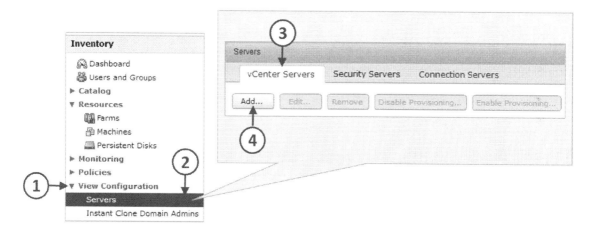

[213]

2. You will now see the **vCenter Server Information** screen, as shown in the following screenshot:

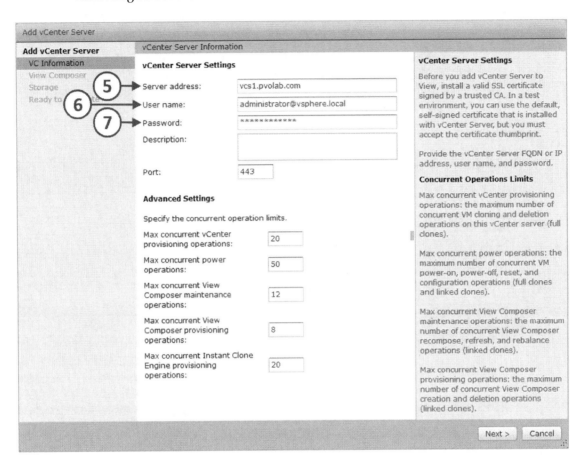

3. In the **Server address** box (**5**), type in the address of the vCenter Server. In the example lab, this is **vcs2.pvolab.com**, the address of the vCenter managing the virtual desktops.

4. Next, in the **User name** box (**6**), type in the vCenter username followed by the password for this account in the **Password** box (**7**). In this example, the administrator account has been used; however, you will probably want to create a specific user account for this.

5. You will now see the following **Invalid Certificate Detected** warning box, as shown in the following screenshot:

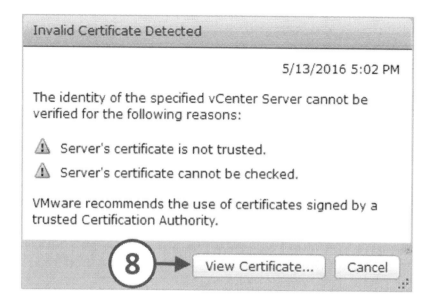

6. Click the **View Certificate…** button (8). You will now see the **Certificate Information** box, as shown in the following screenshot:

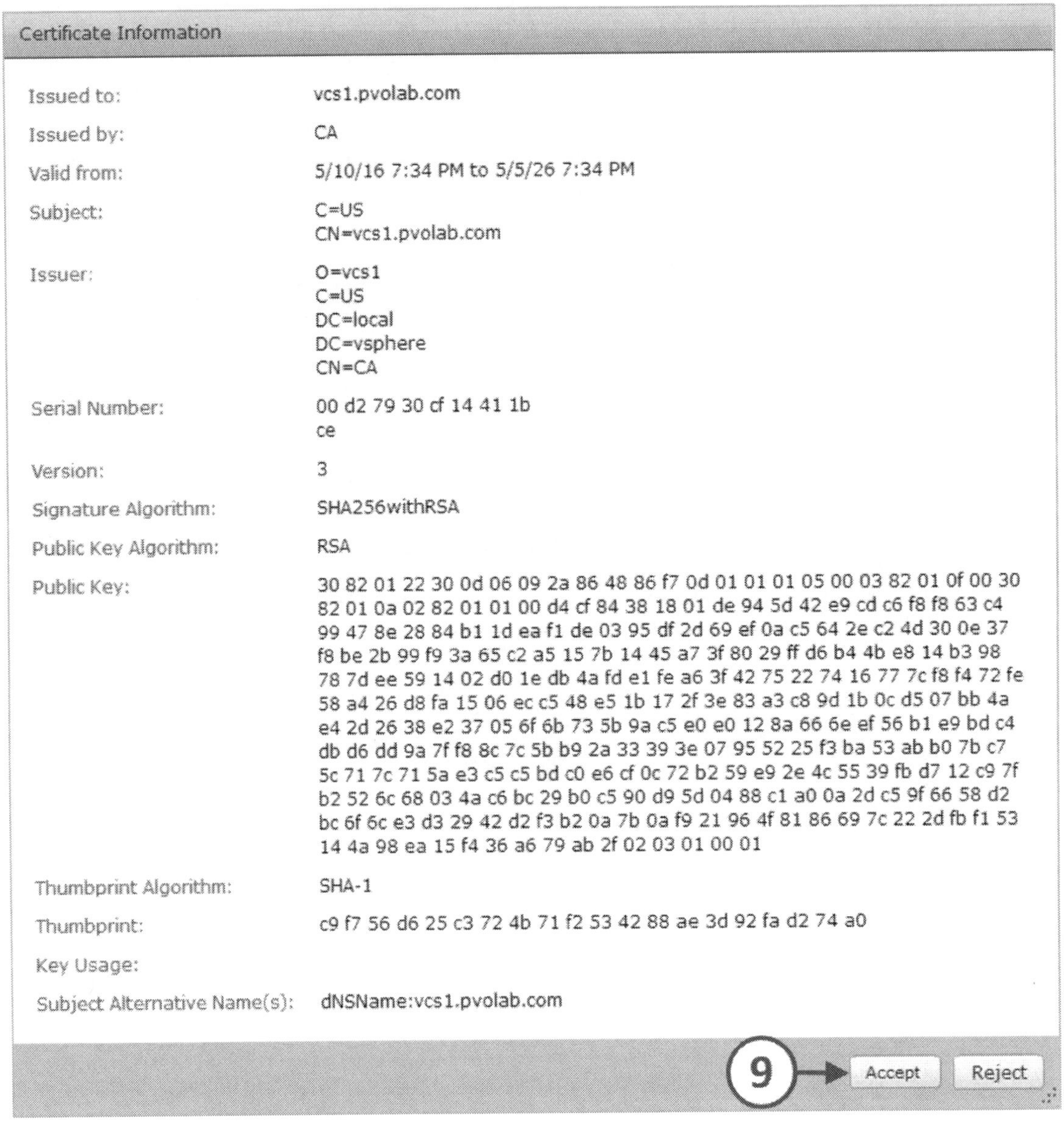

Certificate Information	
Issued to:	vcs1.pvolab.com
Issued by:	CA
Valid from:	5/10/16 7:34 PM to 5/5/26 7:34 PM
Subject:	C=US CN=vcs1.pvolab.com
Issuer:	O=vcs1 C=US DC=local DC=vsphere CN=CA
Serial Number:	00 d2 79 30 cf 14 41 1b ce
Version:	3
Signature Algorithm:	SHA256withRSA
Public Key Algorithm:	RSA
Public Key:	30 82 01 22 30 0d 06 09 2a 86 48 86 f7 0d 01 01 01 05 00 03 82 01 0f 00 30 82 01 0a 02 82 01 01 00 d4 cf 84 38 18 01 de 94 5d 42 e9 cd c6 f8 f8 63 c4 99 47 8e 28 84 b1 1d ea f1 de 03 95 df 2d 69 ef 0a c5 64 2e c2 4d 30 0e 37 f8 be 2b 99 f9 3a 65 c2 a5 15 7b 14 45 a7 3f 80 29 ff d6 b4 4b e8 14 b3 98 78 7d ee 59 14 02 d0 1e db 4a fd e1 fe a6 3f 42 75 22 74 16 77 7c f8 f4 72 fe 58 a4 26 d8 fa 15 06 ec c5 48 e5 1b 17 2f 3e 83 a3 c8 9d 1b 0c d5 07 bb 4a e4 2d 26 38 e2 37 05 6f 6b 73 5b 9a c5 e0 e0 12 8a 66 6e ef 56 b1 e9 bd c4 db d6 dd 9a 7f f8 8c 7c 5b b9 2a 33 39 3e 07 95 52 25 f3 ba 53 ab b0 7b c7 5c 71 7c 71 5a e3 c5 c5 bd c0 e6 cf 0c 72 b2 59 e9 2e 4c 55 39 fb d7 12 c9 7f b2 52 6c 68 03 4a c6 bc 29 b0 c5 90 d9 5d 04 88 c1 a0 0a 2d c5 9f 66 58 d2 bc 6f 6c e3 d3 29 42 d2 f3 b2 0a 7b 0a f9 21 96 4f 81 86 69 7c 22 2d fb f1 53 14 4a 98 ea 15 f4 36 a6 79 ab 2f 02 03 01 00 01
Thumbprint Algorithm:	SHA-1
Thumbprint:	c9 f7 56 d6 25 c3 72 4b 71 f2 53 42 88 ae 3d 92 fa d2 74 a0
Key Usage:	
Subject Alternative Name(s):	dNSName:vcs1.pvolab.com

9 → Accept   Reject

7. Click the **Accept** button (**9**).

8. The next screen is the **View Composer Settings** screen, as shown in the following screenshot:

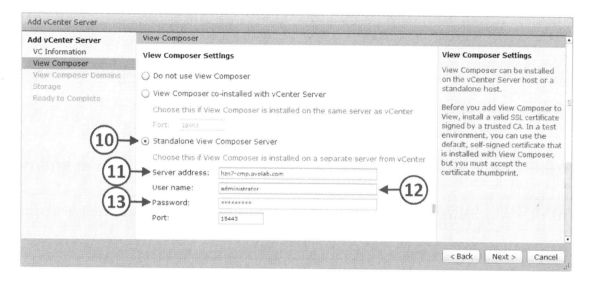

10. You have three options to configure View Composer: Do not use View Composer, View Composer installed on the same server as vCenter, and a Standalone View Composer.

11. For the example lab, View Composer is going to installed on a standalone server, so click the radio button for the **Standalone View Composer Server** (**10**).

12. Next you need to enter the details of the View Composer Server. In the **Server address** box (**11**), type in the server address. In the example lab, this is **hzn7-cmp.pvolab.com**. Then, type the username for this server in the **User name** box (**12**), followed by the password for this user account in the **Password** box (**13**).

13. When you have completed the details, click the **Next >** button.

14. As with adding the vCenter Server, you will again see the following **Invalid Certificate Detected** warning box, as shown in the following screenshot:

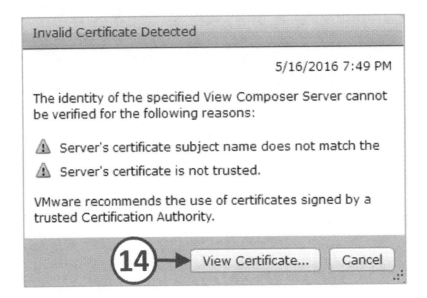

15. Click the button for **View Certificate... (14)**. You will then see the **Certificate Information** screen, as shown in the following screenshot:

Certificate Information

Issued to:	HZN7-CMP
Issued by:	HZN7-CMP
Valid from:	5/16/16 3:25 PM to 5/16/18 3:25 PM
Subject:	C=US ST=CA L=CA O=VMware Inc. OU=VMware Inc. CN=HZN7-CMP EMAILADDRESS=support@vmware.com
Issuer:	C=US ST=CA L=CA O=VMware Inc. OU=VMware Inc. CN=HZN7-CMP EMAILADDRESS=support@vmware.com
Serial Number:	19 f3 2e 79 15 1f 85 9e 4e 00 a0 d7 eb 91 94 d4
Version:	3
Signature Algorithm:	SHA1withRSA
Public Key Algorithm:	RSA
Public Key:	30 82 01 22 30 0d 06 09 2a 86 48 86 f7 0d 01 01 01 05 00 03 82 01 0f 00 30 82 01 0a 02 82 01 01 00 ad bb 8b de 40 7e 66 94 0f db e1 6f 7b a5 6e c2 97 51 77 7f 3f de cb 96 95 fb 6a 2b 37 13 04 99 28 37 39 ba ee 1b 37 44 66 ec e6 07 56 e9 1a bd d3 e3 00 18 51 be 5f b0 1b 3b 3d 38 f5 eb b1 66 af 06 2a bb cf ac 65 53 a0 0d 20 0a e2 4f b2 1d 86 bb 5b aa 64 45 c5 65 cd c0 32 69 03 fe 72 28 c7 dd 38 8d 68 19 f1 3d f9 d1 d7 47 7a 68 ca 92 b6 68 34 70 e2 ae 5c 32 ec 5a f1 fa 8f 00 cb 7b 10 a4 98 36 b8 ea c0 76 bd 1a 37 44 be 09 c7 df 7c 15 7d c4 69 0d 8e 28 82 af a5 4a 47 12 0c 56 c8 f3 fd 37 27 d3 29 19 97 79 11 18 0a 22 6a 6d 5b ec 52 33 0a 9a c3 f4 b3 f8 33 67 50 d6 e4 5b 3c c4 da 31 2d 5e 92 cc b1 cf 23 32 e4 ed 26 63 f3 86 23 3a 1f 5b 4d 89 14 3a 08 0a cb 05 13 3a aa 05 26 80 71 c9 92 c8 94 b1 a8 b7 1e 48 fd ea 31 f9 2e 29 4a 50 6a de 72 ea da d2 db ac 18 f5 02 03 01 00 01
Thumbprint Algorithm:	SHA-1
Thumbprint:	50 cb 86 a2 72 50 4b 26 7e 7c 65 58 48 d9 1b 80 77 af ed d9
Key Usage:	
Subject Alternative Name(s):	

(15) → Accept | Reject

16. Click the **Accept** button (15). You will now see the **View Composer Domains** configuration screen, as shown in the following screenshot:

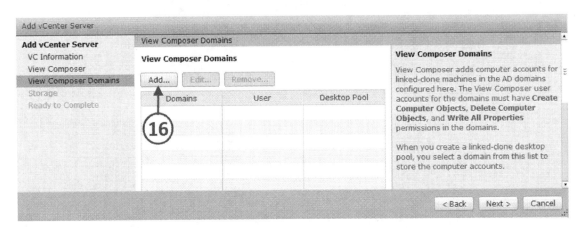

17. This allows View Composer to add computer accounts to Active Directory. Click the **Add...** button (**16**). You will now see the **Add Domain** configuration box, as shown in the following screenshot:

18. In the **Full domain name** box, type in the domain name. In the example lab, this is pvolab.com. Then, in the **User name** box, type the username that has the ability to create and delete computer objects in Active Directory. In the example lab, we will use the administrator account.

19. Finally, in the **Password** box, type in the password for the administrator account.

20. Click the **OK** button when you have entered the information.

21. You will now return to the **View Composer Domains** configuration screen, which now shows the configured domain:

23. Click the **Next >** button to continue.

24. You will now see the **Storage Settings** configuration screen. There are two main elements to configure. The first option is to configure whether or not you want to reclaim VM disk space for your virtual desktops. If this is selected, the virtual machines will be configured with space-efficient disks, which will allow reclamation of unused space on each desktop.

25. The second option is to configure the View Storage Accelerator. This allows a specific amount of the memory host to be utilized as a read cache to reduce the storage overheads on the shared or local storage used to run the virtual machines.

26. By default, this will be set to 1 GB of memory per server, and can be increased to up to 2 GB per server, or alternatively, if you check the box for **Show all hosts**, you can then select individual hosts and configure the cache size differently on each host server.

27. In the example lab, we are going to enable the options for **Reclaim VM disk space** and **Enable View Storage Accelerator**, as shown in the following screenshot:

28. Click the **Next >** button to continue.
29. You will now see the **Ready to Complete** screen:

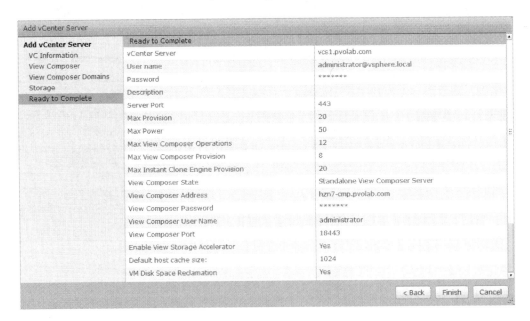

30. Finally, click the **Finish** button to complete the configuration. You will return to the View Administrator screen, which now shows the vCenter Server that was just added, as shown in the following screenshot:

In the following section, we are going to configure the viewevents database

Configuring the viewevents database

The final piece of the initial configuration tasks is to configure the viewevents database. This is where View stores all the events that take place on the Connection Servers.

A database called **viewevents** was created at the start of this chapter, and now we are going to use it in the configuration:

1. From the View Administrator main screen and the **Inventory** section, expand the option for **View Configuration**, and then select **Event Configuration (1)**.

2. Then, on the **Event Database** screen, click the **Edit...** button (**2**). You will now see the **Edit Event Database** dialog box, as shown in the following screenshot:

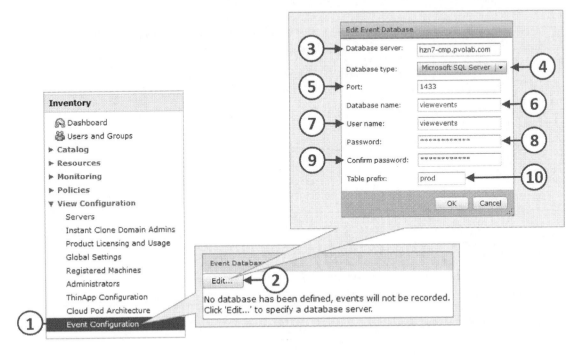

3. In the **Database server** box (**3**), enter the name of the SQL server that is hosting the events database. In the example lab, it's on the same server as View Composer, so enter the name **hzn7-cmp.pvolab.com** as the server name.

4. Ensure that **Microsoft SQL Server** is selected from the drop-down menu from the **Database type** box (**4**). The other option is to set up an Oracle database.

5. Leave the **Port** setting (**5**) as the default port of 1443, and in the **Database name** box (**6**), type in the name of the database. In the example lab, the database is called **viewevents**.

6. In the **User name** box (**7**), type in the username for this database, and in the **Password** box (**8**), type in the password for this user, and then type it in again in the **Confirm password** box (**9**).

7. Finally, in the **Table prefix** box (**10**), you can enter a prefix name. This allows you to use the same events database for multiple installations. Once you have entered the configuration information, click the **OK** button. Once completed, you should see the following:

Event Database

Clear...   Edit...

Database server type: Microsoft SQL Server

Database server: hzn7-cmp.pvolab.com

Port: 1433

Database name: ViewEvents

User name: ViewEvents

Table prefix:

You have now successfully completed the initial Connection Server configuration tasks.

Installing the View Replica Server

Next we are going to deploy a second View Connection Server. Additional View Connection Servers are referred to as **Replica Servers**. This is due to the way in which View shares its configurations between multiple View Connection Servers using the ADAM database.

Additional Connection Servers are generally deployed for availability reasons, as discussed in previous chapters. For test purposes, you could roll out a single View Connection Server.

This second instance of the Connection Server is going to be installed on the virtual machine with the hostname **HZN7-CS2**, which was built at the start of this chapter, and will also need a static IP address assigned to it and to be joined to the domain:

1. Open a console to the HZN7-CS2 virtual machine, and then locate the Horizon View installation software. In the example lab, this was saved to a shared folder on the Domain Controller. As the screenshots are almost identical to those from the first Connection Server installation, we will only highlight and show the differences during this installation.

2. Launch the `VMware-viewconnectionserver-x86_64-7.0.0-3633490` file to start the installation. This is the same installer application as you used for the first Connection Server, but it will be configured differently to reflect the fact that this is a Replica Server.

3. If you see the **Open File – Security Warning message**, click the **Run** button.

4. You will now see the **Welcome to the Installation Wizard for VMware Horizon 7 Connection Server** screen.

5. Click the **Next >** button to start the installation. You will now see the **License Agreement** screen.

6. Click the radio button for **I accept the terms in the license agreement**, and then click the **Next >** button. You will now see the **Destination Folder** screen.

7. Leave the folder as the default setting and then click the **Next >** button to continue.

8. You will now see the **Installation Options** screen, as shown in the following screenshot:

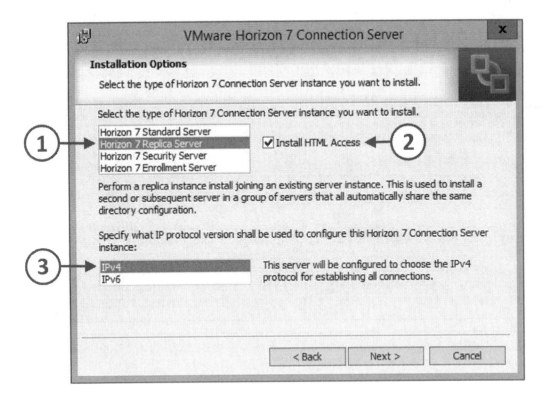

9. As this is the second Connection Server, or Replica Server, from the list of Horizon 7 Connection Server roles, select the option for **Horizon 7 Replica Server** from the list (**1**).

10. As before, we are going to install HTML access, so check the box for **Install HTML Access** (**2**). This will allow users to access their desktops using the Blast Protocol from an HTML 5 web browser. The final option on this screen is to select which IP protocol to use, either IPv4 or IPv6. For the example lab, select the **IPv4** option (**3**).

11. Click the **Next >** button to continue.

12. You will now see the **Source Server** configuration screen, as shown in the following screenshot:

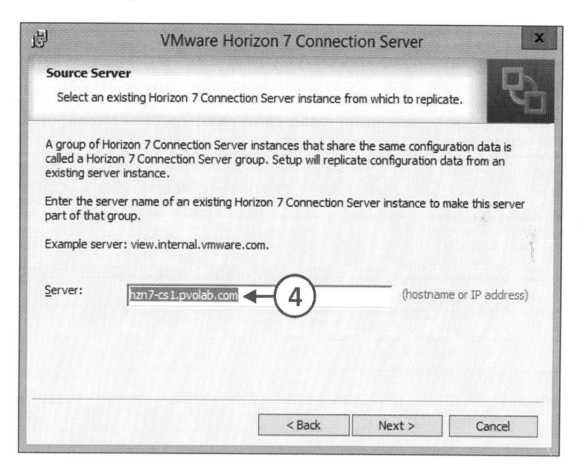

13. In the **Server** box, type in the address of the first Connection Server (**4**). In the example lab, this is **hzn7-cs1.pvolab.com**.

14. Click the **Next >** button to continue. You will see the **Firewall Configuration** screen.

15. Click the radio button for **Configure Windows Firewall automatically**, and then click the **Next >** button to continue. You will see the **Ready to Install the Program** screen.

16. Click the **Install** button to start the process.

17. Once the Replica Server has been installed, you will see the **Installer Completed** screen. Click the **Finish** button on this screen to close the installer.

18. To check that the Replica Server has been installed correctly and that it is up and running, log in to the View Administrator:

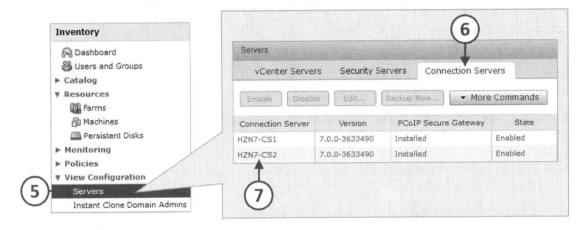

19. From the **Inventory** menu, expand the **View Configuration** section, and then click on **Servers** (**5**). Click the **Connection Servers** tab (**6**). You will now see the Replica Server **hzn7-cs2** listed (**7**).

You have now successfully configured the Replica Server.

Now that you have two Connection Servers, don't forget that Horizon View, as standard, includes no method to load balance Connection Servers or security servers. As such, you should work with the relevant documentation from your load balancing manufacturer to configure your load balancers to work with your View Connection Servers as required. This allows users to be load balanced for availability and scale.

Installing the View Security Server

The next component that we are going to install is the Security Server, so that you can allow external access to your end users.

The Security Server in another instance of the Connection Server and is going to be installed on the virtual machine with the hostname **HZN7-SS1**, which was built at the start of this chapter, and will also need a static IP address assigned to it and to **NOT** be joined to the domain.

 Don't forget that a security server has a one-to-one relationship with a Connection Server, if you wish to roll out a number of security servers; you will want to have multiple View Connection Servers.

It is also recommended that you have dedicated external View Connection Servers ready to pair with your security servers and separate View Connection Servers for internal connections. This will allow you to specify which users can access desktops from outside the organization by using the tagging functionality, which we will discuss later in this chapter and in Chapter 7, *Managing and Configuring Desktop Pools*.

Preparing View Administrator for the Security Server

Before we start with the installation, you need to prepare the Connection Server for the Security Server by creating a pairing password. This password will be used to connect the two servers together securely. It's the same kind of process you would use to pair your Bluetooth cell phone to the hands-free system in your car.

1. From the **Inventory** menu, expand the **View Configuration** section and then click on **Servers**. Now click the **Connection Servers** tab. You will now see the Connection Server details, as shown in the following screenshot:

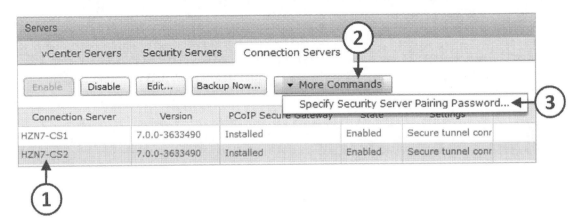

2. Click to select the Connection Server you want to pair the Security Server with. In the example lab, we are going to pair it with the Connection Server called **hzn7-cs2 (1)**.

3. Now click the **More Commands** button (**2**) and select the option for **Specify Security Server Pairing Password... (3)**. You will now see the **Specify Security Server Pairing Password** screen, as shown in the following screenshot:

Specify Security Server Pairing Password

This password is a one-time password that allows a security server to be paired with this connection server. It is invalidated when any authentication attempt is made for pairing.

This password will also be invalidated based on the password timeout value below.

⚠ This View environment is configured to enable IPsec for communication between the HZN7-CS2 Connection Server and the security server. IPsec requires the Windows Firewall to be turned on for the active profile used for pairing the Connection Server to the Security Server.

Please ensure the Windows Firewall for the active profile on the HZN7-CS2 Connection Server is turned on before continuing. You can turn the Windows Firewall on for the active profile from "Windows Firewall with Advanced Security" under "Administrative Tools".

Pairing password: ********

Confirm password: ********

Password timeout: 60   Minutes ▼

OK   Cancel

4. In the **Pairing password** box, type in the password you want to use. You will need to remember this password, as you will enter it again during the installation of the Security Server. Type the password again in the **Confirm password** box, and then in the **Password timeout** box, enter a time for this password to be valid for.

5. Click **OK** once you have configured the pairing password.

You can now go ahead and start the installation of the Security Server.

Security Server installation process

Open a console to the **HZN7-SS1** virtual machine, and then locate the Horizon View installation software. In the example lab, this was saved to a shared folder located on the Domain Controller:

1. Launch the `VMware-viewconnectionserver-x86_64-7.0.0-3633490` file to start the installation. This is the same installer application as you used for the first Connection Server, but it will be configured differently to reflect the fact that this is a Security Server.

2. If you see the **Open File – Security Warning message**, click the **Run** button.

3. You will now see the **Welcome to the Installation Wizard for VMware Horizon 7 Connection Server** screen.

4. Click the **Next >** button to start the installation. You will now see the **License Agreement** screen.

5. Click the radio button for **I accept the terms in the license agreement**, and then click the **Next >** button. You will now see the **Destination Folder** screen.

6. Leave the folder as the default setting and then click the **Next >** button to continue. You will now see the **Installation Options** screen, as shown in the following screenshot:

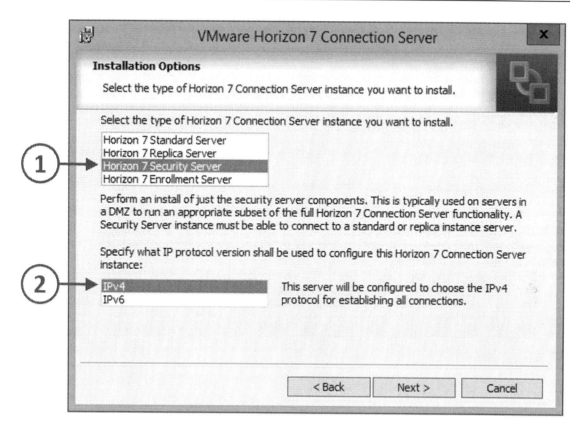

7. From the list of Horizon 7 Connection Server roles, select the option for **Horizon 7 Security Server** from the list (**1**).

8. The final option on this screen is to select which IP protocol to use, either IPv4 or IPv6. For the example lab, select the **IPv4** option (**2**).

9. Click the **Next >** button to continue.

10. You will now see the **Paired Horizon 7 Connection Server** screen, as shown in the following screenshot:

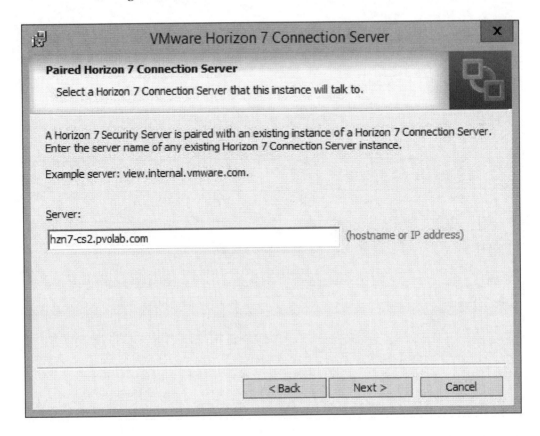

11. In the **Server** box, enter the details of the Connection Server to pair with. In the example lab, we are going to pair with the server called **hzn7-cs2.pvolab.com**.

12. Click the **Next >** button to continue.

13. You will now see the **Paired Horizon 7 Connection Server Password** screen. In the password box, type in the password that you specified when you configured the View Administrator in the previous section. This is shown in the following screenshot:

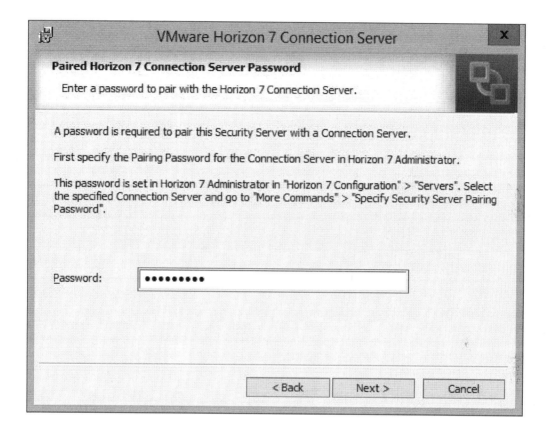

14. Click the **Next >** button to continue. You will now see the **Horizon 7 Security Server Configuration** screen where we can configure the network-specific details for the Security Server, as shown in the following screenshot:

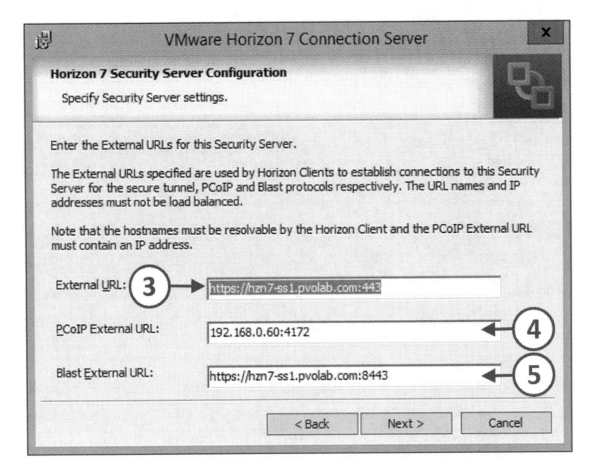

15. In the **External URL** box (3), enter the address that users will use to connect their client to over an Internet connection. In the preceding example, this has been left as the default; however, you will probably want to change this to something more user-friendly.
16. In the **PCoIP External URL** box (4), enter the IP address for the external PCoIP connection. This must contain an IP address rather than a URL as the box suggests.

17. Finally, in the **Blast External URL** box (**5**), enter the address for the Blast protocol. This is used for HTML5 access to the desktop.

18. Click the **Next >** button to continue. You will now see the **Firewall Configuration**.

19. Click the radio button for **Configure Windows Firewall automatically,** and then click the **Next >** button to continue. You will see the **Ready to Install the Program** screen.

20. Click the **Install** button to start the process.

21. Once the Security Server has been installed, you will see the **Installer Completed** screen. Click the **Finish** button on this screen to close the installer.

22. To check that the Replica Server had been installed correctly and that it is up and running, log in to the View Administrator.

23. From the **Inventory** menu, expand the **View Configuration** section, and then click on **Servers** (**6**). Click the **Security Servers** tab (**7**). You will now see the Security Server **HZN7-SS2** listed (**8**):

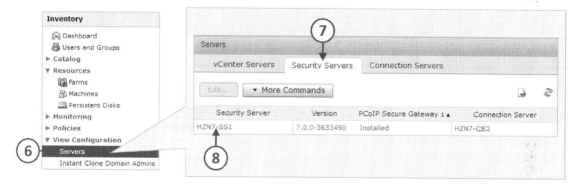

You have now successfully configured the Security Server.

As mentioned earlier, we recommend installing Security Servers in conjunction with dedicated external View Connection Servers, so that you can limit access to the desktops from external connections by using the tagging functionality.

The first step in achieving this is by tagging your external Connection Servers.

1. From the **Inventory** menu, expand the **View Configuration** section, and then click on **Servers** (9). Click the **Connection Servers** tab (10) and then highlight the Connection Server that is paired with the Security Server for the external connections. In the example lab, this the server called **HZN7-CS2** (11).

2. Right-click and then, from the contextual menu, click on **Edit...** (12), as shown in the following screenshot:

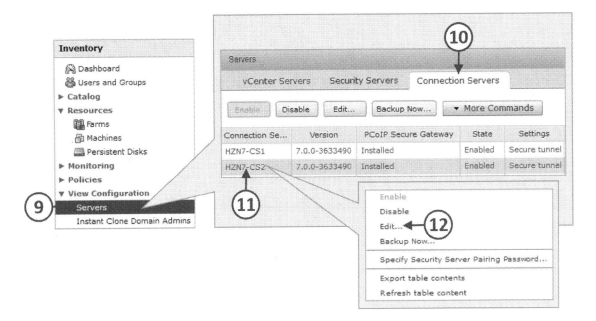

3. You will now see the **Edit Connection Server Settings** screen, as shown in the following screenshot:

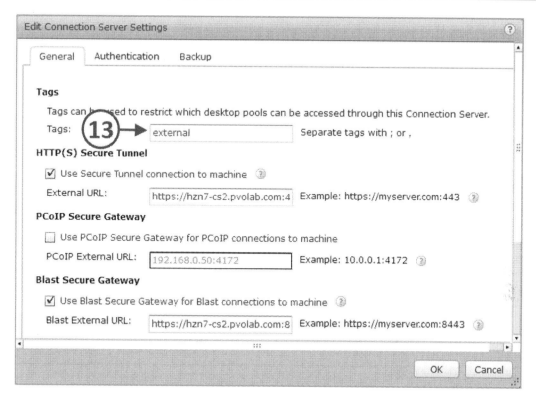

4. In the **Tags** box (13), type in the name for this tag. In the example lab, this tag is called external. This means that only a desktop pool with this tag can connect via this Connection Server.

Installing the View Enrollment Server

The final component we are going to install is the **Enrollment Server**.

As with the first Connection Server, Security Server, and Replica Server, the Enrolment Server is another instance of the Connection Server and is going to be installed on the virtual machine with the hostname **HZN7-ENROL**, which was built at the start of this chapter, and will also need a static IP address assigned to it and to be joined to the domain:

1. Open a console to the HZN7-ENROL virtual machine, and then locate the Horizon View installation software. In the example lab, this was saved to a shared folder on the Domain Controller.

2. Launch the file VMware-viewconnectionserver-x86_64-7.0.0-3633490 to start the installation. This is the same installer application as you used for the first Connection Server, but it will be configured differently to reflect the fact that this is an Enrollment Server.

3. If you see the **Open File – Security Warning message**, click the **Run** button.

4. You will now see the **Welcome to the Installation Wizard for VMware Horizon 7 Connection Server** screen.

5. Click the **Next >** button to start the installation. You will now see the **License Agreement** screen.

6. Click the radio button for **I accept the terms in the license agreement**, and then click the **Next >** button. You will now see the **Destination Folder** screen.

7. Leave the folder as the default setting and then click the **Next >** button to continue. You will now see the **Installation Options** screen, as shown in the following screenshot:

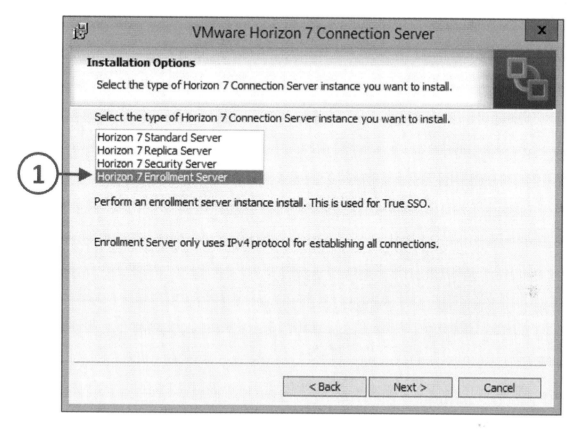

8. From the list of Horizon 7 Connection Server roles, select the option for **Horizon 7 Enrollment Server** from the list (1).

9. Click the **Next >** button to continue.

10. You will now see the **Firewall Configuration** screen, as shown in the following screenshot:

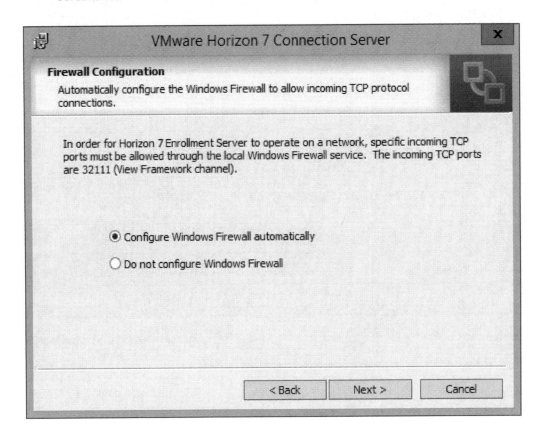

11. Click the **Next >** button to continue.
12. You will see the **Ready to Install the Program** screen.
13. Click the **Install** button to start the process. Once the Enrollment Server has been installed, you will see the **Installer Completed** screen. Click the **Finish** button on this screen to close the installer.

14. As there is no user interface or console for the Enrollment Server, to check whether or not it's running, we are going to check the Windows Services console. To do this, press the Windows key and *R* to open a **Run** dialog box. In the box, type `services.msc`. You will now see the **Services** screen, as shown in the following screenshot:

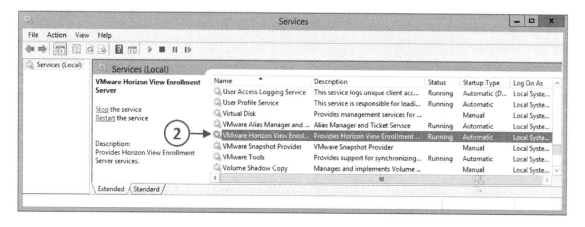

15. Scroll down and check that **VMware Horizon View Enrollment Server** (2) is running. When you are happy it's running, close the **Services** screen.

You have now successfully installed the View Enrollment Server.

Configuring View for GPU-enabled Virtual Desktops

In `Chapter 2`, *An Overview of Horizon View Architecture and Components*, we discussed the ability of Horizon View virtual desktop machines to be configured to use hardware installed in the ESXi host server hosting those desktops. In this case, the hardware in question is a graphics card.

As we discussed earlier, an advanced feature of Horizon View is the ability to use dedicated hardware installed in the ESXi host servers, configured with PCI pass-through so that the virtual desktop machine can *see* the hardware.

In this section, we will perform the initial steps to install a NVIDIA GRID GPU card onto one of the host servers. Later on, in Chapter 6, *Building and Optimizing the Virtual Desktop OS*, we will create a virtual desktop machine image, which will have a dedicated assignment and access to the GPU resource.

 If you are going to be using vGPU, you will need vSphere 6 installed as the hypervisor to support this.

Configuring the ESXi hosts

Before you build the virtual desktop machine, you need to have the graphics card physically installed and configured on the ESXi host in preparation for building the new virtual desktop machines that will use it.

In the example lab, we are using the NVIDIA GRID K2 card. These cards are available via the OEM route and come ready-configured from the server vendors due to them requiring additional power connectors, cooling fans, and specific BIOS settings.

 It's worth checking these before you start, as just retrofitting the cards to an existing server might mean that they do not work. You will find the list of certified servers at http://www.nvidia.com/object/grid-partners.html.

With the hardware installed, log in to the vSphere Web Client, select the host onto which the card has been installed, and complete the following steps:

1. Log in to the vSphere Web Client and then navigate to the host server with the NVIDIA card installed. In the example lab, this the host **esx-1.pvolab.com (1)**, as shown in the following screenshot:

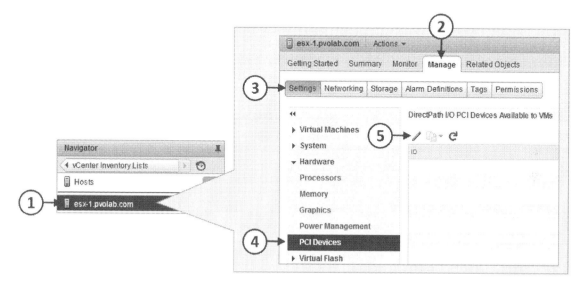

2. Click the **Manage** tab (**2**), and then the **Settings** button (**3**). Expand the **Hardware** section and then click **PCI Devices** (**4**). Now click the pencil icon (**5**) to edit the settings.

3. You will now see the **Edit PCI Device Availability** screen, as shown in the following screenshot:

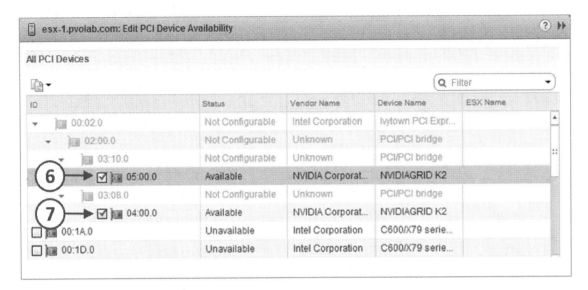

4. As you can see, this host server is configured with two NVIDIA GRID K2 graphics cards. Check the boxes (**6**) and (**7**) to enable the cards.

You have now configured the ESXi host server to use the NVIDIA GRID K2 GPU cards. These will be used when we build the virtual desktop machines later in this book, in Chapter 6, *Building and Optimizing the Virtual Desktop OS*.

In the final section of this chapter, we are going to initialize and configure the Cloud Pod Architecture feature.

Configuring the Cloud Pod Architecture

In Chapter 3, *Design and Deployment Considerations*, we discussed the Cloud Pod Architecture and its ability to deliver multi-site View deployments to allow for scalability and also disaster recovery scenarios. We are now going to look at how to set up a cloud pod using the example lab.

In the example lab, we have built and configured another Connection Server, called **HZN7-CS1B**, which we will use to represent a second pod, located at a second site.

This server is installed as a Connection Server and not a Replica Server, as it needs to be the first server in a different pod.

The following diagram illustrates the installation we are going to follow using the example lab:

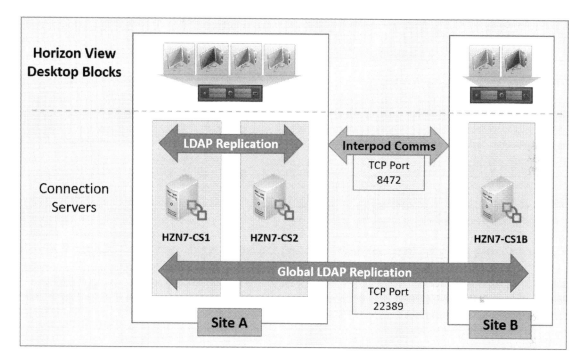

The first step of the process it to initialize the Cloud Pod from the first Connection Server.

Initializing the Cloud Pod

From the View Administrator console, in the Inventory pane on the left, expand the View Configuration section and click **Cloud Pod Architecture** (1). Then click the option for **Initialize the Cloud Pod Architecture feature** (2), as shown in the following screenshot:

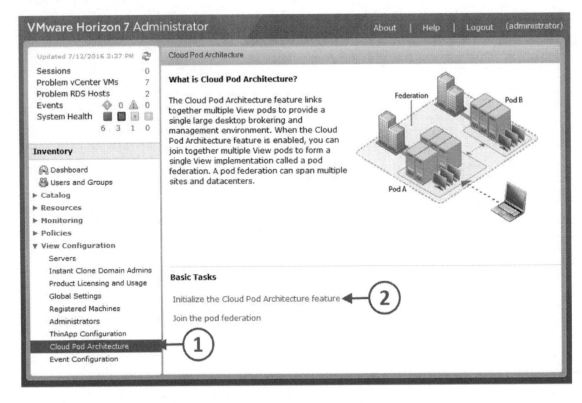

You will now see the **Initialize** dialog box, as shown in the following screenshot:

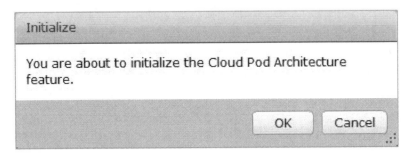

Click the **OK** button to start the initialization. You will now see the initialization process start, and a visual representation of the progress displayed as a % bar across the screen, as well as the status being shown as **Pending**, as shown in the following screenshot:

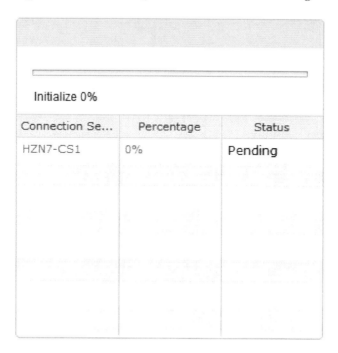

Once the Cloud Pod Architecture feature has complete its initialization, you will see the **Reload** dialog box, as shown in the following screenshot:

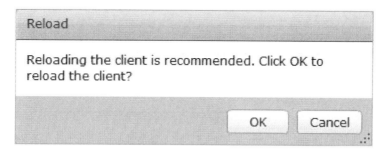

Click the **OK** button to reload the client. You will now see the Cloud Pod Architecture screen in the View Administrator, as shown in the following screenshot:

As you can see, a Pod Federation has been created called **Horizon Cloud Pod Federation**. You can change this name by clicking the **Edit...** button, should you need to.

You will also see that the pods are listed, along with the site information. In the example lab, we only have the HZN7-CS1 Connection Server listed, as this is the first Connection Server to have the Cloud Pod Architecture installed.

The next step is to connect the Connection Server in the second pod to the federation.

Connecting the second pod to the Cloud Pod

The next step in the process is to connect or join your other pods to the pod federation.

Log in to the View Administrator console on the second Connection Server. This is called **HZN7-CS1B**. This is the Connection Server on the second site in the example lab.

Again, from the View Administrator console, in the Inventory pane on the left, expand the View Configuration section and click **Cloud Pod Architecture** (**1**), but this time, click the option for **Join the pod federation** (**2**), as shown in the following screenshot:

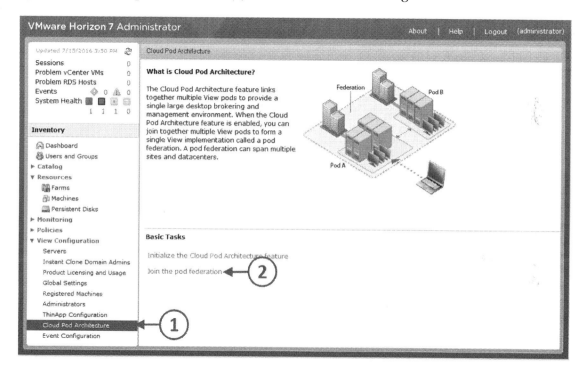

You will now see the **Join** dialog box.

Here you need to enter the details of a Connection Server that is in a pod that has had the Cloud Pod Architecture initialized. In the example lab, this was the **HZN7-CS1** Connection Server that we initialized in the previous section, so we will enter those details into the Join box, as shown in the following screenshot:

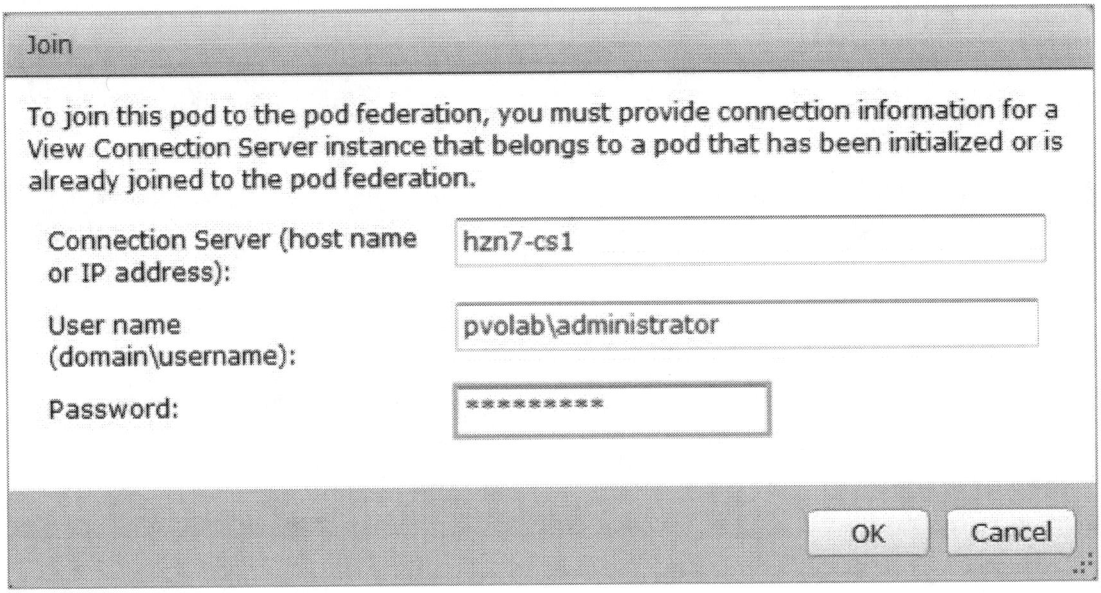

In the **Connection Server** box, type in the name of the Connection Server. As we have said previously, in the example lab this is **HZN7-CS1**.

In the **User name** box, type in the username that has admin access to join the pod. In the example lab, we will just use the administrator account.

Enter the user details in the format domain\username, so in the example lab, this would be pvolab\administrator. Finally, enter the password and then click the **OK** button.

You will now see the join process start and a visual representation of the progress displayed as a % bar across the screen, as well as the status being shown as **Pending**, as shown in the following screenshot:

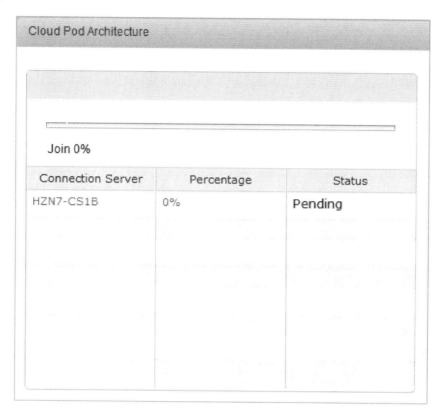

Once the Cloud Pod Architecture feature has completed the join to the pod federation, you will see the **Reload** dialog box, as shown in the following screenshot:

Click the **OK** button to reload the client. You will now see the Cloud Pod Architecture screen in the View Administrator, as shown in the following screenshot:

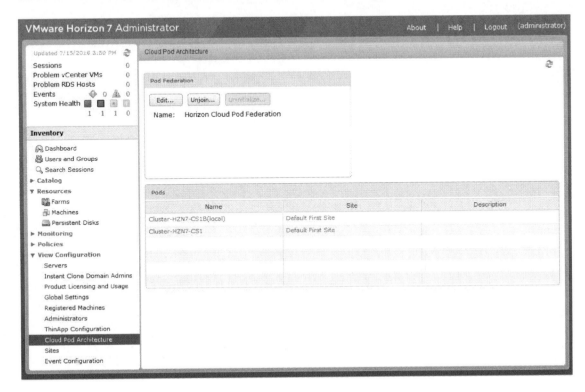

As you can see, both pods are now listed, along with the site information. In the example lab, we now have the **HZN7-CS1** and **HZN-CS1B** Connection Servers listed.

If you were to look at the **Sites** screen now, you would see that the site is listed along with the number of pods that make up that site, as well as the details of the pods in the site.

You will also be able to see the Global Entitlements, as shown in the following screenshot:

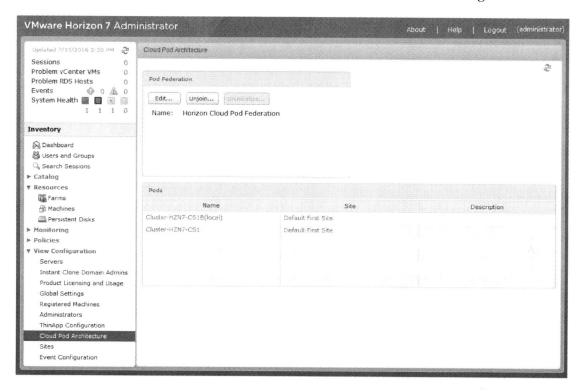

Now that you have created a pod federation by initializing the Cloud Pod Architecture feature and added a second pod to the pod federation, you can create Global Entitlements, which we will cover in the following section.

Entitling users to the Cloud Pod

In this section, we are going to add a Global Entitlement by creating a desktop pool and then entitling a user to connect to desktops within the pool.

From the View Administrator console, in the **Inventory** pane on the left, expand the **Catalog** section and then click on **Global Entitlement (1)**.

Next click the **Add...** button(**2**), as shown in the following screenshot:

You will now see the **Add Global Entitlement** dialog box, and the first section where you choose the type of entitlement you want to create, as shown in the following screenshot:

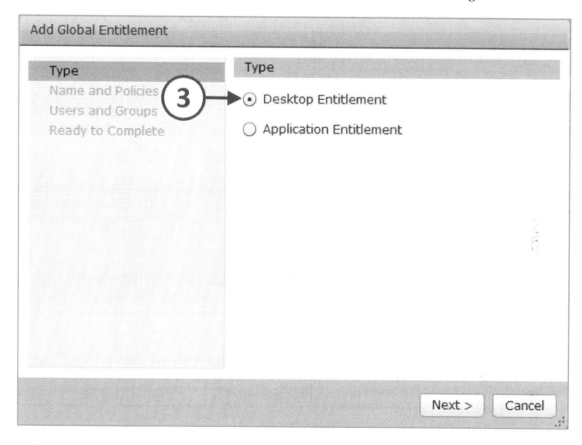

In this example, we are going to create a desktop entitlement, so click the radio button for **Desktop Entitlement** (3), and then click the **Next >** button.

You will now see the **Name and Policies** configuration screen.

First, enter a name for this desktop pool, followed by a description.

Next, in the **Policies** section, you can specify the user assignment and whether the desktop pool is floating or dedicated, and then in the **Scope** section, you can choose where the desktops are delivered from, either from **All sites**, **Within site**, or **Within pod**.

You can also select whether or not to use the home site. The final settings on this configuration screen allow you to set the display protocol, allow users to reset their machine, and have HTML access. The options are shown in the following screenshot:

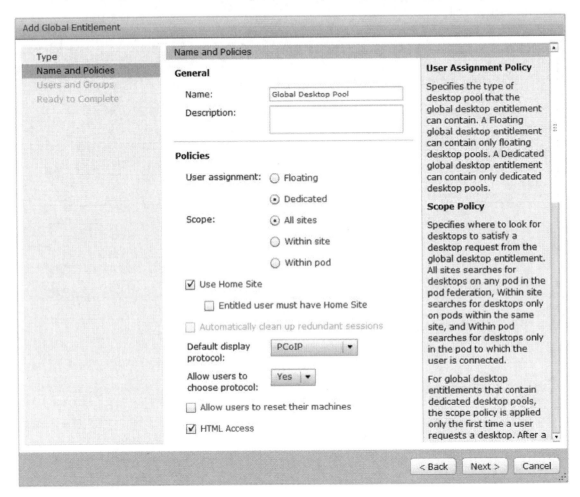

Once you have configured the options, click the **Next >** button. You will now see the **Users and Groups** configuration screen, as shown in the following screenshot:

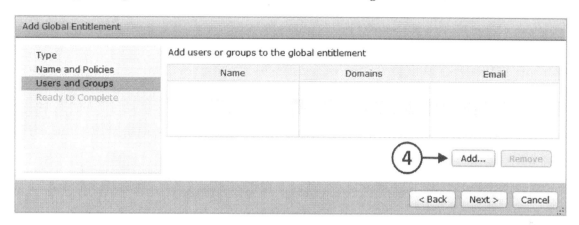

Click the **Add...** button (**4**). You will now see the **Find User or Group** configuration screen, as shown in the following screenshot:

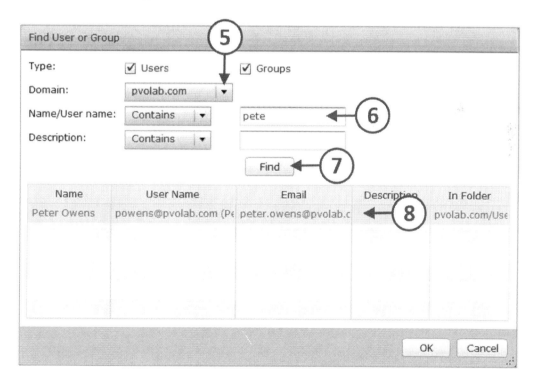

On the **Domain** box, click the dropdown (**5**) and select the domain in which the user resides. In the example lab, this is pvolab.com. Then, in the **Name/User name** box (**6**), enter the name of the user you want to entitle to this pool, and then click the **Find** button (**7**). The details of the user are then displayed. Click to highlight and select the user (**8**), and then click the **OK** button.

You will return to the **Users and Groups** screen, which now shows the selected user, as shown in the following screenshot:

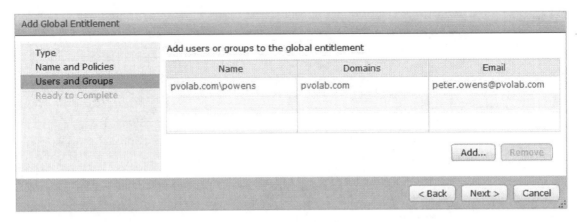

Click the **Next >** button to continue.

You will now see the **Ready to Complete** screen, as shown in the following screenshot:

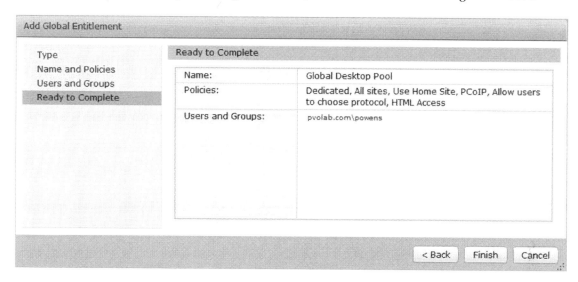

Check the details have been entered correctly and then click the **Finish** button.

You will return to the **Global Entitlements** screen, which now shows the Global Desktop Pool and the number of assigned users, as shown in the following screenshot:

You have now successfully configured a Cloud Pod federation.

Summary

In this chapter, we have walked you through installing and configuring the key server components of your Horizon View Environment, including the View Composer Server, the View Connection Server, the Replica Server, the Security Server, and the Enrollment Server.

We have discussed the initial configuration items that you will need to undertake, such as licensing your environment, connecting your vCenter and View Composer Servers, and configuring the View Security Server for external connections. We have also looked at the configuration items needed to prepare your environment for advanced graphics with NVIDIA GRID.

The final part of this chapter covered how to initialize and configure the Cloud Pod Architecture feature.

Having completed this chapter, you should now have built a fully functioning View deployment, which is ready to deliver virtual desktop machines to your end users. The next steps are to start building the virtual desktops, preparing them for delivery before configuring Horizon View to deliver them.

Before we do, we are going to look at security considerations in the next chapter, Chapter 5, *Securing Horizon View with SSL Certificates and True SSO*, where we will configure SSL certificates across our environment to ensure it is secure, and look at configuring the True SSO feature.

5
Securing Horizon View with SSL Certificates and True SSO

In this chapter, we will discuss the security aspect of VMware Horizon View 7, and in particular, how we deliver secure communication not only with the end user client, but also between the different View infrastructure components in the data center. To deliver this secure communication, we are going to look at two options.

We will start with **Secure Sockets Layer** (**SSL**) certificates and give an overview of what SSL is, before learning how to create/issue a certificate and configure Horizon View to use it.

The second option that will be covered in this chapter is **True SSO**. True SSO provides users a way of authenticating their virtual desktops that keeps all their usual domain privileges, but doesn't require them to provide their Active Directory credentials.

You will more than likely have SSL certificates already set up in your environment, but for this chapter, we're going to set up a test environment using a server in the example lab.

Horizon View and SSL certificates

Let's start by defining SSL: **SSL** is an encryption technology developed by Netscape. It is used to create an encrypted connection between a web server and the web browser from where you will view the web pages. By using SSL, you can securely view the information sent to your browser, knowing that nobody else can access it.

SSL works by means of an SSL certificate that is installed on a server and is used to identify you. So the question is, "How do you know whether you are using a secure connection to connect to the server?" If you have a secure connection, you will see a padlock icon in your browser or the address bar will be colored green.

 To ensure you have a secure connection, you can also access the site using `https://` in your browser rather than the usual `http://`.

SSL certificates are provided by **Certificate Authorities (CAs)**.

What is a Certificate Authority?

A **Certificate Authority** is a service that issues digital certificates to organizations or people after validating them. Certification authorities keep detailed records of the certificates that have been issued and any other information that was used when the certificate was issued. These are regularly audited to ensure compliance.

You can obtain a certificate authority from different organizations, or you can create your own from a Root CA.

Why do I need SSL for Horizon View?

If you are transmitting sensitive information from a website to an endpoint device, you need to secure the information with encryption; otherwise, data could be compromised.

As Horizon View is essentially like a web service to which end users connect from their endpoint device to the View Connection Server, you need to ensure that this connection is secured. In this case, SSL is used to establish the secured link between the client device and the virtual desktop machine, although, with View, no actual data is transmitted. The pixels from your virtual desktop machine are transmitted, and if a third-party intercepts this transmission, they could potentially see your screen by redrawing these pixels. SSL is also used for communication between the Horizon View components, such as the Connection Servers and Replica Servers.

Having an SSL certificate installed is a requirement for Horizon View.

SSL certificates for Horizon View

By default, Horizon View comes with self-signed certificates that are fine for a proof of concept or a small-scale pilot, but for a production environment, you need to have proper certificates.

The use of certificates became a requirement with View 5.1, where they were used for the Horizon View components to communicate, such as the Connection Server, Replica Server, and View Composer, as well as the underlying infrastructure of the ESXi hosts and Virtual Center Servers. Each of these components needs to have a certificate installed along with the client device that is connecting to it.

In the following section of this chapter, we will briefly cover how to set up certificates by installing a Root CA in our example test environment to get you started with Horizon View. However, we strongly recommend that you engage with your security team to deploy the correct type of certificate for your organization/environment.

Installing a Root CA

In this section, we are going to walk through the steps to set up a server that will act as our Root CA. For our example lab, we will use a server named **HZN7-CERTS**:

1. Open a console to the HZN7-CERTS server and launch the **Server Manager**.

2. Click on **Add roles and features (1)**, as shown in the following screenshot:

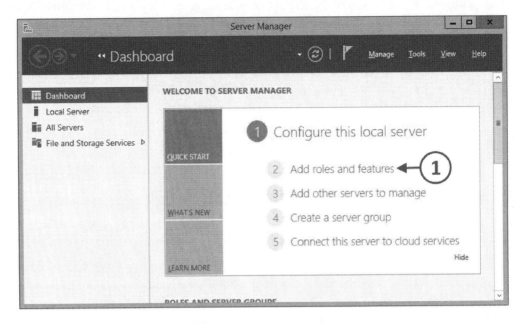

3. You will now see the **Add Roles and Features Wizard** and the **Before You Begin** screen. Click the **Next >** button to continue.

4. Next, you will see the **Installation Type** screen. Click the radio button for **Role-based or feature-based installation (2)**, as shown in the following screenshot:

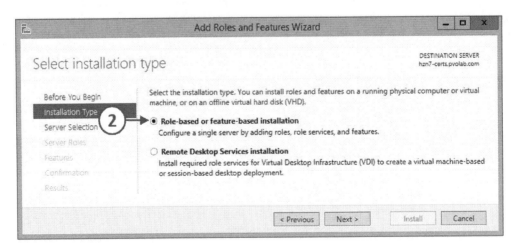

5. Click the **Next >** button to continue.

6. You will now see the **Server Selection** screen, as shown in the following screenshot:

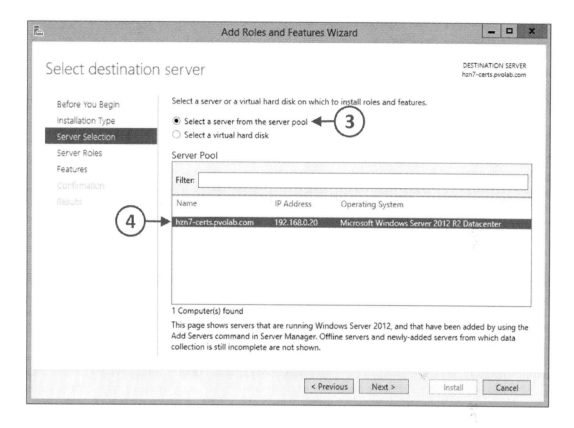

7. Click the radio button for **Select a server from the server pool** (3), and then highlight the **hzn7-certs.pvolab.com** server from the list (4).

8. Click the **Next >** button to continue. You will now see the **Server Roles** screen:

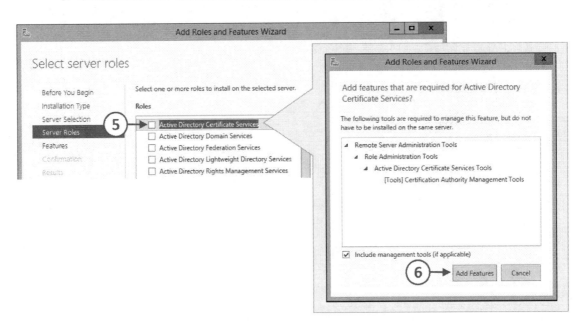

9. Check the box for **Active Directory Certificate Services** (5), and then in the pop-up box for **Add features that are required for Active Directory Certificate Services**, click the **Add Features** button (6).

10. You return to the **Server Roles** screen, which now shows a tick in the box for **Active Directory Certificate Services**. Click the **Next >** button to continue.

11. You will now see the **Features** configuration screen. Click the **Next >** button to continue.

12. The next screen is the **Active Directory Certificate Services** screen, as shown in the following screenshot:

13. Click the **Next >** button to continue. You will now see the **Role Services** screen:

14. Check the box for **Certification Authority (7)**, and click the **Next >** button to continue.

15. On the **Confirmation** screen, check the box for **Restart the destination server automatically (8)**, and then click the **Install** button.

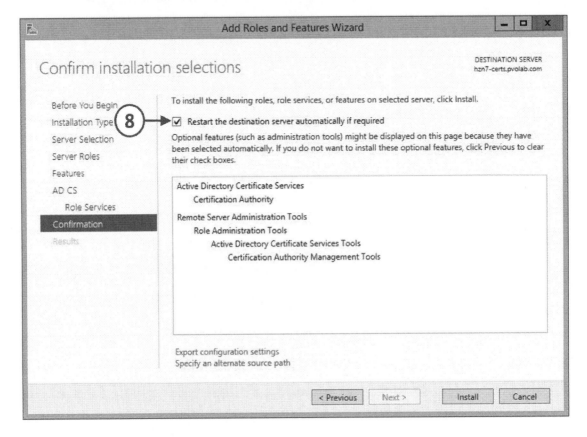

16. The certificate services feature is now installed. Once successfully completed, there are some post-installation configuration tasks to complete.

17. From the menu bar along the top of the **Server Manager Dashboard**, click the yellow triangle warning box, and from the options that pop up, click the **Configure Active Directory Certificate Services** entry (9), as shown in the following screenshot:

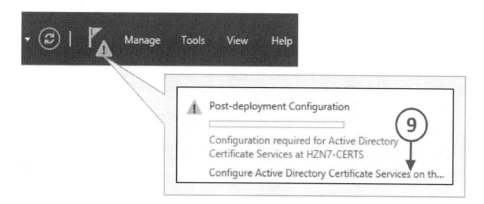

18. You will now see the **AD CS Configuration** screen and the **Credentials** configuration section, as shown in the following screenshot:

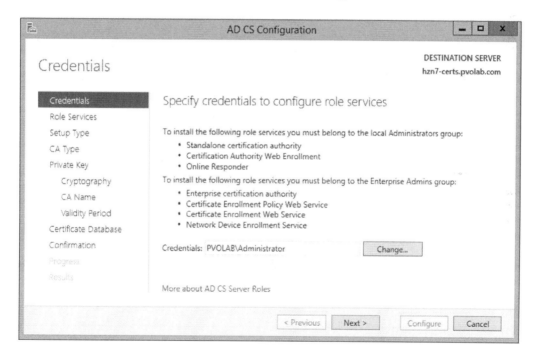

19. Click the **Next >** button to continue. You will now see the **Role Services** configuration screen, as shown in the following screenshot:

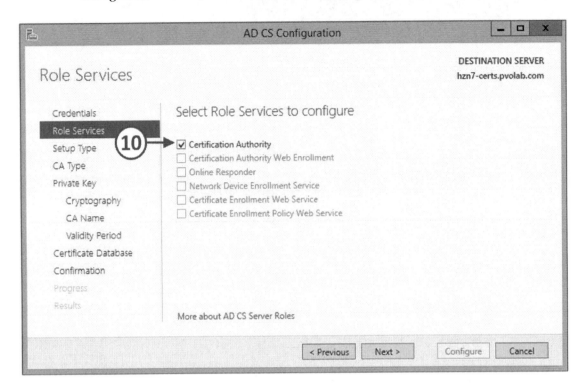

20. Check the **Certification Authority** box (**10**) and click the **Next >** button to continue.

21. You will now see the **Setup Type** configuration screen, as shown in the following screenshot:

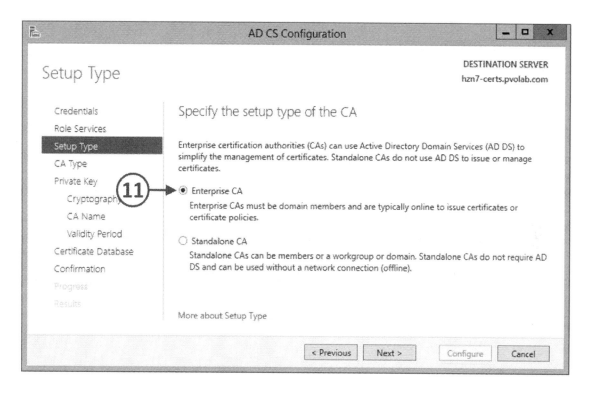

22. Click the radio button to select the **Enterprise CA** option (**11**), and click the **Next >** button to continue. You will now see the **CA Type** configuration screen:

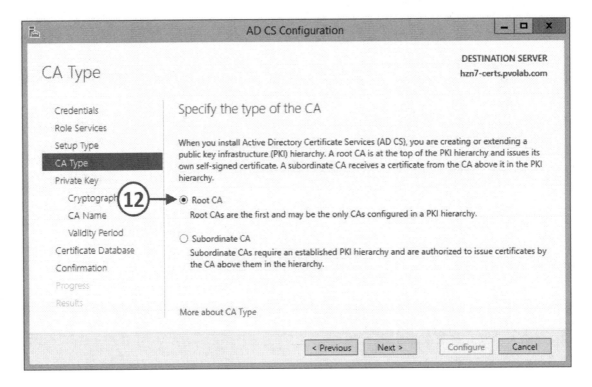

23. Click the radio button to select the **Root CA** option (**12**), and click the **Next >** button to continue.

24. You will now see the **Private Key** configuration screen, as shown in the following screenshot:

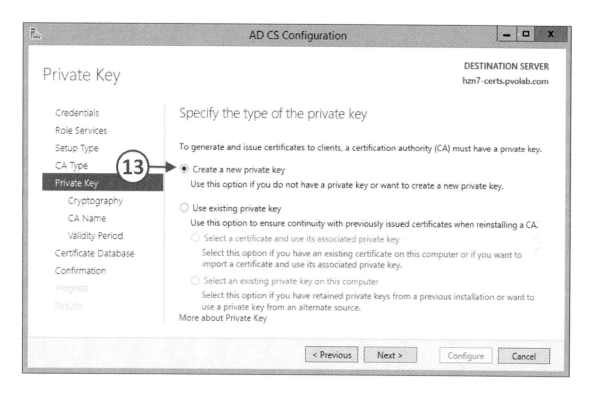

25. Click the radio button to select the **Create a new private key** option **(13)**, and click the **Next >** button to continue. You will now see the **Cryptography** configuration screen:

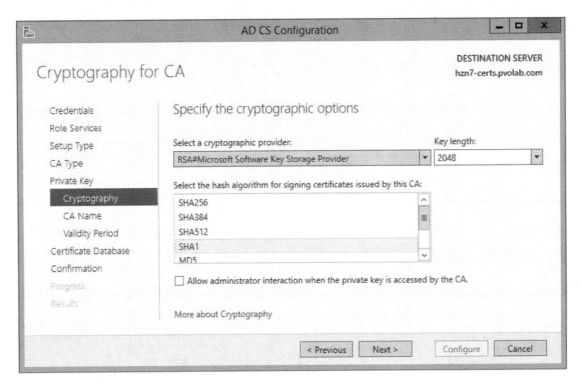

26. Accept the default settings and click the **Next >** button to continue.

27. You will now see the **CA Name** configuration screen, as shown in the following screenshot:

28. Accept the default settings and click the **Next >** button to continue.

29. You will now see the **Validity Period** configuration screen, as shown in the following screenshot:

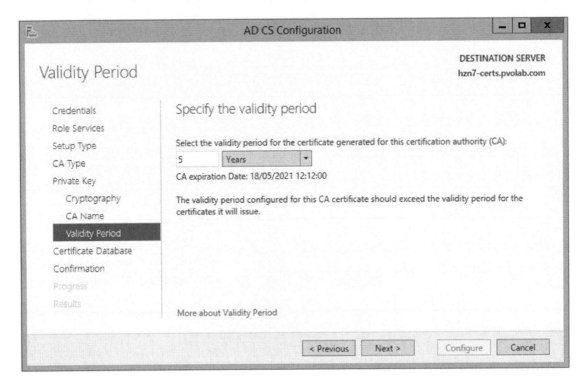

30. Accept the default settings and click the **Next >** button to continue.

31. You will now see the **Certificate Database** configuration screen, as shown in the following screenshot:

32. Accept the default settings and click the **Next >** button to continue. You will now see the **Confirmation** screen, as shown in the following screenshot:

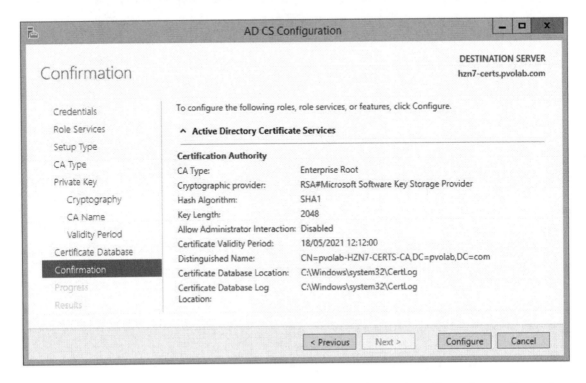

33. Click the **Configure** button to complete the configuration. Once the configuration has successfully completed you will see the following message:

34. Click the **Close** button to close the Server Manager.

Now that we have our certificate server set up and running, we can start configuring the Horizon View software infrastructure components and clients to use it.

We will start by installing the certificate on the Horizon View Connection Server first.

Installing a certificate on the Connection Server

With the certificate server installed and configured, we are now going to install the certificate on the View Connection Server.

1. Open a console to the View Connection Server named **HZN7-CS1**, press the Windows key and the letter *R* to launch a **Run** command box, and type mmc into the **Open** box (1) to launch the **Microsoft Management Console (MMC)**, as shown in the following screenshot:

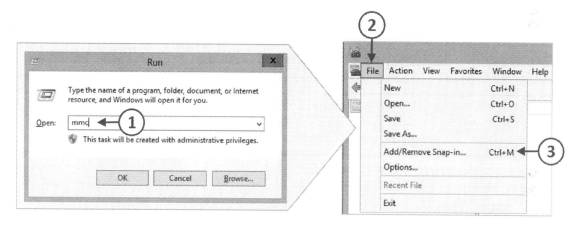

2. On the **MMC** console screen, click **File (2)**, and then **Add/Remove Snap-in... (3)**.
3. You will now see the **Add or Remove Snap-ins** screen.

4. From the **Available snap-ins** section on the left, click to highlight the **Certificates** entry (**4**), and then click the **Add >** button (**5**). This is shown in the following screenshot:

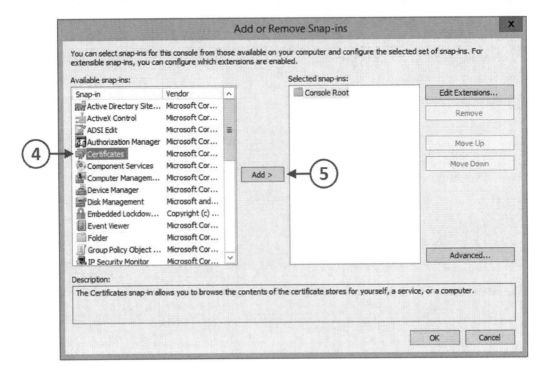

5. You will now see the **Certificates snap-in** box appear, as shown in the following screenshot:

6. Click the radio button for the **Computer account** option (**6**), and then click the **Next >** button to continue. You will now see the **Select Computer** configuration box, as shown in the following screenshot:

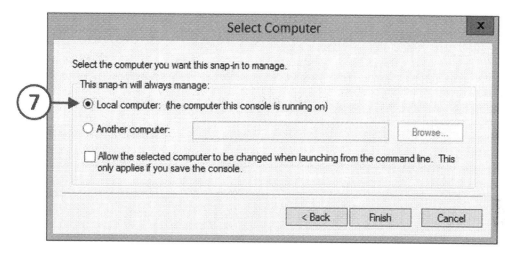

7. Click the radio button for the **Local computer** option (**7**), and then click the **Finish** button. You will return to the **Add or Remove Snap-ins** screen, which now shows the certificates snap-in as being selected.
8. Click **OK** to close the **Add or Remove Snap-ins** screen.

Now you have the certificates option in the management console, as shown in the following screenshot:

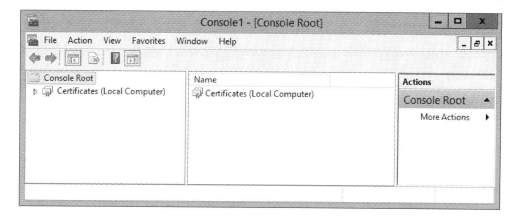

The next task is to request a certificate from the Root CA:

1. From the **Console Root**, expand the **Certificates (Local Computer)** folder, and then right-click on the **Personal** folder **(8)**. From the contextual menu, navigate to **All Tasks (9)** and then select **Request New Certificate… (10)**, as shown in the following screenshot:

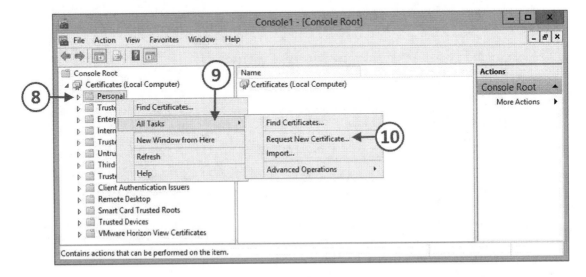

2. You will now see the **Before You Begin** section on the **Certificate Enrollment** screen. Click the **Next** button to continue.

3. You will now see the **Select Certificate Enrollment Policy** screen, as shown in the following screenshot:

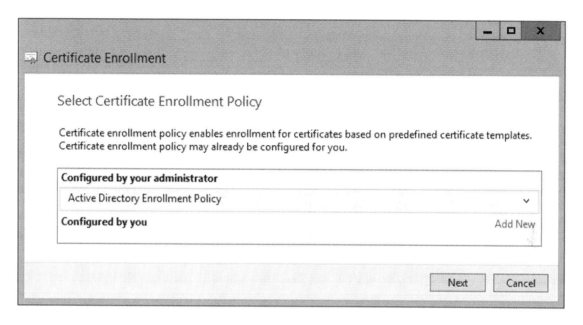

4. Click the **Next** button to continue. You will now see the **Request Certificates** screen.

5. In the **Active Directory Enrollment Policy** box, check the box for **Computer (11)**. We will use this policy template for our certificate; however, you can create your own template on the Root CA server.

6. Now click on the arrow next to **Details (12)**, and then click the **Properties** box **(13)** so that we can configure the properties of the certificate.

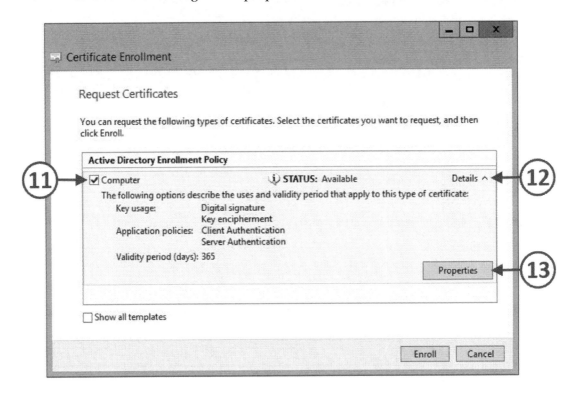

7. You will now see the **Certificate Properties** configuration box, as shown in the following screenshot:

8. Click the **General** tab (**11**), and then in the **Friendly name** box (**15**), type in a friendly name for this certificate. In the example lab, we will call this **vdm**.

9. Next, click on the **Private Key** tab (**16**), as shown in the following screenshot:

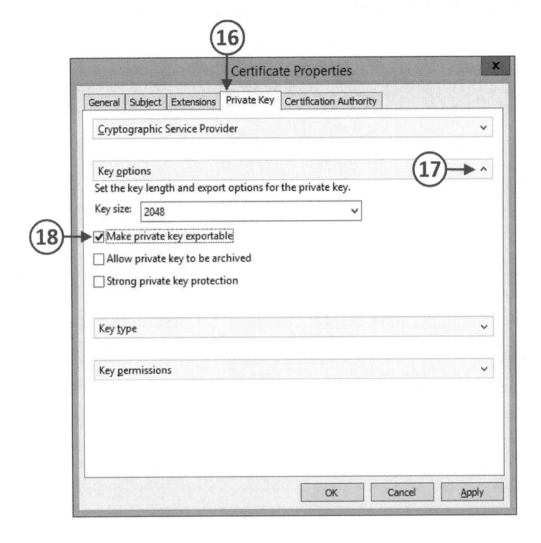

10. Click the down arrow for **Key options** (**17**) to expand the configuration options, and check the box for **Make private key exportable** (**18**).

11. Finally, click on the **Certification Authority** tab (**19**), as shown in the following screenshot:

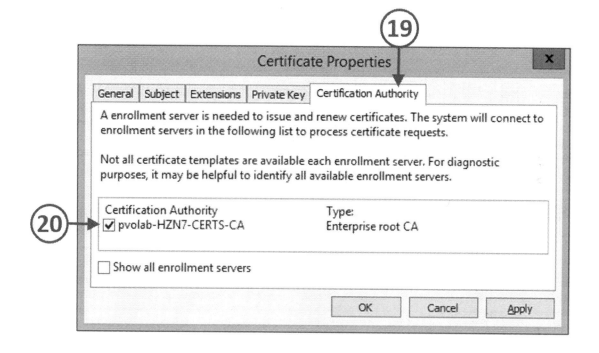

12. Check the box to select the enrollment server **pvolab-HZN7-CERTS-CA** (20). Once the configuration has been completed, click the **OK** button. You will return to the **Request Certificates** screen, as shown in the following screenshot:

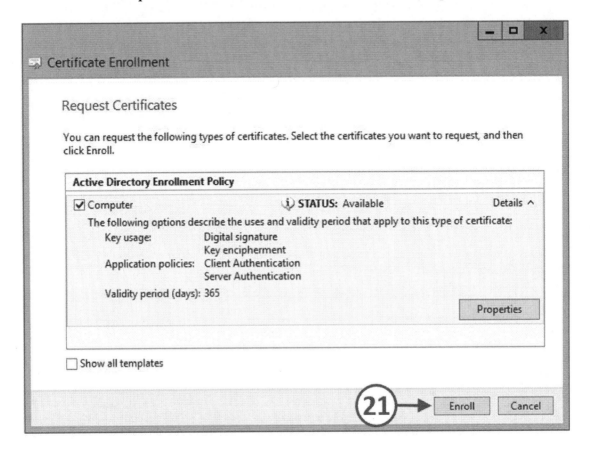

13. Click the **Enroll** button (**21**) to continue and enroll the Connection Server. If the enrollment is successful, then you will see the following screenshot:

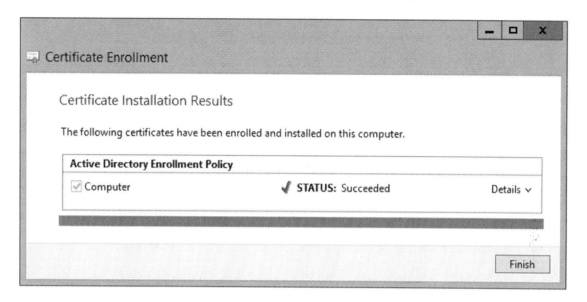

14. Click the **Finish** button to complete the certificate enrollment process.

Don't forget that you need to complete the certificate enrollment process on all the Horizon View components.

In the next section, we will take a look at what to do now that we have our Root CA certificate server and the certificate is installed on our Connection Servers.

Post-certificate enrollment configuration tasks

Even though you have installed a certificate server and installed a valid certificate on the Connection Server, there are still a few things to configure.

If you were to try and connect to the View Administrator using your browser, you will still see an error message saying there is a problem with the website's security certificate:

There is a problem with this website's security certificate

We recommend that you close this webpage and do not continue to this website.

The security certificate for this site doesn't match the site's web address and may indicate an attempt to fool you or intercept any data you send to the server.

⬛Go to my homepage instead

⊗Continue to this webpage (not recommended)

If you remember from the beginning of this chapter, we also discussed accessing web pages using `http://`, or `https://` for secure web pages. If the address bar in your browser is red, as shown in the following screenshot, then the connection is not secure and there are no certificates installed:

You can, of course, ignore these errors and just click **Continue to this website (not recommended)**,which allows you to continue past the warning and log on to View Administrator.

However, when you log on, you will see that, in the **System Health** section of the **View Administrator Dashboard**, there is also a red warning box. As far as View is concerned, if you don't have a valid certificate installed; the health warning tells you that the connections will be untrusted and therefore that's a bad thing!

1. In the View Administrator, click on **Dashboard(1)**, and then in the **System Health** box, click on the down arrows to expand the options for **View components**, and then **Connection Servers**, and click on the link for the **HZN7-CS1** Connection Server (**2**). You will see the following:

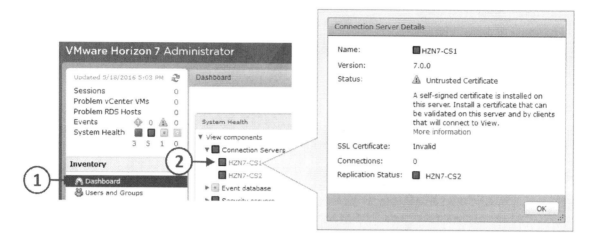

2. The users will also see a similar issue when they connect, as shown in the following screenshot of the Horizon Client:

3. In order for View to pick up the recently installed certificate, you need to restart the View Connection Server service in Windows services. To do this, press the Windows key and *R* to open a **Run** dialog box. In the **Run** dialog box, type `services.msc` to open the Services screen. Scroll down to **VMware Horizon View Connection Server (3)**, as shown in the following screenshot:

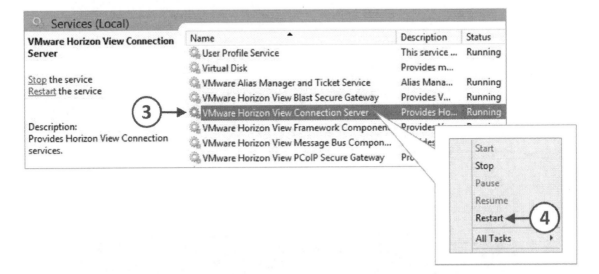

4. Right-click, and then from the contextual menu, click **Restart (4)**.
5. Once the **VMware Horizon View Connection Server** service has restarted, log in to the View Administrator.
6. From the **Dashboard**, click on expand **Connection Servers** and then click on the Connection Server **HZN7-CS1 (5)**. You will now see that the SSL certificate is valid and the error boxes have changed from red to green:

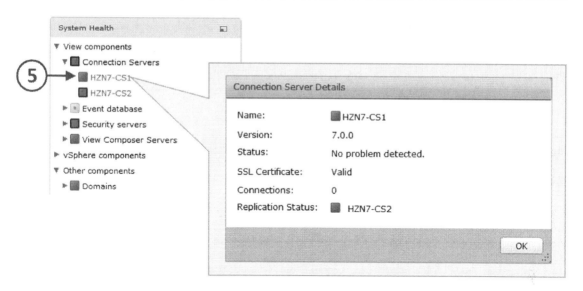

7. We have now finished configuring certificates. Click on **OK** to close the dialog box for the **Connection Server Details** and then log out of the View Administrator.

Don't forget that you need to install the certificate on all of the Horizon View components, such as any replica servers, security servers, and View Composer servers.

Horizon View True SSO

In Chapter 2, *An Overview of Horizon View Architecture and Components*, we introduced you to the True SSO feature and its architecture. In this section, we are going to look at how to configure it.

To set up **True SSO**, you first need to configure a Certificate Authority, which we have already configured earlier on in this chapter in the *Installing a Root CA* section. There are a number of steps to configure this as described.

Preparing AD for True SSO

Next, create an **Active Directory (AD)** group for the Enrollment Server. Open a console to your Domain Controller, in the example lab this is the machine called **dc.pvolab.com**, and launch the **Active Directory Users and Computers** configuration screen, as shown in the following screenshot:

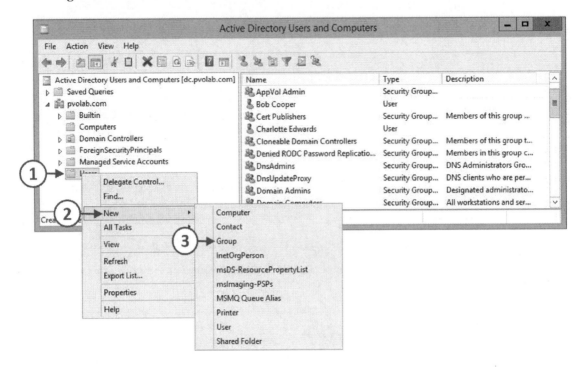

1. Click **Users** (1), right-click, and from the contextual menu, click on **New** (2). Then click **Group** (3).

2. You will now see the **New Object – Group** dialog box. In the **Group name** box
   (**4**), type in a name for the new group. In the example lab, this is called
   Enrollment Servers. In the **Group scope** box, click the radio button for **Universal**
   (**5**), and in the **Group type** box, click the radio button for **Security** (**6**), as shown in
   the following screenshot:

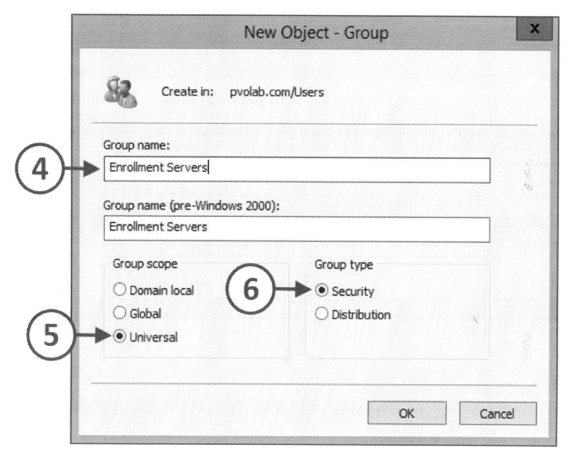

3. Once configured, click the **OK** button.

Next, you need to add the Enrollment Server into this newly created group:

1. In the **Active Directory Users and Computers** configuration screen, click on **Computers** (7), and then double-click on the Enrollment Server. In the example lab, this is the computer called **HZN7-ENROL**, as shown in the following screenshot:

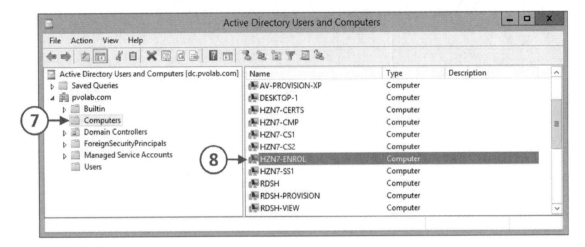

2. You will now see the **HZN7-ENROL Properties** dialog box.

3. Click the **Member of** tab (**9**), and then click the **Add...** button (**10**), as shown in the following screenshot:

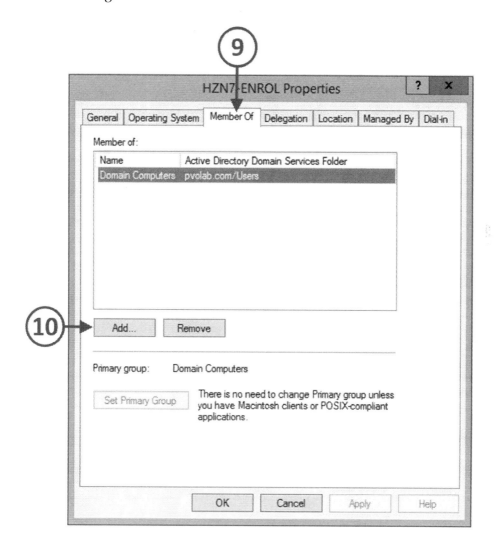

4. You will now see the **Select Groups** dialog box, as shown in the following screenshot:

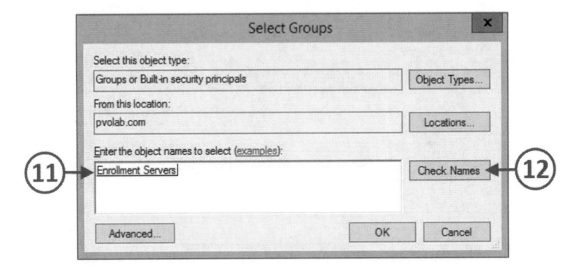

5. In the **Enter the object names to select** box, type in the name of the group you created for the Enrollment Servers. You can just type the first part of the name and then click the **Check Names** button (**12**). With the correct group name in the **Enter the object names to select** box (**11**), click the OK button to continue.

6. You will return to the **HZN7-ENROL Properties** dialog box, which now shows that the Enrollment Server called HZN7-ENROL is a member of the Enrollment Servers group:

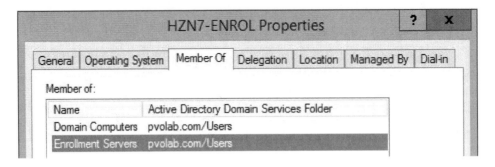

With the Domain Controller elements configured, the next step is to create a new certificate template.

Creating a Certificate Template for True SSO

To create a Certificate Template, let's follow these steps:

1. Open a console to the certificate server, and launch the **Certificate Management Console**. In the example lab, this is the server called **HZN7-CERTS**.
2. Click on the **Certificate Templates** folder (**13**), right-click, and then from the contextual menu, click on **Manage** (**14**), as shown in the following screenshot:

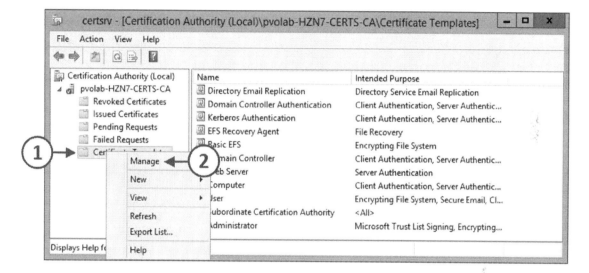

3. You will now see the **Certificate Templates Console**.

4. Scroll down the **Template Display Name** pane until you find the template for **Smartcard Logon**. Click to highlight it (**15**), right-click, and then from the contextual menu, click on **Duplicate Template** (**16**). This is shown in the following screenshot:

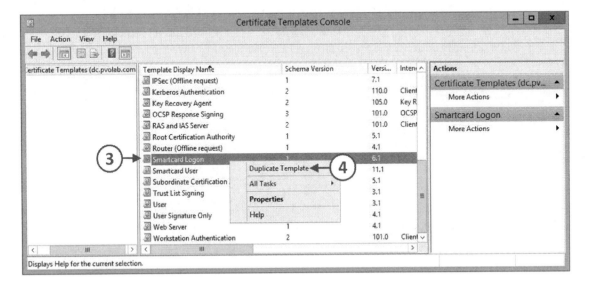

5. You will now see the **Properties of New Template** configuration box, as shown in the following screenshot:

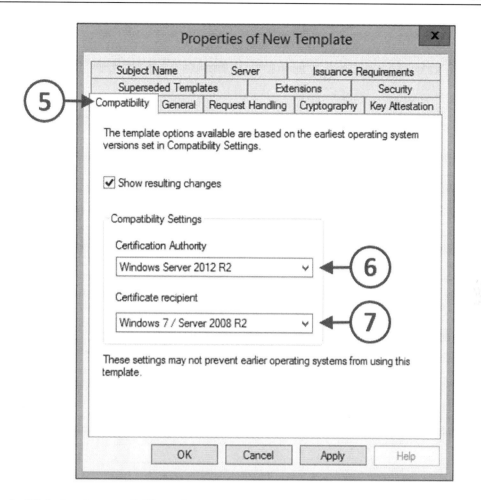

6. Click the **Compatibility** tab (5). In the **Compatibility Settings** section, from the drop-down menu for **Certification Authority** (6), select the appropriate setting for the server version that is running as the CA. In the example lab, the CA server is running **Windows Server 2012 R2**.

7. Next, from the drop-down menu for **Certificate Recipient (7)**, select the appropriate setting for the machines that will be in receipt of this certificate. In the example lab, we will set this to **Windows 7 / Server 2008 R2**.

 When changing these settings, you will see a dialog box appear warning you about compatibility changes, and changes to the template that you are about to make. Click **OK** to accept these messages and to continue.

8. Now click on the **General** tab box **(8)**, as shown in the following screenshot:

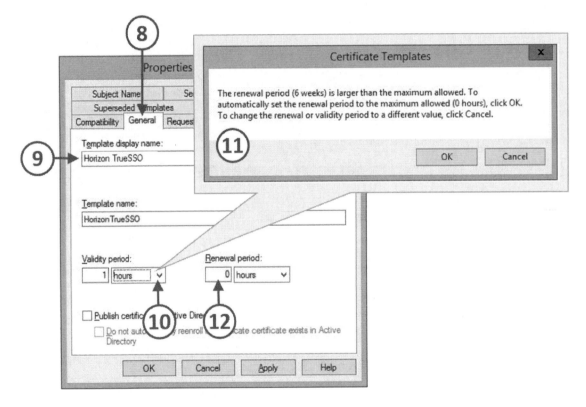

9. In the **Template display name** box **(9)**, type in a name for the new certificate template. In the example lab, this is called **HorizonTrueSSO**.

10. Next, you need to configure a validity time. From the drop-down menu under **Validity period (10)**, select the option for **hours**. You will then see the **Certificate Templates** warning box **(11)**.

11. Click **OK** to accept. Accepting the warning will automatically set the **Renewal period** to 0 hours (**12**).

12. Now click on the **Request Handling** tab box (**13**).

13. In the drop-down box next to **Purpose** (**14**), click and select the option for **Signature and smartcard logon**. You will then see the **Certificate Templates** warning box (**15**), which warns you that you are about to change the purpose of the certificate. Click **Yes** to accept the warning message and close the dialog box, as shown in the following screenshot:

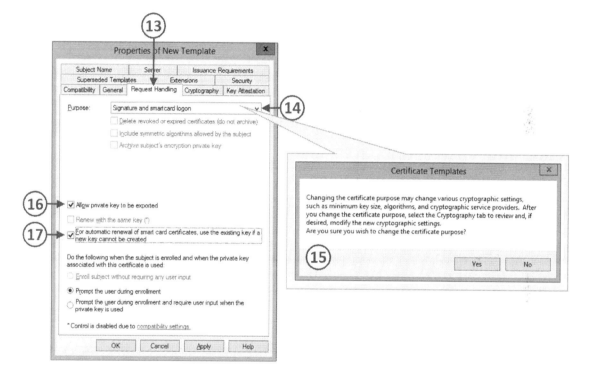

14. Finally, on this screen, check the box for **Allow private key to be exported** (**16**), and also check the box **for Automatic renewal of smartcard certificates** (**17**).

15. Next, click the **Cryptography** tab (**18**), as shown in the following screenshot:

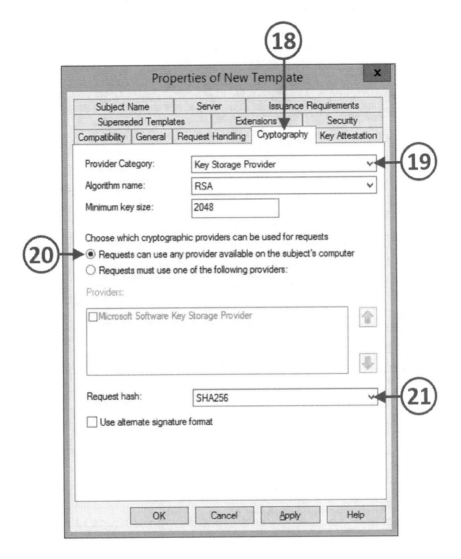

16. In the **Provider Category** box, click the drop-down arrow (**19**) and select the option for **Key Storage Provider**. Then click the radio button for **Requests can use any provider available** (**20**), and then in the **Request hash** box, click the drop-down arrow (**21**) and select the option for **SHA256**.

17. The next tab to configure is the **Subject Name** tab (**22**), as shown in the following screenshot:

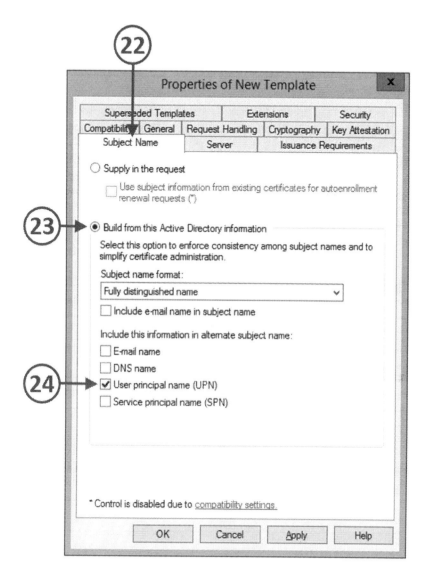

18. Click the radio button for **Build from this Active Directory information (23)**, and then check the box for **User principal name (UPN) (24)**.

19. The next tab to configure is the **Server** tab **(25)**, as shown in the following screenshot:

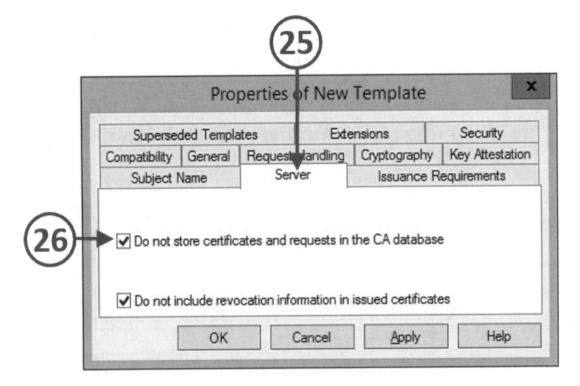

20. Check the **Do not store certificates and requests in the CA database** box **(26)**.

21. Now click the **Issuance Requirements** tab **(27)**. Check the box for **This number of authorized signatures (28)**, and ensure the value for this option is set to **1**.

22. From the **Application policy** box, click the drop-down arrow (**29**) and select the option for **Certificate Request Agent**. Finally, on this tab, click the radio button for **Valid existing certificate** (**30**), as shown in the following screenshot:

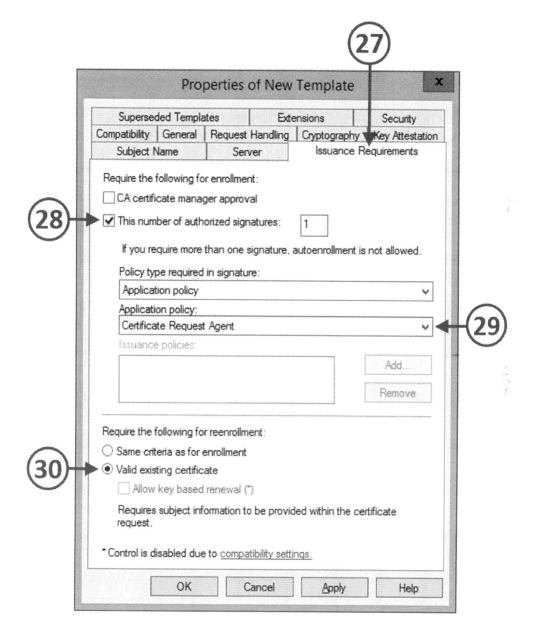

23. For the final part of the **Properties of New Template** configuration, click the **Security** tab (**31**).

24. Highlight the **Enrollment Servers** group (**32**), and then click the **Add...** button (**33**).

25. You will now see the **Select Users, Computers, Service Accounts or Groups** dialog box pop up. In the **Enter the object names to select** box (**34**), type in the name of the Enrollment Servers group.

26. You can just type the first few letters of the group name and then click the **Check Names** button (**35**). Select the **Enrollment Servers** group (**34**).

27. Finally, in the **Permissions for Enrollment Servers** section, check the box under the **Allow** heading for **Read** (**36**) and **Enroll** (**37**). This is shown in the following screenshot:

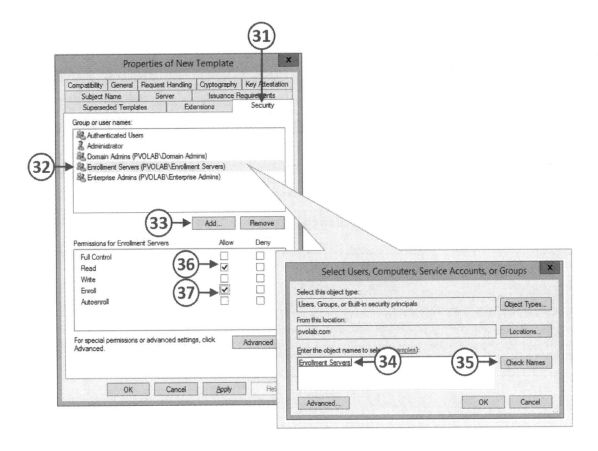

28. Once you have finished configuring the **Properties of New Template**, click **OK** to finish configuring and to close the dialog box.

The next step is to issue the newly created certificate template.

Issuing the TrueSSO certificate template

Now that the certificate template has been created, the next task is to issue it.

1. From the **Certificate ManagementConsole** screen, click on the **Certificate Templates** folder (**1**), right-click, and then from the contextual menu, click on **New** (**2**), and then select the option for **Certificate Template to Issue** (**3**). This is shown in the following screenshot:

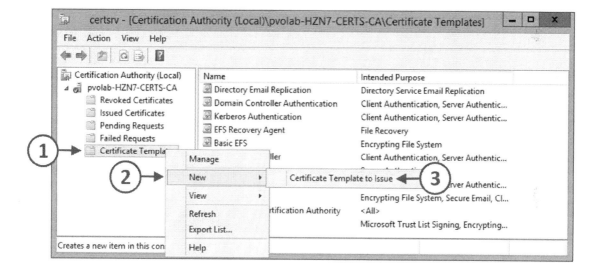

2. You will now see the **Enable Certificate Templates** dialog box, as shown in the following screenshot:

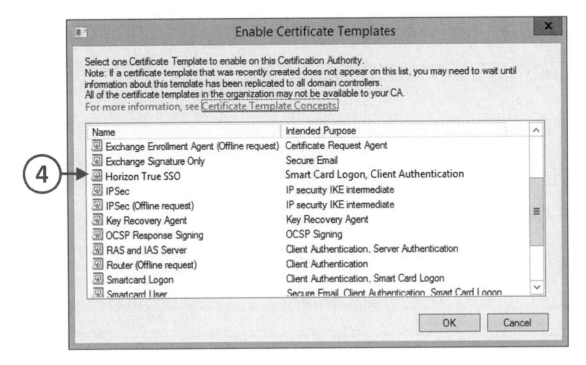

3. Click on **Horizon True SSO** (4), and click the **OK** button.
4. You will return to the **Enable Certificate Templates** dialog box.
5. Next, we need to enable the Enrollment Agent. As in the previous step, from the **Certificate Management** console screen, click on the **Certificate Templates** folder (**1**), right-click, and then from the contextual menu, click on **New** (**2**), and then select the option for **Certificate Template to Issue** (**3**).

6. You will now see the **Enable Certificate Templates** dialog box. Click on the option for **Enrollment Agent (Computer)** (5), as shown in the following screenshot:

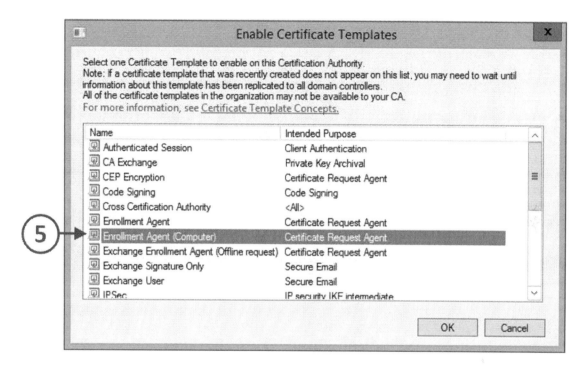

7. Now click the **OK** button.
8. You will return to the **Enable Certificate Templates** dialog box. You can now exit the **Certificate Management Console**.

> You need to check that the **Enrollment Agent (Computer)** template has the same security settings as the **Template for TrueSSO** template was configured with. This means it needs to the Enrollment Servers Security group adding and has been granted read and enroll permissions.

The final few configuration tasks are command line-based, so from the desktop of the certificate server, press the Windows key and *R* to open a **Run** dialog box. In the **Run** dialog box, type cmd to open a command prompt box.

The first thing you need to do is to configure the **Certificate Authority** for non-persistent certificate processing. To do this, at the command prompt, type the following command:

```
certutil -setreg DBFlags +DBFLAGS_ENABLEVOLATILEREQUESTS
```

```
C:\>certutil -setreg DBFlags +DBFLAGS_ENABLEVOLATILEREQUESTS
HKEY_LOCAL_MACHINE\SYSTEM\CurrentControlSet\Services\CertSvc\Configuration\DBFla
gs:

Old Value:
    DBFlags REG_DWORD = b0 (176)
        DBFLAGS_MAXCACHESIZEX100 -- 10 (16)
        DBFLAGS_CHECKPOINTDEPTH60MB -- 20 (32)
        DBFLAGS_LOGBUFFERSHUGE -- 80 (128)

New Value:
    DBFlags REG_DWORD = 8b0 (2224)
        DBFLAGS_MAXCACHESIZEX100 -- 10 (16)
        DBFLAGS_CHECKPOINTDEPTH60MB -- 20 (32)
        DBFLAGS_LOGBUFFERSHUGE -- 80 (128)
        DBFLAGS_ENABLEVOLATILEREQUESTS -- 800 (2048)
CertUtil: -setreg command completed successfully.
The CertSvc service may need to be restarted for changes to take effect.

C:\>
```

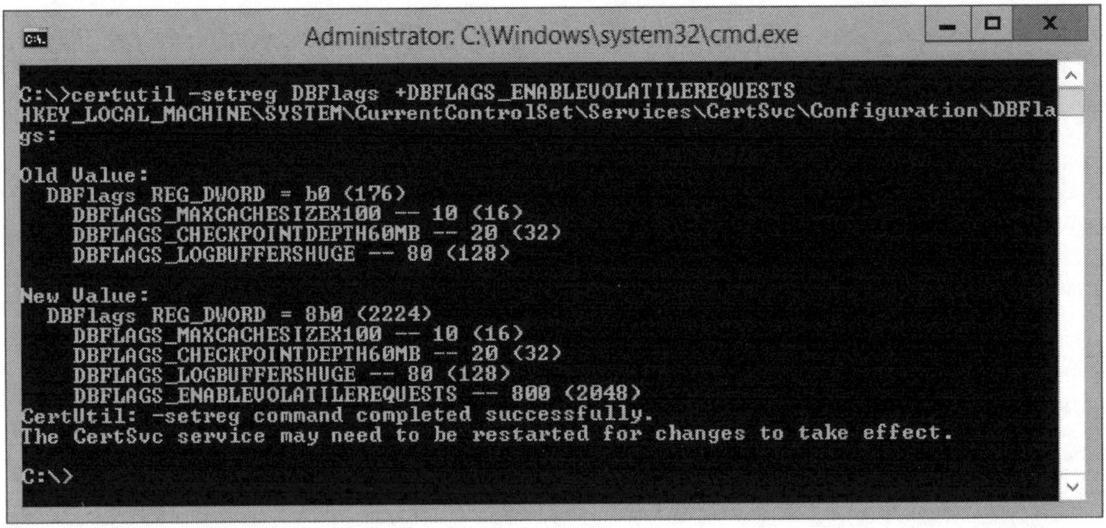

The previous screenshot shows the output of the command and shows that it completed successfully.

The second thing you need to do is to configure the **Certificate Authority** to ignore offline CRL (Certificate Revocation Lists) errors. To do this, at the command prompt, type the following command:

```
certutil -setreg ca\CRLFlags +CRLF_REVCHECK_IGNORE_OFFLINE
```

You will see the following screen showing the command successfully executing:

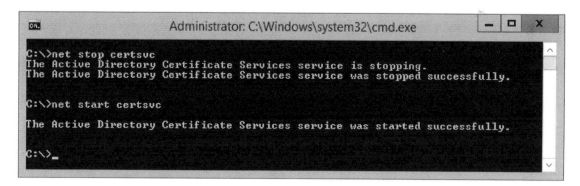

Finally, as it states in the command prompt, you need to restart the certificate service. To do this, at the command prompt, run the following two commands one after the other:

```
net stop certsvc
net start certsvc
```

You will see the following screen showing that the certification service was successfully stopped and then started again:

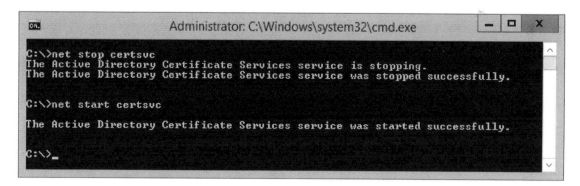

The next step in the process is to deploy the certificates on the Enrollment Server and the Connection Server.

Certificate deployment

The next task to perform is to deploy the **Enrollment Agent (Computer) certificate** on the Enrollment Server.

By deploying the Enrollment Agent (Computer) certificate on this server, you are authorizing this Enrollment Server to act as an Enrollment Agent and to be able to generate certificates on behalf of the end users.

If you are following the example lab, then in `Chapter 4`, *Installing and Configuring Horizon View*, you will already have an Enrollment Server built, which is called HZN7-ENROL. Open a console to this server:

1. Press the Windows key and the letter *R* to launch a **Run** command box, and type **mmc** into the **Open** box (**1**) to launch the Microsoft Management Console, as shown in the following screenshot:

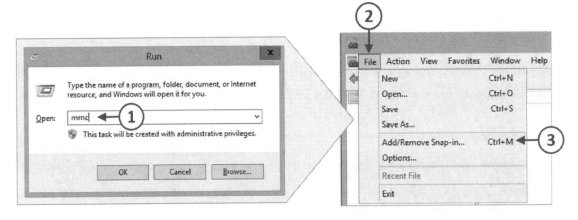

2. On the **MMC** console screen, click **File (2)**, and then **Add/Remove Snap-in... (3)**.
3. You will now see the **Add or Remove Snap-ins** screen.

4. From the **Available snap-ins** section on the left, click to highlight the **Certificates** entry (**4**), and then click the **Add >** button (**5**). This is shown in the following screenshot:

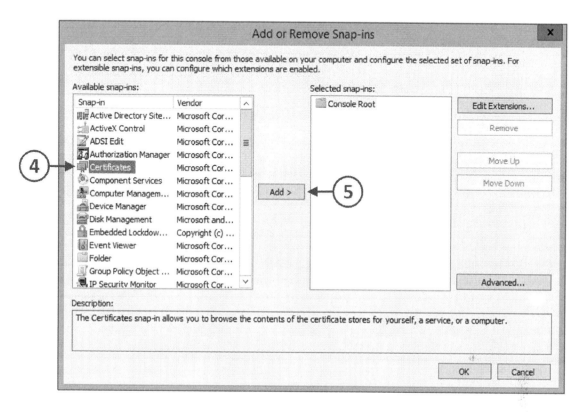

5. You will now see the **Certificates snap-in** box appear, as shown in the following screenshot:

6. Click the radio button for the **Computer account** option (**6**), and then click the **Next >** button to continue. You will now see the **Select Computer** configuration box, as shown:

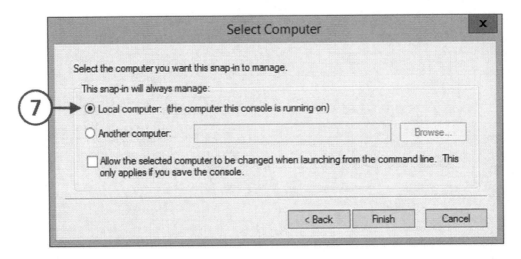

7. Click the radio button for the **Local computer** option (**7**), and then click the **Finish** button. You will return to the **Add or Remove Snap-ins** screen, which now shows the certificates snap-in as being selected.

8. Click **OK** to close the **Add or Remove Snap-ins** screen. Now you have the certificates option in the management console, as shown in the following screenshot:

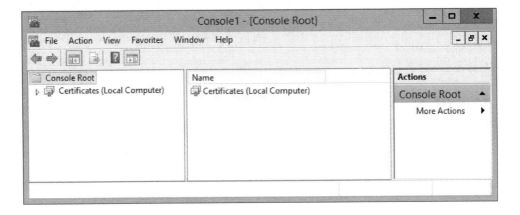

9. The next task is to request the **Enrollment Agent (Computer)** certificate.

10. From the **Console Root**, expand the **Certificates (Local Computer)** folder, and then right-click on the **Personal** folder (8). From the contextual menu, navigate to **All Tasks (9)** and then select **Request New Certificate… (10)**, as shown in the following screenshot:

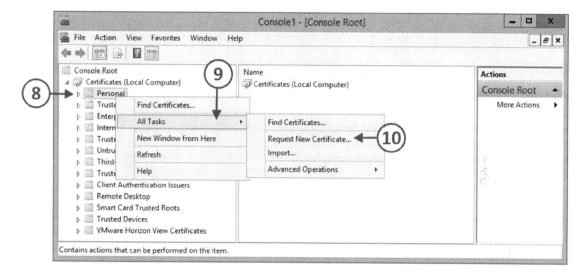

11. You will now see the **Before You Begin** section on the **Certificate Enrollment** screen. Click the **Next** button to continue.

12. You will now see the **Select Certificate Enrollment Policy** screen. Click the **Next** button to continue. The next screen you will see is the **Request Certificates** screen, as shown in the following screenshot:

13. Click the **Enroll** button to request the certificate. You should then see that the certificate has successfully been enrolled.

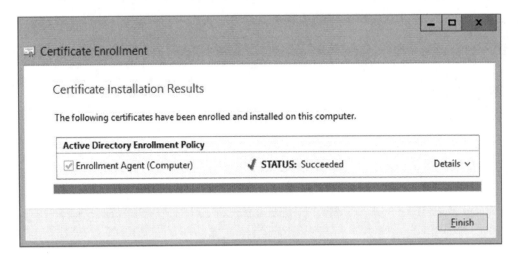

14. Click the **Finish** button to complete the configuration and close the Certificate Enrollment dialog box, and then close the Certificate Management console.

The next task is to import the **Enrollment Service Client Certificate**, which you need to first export from the Connection Server before importing it onto the Enrollment Server.

Deploying the Enrollment Service Client Certificate from the Connection Server pairs the Connection Server with the Enrollment Server. If you don't do this, then any connection request that is made to the Enrollment Server will be rejected, with the result that no certificate will be generated. The Enrollment Service Client Certificate is automatically generated on the Connection Server when the Connection Server service starts up.

So let's export the certificate from the Connection Server:

1. Open a console to the Connection Server. In the example lab, this is the server called **HZN7-CS1**. Launch the MMC console and add the Certificates snap-in as we covered previously, and then launch the Certificates Management Console, as shown in the following screenshot:

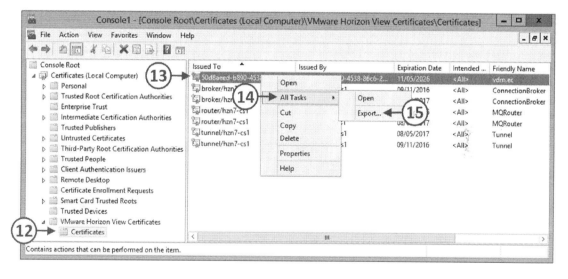

2. From the **Console Root** section in the left-hand pane, navigate to the **VMware Horizon View Certificates** folder, expand it by clicking the arrow, and then click the **Certificates** folder (**12**).

3. Click and select the certificate that contains the friendly name **vdm.ec (13)**, right-click, then from the contextual menu click on **All Tasks (14)**, and then select the option for **Export… (15)**. You will now see the **Welcome to the Certificate Export Wizard** screen. Click the **Next** button to continue.

4. You will now see the **Export Private Key** dialog box. Click the radio button for the **No, do not export the private key** option **(16)**, and then click the **Next** button.

5. In the **Export File Format** dialog box, accept the default selected format option and click the **Next** button to continue.

6. The **File to Export** dialog box is now shown. Type in a name for the file that you are going to save this certificate as in the **File name** box. In the example lab, this has been called **cs-cert**, as shown in the following screenshot:

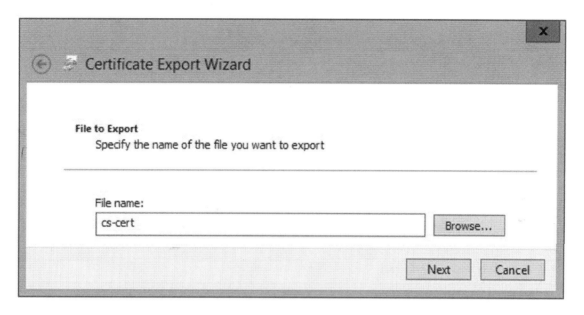

This file has been saved in a shared folder called cert on the Domain Controller, as it needs to be accessible from the Enrollment Server when we come to import it.

1. Click the **Next** button to continue.

2. You will now see the **Completing the Certificate Export Wizard** dialog box, as shown in the following screenshot:

3. Click the **Finish** button to complete the certificate export process. You will see a message saying the export was successful.

The next task is to import the certificate into the Enrollment Server.

Open a console to the Enrollment Server. In the example lab, this is the server called HZN7-ENROL. Launch the MMC console and add the Certificates snap-in as we covered previously, and then launch the Certificates Management Console, as shown in the following screenshot:

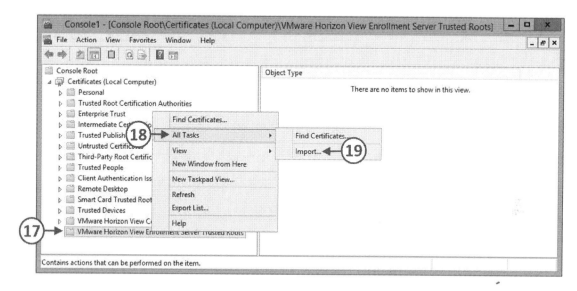

1. From the **Console Root** section in the left-hand pane, navigate to the **VMware Horizon View Enrollment Server Trusted Roots** folder (**17**), highlight it and right-click. From the contextual menu, click on **All Tasks** (**18**), and select the option for **Import...** (**19**).

2. You will now see the **Welcome to the Certificate Import Wizard** screen. Click the **Next** button to continue.

3. The **File to Import** dialog box is now shown. Type in the name for the file that you are going to import in the **Filename** box. In the example lab, this was the file called **cs-cert** that was saved to the shared folder, as shown in the following screenshot:

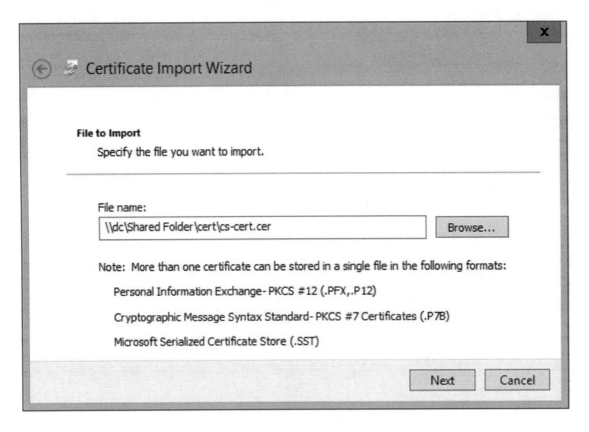

4. Click the **Next** button to continue. On the next screen, **Certificate Store**, you need to select the store in which the certificate will be stored.

5. In the **Certificate Store** dialog box, click the radio button for **Place all certificates in the following store** (20), and then ensure that the Certificate Store is set to **VMware Horizon View Enrollment Server Trusted Roots**, as shown in the following screenshot:

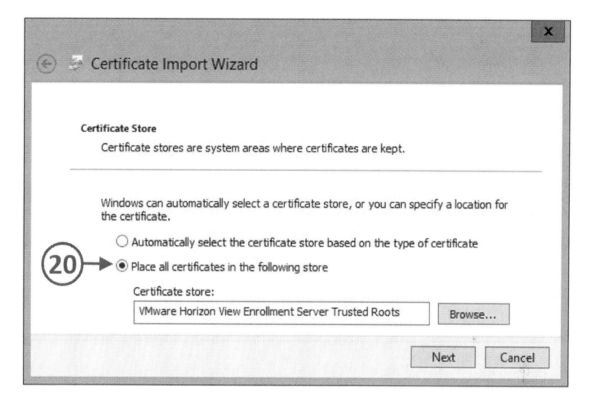

6. Click the **Next** button to continue.

7. You will now see the **Completing the Certificate Import Wizard** dialog box, as shown in the following screenshot:

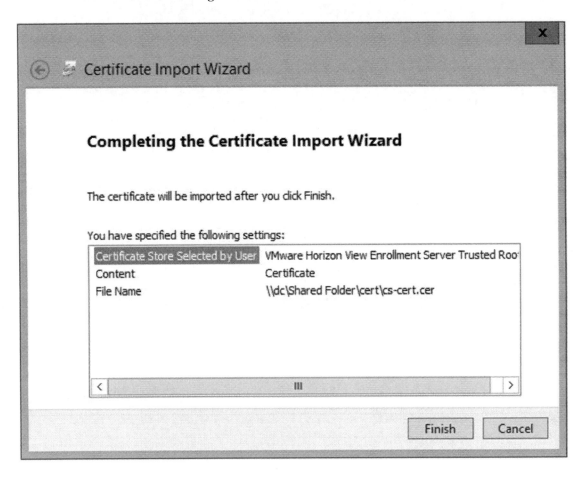

8. Click the **Finish** button to import the certificate. You should then see a message stating that the import was successful.

Once imported, you will see the certificate in the Certificate Management Console, as shown in the following screenshot:

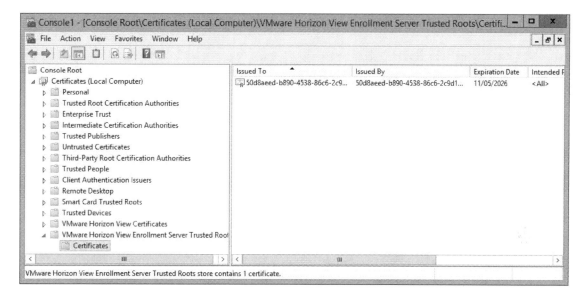

Having successfully imported the certificate, you can now close the Certificate Management Console.

Configuring True SSO on the Connection Server

Now that you have all the necessary certificates in place, the next step is to set up the True SSO feature on the Connection Server:

1. This setup process is command line-driven and uses the **vdmUtil** command, so the first step is to open a command prompt window on the Connection Server.

2. The first command you need to run adds the Enrollment Server to the View environment. This allows you to query the Enrollment Server and gather information about the domain and other useful information such as available templates, CA name, and so on. We will need this information during the configuration process.

3. From the command line, type the following command:

   vdmUtil --authAs administrator --authDomain PVOLAB --authPassword
   password --truesso --environment --add --enrollmentServer
   hzn7-enrol.pvolab.com

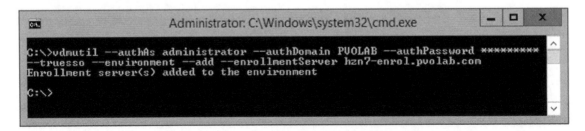

You will see that the Enrollment Server has now been successfully added to the environment:

1. The next command provides you with detailed information about the various Horizon components in your environment. This will help with the configuration of True SSO.

2. From the command line, type the following command:

   vdmUtil --authAs administrator --authDomain PVOLAB --authPassword
   password --truesso --environment --list --enrollmentServer
   hzn7-enrol.pvolab.com --domain pvolab.com

You will see the following output, as shown in the following screen:

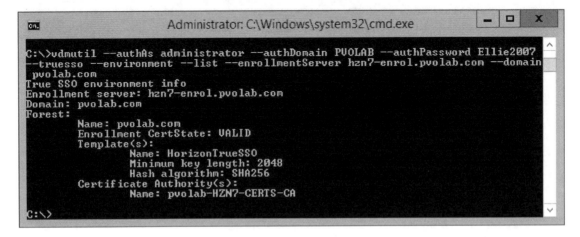

We can now use this information to create a True SSO connector. A True SSO Connector specifies the details of Enrollment Servers, Certificate Authorities, and Certificate Templates to be used. When a Connection Server receives a request to launch a desktop for an end user, it will look up the True SSO Connector for the domain the user belongs to and uses the components that you configure to obtain the Certificate.

From the command line, type the following command:

```
vdmUtil --authAs administrator --authDomain PVOLAB --authPassword password
--truesso --create --connector --domain pvolab.com --template
HorizonTrueSSO --primaryEnrollmentServer hzn7-enrol.pvolab.com --
certificateServer pvolab-hzn7-certs-ca --mode enabled
```

```
C:\>vdmutil --authAs administrator --authDomain PVOLAB --authPassword Ellie2007
--truesso --create --connector --domain pvolab.com --template HorizonTrueSSO --p
rimaryEnrollmentServer hzn7-enrol.pvolab.com --certificateServer pvolab-hzn7-cer
ts-ca --mode enabled
Connector created
Domain: pvolab.com
Mode: ENABLED

C:\>_
```

You will now see that the connector has been successfully created and enabled.

1. Now log in to the View Administrator and check that True SSO is working. From the dashboard screen, under the **System Health** section, click the arrow to expand the True SSO section (21), and then click the link for pvolab.com (**22**).

2. You will see the **True SSO Domain Details** box, as shown in the following screenshot:

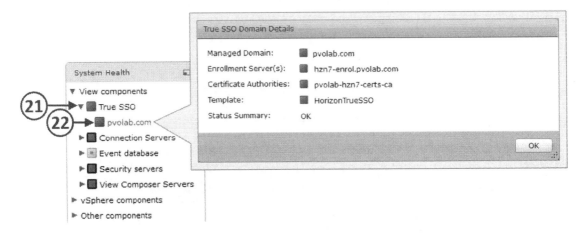

3. Click the **OK** button to close the box and then log out of the View Administrator.

You have now successfully configured the View elements for True SSO. The real benefit of the True SSO feature is when used in conjunction with vIDM, allowing a user to single sign-on to their virtual desktop machine or applications from the vIDM portal.

Summary

In this chapter, we have discussed some of the security aspects of deploying Horizon View. We started off by describing what an SSL certificate is and why Horizon View uses them, before going on to show this practically by installing and configuring a Root CA server and then configuring the View components in the example lab to use these certificates.

The second part of this chapter explored the True SSO feature of Horizon View. Again, we demonstrated this practically by configuring the certificates server to use this feature, and then configuring the Horizon View Enrollment Server and Connection Server so that they "trust" each other when it comes to the user login process.

6
Building and Optimizing the Virtual Desktop OS

Having built the Horizon View infrastructure and its components, in this chapter, we will look at how to create and configure virtual desktop machines, install a desktop operating system on them based on best practice for virtual desktop machines, and then configure that operating system to run at its optimum performance levels.

The steps involved in building the core operating system for a virtual desktop machine are not too dissimilar to the process of building a physical desktop machine. However, there are some additional tasks and software components that we need to install on the operating system to turn it into a true virtual desktop machine that's fit for a Horizon View environment.

The following screenshot shows an outline of the key steps that we will follow in this chapter to building the virtual desktop machines:

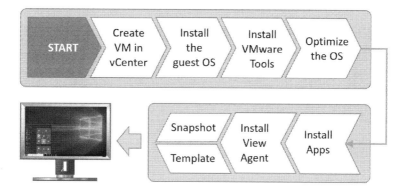

In the following sections of this chapter, we will cover each of these steps in more detail and also build several images along the way, using the example lab.

One virtual desktop machine will be a Windows 7 desktop, which will be configured with a **floating desktop assignment** built using Linked Clones, and a second virtual desktop machine, also running Windows 7, will be configured with a **dedicated assignment** and built from a Full Clone.

Finally, we will also look at creating an Instant Clone Windows 10-based desktop, before finishing the chapter with a look at delivering a Linux-based virtual desktop machine.

In a physical desktop environment, there are a number of ways in which the operating system can be built and deployed. For example, you could use the **Microsoft Deployment Toolkit (MDT)**, or maybe the **Microsoft System Center Configuration Manager (SCCM)**. Both of these options can be used along with all the other tools available to build desktop images, including VMware's own Mirage product, of course.

So, we just talked about a couple of options that you can use to build your desktop images, but let's just highlight the one that you should not use, and that's a **physical-to-virtual tool (P2V)**, which turns your physical image into a virtual one.

Best practice is to build a new virtual desktop image from scratch, so it starts off life as being designed to be a virtual machine from day one. After all, you would potentially build a new image for a new hardware platform and that's what you are doing in reality.

There are a few reasons for not using your physical image to create your virtual desktop image. One of the reasons is the size of the image, which more than likely will have become bloated with numerous patches and updates being applied over the last year or so. You want your VDI image to be lean and fresh, with just the most recent and relevant software installed.

Another reason is that there might be some hardware drivers or other hardware-based software elements within the image, such as a desktop hardware management solution like **Intel Active Management Technology (AMT)**, that relies on firmware and other components built into the chipset of the physical machine. As you are now using a virtual desktop machine, this type of hardware is not present, and therefore, you do not require it to be installed.

The worst case scenario is that by having this type of solution installed it will affect the overall performance of your virtual desktop machine.

Virtual desktop hardware requirements

Before we get on with the build process, we need to look at the specifications of the virtual desktop machine from a hardware perspective and what we need to configure it.

The following screenshot lists the requirements for you:

Hardware Component	Setting
CPU Requirements	Dual CPU for intensive workloads
	Single CPU for everything else
Memory	2 GB for 32-bit OS (3 GB maximum)
	4 GB for 64-bit OS and high-end graphics
SCSI Controller	LSI Logic SAS
Graphics Card	N/A as it will be overridden by pool settings
Diskette Drive	Set to disabled
Network Card	VMXNET 3
Optical Drive	Set to client device to mount ISO images
Serial and Parallel Port	Set to disabled

You should be able to work out the requirements for your environment by using your assessment data captured at the start of the project. The one thing to bear in mind is that you can quite easily change the configuration should you need to.

> Another important factor when configuring the size of the hardware is not to fall into the trap of over-sizing your virtual desktop machines. For example, if you only need one CPU, then only give the virtual desktop machine one CPU. As previously mentioned, this is why your assessment data is critical.

The virtual desktop machine should be configured using the guidelines for the hardware specifications outlined in the previous table.

Creating a Windows 7 virtual desktop machine

In this section, we will build a virtual desktop machine with Windows 7 as the operating system. We will follow the steps outlined at the beginning of this chapter to optimize and prepare the image to be used as a floating-assigned, linked-clone virtual desktop machine.

Creating the virtual desktop machine container

The first thing we need to do is build and configure the actual virtual desktop machine on our **vCenter Server**. This will define the virtual hardware configuration. To define the configuration, follow these steps:

1. Open a browser and log in to the vSphere Web Client for the vCenter **vcs1.pvolab.com**, as shown in the following screenshot:

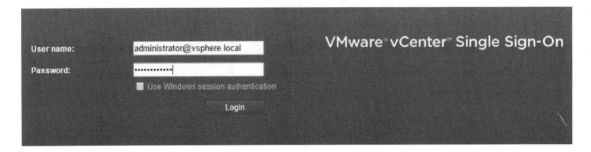

2. Once logged in, you will see the **vSphere Web Client** home page, as shown in the following screenshot:

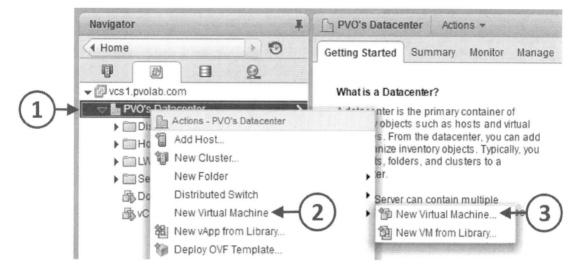

3. Navigate to the data center where you want to create the virtual desktop. In the example lab, the data center is called **PVO's Datacenter** (1).

4. Click and highlight the data center name, right-click, and from the contextual menu, hover your mouse over the option for **New Virtual Machine** (2) until another menu appears, and then from that menu, select the option **New Virtual Machine** (3).

5. The **New Virtual Machine** configuration window will now open, as shown in the following screenshot:

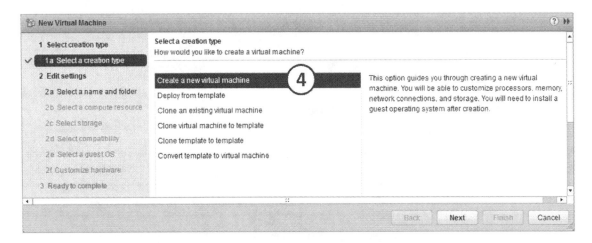

6. Click on **Create a new virtual machine** (**4**), and then click the **Next** button.
7. You will now see the **Select a name and folder** screen, as shown in the following screenshot:

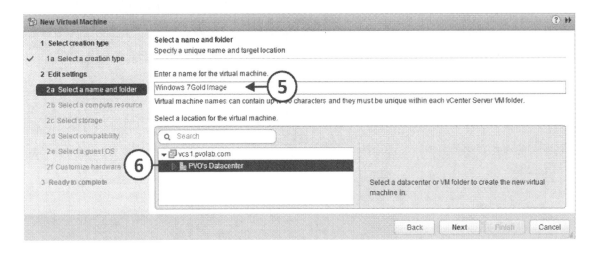

8. In the **Enter a name for the virtual machine** box (**5**), type in a name for the new virtual desktop machine. In the example lab, this is called **Windows 7 Gold Image**.

9. Then, in the **Select a location for the virtual machine** section, click to highlight the data center where you want this virtual machine to be created (**6**). In the example lab, this machine is going to be created in the data center called **PVO's Datacenter**.

10. Click the **Next** button to continue.

11. You will now see the **Select a compute resource** screen, as shown in the following screenshot:

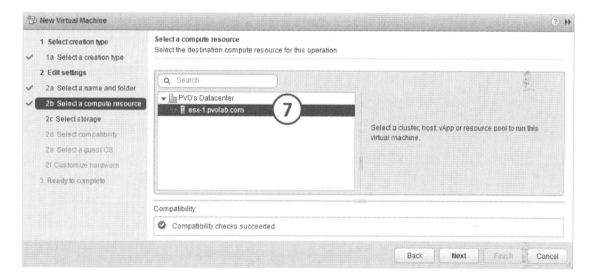

12. Expand the data center called **PVO's Datacenter** and then click on the ESX server you want to host this virtual desktop. In the example lab, **esx-1.pvolab.com** (**7**) is going to be the host server.

 As this is going to be our gold/master image or parent virtual desktop machine, it's probably not as important with regard to the location when compared to the live production virtual desktop machines. So for the example lab, we will use the management block to host this virtual desktop machine.

13. Click the **Next** button to continue.
14. You will now see the **Select storage** screen, as shown in the following screenshot:

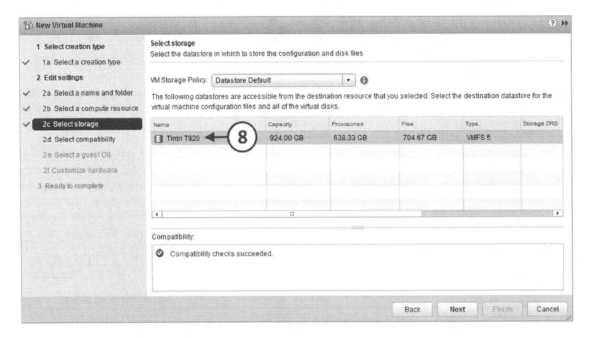

15. Select the datastore where this virtual desktop machine will be stored. In the example lab, the virtual desktop machine is stored on the **Tintri T820 (8)**.
16. Click the **Next** button to continue.
17. You will now see the **Select compatibility** screen. This is where we will choose the virtual machine version for our virtual desktop machine. As the page says, for the best performance, you should use Version 11, which means using vSphere 6 as the hosting platform. We also need vSphere 6, as that is the platform that supports features such as Instant Clones and vGPU.

 If you choose hardware version 9 or greater, remember that you will need to manage this virtual desktop machine by using the vSphere Web Client and not the old C# console.

18. From the drop-down menu (**9**), select **ESXi 6.0 and later**, as shown in the following screenshot:

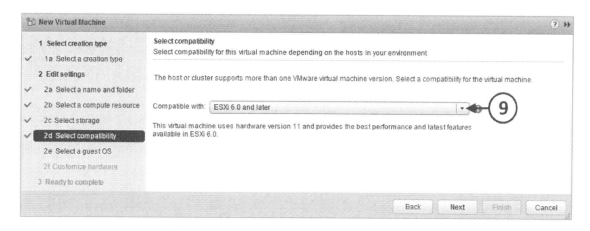

19. Click the **Next** button to continue.
20. You will now see the **Select a guest OS** screen, as shown in the following screenshot:

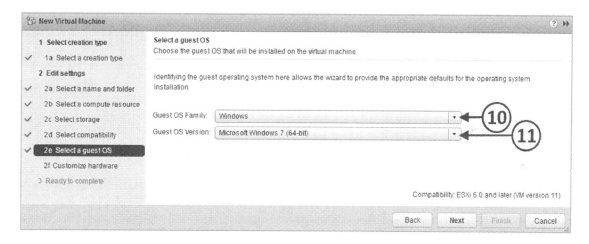

21. The next step is to choose the operating system for the virtual desktop machine. In the example, this is the first virtual desktop machine, which we will build as a Windows 7 Professional 64-bit image.
22. From the **Guest OS Family** box, click the arrow for the drop-down menu (**10**) and select **Windows**. Then, from the **Guest OS Version** box, click the arrow for the drop-down menu (**11**) and select **Microsoft Windows 7 (64-bit)**. The guest OS selection is important, as it determines which drivers get installed when VMware Tools is installed.

23. Click the **Next** button to continue.

24. You will now see the **Customize Hardware** screen where you will configure the virtual hardware specification for the virtual desktop machine, as shown in the following screenshot:

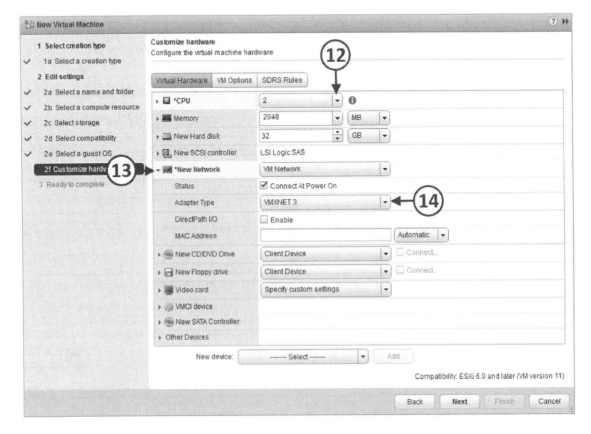

25. There are a couple of things to change on this configuration screen. First, this virtual machine is going to have 2 vCPUs. In the **CPU** box, click the down arrow (**12**) and select **2** from the drop-down menu.

26. Next, expand the **New Network** option by clicking the arrow (**13**), and then in the **Adapter Type** box, click the down arrow (**14**), and select the option for **VMXNET 3**.

27. In the last part of the hardware configuration, you need to change one of the boot options so that the next time the virtual desktop machine powers on and boots, it goes straight into the BIOS setup screen. You could, of course, open a console to the virtual desktop machine and press the *F2* key as it boots; however, that screen can flash past so quickly you might miss it, so the former option is easier.

28. The reason you need to select this option and go into the BIOS setup screen is because we need to change some of the configuration settings so that this virtual desktop machine behaves as a virtual machine rather than a physical desktop PC.

29. We will cover this a bit later when we power on the newly created virtual desktop machine for the first time.

30. To configure the boot options, click the **VM Options** tab (**15**), and then expand the arrow for ***Boot Options** (**16**). In the **Force BIOS Setup (*)** section (**17**), check the box for **The next time the virtual machine boots, force entry into the BIOS setup screen**:

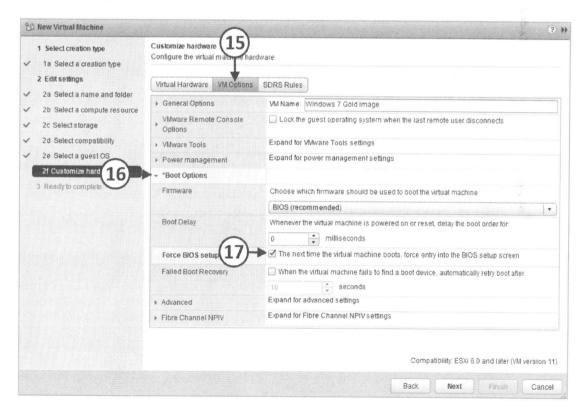

31. Once you have completed the configuration, click the **Next** button to continue. You will now see the **Ready to complete** screen, as shown in the following screenshot:

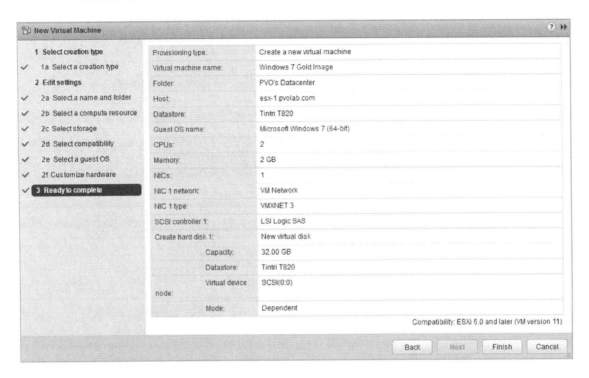

32. Click the **Finish** button to complete the configuration.

33. If you check the **Recent Tasks** box, you will see that the virtual desktop machine has been successfully created, as shown in the following screenshot:

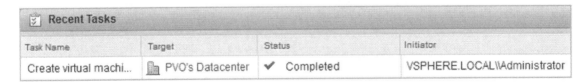

34. With the virtual desktop machine now built and configured, it's time to power it on and continue the build process. Navigate to the virtual desktop machine in the inventory. You should see an entry called **Windows 7 Gold Image** (**18**).

35. Highlight the virtual desktop machine, right-click, and from the contextual menu, click on **Power** (**19**) and then click on **Power On** (**20**), as shown in the following screenshot:

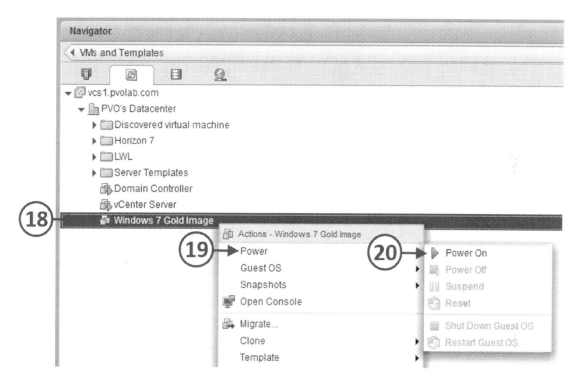

The virtual desktop machine will now power on and boot into the BIOS setup screen, as that's what we configured to happen on the next boot. Any subsequent boot ups will boot as normal into the operating system, once it's installed. In the next section, we will make the configuration changes to the machine BIOS.

Updating the virtual desktop machine BIOS

With the virtual desktop machine now powered on and booted into the BIOS setup screen, launch a console to it so that you can perform the configuration steps:

1. Highlight the **Windows 7 Gold Image** virtual desktop machine in the **Inventory** section, and then click the **Summary** tab (1). Then click the **Launch Remote Console** link (2), as shown in the following screenshot:

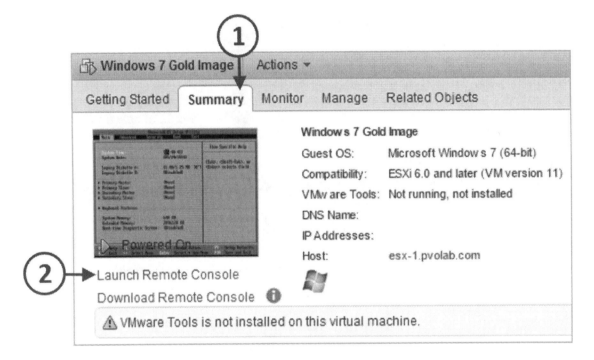

2. You will now see the **PhoenixBIOS Setup Utility** screen of the virtual desktop machine:

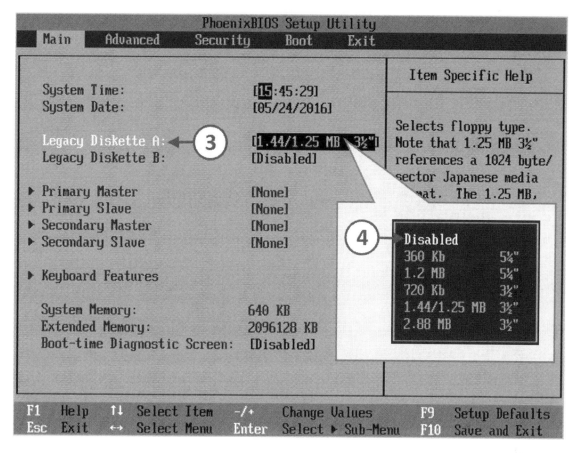

3. The first thing you need to do is to disable the floppy drive. On the **Main** section of the BIOS setup screen, use the cursor keys to move down and highlight the option for **Legacy Diskette A:(3)**, and then press Enter.

4. You will now see a pop-up box displaying the diskette options. Use the cursor keys again to highlight the **Disabled** option (4) and then press Enter.

5. Next, you need to navigate to the **Advanced** section of the BIOS setup screen. To do this, press the right arrow cursor key to move across the tabs along the top, until **Advanced** is highlighted (**5**), as shown in the following screenshot:

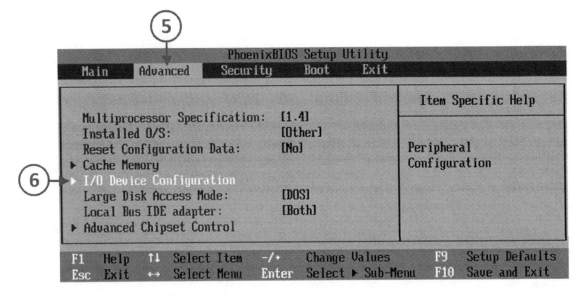

6. Using the down arrow cursor, move down to the option for **I/O Device Configuration** (**6**) and press *Enter*.
7. You will now see the **Advanced** configuration screen:

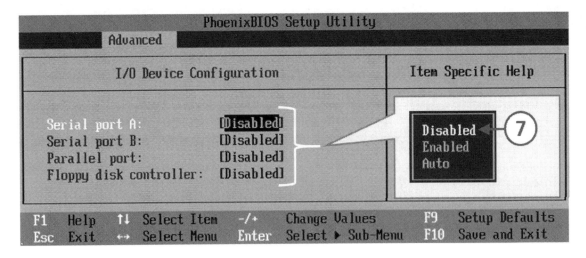

8. Move the cursor to the entry for **Serial port A:** and press Open a command prompt window by pressing the Windows key and *R*, and then in the Run dialog. From the pop-up box, select the option for **Disabled** (7).

9. Follow the same procedure to disable the options for **Serial port B:**, **Parallel port:**, and **Floppy disk controller:**, until all options have been set to **Disabled**. Once you have completed these configuration changes, press the *F10* key to save and exit.

10. You will see the following **Setup Confirmation** box, as shown in the following screenshot:

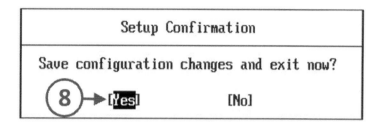

11. Confirm the configuration changes by selecting **Yes** (8), and then pressing *Enter*. The BIOS changes are now saved and the virtual desktop machine is rebooted automatically.

Operating system installation options

There are a couple of options you can use to build the operating system for the virtual desktop machines. The first option is to use something such as MDT, SCCM, or VMware's own Mirage product (used for Full Clone desktops) to deploy an image you have already built for VDI, but for the example lab, we will use a different option, which is to build the image manually by using the installation media to show the different tasks you need to perform in order to optimize the image for VDI.

This build process is no different to how you build any other virtual machine on vSphere, so therefore, we will just briefly cover some of this as a quick reminder for those already familiar with working on the vSphere platform, and in enough detail that those that are new to the technology can quickly get their first virtual desktop machine image built.

Installing the guest operating system

The first thing you need to do in order to start the installation of the guest operating system is to attach the installation media to the virtual desktop machine:

1. From the vSphere Web Client, in the **Inventory** section, highlight the **Windows 7 Gold Image** virtual desktop machine. Click on the **Summary** tab and then, in the **VM Hardware** section, click on the down arrow next to the entry for **CD/DVD drive 1 (1)**:

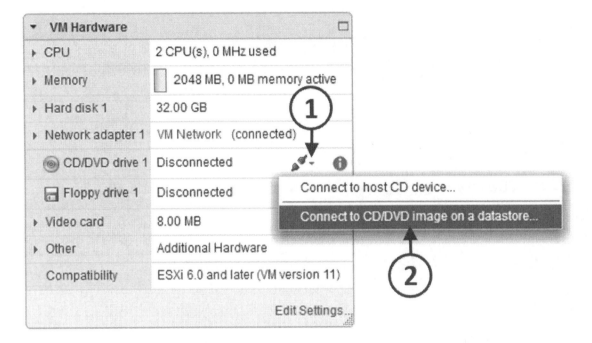

2. From the menu that pops up, select **Connect to CD/DVD image on a datastore...** (2).

3. In the example lab, we've copied the software ISO images for the operating systems that we are going to build onto a datastore on the ESXi host servers, into a folder called **ISO Images**. Click on the folder (**3**), highlight the Windows 7 ISO image (**4**), and click **OK**:

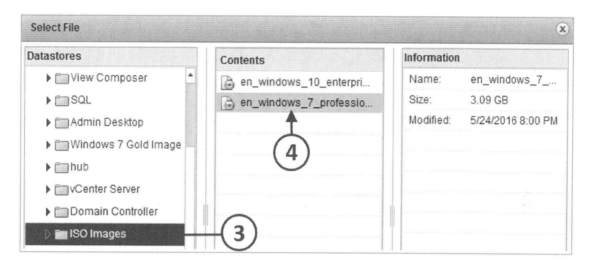

4. Once you have attached the ISO image, and as the virtual desktop machine is still powered on with a console attached, reboot the virtual machine.

5. You will see the virtual machine reboot and then boot from the attached ISO image, launching the Windows 7 installer, as shown in the following screenshot:

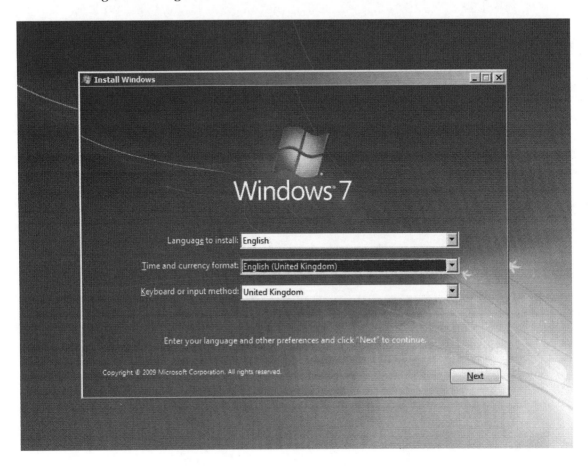

We won't cover how to install Windows 7, so carry on with a basic installation. Once the installation is complete, make sure you apply any updates and patches and then join the virtual desktop machine to the domain.

The reason you need to join the virtual desktop machine to the domain, even though this machine is effectively the template, is so that all the software components, DLL files, and so on that are needed on the machine for it to be domain-joined are present. Otherwise, when you create the Linked Clones from this parent image and try to join them to the domain, the virtual desktop machines will ask for the installation media to be inserted. That's OK for one or two desktops and when testing, but not for thousands in production.

Once you are happy that the operating system for the parent image has been patched and is joined to the domain, you can start installing some of the VMware-specific virtual machine tools and Horizon View components, starting with VMware Tools.

Installing VMware Tools

VMware Tools is installed to enhance the usability of the virtual desktop machine. It installs VMware-specific device drivers that allow it to run as a virtual desktop machine, replacing the physical hardware equivalents. The installation of VMware Tools is initiated from the vSphere Web Client:

1. As we did in the previous section, highlight the **Windows 7 Gold Image** virtual desktop machine in the **Inventory** section, and then click on the **Summary** tab (**1**). Next, click on **Install VMware Tools** link (**2**), as shown in the following screenshot:

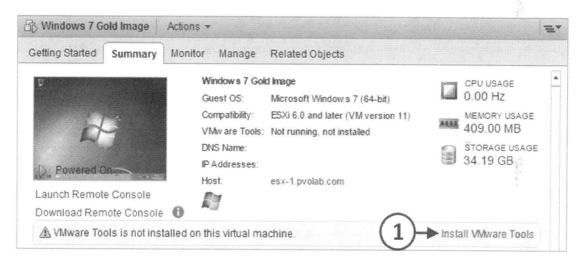

2. Initiating the installation from the vSphere Web Client effectively mounts the VMware Tools installation media as a virtual CD drive on the virtual desktop machine.

3. You will see the following **Install VMware Tools** dialog box pop up, as shown in the following screenshot:

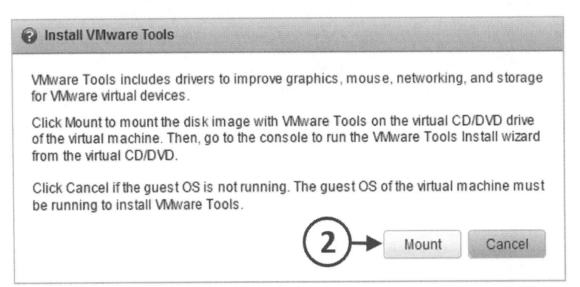

4. Click the **Mount** button (**2**) to mount the installation media as shown in the previous screenshot, and then switch back to the console view of the virtual desktop machine.
5. You will now see the **AutoPlay** dialog box showing that the VMware Tools DVD drive has been mounted and the installation program is available to launch, as shown in the following screenshot:

6. Click **Run setup64.exe (3)** to launch the VMware Tools installer.

7. If you see the **User Account Control** box pop up warning you about making changes to the computer, ignore it by clicking on the **Yes** button.

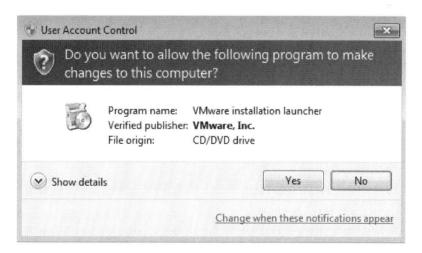

8. You will now see the **Welcome to the installation wizard for VMware Tools** dialog box, as shown in the following screenshot:

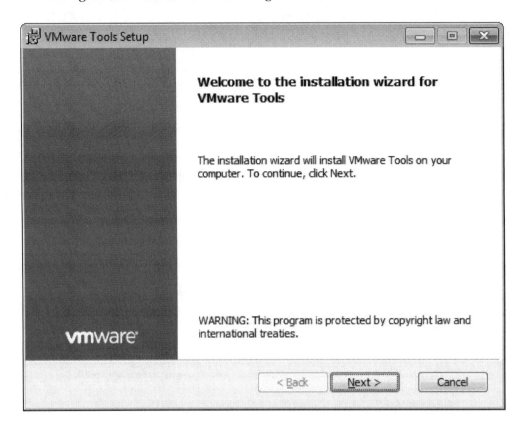

9. Click the **Next >** button to continue the installation. You will now see the **Choose Setup Type** dialog box, as shown in the following screenshot:

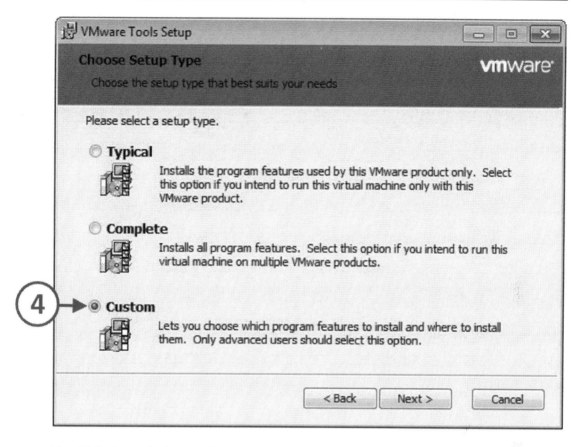

10. Click the radio button for **Custom** (4), and then click the **Next >** button to
    continue.

 You could normally just perform a **Typical** installation, but for the
purposes of this book we are going to look at the **Custom** option, as it
shows you all the drivers that get installed during install.

11. You will now see the **Custom Setup** dialog box, as shown in the following screenshot:

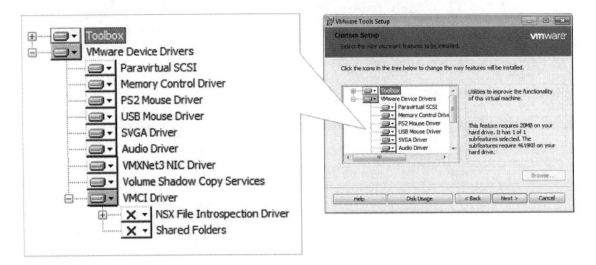

12. VMware Tools will install the following VMware device drivers:
    - **Paravirtual SCSI**: This is for PVSCSI adapters to enhance the performance of virtualized applications.
    - **Memory Control Driver**: This allows memory management of the virtual desktop machine when running on an ESXi host.
    - **PS2/USB Mouse Driver**: This virtual mouse driver improves the performance of the mouse in a virtual desktop machine.
    - **SVGA Driver**: This enables 32-bit displays, high resolution, and faster graphics performance. It installs a virtual SVGA driver that replaces the standard VGA driver. On Windows Vista or later versions, the VMware SVGA 3D (Microsoft – WDDM) driver is also installed, adding support for Windows Aero.
    - **Audio Driver**: This is required for all 64-bit guest operating systems to enable sound capabilities.
    - **VMXNET3 NIC Driver**: This improves network performance and is recommended for virtual desktop machines.
    - **Volume Shadow Copy**: This allows taking backup copies or snapshots of the virtual desktop machine.

- **VMCI Driver**: This allows faster communication between virtual machines.
- **NSX File Introspection Driver**: This installs the agent to use antivirus offload scanning.

13. Other options in this dialog box allow you to change where VMware Tools is installed, and to check the disk space requirements so that you can check the amount of disk space that VMware Tools needs to install your chosen options.

14. Click the **Next >** button to continue.

15. You will now see the **Ready to install VMware Tools** dialog box. Click the **Install** button to start the install process, as shown in the following screenshot:

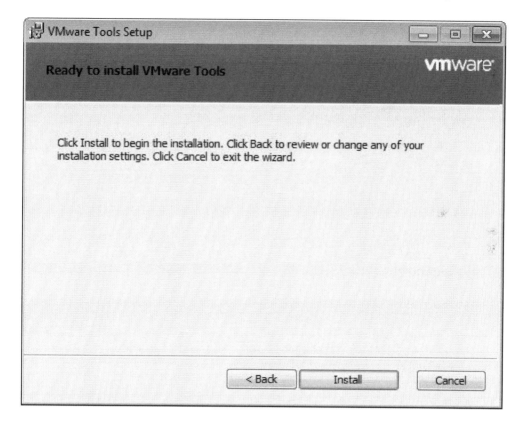

16. Once completed, you will see the **Completed the VMware Tools Setup Wizard** dialog box. Click on the **Finish** button to complete the installation process, as shown in the following screenshot:

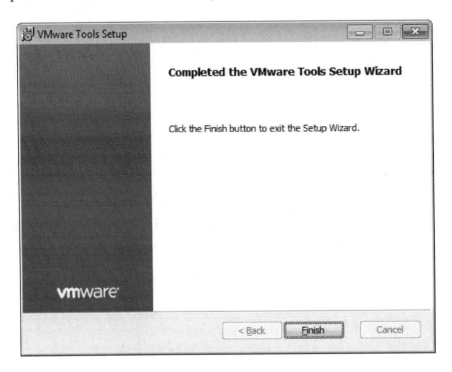

17. On completion, you will be prompted to restart the virtual desktop machine in order to start the VMware Tools services. From the following dialog box, click the **Yes** button to reboot.

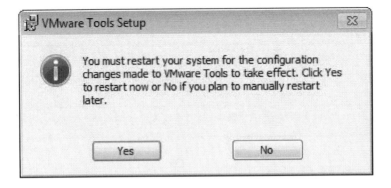

18. Once the virtual desktop machine has restarted, check that VMware Tools services are up and running by clicking on the taskbar and checking for the **vm** icon (**5**), as shown in the following screenshot:

You can also launch the Services console from the virtual desktop machine and check that the service is running from there, as shown in the following screenshot:

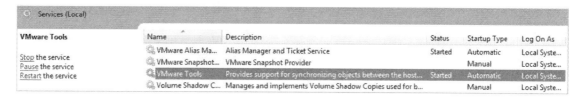

You have now successfully installed VMware Tools. The next step of the process is to install any core applications that you want to include as part of the parent image.

Installing applications for the parent image

The next stage of the process is to install any applications that you want to have as part of your parent image. These are typically applications that will be used by every user in your organization. You could also deliver applications using other technologies, such as *ThinApp*. Ideally, you would want to try and deliver applications on demand rather than install them into operating system images.

Installing the Horizon View Agent

The **Horizon View Agent** is installed on each virtual desktop machine and is used for communication between the Horizon View Client and the virtual desktop machine. It also adds components for things such as View Persona Management and USB redirection. We will cover these different components in more detail in this section as we install the agent on the virtual desktop machine. Follow these steps:

1. Open a console to the Windows 7 Gold Image virtual desktop machine, and from the desktop, navigate to the installation file for the View Agent. In the example lab, the installation software is in the shared folder, as shown in the following screenshot:

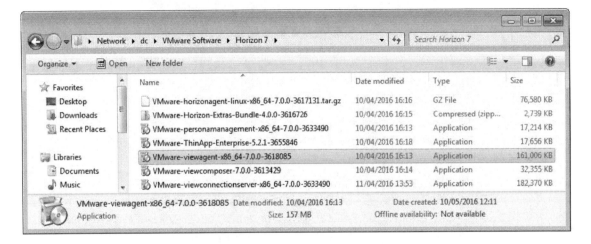

2. Launch the file `VMware-viewagent-x86_64-7.0.0-36180859` to start the installation, and if you see the **Open File – Security Warning message**, click the **Run** button.

3. You will now see the **Welcome to the Installation Wizard for VMware Horizon Agent** screen, as shown in the following screenshot:

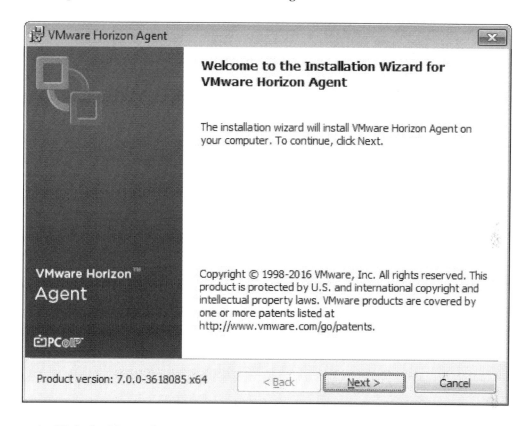

4. Click the **Next >** button to continue.

5. You will now see the **License Agreement** page, as shown in the following screenshot:

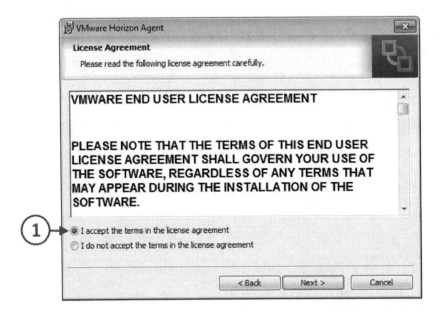

6. Click on the radio button for **I accept the terms in the license agreement** (1).
7. Click the **Next >** button to continue.
8. You will now see the **Network protocol configuration** dialog box, as shown in the following screenshot:

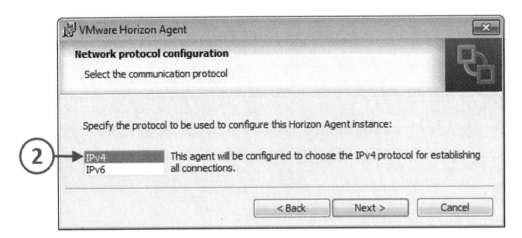

9. As this lab is using **IPv4**, from the options box, click **IPv4** (2), and then click the **Next >** button to continue.

10. You will now see the **Custom Setup** page.

11. On the Custom Setup page, you can choose the features and functions you want to install. Not all of these features are installed by default, so on this screen you might want to review some of them and select/deselect them from the installation process as you might not want to use some of the features. You can always install them again later if need be.

12. Those features not installed by default are marked with a red **X**. The features are shown in the following screenshot:

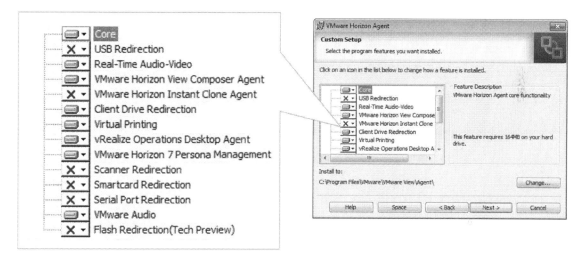

13. You can choose to install the following features:

- **USB Redirection**: This allows a USB device to be plugged into the endpoint device and then redirect the USB traffic to the virtual desktop machine
- **Real-Time Audio-Video**: This allows you to redirect locally-connected audio and video devices (such as USB webcams) to your virtual desktop machine
- **VMware Horizon View Composer Agent**: This allows the virtual desktop machine to be run as a Linked Clone desktop
- **VMware Horizon Instant Clone Agent**: This allows the virtual desktop machine to be run as an Instant Clone desktop
- **Client Drive Redirection**: Allows View Clients to share local drives with remote desktops and applications (IPv4 only)

- **Virtual Printing**: This allows users to print to printers without the need to install print drivers
- **vRealize Operations Manager Agent**: This allows the virtual desktop machine to be monitored by vRealize Operations Manager for Horizon View
- **VMware Horizon View Persona Management**: This synchronizes a user's profile from the virtual desktop machine to a repository on a central server, meaning that a profile can be delivered to a floating assigned desktop to personalize it for that user so that they can access their profile
- **Scanner Redirection**: Allows you to redirect a local scanner to the virtual desktop machine
- **Smartcard Redirection**: This allows users to use a smartcard for authentication
- **Serial Port Redirection**: This allows users to redirect the local serial port to the virtual desktop machine
- **VMware Audio**: Enables sound on the local device
- **Flash Redirection (Tech Preview)**: Offloads the processing of Flash-based content to the local device

14. When you are happy with the features you have chosen to install, click on the **Next >** button to continue.
15. On the next screen, you will see the **Remote Desktop Protocol Configuration** dialog box. You need remote desktop support enabled for the View Agent to work. You could always enable this using a Group Policy.
16. Click on the radio button for **Enable the Remote Desktop capability on this computer (3)**, as shown in the following screenshot:

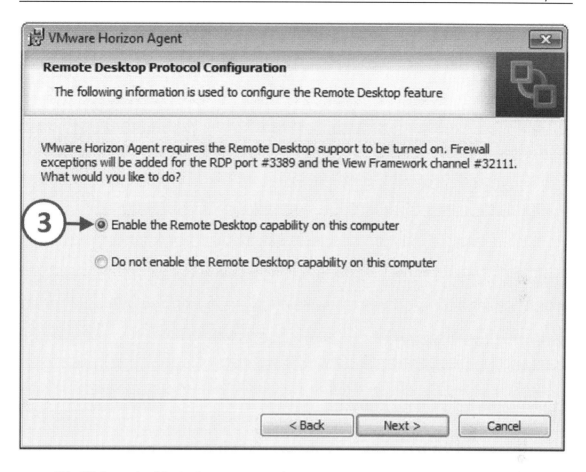

17. Click on the **Next >** button to continue.

18. You will now see the **Ready to Install the Program** dialog box, as shown in the following screenshot:

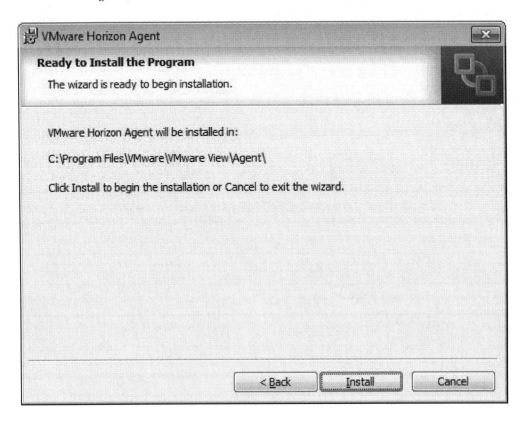

19. Click the **Install** button to start the installation.

20. Once the installation has finished, you will see the **Installer Completed** dialog box, as shown in the following screenshot:

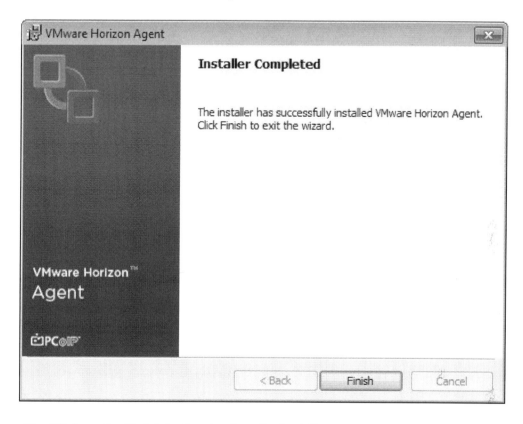

21. Click on the **Finish** button to close the installer.

Finally, you will be prompted to reboot the virtual desktop machine. Click on the **Yes** button to reboot. You will now have successfully installed the Horizon View Agent.

In the next section, we will start optimizing the parent image to run as a virtual desktop machine.

Optimizing the guest operating system

There are various automated tools and manual processes to optimize the virtual desktop operating systems.

Previously, the optimization process was delivered via a set of scripts that you would manually execute on the virtual desktop machine that is being used to create the gold image from. However, in this chapter, we will take a look at the GUI-based **VMware Optimization Tool** this is available to download as a fling.

 A **fling**, in VMware terms, is a free piece of software for end users to try out and provide feedback to VMware. Often, these products make it into production as products in their own right, or they form part of a new feature of an already existing product. The only thing to bear in mind, should you choose to use them in your production environment, is that these product flings don't have any official support; however, you will find a number of blogs that may help.

Download the optimization tool and save it in the shared folder. You can download the tool from the following link: `https://labs.vmware.com/flings/vmware-os-optimization-tool`.

Once downloaded, let's take a few minutes just to see how this tool works.

VMware OS Optimization Tool is an application that you can execute on the virtual desktop machine you are optimizing. It also has the ability to analyze and optimize remote systems.

1. From the Windows 7 virtual desktop machine being used to create the parent image, navigate to the shared software folder, locate the **VMware OS Optimization Tool** application, as shown in the following screenshot:

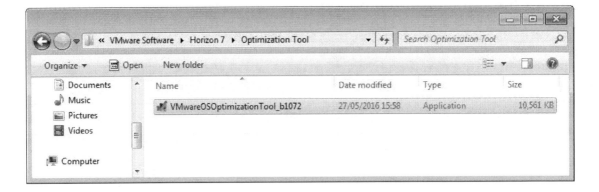

2. Launch the `VMwareOSOptimizationTool_b1072` file to launch the optimization tool. If you see the **Open File – Security Warning message**, click the **Run** button to continue. You will now see the tool launch, as shown in the following screenshot:

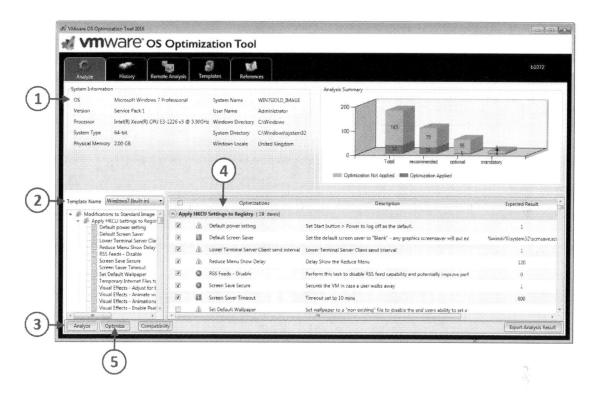

3. At the top of the screen (**1**), you can see the details of the virtual desktop machine's operating system and hardware configuration.

4. The next section is **Template Name** (**2**) and is where you choose the template you want to use for the optimization. From the drop-down menu, you select the relevant operating system template that you want to apply to this image. You have the ability to create new templates using this tool by clicking on the **Templates** tab from the list of tabs across the top of the screen.

5. To start the process, the tool firstly analyzes the differences between the current virtual machine state and the optimizations contained within the chosen template. Click on the **Analyze** button (**4**) to start the process.

6. The tool will run the analysis and then come back with a report showing the components that need to be optimized (**4**). At this stage, you can select or deselect options before you actually run the optimization. Scroll through the analysis results to understand what is going to be changed.

7. When you are happy with the options, click the **Optimize** button (**5**) to start the optimization process. The image will now be optimized as per the settings and configuration details contained within the template that you chose.

8. If you want to see the results of what has been changed during the optimization process, click on the **Optimize** tab (**6**), as shown in the following screenshot:

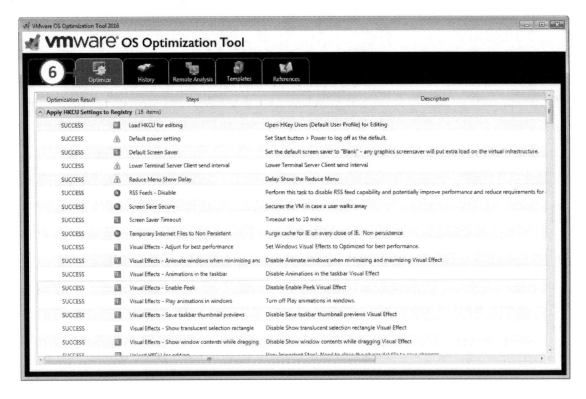

For more detailed information on how to optimize the desktop operating system for running in a virtual environment, have a look at the following link: `http://tinyurl.com/7 rzfw6b`.

Once you have completed the optimization process, exit the tool. In the next section, we will look at what's next for the example lab-based virtual desktop machine.

Post-optimization tasks

One of the final things to do is to release the IP address, if you have been using DHCP, so that when the new virtual desktop machines are created from this parent image, they don't have a duplicate IP address and therefore will obtain a new IP address.

Open a command prompt window by pressing the Windows key and *R*, and then in the **Run** dialog box, type **cmd**.

In the command prompt window that now opens, type `ipconfig /release`, as shown in the following screenshot:

Before shutting down the virtual desktop machine and completing the image build, there are just a few other housekeeping tasks to perform.

The key one is not to forget to tidy up behind you. For example, empty the Recycle Bin and delete any browser history or temporary files. Basically, delete everything that is not part of that parent image. Once you are happy that the image is optimized to your specific requirements, you can shut down the virtual desktop machine.

With the image build for Windows 7 now complete, we will finalize the preparation of this image ready for delivery later on in this chapter.

Creating a Windows 10 virtual desktop machine

For the example lab, we will repeat the build and optimization process to build a second parent image, but this time, we are going to build a Windows 10 virtual desktop machine. In the next section, we will repeat the process described in the previous section and build a Windows 10 virtual desktop machine.

Just as a reminder, the process for building the virtual desktop machine is shown in the following image:

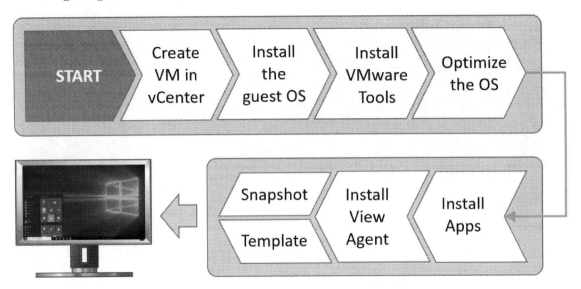

Once built, this Windows 10 parent image will then be used to create an Instant Clone, virtual desktop machine pool.

Rather than go through every step again screenshot by screenshot, we will list the steps we followed when creating the Windows 7 parent image and then just show the screenshots to highlight the differences. You can refer to the previous section to get more details.

Creating the virtual desktop machine container

As with creating the previous virtual desktop machine, the first thing we need to do is build and configure the actual virtual desktop machine on the vCenter Server. This will define the virtual hardware configuration. To define the configuration, follow these steps:

1. Open a browser and log in to the vSphere Web Client for the vCenter **vcs1.pvolab.com**

2. Navigate to the data center where you want to create the virtual desktop. In the example lab, the data center is called **PVO's Datacenter**.

3. Click and highlight the data center name, right-click, and from the contextual menu, hover your mouse over the option for **New Virtual Machine** until another menu appears, and then from that menu, select the option **New Virtual Machine**.

4. The **New Virtual Machine** configuration window will now open.

5. Click on **Create a new virtual machine**, and then click the **Next** button. You will now see the **Select a name and folder** screen.

6. In the **Enter a name for the virtual machine** box (1), type in a name for the new virtual desktop machine. In this example, this is called **Windows 10 Gold Image**.

7. Then, in the **Select a location for the virtual machine** section (2), click to highlight the data center where you want this virtual machine to be created. In the example lab, this machine is going to be created in the data center called **PVO's Datacenter**:

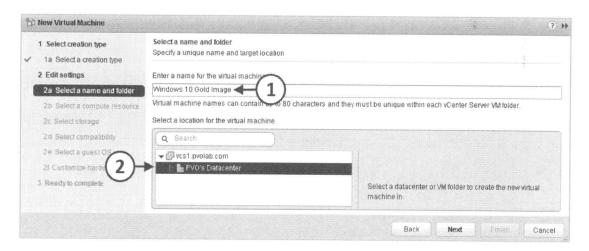

8. Click the **Next** button to continue.

9. You will now see the **Select a compute resource** screen.

10. Expand the data center called **PVO's Datacenter** and then click on the ESX server you want to host this virtual desktop. In the example lab, **esx-1.pvolab.com** is going to be the host server.

11. Click the **Next** button to continue. You will now see the **Select storage** screen.

12. Select the datastore where this virtual desktop machine will be stored. In the example lab, the virtual desktop machine is stored on the **Tintri T820**.

13. Click the **Next** button to continue.

14. You will now see the **Select compatibility** screen. This is where we will choose the virtual machine version for our virtual desktop machine. As the page says, for the best performance you should use Version 11, which means using vSphere 6 as the hosting platform. We also need vSphere 6, as that is the platform that supports features such as Instant Clones and vGPU.

15. If you choose hardware version 9 or greater, remember that you will need to manage this virtual desktop machine by using the vSphere Web Client and not the old C# console.

16. From the drop-down menu, select **ESXi 6.0 and later** and then click the **Next** button to continue. You will now see the **Select a guest OS** screen.

17. The next step is to choose the operating system for the virtual desktop machine. In this example, this is the second virtual desktop machine, which we will build as a Windows 10 machine.

18. From the **Guest OS Family** box, click the arrow for the drop-down menu (**3**), and select **Windows**. Then, from the **Guest OS Version** box, click the arrow for the drop-down menu (**4**) and select **Microsoft Windows 10 (64-bit)**. The guest OS selection is important, as it determines which drivers get installed when VMware Tools is installed:

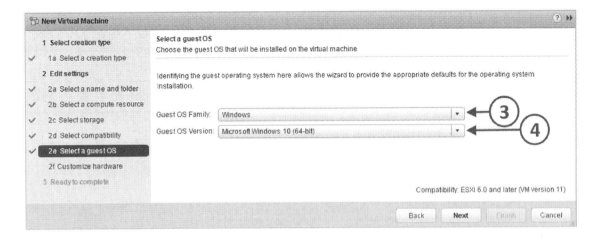

19. Click the **Next** button to continue.

20. You will now see the **Customize Hardware** screen where you will configure the virtual hardware specification for the virtual desktop machine.

21. There are a couple of things to change on this configuration screen. First, this virtual machine is going to have two vCPUs. In the **CPU** box, click the down arrow and select **2** from the drop-down menu.

22. Next, expand the **New Network** option by clicking the arrow and then on the **Adapter Type** box, click the down arrow, and select the option for **VMXNET 3**.

23. In the last part of the hardware configuration, as with the previous configuration, you need to change one of the boot options so that the next time the virtual desktop machine powers on and boots, it goes straight into the BIOS setup screen.

24. To configure the boot options, click the **VM Options** tab, and then expand the arrow for **Boot Options**. In the **Force BIOS Setup (*)** section, check the tick box for **The next time the virtual machine boots, force entry into the BIOS setup screen**.

25. Once you have completed the configuration, click the **Next** button to continue. You will now see the **Ready to complete** screen.

26. Click the **Finish** button to complete the configuration. With the Windows 10 virtual desktop machine now built and configured, it's time to power it on and continue the build process by configuring the BIOS settings.

Updating the virtual desktop machine BIOS

As with the Windows 7 virtual desktop machine, you need to power on the newly created Windows 10 virtual desktop machine and make some configuration changes to the BIOS.

Make exactly the same changes as made previously and disable floppy drives, serial ports, and parallel ports. Once complete, save the changes and restart the virtual desktop machine.

Installing the guest operating system

With the BIOS updated, you can now go ahead and install the guest operating system:

1. Ensure that the virtual desktop machine is powered on and then from the vSphere Web Client, in the **Inventory** section, highlight the **Windows 10 Gold Image** virtual desktop machine. Click on the **Summary** tab and then, in the **VM Hardware** section, click on the down arrow next to the entry for **CD/DVD drive 1**.

2. From the menu that pops up, select **Connect to CD/DVD image on a datastore....**

3. In the example lab, we've copied the software ISO images for the operating systems that we are going to build onto a datastore on the ESXi host servers, into a folder called **ISO Images**.

4. Click on the **Tintri T820** folder to expand it and then highlight the **ISO Images** folder, highlight the Windows 10 ISO image file, and click **OK**. The Windows installer will launch.

5. Follow the Windows 10 installation steps until you have built the operating system. Once built, apply any updates and patches and don't forget to join the virtual desktop machine to the domain.

Installing VMware Tools

The next step is to install VMware Tools. Follow the steps outlined during the Windows 7 virtual desktop machine build, using the same details.

Installing applications for the parent image

The next step is to install any applications that will form a part of the parent image. This is the same process as we covered previously when building the Windows 7 image.

Installing the Horizon View Agent

Now we can install the Horizon View Agent. The installation process is again no different from the one we worked through during our Windows 7 build, so please refer to the previous section for more details.

Optimizing the guest operating system

As with the Windows 7 build, you will need to optimize the operating system for running in a virtual desktop environment.

You can use the VMware Optimization Tool; however, at the time of writing this book, Windows 10 support is listed as beta.

Post-optimization tasks

Now that we have completed all the build tasks, all that remains is releasing the IP address and then clearing up any temporary files, browser histories, and so on. Once we have finished these, power off the virtual desktop machine, which is ready for us to prepare the image as our virtual desktop machine template.

Creating a GPU-enabled virtual desktop machine

In this section, we are going to build a second Windows 7 virtual desktop machine, but this time for use with a dedicated hardware-based NVIDIA GPU card. As we discussed previously, there are three models for delivering high-end graphics. For this example, we will set up a virtual desktop machine to use vDGA.

Creating the virtual desktop machine container

The first step, as with the build process covered previously for Windows 7, is to build the virtual machine itself. We will follow the steps previously described in this chapter to build a Windows 7 virtual desktop machine, up to the point where we configure the virtual hardware differently, as we need to add in the GPU card at this point:

1. Follow the steps to build a Windows 7 machine, as described in the previous section, Creating a Windows 7 virtual desktop machine, until you get to the **Customize Hardware** section, as shown in the following screenshot:

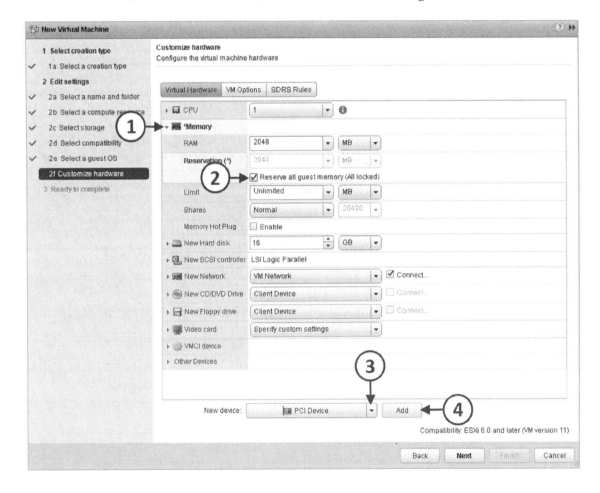

2. In the **2f Customize Hardware** section, under the **Virtual Hardware** tab, click on the drop-down arrow for **Memory (1)**, and check the box for **Reserve all guest memory (2)**.

If you do not configure memory reservation, then the virtual desktop machine will fail to power on, as it can't guarantee that the memory will be available.

3. Next, at the bottom of the box, in the **New PCI device** section **(3)**, click the drop-down arrow and from the list of options, click on **PCI Device**, and then click the **Add** button **(4)** to add the new PCI device.

4. You will now see the following dialog box, which shows the available PCI devices. These devices were configured for PCI pass through when the ESXi hosted was configured in `Chapter 4`, *Installing and Configuring Horizon View*:

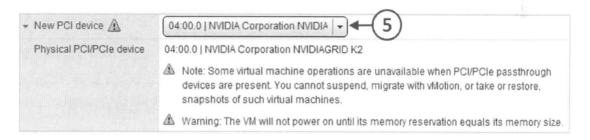

5. From the **New PCI Device** drop-down menu **(5)**, click the down arrow and select one of the two NVIDIA cards from the drop-down box. It's also worth noting the warning information around some of the operations that are not available on the virtual desktop machine.

You will also need to follow these steps for each vDGA-enabled virtual desktop machine you want to create and build. You need to do this because, being a 1:1 assignment, each machine has its own dedicated GPU memory address.

The final step in the building of the virtual desktop machine process is to add an entry to the virtual machine configuration file (VMX file). This is only a requirement if your virtual desktop machine has more than 2 GB of memory configured. This is a limitation of the 32-bit hardware and 32-bit operating systems that cause a PC to appear to have less memory available than is actually installed.

There is an amount of system memory that is hidden and unavailable, which varies depending on the chipset, BIOS, physical memory installed, the amount of video RAM installed on the graphics cards, and the number and type of PCI cards configured. More than 1 GB of the 32-bit system memory can be unavailable when 4 GB of physical memory and multiple 3D cards with large amounts of video memory are installed.

Edit the VMX file and add the line `pciHole.start = "2048"`, as shown in the following screenshot:

```
pciHole.start = "2048"
pciPassthru0.present = "TRUE"
pciPassthru0.deviceId = "11bf"
pciPassthru0.vendorId = "10de"
pciPassthru0.systemId = "51baead3-61b2-2958-6a0d-90b11c18c094"
pciPassthru0.id = "07:00.0"
pciPassthru0.pciSlotNumber = "192"
```

With these steps complete, follow the steps to update the BIOS settings before moving on to installing the guest operating system and optimizing it.

Installing the operating system for GPU-enabled desktops

In the example lab, we are going to build a Windows 7 virtual desktop machine to deliver high-end graphics. To install the operating system, follow the steps described in the Installing the guest operating system section under the Creating a Windows 7 virtual desktop machine section of this chapter, but with one difference.

After you have installed the Horizon View Agent, you need to install the NVIDIA drivers on the virtual desktop machine. The drivers can be downloaded from the following link: `http://tinyurl.com/mzf2b33`.

> When you install the NVIDIA driver software, make sure you select all the components to be installed and don't use the express option. Express will miss out some of the key components that need to run in a virtual desktop machine.

Once you have the drivers installed, complete the operating system setup by installing any additional applications and then performing the optimization steps. It's probably worth checking that the graphics card has been installed correctly, by checking the device manager of the virtual desktop machine, as shown in the following screenshot:

You should now have a GPU-enabled virtual desktop image ready to be prepared for delivery to end users, which we will cover later in this chapter.

Due to the nature of GPU-enabled virtual desktop machines, the best way to deploy additional machines will be by cloning the virtual desktop machines and then making sure that each one is assigned to its own GPU resource.

Completing the GPU-enabled desktop build

With the operating system now built and the NVIDIA components installed, you can follow the remaining tasks to complete the build. These are all covered in the previous section and are listed as follows:

- Installing VMware Tools
- Installing applications for the parent image
- Installing the Horizon View Agent
- Optimizing the guest operating system
- Post-optimization tasks

With these tasks complete, you will now have three virtual desktop machines built to use as the parent image ready to create new virtual desktop machines to deliver to your end users.

Before we look at the final preparation steps, we are going to create one final virtual desktop machine, this time using a Linux-based operating system.

Linux virtual desktop machines

The final virtual desktop that we are going to build is for Linux operating system, and for this example, *CentOS* is going to be the **Linux distribution** that is used.

The process is almost the same as that used for installing a Windows-based operating system; however, there are some differences when it comes to installing the Horizon View Agent. The process starts with creating the virtual desktop machine itself.

Creating the virtual desktop machine container

As with creating the previous virtual desktop machines, the first thing we need to do is build and configure the actual virtual desktop machine on the vCenter Server. This will define the virtual hardware configuration. To define the configuration, follow these steps:

1. Open a browser and log in to the vSphere Web Client for the vCenter **vcs1.pvolab.com.**
2. Navigate to the Data center where you want to create the virtual desktop. In the example lab, the data center is called **PVO's Datacenter**.
3. Click and highlight the data center name, right-click, and from the contextual menu, hover your mouse over the option for **New Virtual Machine** until another menu appears, and then from that menu, select the **New Virtual Machine** option.
4. The **New Virtual Machine** configuration window will now open.
5. Click on **Create a new virtual machine**, and then click the **Next** button. You will now see the **Select a name and folder** screen.
6. In the **Enter a name for the virtual machine** box (**1**), type in a name for the new virtual desktop machine. In this example, this is called **Linux Desktop**.

7. Then, in the **Select a location for the virtual machine** section (**2**), click to highlight the data center where you want this virtual machine to be created. In the example lab, this machine is going to be created in the data center called **PVO's Datacenter**:

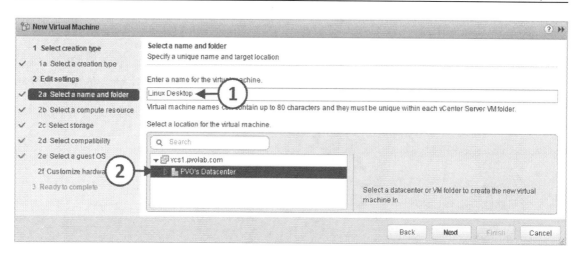

8. Click the **Next** button to continue.

9. You will now see the **Select a compute resource** screen.

10. Expand the data center called **PVO's Datacenter** and then click on the ESX server you want to host this virtual desktop. In the example lab, **esx-1.pvolab.com** is going to be the host server.

11. Click the **Next** button to continue. You will now see the **Select storage** screen.

12. Select the datastore where this virtual desktop machine will be stored. In the example lab, the virtual desktop machine is stored on the **Tintri T820**.

13. Click the **Next** button to continue.

14. You will now see the **Select compatibility** screen. This is where we will choose the virtual machine version for our virtual desktop machine. As the page says, for the best performance, you should use Version 11, which means using vSphere 6 as the hosting platform. We also need vSphere 6, as that is the platform that supports features such as Instant Clones and vGPU.

15. If you choose hardware version 9 or greater, remember that you will need to manage this virtual desktop machine by using the vSphere Web Client and not the old C# console.

16. From the drop-down menu, select **ESXi 6.0 and later** and then click the **Next** button to continue. You will now see the **Select a guest OS** screen.

17. The next step is to choose the operating system for the virtual desktop machine. In this example, this is the second virtual desktop machine, which we will build as a Windows 10 machine.

18. From the **Guest OS Family** box, click the arrow for the drop-down menu (3), and select **Linux**. Then, from the **Guest OS Version** box, click the arrow for the drop-down menu (4) and select **CentOS 4/5/6/7 (64-bit)**. The guest OS selection is important, as it determines which drivers get installed when VMware Tools is installed:

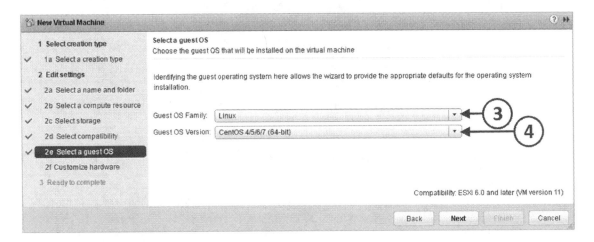

19. Click the **Next** button to continue.

20. You will now see the **Customize Hardware** screen, where you will configure the virtual hardware specification for the virtual desktop machine.

21. There are a couple of things to change on this configuration screen. First, this virtual machine is going to have 2 vCPUs. In the **CPU** box, click the down arrow and select **2** from the drop-down menu.

22. Unlike the Windows virtual desktop machines, the network adapter is automatically configured for **VMXNET 3**.

23. In the last part of the hardware configuration, as with the previous configuration, you need to change one of the boot options so that the next time the virtual desktop machine powers on and boots, it goes straight into the BIOS setup screen.

24. To configure the boot options, click the **VM Options** tab, and then expand the arrow for **Boot Options**. In the **Force BIOS Setup (*)** section, check the box for **The next time the virtual machine boots, force entry into the BIOS setup screen**.

25. Once you have completed the configuration, click the **Next** button to continue. You will now see the **Ready to complete** screen.

26. Click the **Finish** button to complete the configuration. With the Linux virtual desktop machine now built and configured, it's time to power it on and continue the build process by configuring the BIOS settings.

Updating the virtual desktop machine BIOS

As with the other virtual desktop machines that we have created previously, you need to power on the newly created Linux virtual desktop machine and make some configuration changes to the BIOS settings.

Make exactly the same changes as made previously, and disable floppy drives, serial ports, and parallel ports. Once complete, save the changes and restart the virtual desktop.

Installing the guest operating system

With the BIOS updated, you can now go ahead and install the guest operating system:

1. Ensure that the virtual desktop machine is powered on and then, from the vSphere Web Client, in the **Inventory** section, highlight the **Linux Desktop** virtual desktop machine. Click on the **Summary** tab and then, in the **VM Hardware** section, click on the down arrow next to the entry for **CD/DVD drive 1**.

2. From the menu that pops up, select **Connect to CD/DVD image on a datastore...**.

3. In the example lab, we've copied the ISO images for the operating systems that we are going to build onto a datastore on the ESXi host servers, in a folder called **ISO Images**.

4. Click on the **Tintri T820** folder to expand it and then highlight the **ISO Images** folder, highlight the **CentOS-7-x86_64-DVD-1511.iso** file and click **OK**. The CentOS installer will now launch.

Follow the CentOS installation steps until you have built a CentOS desktop operating system instance.

 Ensure that when you are building this virtual machine, you select the option for Desktop or Minimal Desktop.

Once built, apply any updates and patches, as well as install any applications you want to add as part of the image.

Installing VMware Tools

The next step is to install VMware Tools. In this particular example, VMware Tools is automatically installed on the CentOS operating system as part of the build.

Installing the Horizon View Agent

Now we can install the Horizon View Agent. The installation process is a little different to previous installations, as this is a Linux-based operating system:

1. You can either download the Horizon View Agent for Linux installer from the VMware download website, using the Linux desktop, or in the example lab, the installer was copied onto the Linux desktop using WinSCP.
2. The `file.tar` file **VMware-horizonagent-linux-x86_64-7.0.0-3617131.tar.gz (1)** is copied, and then extracted to get the installer, as shown in the following screenshot:

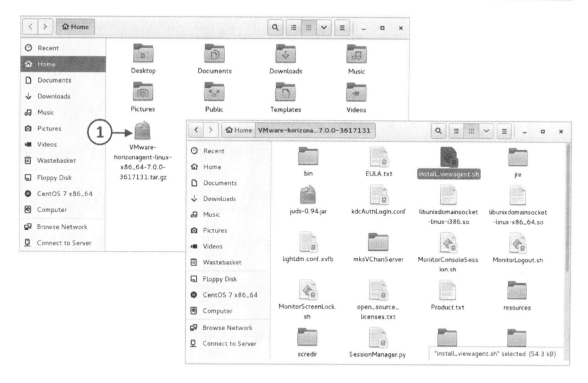

3. With the software extracted, the next task is to run the installer script.

4. From the desktop of the Linux virtual desktop, open a Terminal session by clicking **Applications**, **Favourites** (1) and then **Terminal** (2), as shown in the following screenshot:

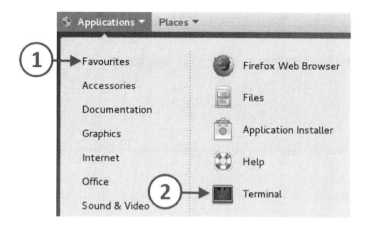

5. Once you have an open Terminal session, change to the directory where the VMware View Agent software was extracted to, as shown in the following example:

```
Desktop     Pictures    VMware-horizonagent-linux-x86_64-7.0.0-3617131
Documents   Public      VMware-horizonagent-linux-x86_64-7.0.0-3617131.tar.gz
Downloads   Templates
Music       Videos
[root@linux-desktop pvo]# cd VMware-horizonagent-linux-x86_64-7.0.0-3617131/
```

6. Next, launch the installer script using the following syntax and options, as shown in the following screenshot:

```
pvo@linux-desktop:~
File  Edit  View  Search  Terminal  Help
[pvo@linux-desktop ~]$ ./install_viewagent.sh -b hzn7-cs1.pvolab.com
-d pvolab.com -u administrator -p xxxxxxxxxx
```

7. The switch options used are as follows:

Syntax	Description
-b connectionserver.domain.com	Fully qualified name of the connection server
-d domain.com	Name of your domain
-u username	Username of account that has Agent Registration Administrators permission on the connection server
-u password	Password for the above account

8. When the installer scripts launch, you will first see the EULA message. At the bottom of the screen, you will see the **Are you sure you want to install linux agent y/n?** prompt. Type **Y** and then press **Enter**:

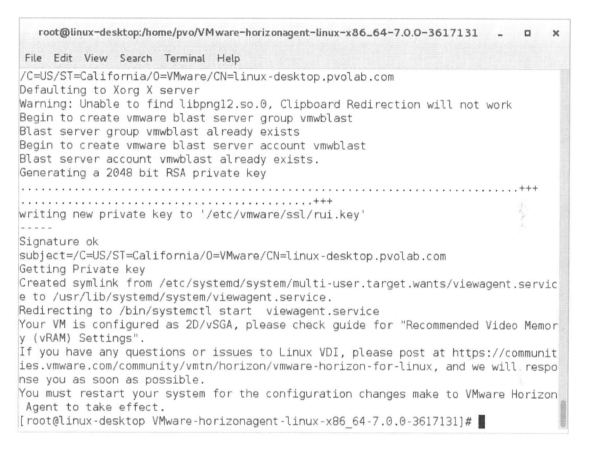

The Horizon Agent for Linux has now been successfully installed. As requested, restart the virtual desktop machine to complete the installation.

Optimizing the guest operating system

Unlike with Windows-based operating systems, there is no automated optimization tool available; however, you should still look at optimizing the image by switching off any tasks or applications that take up unnecessary resources, such as disk I/O or CPU cycles. You also need to ensure that you configure the operating system to work with Active Directory authentication.

Post-optimization tasks

Now that we have completed all the build tasks, all that remains is ensuring there is no fixed IP address and that DHCP has been selected, and then clearing up any temporary files, browser histories, and so on. Once you have finished these tasks, power off the virtual desktop machine, which is ready for us to prepare the image as our virtual desktop machine template.

Preparing virtual desktops for delivery

Now that we have our fully optimized virtual desktop machine parent images that can be used by Horizon View, the next stage of the process is to prepare them for delivery to the end users. There are two different ways in which a desktop needs to be prepared, depending on whether you are using a Full Clone desktop or a linked/instant clone desktop.

Pool design – a quick recap

We will cover creating desktop pools in more detail in Chapter 7, *Managing and Configuring Desktop Pools*, but for now, let's just have a quick recap around pool design and where the images that we created in this chapter are going to be used.

You will typically have a desktop pool for each type of virtual desktop machine you want to deliver, probably categorized by use case or department. In this chapter, we have built several different types of virtual desktop machines, which will be used in the following desktop pools:

- **Windows 7**: This is to be used as a floating assignment, Linked Clone desktop
- **Windows 7**: This is to be used as a dedicated, Full Clone with hardware-enabled GPU
- **Windows 10**: This is to be used as a floating assignment, Instant Clone desktop
- **CentOS 7**: This is to be used as a dedicated Linux desktop

As we have Linked Clone, Full Clone, and Instant Clone desktops, the preparation method for each is different. We will cover this in the following sections.

Creating a snapshot for Linked Clones

The first virtual desktop machine we are going to prepare for delivery is for the Windows 7 floating, Linked Clone virtual desktop machine. To prepare this image for delivery, we will need to take a snapshot of the virtual desktop machine using vCenter and the vSphere Web Client. Once you have taken the snapshot, it can then be used by the View Administrator to create a new desktop pool for virtual desktop machines using Linked Clones. It will be used to create the replica in View Composer:

1. To create the snapshot, log in to the vSphere Web Client and navigate to the **Windows 7 Gold Image** virtual desktop machine (**1**), ensuring that it's powered off.

2. Click on the virtual desktop machine to highlight it, right-click, and from the menu that pops ups, move the cursor to hover over **Snapshots (2)**, and then select the option for **Take Snapshot... (3)**, as shown in the following screenshot:

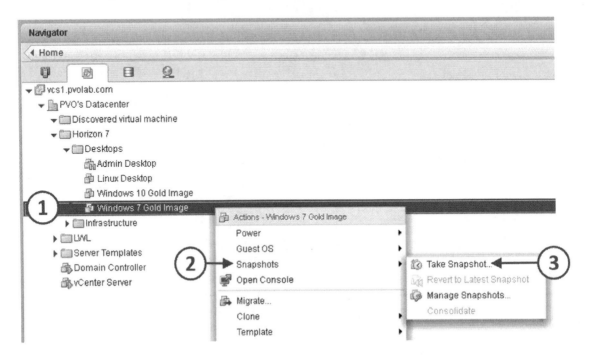

3. You will now see the **Take VM Snapshot for Windows 7 Gold Image** dialog box, as shown in the following screenshot:

4. Type in a name for this snapshot in the **Name** box, and then type in a description to describe the purpose of the snapshot in the **Description** box.
5. Click the **OK** button when you are ready to create the snapshot.
6. To check that the snapshot has been taken, navigate to the snapshot manager.
7. To do this, from the vSphere Web Client, highlight the **Windows 7 Gold Image** virtual desktop machine. Right-click, and from the menu that pops up, move the cursor to hover over **Snapshots (2)**, and then select the option for **Manage Snapshots....**

8. You will now see the **Manage VM Snapshots for Windows 7 Gold Image** dialog box, where you will be able to see the snapshot that was just taken, as shown in the following screenshot:

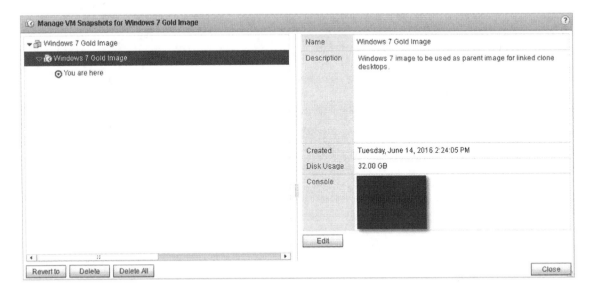

9. You will now be able to see how many snapshots have been taken and also when they were created. This will help with the version control of your parent images.

10. Click on **Close** to close the snapshot manager.

You have now successfully taken a snapshot that can be used as the base image for all virtual desktop machines that are created from it. We will see how this snapshot is used to deliver the Linked Clone virtual desktop machines in `Chapter 7`, *Managing and Configuring Desktop Pools*.

Creating a snapshot for Instant Clones

The next image to prepare for delivery is the Windows 10 image. As this is going to be used with an Instant Clone desktop pool, then the base image again starts off life as a snapshot of the parent image.

To create the snapshot, follow the process described in the previous section to create a new snapshot of the **Windows 10 Gold Image** virtual desktop machine.

Creating a template for Full Clones

For the second Windows 7 virtual desktop machine (with GPU enabled), and the CentOS Linux virtual desktop machines, you need to perform the tasks as described in this section.

To use these virtual desktop machines as parent virtual desktop machines for Full Clone desktops, you will first need to convert them into a virtual machine template, or use the clone to template feature using vCenter and the vSphere Web Client.

Once that's completed, you can then use the View Administrator to create new desktop pools (one for Linux and one for Windows 7 GPU), based on the virtual desktop machines using these templates for each desktop pool.

In the example lab, we will use the Windows 7 image. The process for creating the Linux virtual desktop machine is exactly the same, so repeat these instructions to create the template for that particular operating system. However, the pool configuration will be different for each one, as we will see in Chapter 7, *Managing and Configuring Desktop Pools*:

1. To create the snapshot, log in to the vSphere Web Client and navigate to the **Windows 7 Gold Image** virtual desktop machine (**1**), ensuring that it's powered off.

2. Click on the virtual desktop machine to highlight it, right-click, and from the menu that pops ups, move the cursor to hover over **Clone (2)**, and then select the option for **Clone to Template... (3)**, as shown in the following screenshot:

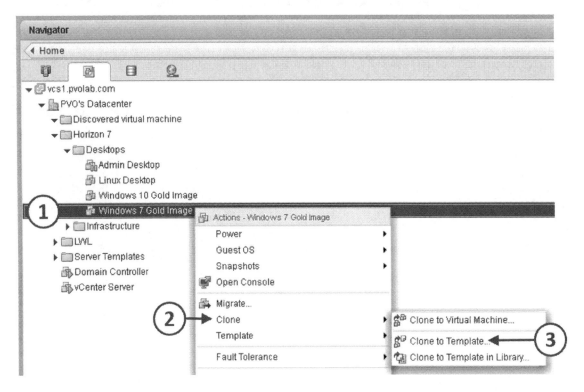

3. You will now see the **Windows 7 Gold Image – Clone Virtual Machine to Template** configuration dialog box.
4. In the **Enter a name for the template** box (4), type in a name for the template. In the example lab, this is called **Windows 7 Gold Image Template**.

5. Then, in the **Select a location for the template** section, click to highlight the data center where you want this virtual machine to be created (6). In the example lab, this machine is going to be created in the data center called **PVO's Datacenter**, as shown in the following screenshot:

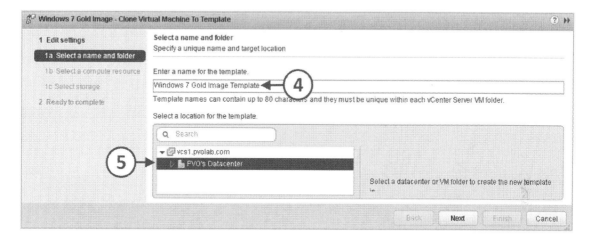

6. Click the **Next** button to continue.
7. You will now see the **Select a compute resource** screen. Expand the data center called **PVO's Datacenter** and then click on the ESX server you want to host this template. In the example lab, **esx-1.pvolab.com** is going to be the host server.
8. Click the **Next** button to continue.
9. You will now see the **Select storage** screen. Select the datastore where this template will be stored. In the example lab, the template is stored on the **Tintri T820** datastore.
10. Click the **Next** button to continue. You will now see the **Ready to complete** screen.
11. Click the **Finish** button to complete the configuration and to create the virtual desktop machine template for Windows 7.

You have now successfully created a template that can be used as the parent image from which to create new virtual desktop machine from. Repeat the same process and create a template for the Linux desktop virtual machine, and call the template Linux Desktop Template. Once completed, if you navigate to the VMs and Templates view in vCenter, you will see the following:

> 🗔 Linux Desktop Template
> 🗔 Windows 7 Gold Image Template

We will use these templates in Chapter 7, *Managing and Configuring Desktop Pools*, to start creating virtual desktop machines for the end users.

Summary

In this chapter, we have built several virtual desktop machine images that will act as the parent images from which all the virtual desktop machines in the environment will be created.

To build the virtual desktop machines, we outlined a process to follow a process in which you started by creating the virtual hardware containers, installing the guest operating systems, optimizing them to run as Horizon View virtual desktop machines, and then prepared them by creating either templates or snapshots ready to be used to create virtual desktop machines to be delivered to the end users.

In the next chapter, we will configure the View Administrator and create the desktop pools, ready to deliver our virtual desktop machines to our end users, which will allow them to connect and start using the different virtual desktop machines.

7
Managing and Configuring Desktop Pools

Now that you have prepared a number of desktop images in the previous chapter, the next step is to configure desktop pools that will deliver these desktops to the end users, and so in this chapter, we will look at how to create and manage desktop pools within Horizon View. In Chapter 2, *An Overview of Horizon View Architecture and Components*, and Chapter 3, *Design and Deployment Considerations*, we discussed the use cases for the different types of desktop pools within View. To recap, desktop pools are collections of one or more virtual desktop machines that have similar attributes. By this, we mean that they have the same operating system versions, applications, memory, CPU, or other configuration. Different desktop pools can also be built and assigned differently. For example, one pool may be built using Linked Clones, and another could have a dedicated user assignment. The types of pools available are as follows:

- Automated desktop pool
- Manual desktop pool
- RDS desktop pool

So, let's take two minutes to describe what each of these types of pool is used for:

An automated desktop pool is a collection of desktops that are automatically created from a snapshot or a virtual machine template by Horizon View. Desktops within an automated pool may be created on demand or built in advance. They can also be deleted or refreshed on logoff. Automated pools are generally the most widely used pools within Horizon View deployments, as they allow great flexibility for administration.

A manual desktop pool provides access to an existing desktop, whether it is virtual or physical, just so long as it has the View Agent installed on it. A manual pool is used for niche use cases due to the administrative overhead. Also, you would generally use an **image management tool**, such as VMware Mirage or *SCCM*, with these machines to simplify the management as far as possible.

Finally, an RDS desktop pool is a great way of offering high levels of consolidation for task workers within your Horizon View environment. An example of where an RDS desktop might be suitable would be for call center users, where the user is using one or two simple applications and doesn't require a full-blown desktop. We will cover RDS desktops in `Chapter 9`, *Delivering Session-Based Desktops with Horizon View*.

In the following sections, we are going to configure the different pool options using the example lab and the parent desktop images created in the previous chapter.

Automated desktop pools

Automated desktop pools will be the largest use case within our Horizon View environment, and so we will start by looking at how to create and manage them first.

As you start running through the configuration wizards to create the automated desktop pools, you will be asked a number of questions that will further define how the users will use the desktop pool. The first of these questions is, how is the desktop going to be assigned to the end users?

The first option is for creating dedicated desktop assignments. Along with this option, you will get the choice of having an automatic assignment. Dedicated desktops are generally used due to something being stored or configured within the user's desktop that is important for that user, or due to application-specific nuances (for example, a licensing restriction that requires a specific MAC address to be used). This means that every time the user wants to connect to a desktop, they will always be given the same desktop.

 Dedicated desktops can be built as either Full Clones or Linked Clones.

With a dedicated desktop that is built using Linked Clones, you can also add a persistent disk to the virtual desktop to save all the changes that happen to the desktop while the user is using it. If you then need to refresh or recompose the desktop operating system, then the user won't lose the customization or their personal data stored on their desktop, as they are stored on a separate disk. However, you need to keep in mind that there is no easy way to back up the persistent disks and, as such, you might decide to use another tool to protect and update these desktops.

Creating dedicated, Linked Clone desktop pools

In this section, we will now work through the configuration wizard to create the first desktop pool for a dedicated Windows 7 desktop, built as a Linked Clone desktop using the Windows 7 gold image snapshot created in the previous chapter.

To create the pool, we are going to work through following steps using the **Horizon View Administrator console**:

1. From a workstation, open a browser and enter the address details of the View Connection Server. In the example lab, `https://hzn7-cs1.pvolab.com/admin` is the address for the Connection Server.

2. You will now see the **View Administrator** login screen. Log in using the account that was set up for the **View Administrator**. You will now see the Horizon View Administrator dashboard screen:

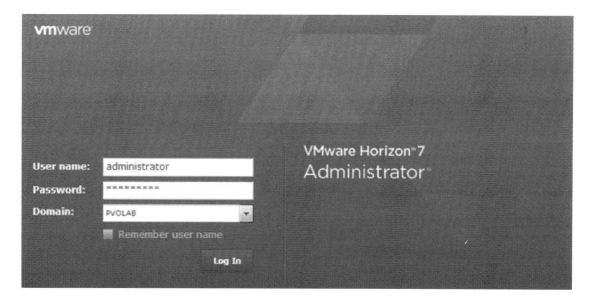

3. From the Horizon View Administrator, click to expand the **Catalog** option (**1**), and then click on **Desktop Pools** (**2**). Then, from the **Desktop Pools** pane, click the **Add** button (**3**), as shown in the following screenshot:

4. You will now see the **Add Desktop Pool** screen. Click the radio button for **Automated Desktop Pool** (**4**), and then click the **Next >** button (**5**), as shown in the following screenshot:

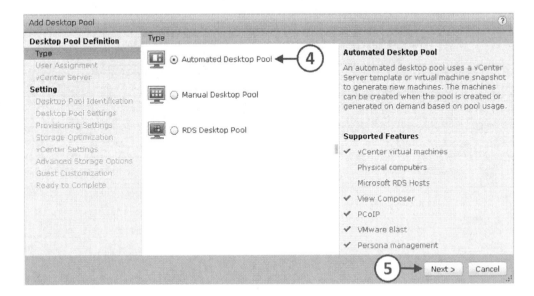

When selecting the various types of desktop pools that are available, the description on the right-hand side will change, reminding you of the differences between types.

5. You will now see the **User Assignment** screen, as shown in the following screenshot:

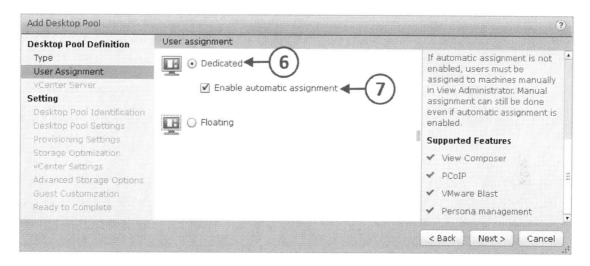

6. Click the radio button for **Dedicated** (6). The **Enable automatic assignment** option (7) will already be selected by default. This means the desktops will be assigned to the users on a first-come-first-served basis, as they log in. If for some reason you need to ensure a user is assigned a specific desktop, then you will need to uncheck this box and manually assign them a virtual desktop machine.

7. Click the **Next>** button (3) to continue the configuration. Next, you will configure how the virtual desktops machines will be built, as shown in the following screenshot:

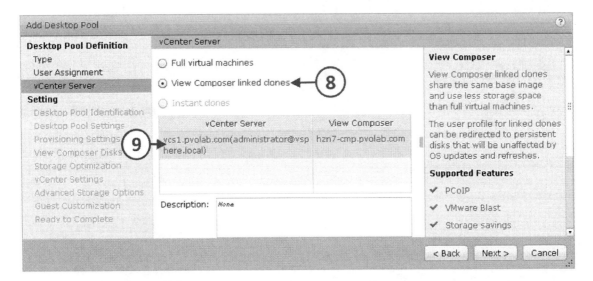

On this configuration screen, you have the option to build either Full Clone or Linked Clone virtual desktop machines.

1. For this first pool, we are going to use Linked Clones, so click the radio button for **View Composer linked clones** (8). Next, you need to select the relevant vCenter Server from the list. In the example lab, the vCenter we are using is **vcs1.pvolab.com** (9).

2. Click the **Next>** button to continue the configuration. The next configuration screen is for the **Desktop Pool Identification**, as shown in the following screenshot:

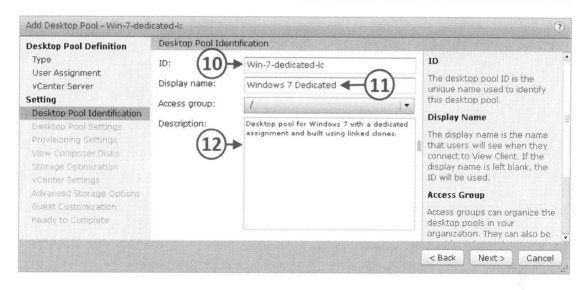

3. In the **ID** box **(10)**, type in an ID for this desktop pool. In the example lab, this is called **Win-7-dedicated-lc**.

You can only use the characters **a-z**, **A-Z**, **0-9**, **–**, and _ in the pool ID.

4. In the **Display name** box **(11)**, type in a name for this pool. Bear in mind that the display name is what is displayed to the end users, so make sure you give it a non-technical name that the users will understand.

5. Finally, in the **Description** box **(12)**, type in a more detailed description, which describes the desktop pool. Click the **Next>** button to continue the configuration.

6. You will now see the **Desktop Pool Settings** configuration screen, as shown in the following screenshot:

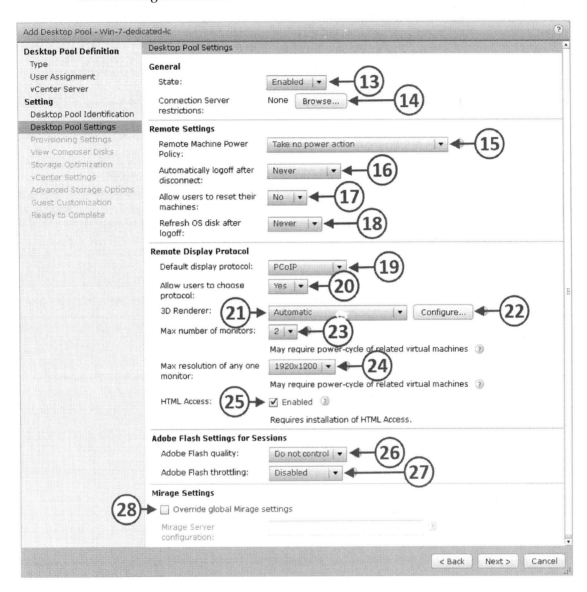

This screen is where we start to configure the settings that will define the way the desktop behaves within the desktop pool for users before they connect, while they use it, and finally, once they disconnect from it.

We are going to configure the desktop pool with the following settings:

1. First, in the **General** section, you can configure the **State** of the desktop pool. From the drop-down menu, select the **Enabled** option (**13**) to enable this pool, meaning that it will be available to users who are entitled to use it and the desktops will be provisioned and made available for the users too. If you set the **State** to **Disabled**, provisioning will not happen and the desktop will not be made available. You might want to set the **State** to **Disabled** if you are pre-configuring a new pool for users.

2. The second option under the **General** section is for **Connection Server restrictions**, where you are able to select tags associated with the Connection Servers to restrict where the users can connect from. Click the **Browse...** button (**14**) to configure the restrictions, as shown in the following screenshot:

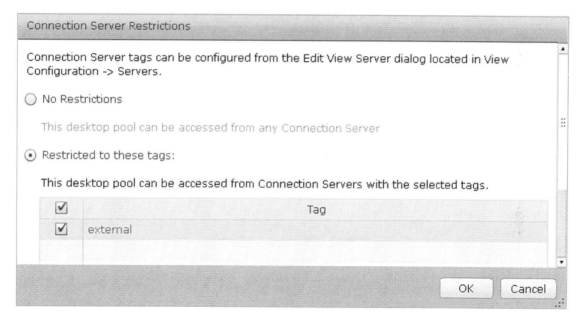

In this example, the restrictions have been configured so that the desktop pool can only be accessed by Connection Servers configured with the external tag:

1. The next section to configure is for the **Remote Settings**. These settings define the power state of the virtual desktops and what happens when users connect and disconnect.

2. Fist we have the **Remote Machine Power Policy** option, which defines the power state of the desktop when users connect and disconnect. Click on the drop-down menu (15) and you will see the following options:

- **Take no power action**: The virtual desktop machines will remain in the last state they were left in. For example, if the desktop was left powered on, then it will remain powered on.
- **Ensure machines are always powered on**: The virtual desktop machines will always be restored to a powered-on status after being shut down by an end user or an administrative task.
- **Power Off** : Virtual desktop machines will be powered off when a user logs off.
- **Suspend:** Virtual desktop machines will be suspended when a user logs off.

Suspend is not available when using NVIDIA GRID vGPU desktops.

When configuring power policies, the most important thing to do is to understand your use case and choose the correct options as appropriate. For example, if you have 200 users all planning to log in within a 10-minute window at 9:00 AM and the desktops are powered off or suspended, this could cause some delay and a large performance spike while the desktops are resumed or powered on. Alternatively, if you are using a dedicated desktop model with a shift-based work pattern and choose to leave the desktops always powered on, this could cause your environment to be over-allocated in terms of desktop resources, as well as potentially requiring more licenses than you actually use.

1. The next setting is for **Automatically logoff after disconnect**. This option allows you to define what happens when a user simply disconnects from their desktop and doesn't choose to log off.
2. Click the drop-down menu (**16**) for the available options, which are described as follows:
   - **Immediately**: When the user disconnects from the virtual desktop machine it is immediately logged off.
   - **Never**: When the user disconnects from the virtual desktop machine it is never logged off.
   - **After**: When the user disconnects from the virtual desktop machine it is logged off after a set period of time. You can choose how many minutes before the desktop will be logged off.

Again, how you configure this setting will very much depend on how your users will use the desktop. Very rarely would you choose to log off the desktop immediately, in case the user has only temporarily disconnected from their desktop or been disconnected due to a network drop out. You should give them at least a 5 to 10-minute window to allow them to reconnect.

1. The next setting to configure is **Allow users to reset their machines (17)**. If this option is set to **Yes**, it means that the users are able to effectively use a reset button to hard reset the virtual desktop machine. This can be a useful feature to allow end users to perform troubleshooting steps without the assistance of IT. However, it can also cause some confusion when the end user believes they are simply resetting the endpoint device but instead are resetting their virtual desktop machine. If this is a Linked clone desktop, then they could end up with a completely new virtual desktop and lose any current work.

2. The final setting in this section is for **Refresh OS disk after logoff**. As this pool is created from Linked Clone images, this option defines how the operating system disk of the Linked Clone behaves when a user logs off.

3. Click the drop-down menu **(18)** for the available options, which are described as follows:

   - **Never**: The operating system disk will never be refreshed automatically; this will result in the Linked Clone growing over time, especially if a persistent disk and/or a disposable disk isn't configured in the later stages of this wizard. By refreshing the OS disk, the disk is refreshed to a snapshot that is taken when the desktop is originally created. Without a persistent disk, redirected profiles, and so on, all user settings/data will be lost.
   - **Always**: The desktop will be refreshed every time the user logs off.
   - **Every**: Allows you to define the number of days after which the desktop will be refreshed.
   - **At**: Allows you to set at what percentage of OS disk utilization the desktop should be refreshed.

Again, as with the other configuration settings, how you configure these settings will depend greatly on your use cases and how your users work:

1. The following section we will configure is for **Remote Desktop Protocol**.
2. The first option in this section is to select the **Default display protocol**. From the drop-down menu (**19**), you have the options of Microsoft RDP, PCoIP, or VMware Blast to choose from, and then with the next setting, **Allow users to choose protocol** (**20**), you can give the users the choice of which protocol they want to use.

Typically, you would use PCoIP or VMware Blast as the default protocol, unless there is a specific use case that determines where RDP must be used, for example, where more than four screens are required or where a user will always be connected behind a very strict outbound firewall.

1. Next you can configure the **3D Renderer** options.

 To enable 3D rendering for this desktop pool, you need to select either PCoIP or VMware Blast as the protocol, and then configure the **Allow users to choose protocol** to be set to **No**. This setting also only applies to Windows 7 virtual desktops or later running on VMs with virtual hardware version 8 or later.

2. Click the drop-down menu (**21**) for the available options, which are described as follows:
   - **Automatic**: ESX reserves GPU resources on a first come, first served basis and, if they can't be fulfilled, will revert to software rendering.
   - **Software**: ESX uses software rendering only.
   - **Hardware**: Like Automatic, ESX reserves GPU resources on a first come, first served basis. If they can't be fulfilled, then the virtual desktop machine will not power on.
   - **Manage using vSphere Client**: 3D memory and the number of monitors will need to be configured using vCenter Server.
   - **NVIDIA GRID VGPU**: As with the preceding option, 3D memory and the number of monitors will need to be configured using vCenter Server.
   - **Disabled**: 3D rendering is not configured.

3. If you selected Automatic, Hardware, or Software as the 3D Renderer option, you will also see a **Configure...** button (**22**). If you click the button, you will see the following **Configure VRAM for 3D guests** box, as shown in the following screenshot:

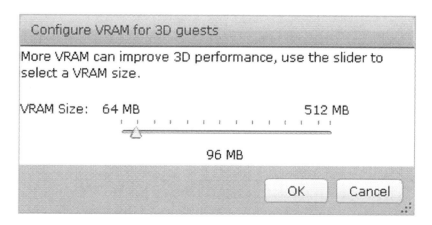

4. In this configuration box, you can move the slider to configure the amount of video memory for the virtual desktop machines to use up to a maximum of 512 MB.

5. The next option is to configure the **Max number of monitors** for each virtual desktop machine. This option is only available if you select PCoIP or VMware Blast as the protocol.

6. Click the drop-down menu next to the Max number of monitors box (**23**) to select the number of monitors. When the 3D renderer is disabled, View will support up to three monitors running at a resolution of *3840 x 2160* on a Windows 7 VM with Aero disabled. For other operating systems, or for Windows 7 with Aero enabled, the number of monitors supported drops to just one, running at the same resolution. When 3D is enabled, only a single monitor is supported, running at a resolution of *3840 x 2160*.

7. In the preceding section, we stated the maximum resolution. In the next configuration option, you can specify a resolution. Again, as previously mentioned, this option is only available if you select PCoIP or VMware Blast as the protocol.

8. If you click on the drop-down menu for **Max resolution for any one monitor** (**24**), you can select from the following resolutions: *1680 x 1050, 1920 x 1200, 2560 x 1600*, and *3840 x 2160*.

9. It's worth remembering that by selecting more monitors and/or higher resolutions, more video memory will be required and, potentially, more CPU resources will be consumed when an end user connects from a source that utilizes these resolutions or multiple monitors. However, with modern servers, the difference may be limited under normal circumstances. So, it is often easiest to select four monitors and the highest resolution.

10. The final setting in the **Remote Display Protocol** section is for **HTML Access**. To enable access to the virtual desktop from a browser, simply check the **Enable** box **(25)** next the **HTML Access** option. This can be useful when users connect from home or other devices where it is not possible to install the relevant client software on their device. For example, from an Internet cafe (do they even still exist?!) or from a Chromebook.

11. Next up are the **Adobe Flash Setting for Session** options. This section defines how a virtual desktop machine behaves when using Adobe Flash. Click the drop-down menu **(26)** for the available options, which are described as follows:

    - **Do not control**: This allows the web page to determine the best setting
    - **Low** (default): Low quality means less bandwidth consumption
    - **Medium**: Medium quality means average bandwidth consumption
    - **High**: High quality means more bandwidth consumption

12. The other configurable setting for Adobe Flash is for **Adobe Flash throttling**. Adobe Flash updates the screen by default, using a timer service to determine the update interval. By changing this time interval setting, you can control the frame rate of the screen updates and therefore reduce the bandwidth requirements.

13. Click the drop-down menu **(27)** for the available options, which are described as follows:

    - **Disabled**: Throttling is turned off
    - **Conservative**: The update interval is set to 100 ms
    - **Moderate**: The update interval is set to 500 ms
    - **Aggressive**: The update interval is set to 2,500 ms

14. The final configuration section to configure on this screen is for **Mirage Settings**. Checking the box for **Over-ride global Mirage settings (28)** allows you to specify a specific Mirage server to manage the virtual desktops in this pool rather than having different desktops managed by different Mirage servers.

15. As in this example we are using Linked Clone desktops, this option is not applicable. Nor does it support Instant Clone desktops.

16. Once you have completed the configuration settings on this screen, click on the **Next >** button to continue to the next configuration screen. This is the **Provisioning Settings** configuration screen, where you are going to configure how the virtual desktop machines are built, as shown in the following screenshot:

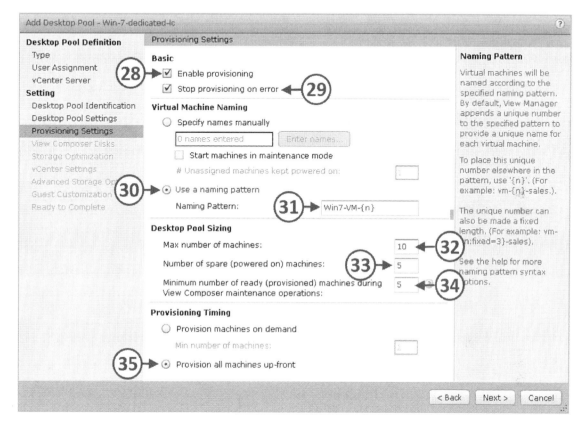

We are going to configure the desktop pool with the following settings:

1. First, in the **Basic** section, tick the **Enable provisioning** box (**28**) to switch provisioning on. Also check the **Stop provisioning on error** box (**29**) below it. Checking this box means that provisioning will halt if there is an error, rather than going ahead and continuing to provision hundreds of virtual desktop machines that have errors.

2. The next section to configure is the **Virtual Machine Naming** section. Here you can choose whether to specify names for the virtual desktop machines either manually or automatically, using a naming pattern. In the example lab, we are going to click the radio button for **Use a naming pattern** (**30**).

3. It is usual to use a naming pattern unless there is some reason your desktops need unique, noncontiguous names. While using the naming pattern, you are able to specify how many digits the unique number should have or where the unique number is to be appended in the name. This can be done simply by using `{n}` somewhere in the name for a single digit, or by adding `{n:fixed=2}` for two digits, `{n:fixed=3}` for three, and so on. This will ensure the desktops appear in numerical order.

4. In the **Naming Pattern** box (**31**), type in a name for the virtual desktop machines. In the example lab, and for this pool, we are going to enter `Win7-VM-{n}`. This will result in the virtual desktop machines being named `Win7-VM-1`, `Win7-VM-2`, and so on.

5. Next is the **Desktop Pool Sizing** section. In this section, you can specify the number of virtual desktop machines that are created and provisioned. In the **Max number of machines** box (**32**), enter the maximum number of machines that can be provisioned in this desktop pool. Then, in the Number of spare (powered on) machines (**33**) box, enter the number of machines that should be powered on and waiting for users to connect to them.

6. Finally, in this section, in the **Minimum number of ready (provisioned) machines during View Composer maintenance operations** box (**34**), enter a number of virtual desktop machines you want to have still available during maintenance.

7. How you configure these options is going to be critical to the success of the pool within your View Solution. You need to ensure that there are enough virtual desktop machines provisioned and available for the users as and when they are required. This also means ensuring that you are able to meet user demand even during maintenance operations.

8. The final section to configure is for Provisioning Timing. You have the option of provisioning machines on demand, as users log in and request them, or you can pre-provision them in advance. Click the radio button for **Provision all machines up-front** (**35**). This means that all the virtual desktop machines, the total number of which is whatever you entered as the maximum number of machines, will be created and provisioned in advance ready for users to connect and log in to.

9. If you are going to provision all the desktops upfront, you need to ensure that you do this at a time when the increase in performance is not going to have a knock-on effect for end users. If you choose to **Provision on-demand**, then you need to ensure there are enough desktops ready-provisioned to meet user demand without causing long delays. This is where making sure you have enough provisioned upfront versus number of spares.

10. Once you have completed the configuration settings on this screen, click the **Next >** button to continue to the next configuration screen. As this desktop pool is going to use virtual desktop machines from Linked Clones, the next configuration screen is the **View Composer Disks** configuration screen.

11. The first section to configure is for **Persistent Disk**. Careful consideration needs to be given as to whether or not you need to utilize these settings within your desktop pool architecture or not.

12. With a persistent disk, the Windows profile will be redirected to a dedicated disk that will be kept even if the OS disk is refreshed. This can be a great way to protect user configuration. However, you might also wish to investigate other solutions for this such as VMware View Persona Management, or Liquidware Labs ProfileUnity, which can offer you similar benefits without the complexity.

13. To configure this setting, click the radio button for **Redirect Windows profile to a persistent disk** (36). Then, in the **Disk size** box (37), enter a size for the persistent disk. Lastly, in the **Drive letter** drop-down box (38), you can select a drive letter for this persistent disk. If you don't want to use this option as you are using another profile management tool, click the radio button for **Do not redirect Windows profile**, as shown in the following screenshot:

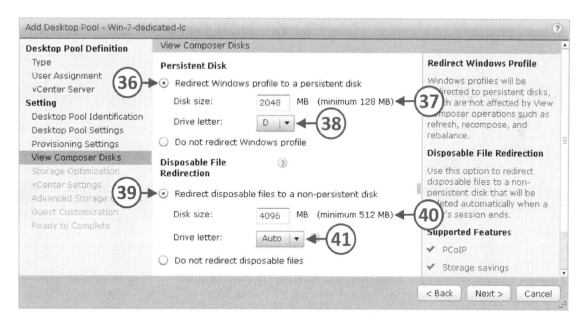

14. The final section on this configuration screen is for **Disposable File Redirection**. The disposable disk contains all page and temporary files and is refreshed after every desktop reboot. This can be a great way to reduce the size of the Linked Clone between desktop refreshes.

15. To configure this setting, click the radio button for **Redirect disposable files to a non-persistent disk** (**39**). Then, in the **Disk size** box (**40**), enter a size for the persistent disk. Lastly, in the **Drive letter** drop-down box (**41**), you can select a drive letter for this persistent disk, or allow this to be automatically selected. Again, as with the previous setting, if you don't want to use this option as you are using another profile management tool, then click the radio button for **Do not redirect disposable files**.

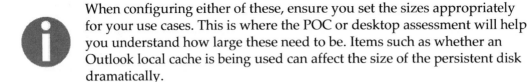 When configuring either of these, ensure you set the sizes appropriately for your use cases. This is where the POC or desktop assessment will help you understand how large these need to be. Items such as whether an Outlook local cache is being used can affect the size of the persistent disk dramatically.

16. Once you have completed the configuration settings on this screen, click the **Next >** button to continue to the next configuration screen.

17. The next configuration screen is the **Storage Policy Management** configuration screen, as shown in the following screenshot:

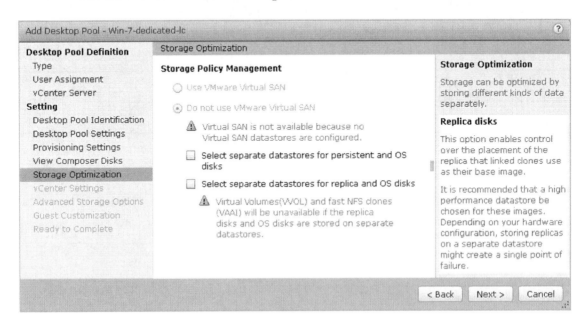

18. On this screen, you are able to configure advanced options with regard to storage management and the placement of the OS, persistent, and replica disks.

19. The first option is to configure VMware Virtual SAN. If there are no Virtual SAN datastores configured, as per the example lab configuration, then this option will not be available.

20. You then have the option to select the location of the various different disks that get created for the virtual desktops in this desktop pool. Horizon View effectively allows you to tier your storage and so, depending on your storage design, you might want to place the replica images on faster, local SSD-based storage and the OS disks on a different tier of storage, such as spinning hard drives.

21. In the example lab, we have a deployed a Tintri T820 hybrid array, which provides the maximum level of performance across the array. As such, there is no reason to place the replica disks on a different datastore to the OS. However, you could choose to place the persistent disks on a different volume to allow a data protection policy to be put in place to protect the data on the persistent disks.

22. In the example lab, we will not select any storage policy options and keep all the disks on the same datastore, so click the **Next >** button to continue to the next configuration screen.

23. The next configuration screen is the **vCenter Settings** configuration screen, as shown in the following screenshot:

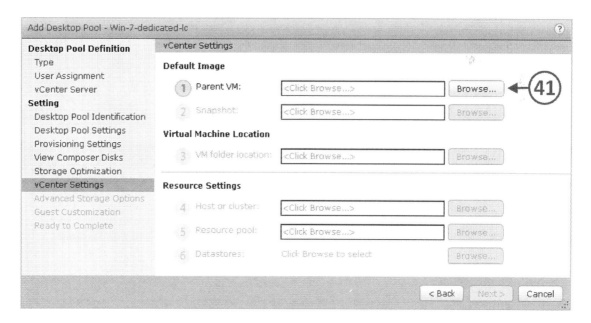

24. The first thing to configure is the details of the **Default Image** to be used as the parent image from which to create the virtual desktop machines for this desktop pool.

25. From here you select a valid VM. Valid means that these will be VMs that contain snapshots and have the Horizon View Agent installed within them. The VMs that will be filtered from the View by default are virtual machines running on ESX/ESXi hosts older than 4.0, VMs that don't have a snapshot, VMs with an unsupported guest OS, VMs already used by another desktop pool, and View Composer Replicas. It is possible to add these VMs to the View by pressing the **Show all partner VMs** button. However, if they are not compatible, you will not be able to select them.

26. In the **Parent VM** box, click the **Browse...** button (**41**). You will then see the **Select Parent VM** configuration box, as shown in the following screenshot:

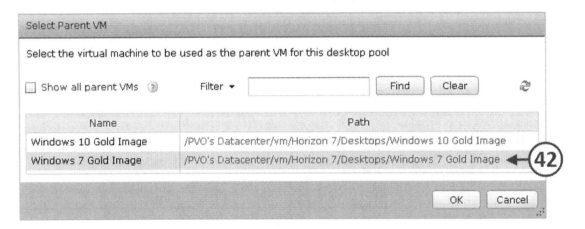

27. In this example, we are going to use the Windows 7 virtual desktop machine, so click the entry for **Windows 7 Gold Image** (**42**) and click the **OK** button.

28. You will return to the **vCenter Settings** configuration screen, where you will see that the details of the **Parent VM** are now entered. As this is a Linked Clone virtual desktop machine, the next configuration task is to configure the details of the snapshot that was created from the parent image.

29. Click the **Browse...** button (**43**), as shown in the following screenshot:

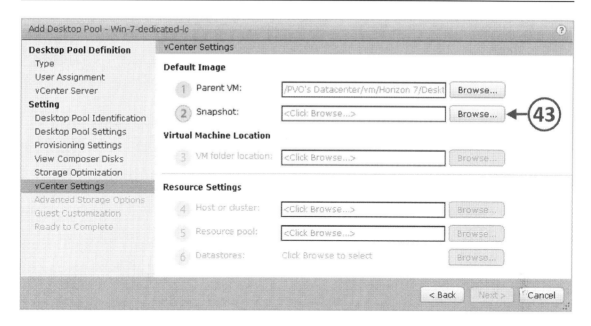

30. You will now see the **Select default image** configuration box, as shown in the following screenshot:

31. Click and select the **Windows 7 Gold Image** snapshot and then click the **OK** button.

32. You will return to the **vCenter Settings** configuration screen, where you will see that the details of the **Snapshot** are now entered.

33. The next section to configure is for the Virtual Machine Location.

35. In the **VM folder location** box, click the **Browse...** button (**44**), as shown in the following screenshot:

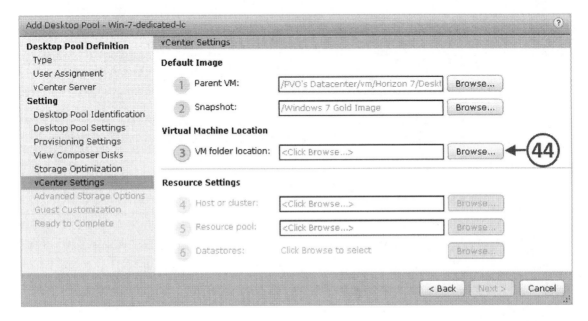

35. You will now see the **VM Folder Location** configuration screen, as shown in the following screenshot:

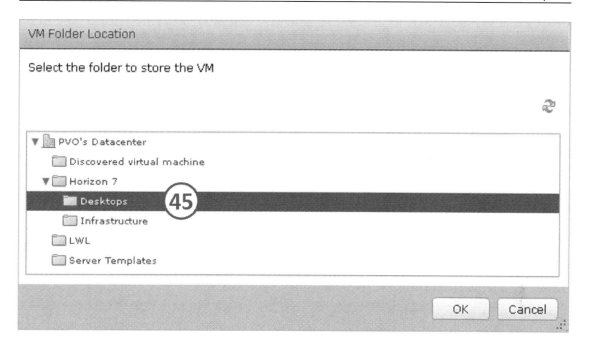

36. Select the folder into which you want to create the newly created virtual desktop machines.

You might want to consider a folder structure for the virtual machines to help with management, otherwise you could end up creating hundreds of different virtual desktop machines that reside in different pools, all in the same folder.

37. In the example lab, the virtual desktop machines are going to be stored in a folder called **Desktops**. Highlight the **Desktops** folder (**45**), and then click the **OK** button.

38. You will return to the **vCenter Settings** configuration screen, where you will see that the details of the **VM folder location** are now entered.

39. The next section is for configuring the **Resource Settings**, which allows you to configure the infrastructure components that will host the newly created virtual desktop machines.

40. In the **Host or cluster** box, click the **Browse...** button (**46**), as shown in the following screenshot:

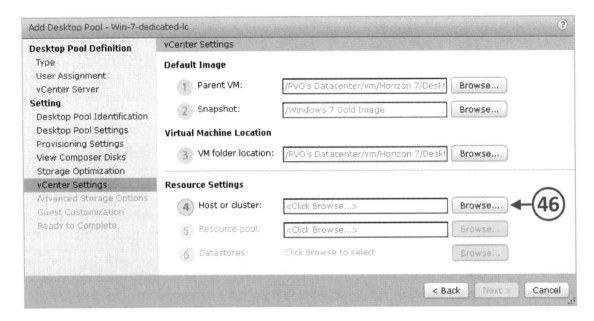

41. You will now see the **Host or Cluster** configuration screen, as shown in the following screenshot:

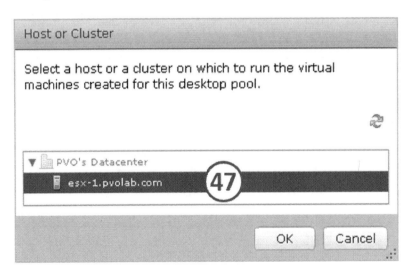

42. Select the host or cluster that will host the virtual desktop machines.

43. In the example lab, this is the ESXi host server called `esx-1`, so click and select the host server **esx-1.pvolab.com** (47), and then click the **OK** button.

 In a production environment, the hosting infrastructure used in this part of the configuration would be part of the desktop block hosting infrastructure.

44. You will return to the **vCenter Settings** configuration screen, where you will see that the details of the host server have now been entered. Next, in the **Resource pool** box, click the **Browse...** button (48):

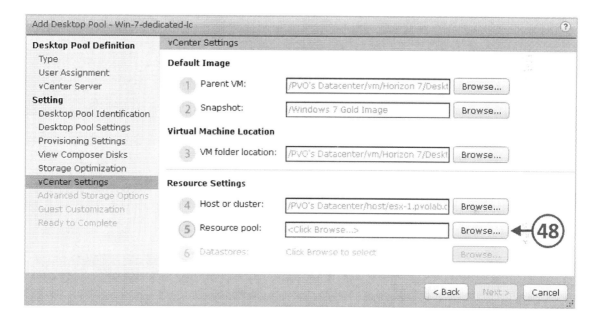

45. You will now see the **Resource Pool** configuration screen, as shown in the following screenshot:

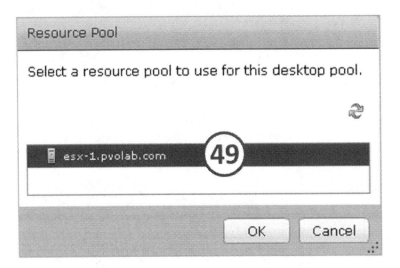

46. Select the resource pool that will be used to host the virtual desktop machines.
47. In the example lab, as there are no resource pools configured, click and select the host server **esx-1.pvolab.com (49)**, and then click the **OK** button.
48. You will return to the **vCenter Settings** configuration screen, where you will see that the details of the host server details have now been entered as the resource pool.
49. The final setting to configure on this configuration screen is the location of the datastores. In the example lab, we are using a single datastore, which was selected from the **Storage Optimization** settings screen. If you have opted to place the different disks on different datastores, you will now see options to configure the location for the OS disk datastore, persistent disk datastore, and replica disk datastore.

50. In the **Datastores** box, click the **Browse...** button **(50)**.

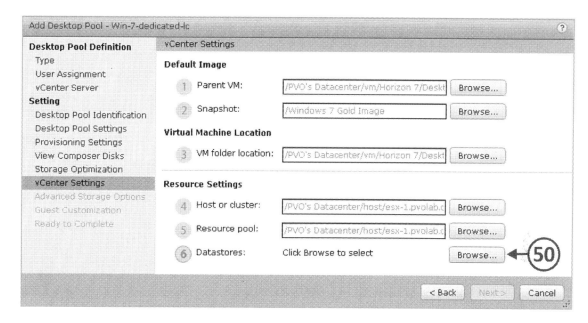

51. You will now see the **Select Linked Clone Datastores** configuration screen, which shows all available datastores, as shown in the following screenshot:

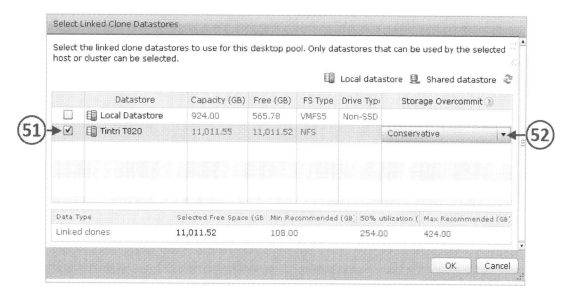

52. Check the box for **Tintri T820 (51)**. You then have the option to configure **Storage Overcommit**. The overcommit level represents the multiplier that, when applied to the capacity of the full desktop, gives you the amount you wish to allow in the datastore.

53. To configure an overcommit, click the drop-down menu **(52)**, from where you can select from the following options:
    - **None**: No overcommit allowed
    - **Conservative**: Allows four times overcommit
    - **Moderate**: Allows seven times overcommit
    - **Aggressive**: Allows fourteen times overcommit
    - **Unbounded**: Has no restriction

54. For example, if the size of your full desktop was 10 GB and you had a 100 GB datastore, then selecting **None** would allow you to provision 10 desktops, **Conservative** would allow you 40 desktops, **Moderate** would allow 70 desktops, **Aggressive** would allow 150 desktops, and **Unbounded** would have no restriction.

> You need to be careful when choosing how you are going to configure the overcommit setting, and the only real way to judge this is to monitor Linked Clone growth during the POC.

55. Once configured, click the **OK** button. You will return to the **vCenter Settings** configuration screen, where you will see that the details of the **Linked Clone Datastores** have now been entered, as shown in the following screenshot:

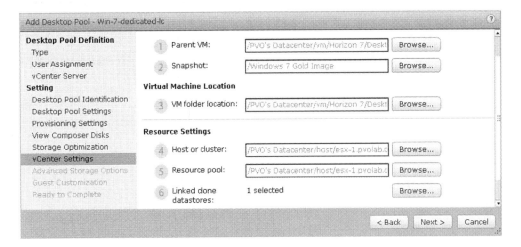

56. Once you have completed the configuration settings on this screen, click the **Next >** button to continue to the next configuration screen.

57. The next configuration screen is the **Advanced Storage Options** configuration screen, as shown in the following screenshot:

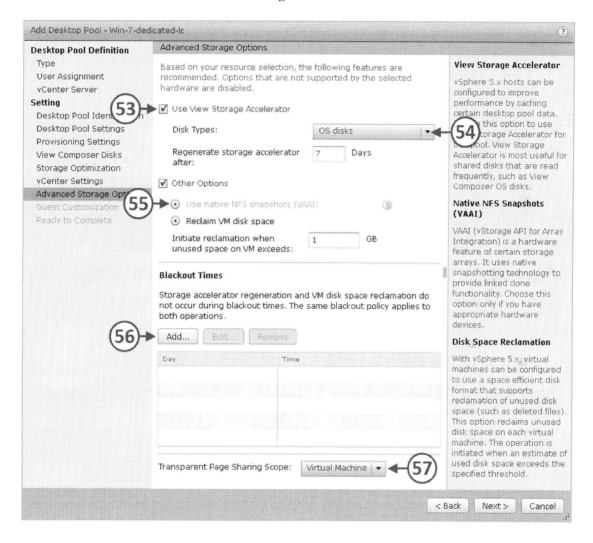

The first option on this configuration screen is for the View Accelerator, which enhances the performance by caching desktop pool data. Tick the **Use View Storage Accelerator** box **(53)** to enable it. You then have the option to select which disks the acceleration applies to. From the **Disk Types** box drop-down menu **(54)**, select the option for either **OS disks** or **OS and persistent disks**. In the example lab, select **OS disks**.

With NFS storage, you can configure VAAI API offloading of the Linked Clones to the storage device. As we are using a Tintri T820 storage array, which supports VAAI, click the radio button for **Use native NFS snapshots (VAAI)** **(55)**.

The other option in this section is for **Reclaim VM disk space**. This feature allows you to reclaim unused disk space.

Finally, the last option on this configuration screen is to configure blackout times for cache regeneration and space reclamation. This should be set to ensure that these operations won't be scheduled during working hours and ensure users are not affected.

1. To configure a blackout time, click the **Add...** button **(56)**. You will now see the **Set Blackout Days** configuration box, as shown in the following screenshot:

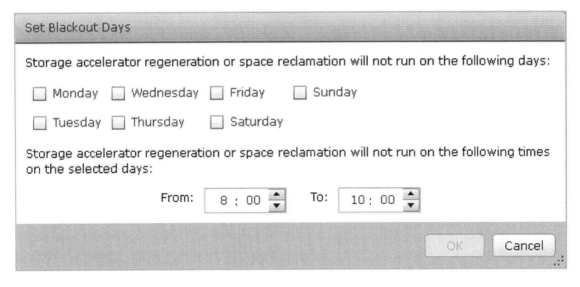

2. To configure a blackout day, tick the box for the days you want to prevent the regeneration or reclamation tasks from running, and then select a time window for the selected days.

3. Once configured, click the **OK** button to return to the **Advanced Storage Options** configuration screen.

4. Now click the **Next >** button to continue to the next configuration screen.

5. The next configuration screen is the **Guest Customization** configuration screen, as shown in the following screenshot:

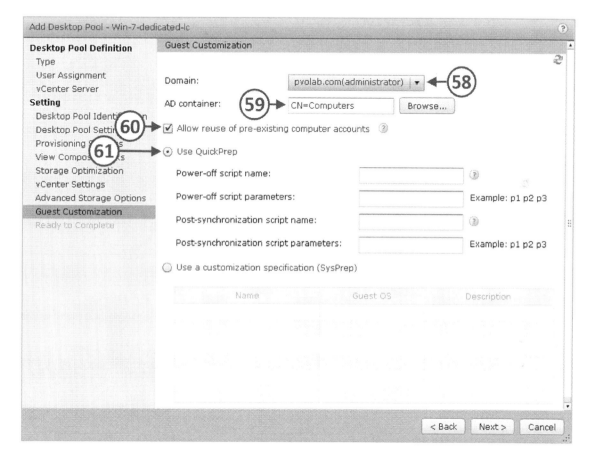

6. In the **Domain** box, from the drop-down menu (**58**), select the domain in which the newly created virtual desktop machines will reside.

7. Then, in the **AD container** box (**59**), type in the container name of where the desktop accounts should be created. By default, this is set to the **Computers** group in AD.

8. Next, tick the box for **Allow reuse of pre-existing computer accounts** (**60**). This means that computer accounts can be reused—useful when creating non-persistent desktops.

9. Finally, click the radio button for **Use QuickPrep**. QuickPrep will allow you to prepare your desktops in a quicker fashion than Sysprep. However, no unique SID will be created. Sysprep will create a new SID, but will take longer for each desktop to prepare. Which one you choose to use will depend on your use cases. It is recommended that you test your configuration during the POC.

10. Now click the **Next >** button to continue to the **Ready to Complete** screen, as shown in the following screenshot:

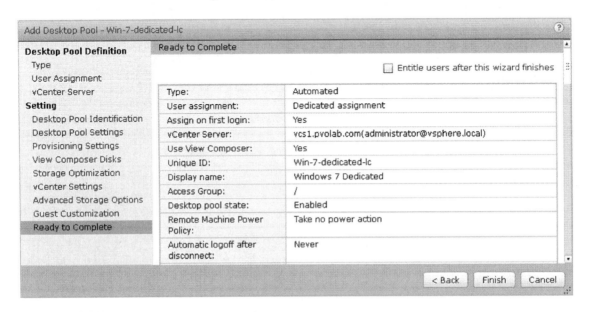

Review your configuration settings, and then click the **Finish** button to create the desktop pool. You have the option of ticking the **Entitle users after this wizard finishes** box at the top of the screen, which will automatically launch the entitlement configuration; however, in the example lab, we will do this later, after we have created some additional desktop pools.

You will now see that the pool has been created, as shown in the following screenshot:

In the following section, we are going to create another automated desktop pool, but this time you will create a pool built using Full clone desktops.

Creating dedicated, Full Clone desktop pools

The process for creating a dedicated, Full Clone desktop pool is pretty much the same as we covered in the previous section, with a few changes, as we configuring a Full Clone virtual desktop machine. As such, in this section we will just highlight the different configuration options:

1. From the Horizon View Administrator screen, click to expand the **Catalog** option, click on **Desktop Pools**, and then from the **Desktop Pools** pane click the **Add** button.

2. Then, on the **Add Desktop Pool** screen, click the radio button for **Automated Desktop Pool**, and then click the **Next >** button to continue to the **Assignment** screen.

3. On the **User Assignment** screen, click the radio button for **Dedicated**. The **Enable automatic assignment** option will already be selected by default. Click the **Next>** button to continue the configuration. You will now see the **vCenter Server** settings screen, as shown in the following screenshot:

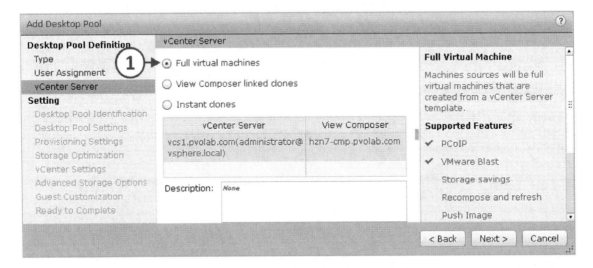

4. For this second pool, we are going to use Full Clones, so click the radio button for **Full virtual machines (1)**, and then select the relevant vCenter Server from the list. Again, in the example lab, the vCenter we are using is **vcs1.pvolab.com**.

5. Click the **Next>** button to continue the configuration. The next configuration screen is for the **Desktop Pool Identification**. Enter an **ID**, **Display name**, and **Description** for this pool that reflect the fact that it's a Windows 7 dedicated, Full Clone desktop pool.

6. Click the **Next >** button to continue. The next screen is for the **Desktop Pool Settings**. Configure your remote settings and remote display protocol and then click the **Next >** button to continue the configuration. Next up is the **Provisioning Settings** screen.

7. Ensure that provisioning is enabled by ticking the **Enable provisioning** box, as well as the box below it for **Stop provisioning on error**. Then enter a naming pattern for the newly created virtual desktop machines. Once completed, click the **Next >** button to continue the configuration.

8. The next configuration screen is for **Storage Optimization**. The only option you have on this screen now is to enable VMware Virtual SAN. As we don't have a VSAN datastore in the lab environment, just click the **Next >** button to continue the configuration to the **vCenter Settings** screen, as shown in the following screenshot:

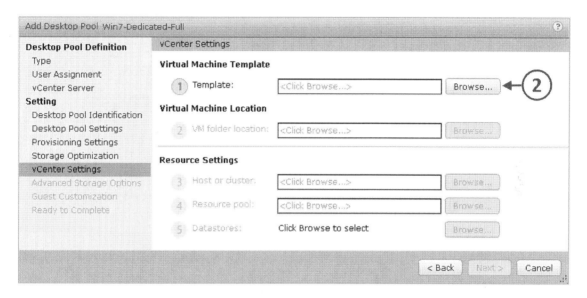

9. In the **Template** box, click the **Browse...** button (**2**). You will now see the Select Template box, as shown in the following screenshot:

10. Select the **Windows 7 Gold Image Template** option from the list and then click the **OK** button. As you are building a Full Clone virtual desktop machine, basically, this is built by deploying a virtual machine from a template.

11. From the **vCenter Settings** screen, click the **Next >** button to continue the configuration. You will now see the **Advanced Storage Options** screen, as shown in the following screenshot:

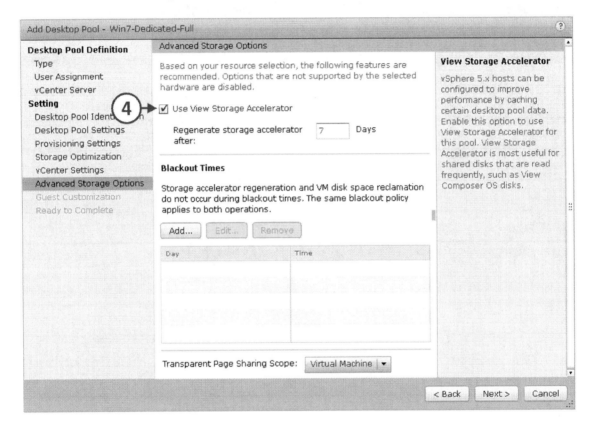

12. Unlike the previous desktop pool that you configured, you only have two options to configure. Check the box for **Use View Storage Accelerator** (4), and then, optionally, configure a blackout time.

13. Click the **Next >** button to continue the configuration. The next configuration screen is for **Guest Customization**, as shown in the following screenshot:

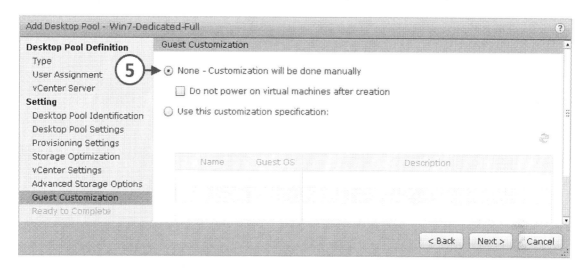

14. Click the radio button for **None – Customization will be done manually** (5). This will mean that you will need to configure each virtual desktop machine as a manual process once they have been created.

15. Ideally, you create a customization script to complete the build of the virtual desktop machines.

16. Now click the **Next >** button to continue to the **Ready to Complete** screen. Review your configuration settings, and then click the **Finish** button to create the desktop pool. You will now see that the pool has been created, as shown in the following screenshot:

In the following section, we are going to create another automated desktop pool, but this time, you will create a pool with a floating assignment, built using Linked Clone desktops.

Creating floating, Linked Clone desktop pools

As with the other pools we have created, the process for creating a floating, Linked Clone desktop pool is pretty much the same as we covered in the previous section, with a few changes to reflect this pool having a floating assignment. As such, in this section we will just highlight the different configuration options:

1. From the Horizon View Administrator screen, click to expand the **Catalog** option, click on **Desktop Pools**, and then, from the **Desktop Pools** pane, click the **Add** button.

2. Then, on the **Add Desktop Pool** screen, click the radio button for **Automated Desktop Pool**, and then click the **Next >** button to continue to the **Assignment** screen.

3. On the **User Assignment** screen, this time click the radio button for **Floating**, as shown in the following screenshot:

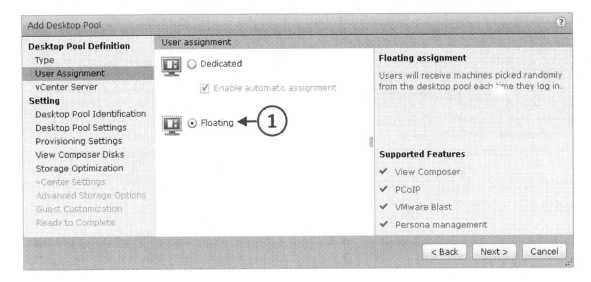

4. Click the **Next >** button to continue.

5. Work through the **vCenter Server, Desktop Pool Identification, Desktop Pool Settings**, and **Provisioning Settings**, as per the previous Linked Clone desktop pool that you created, and stop when you get to the **View Composer Disks** configuration screen, as shown in the following screenshot:

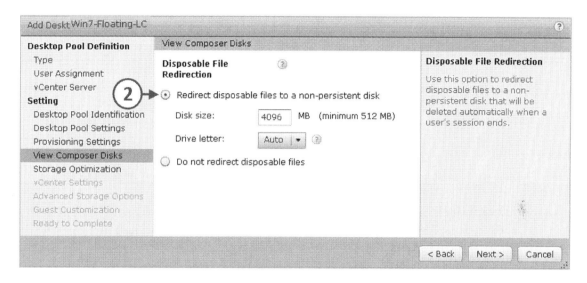

6. Click the radio button for **Redirect disposable files to a non-persistent disk (2)**. You will see that there is no option for a persistent disk on this configuration screen. This is down to the floating assignment that you configured. Basically, there is no persistent disk, hence why it cannot be redirected. To have a persistent disk for a floating desktop assignment, you should consider deploying VMware App Volumes and the Writeable Volume feature.

7. Click the **Next >** button to continue the configuration, and work your way through the rest of the configuration screens to the end. The process is exactly the same as you followed for the previous Linked Clone desktop pool that was created.

8. Once completed, you will see the desktop pool listed in the **Desktop Pools** screen.

In the following section, we are going to create another automated desktop pool, but this time, we will create a pool with a floating assignment, built using Full Clone desktops.

Creating floating, Full Clone desktop pools

As with the other pools we have created, the process for creating a floating, Linked Clone desktop pool is pretty much the same as we covered in the previous section, with a few changes to reflect this pool having a floating assignment. As such, in this section we will just highlight the different configuration options:

1. From the Horizon View Administrator screen, click to expand the **Catalog** option, click on **Desktop Pools**, and then, from the **Desktop Pools** pane, click the **Add** button.

2. Then, on the **Add Desktop Pool** screen, click the radio button for **Automated Desktop Pool**, and then click the **Next >** button to continue to the **Assignment** screen.

3. On the **User Assignment** screen, click the radio button for **Floating**, and then click the **Next >** button to continue the configuration. You will now see the **vCenter Server** settings screen.

4. For this pool, we are using Full Clones, so click the radio button for **Full virtual machines (1)**, and then select the relevant vCenter Server from the list. Again, in the example lab, the vCenter we are using is **vcs1.pvolab.com**.

5. Click the **Next >** button to continue the configuration. The next configuration screen is for the **Desktop Pool Identification**. Enter an **ID**, **Display name**, and **Description** for this pool that reflects the fact that it's a Windows 7 floating, Full Clone desktop pool.

6. Click the **Next >** button to continue. The next screen is for the **Desktop Pool Settings**. Configure your remote settings and remote display protocol, and then click the **Next >** button to continue the configuration. Next up is the **Provisioning Settings** screen.

7. Ensure that provisioning is enabled by checking the **Enable provisioning** box, as well as the box below it for **Stop provisioning on error**. Then enter a naming pattern for the newly created virtual desktop machines. Once completed, click the **Next>** button to continue the configuration.

8. The next configuration screen is for **Storage Optimization**. The only option you have on this screen now is to enable VMware Virtual SAN. As we don't have a VSAN datastore in the lab environment, just click the **Next >** button to continue the configuration to the **vCenter Settings** screen.

9. On the **vCenter Settings** configuration screen, in the **Template** box, click the **Browse...** button. You will now see the **Select Template** box.

10. Select the **Windows 7 Gold Image Template** option from the list and then click the **OK** button. As you are building a Full Clone virtual desktop machine, basically, this is built by deploying a virtual machine from a template.

11. From the **vCenter Settings** screen, click the **Next >** button to continue the configuration. You will now see the **Advanced Storage Options** screen.

12. Check the box for **Use View Storage Accelerator (4)**, and then, optionally, configure a blackout time. Click the **Next >** button to continue the configuration.

13. The next configuration screen is for **Guest Customization**.

14. Click the radio button for **None – Customization will be done manually (5)**. This will mean that you will need to configure each virtual desktop machine as a manual process once they have been created.

15. Now click the **Next >** button to continue to the **Ready to Complete** screen. Review your configuration settings, and then click the **Finish** button to create the desktop pool.

You will now see that the pool has been created, as shown in the following screenshot:

In the final section, we are going to create another automated desktop pool, but this time we will create a pool with a floating assignment, built using Instant Clones.

Creating floating, Instant Clone desktop pools

Before you configure a desktop pool using Instant Clones, you first have to add an **Instant Clone domain administrator**. This account is used to perform the active directory tasks required to create new virtual desktop machines. It's similar to the service account used in View Composer, but as Instant Clones don't use Composer, you need to add the account within the View Administrator. The account needs the following permissions:

- Create Computer Objects
- Delete Computer Objects
- Write All Properties

1. To add the account, from the View Administrator dashboard, expand the option for **View Configuration** from the **Inventory** menu in the left-hand pane, and then click on the option for **Instant Clone Domain Admins (1)**.

2. Then click on the **Add...** button (**2**), as shown in the following screenshot:

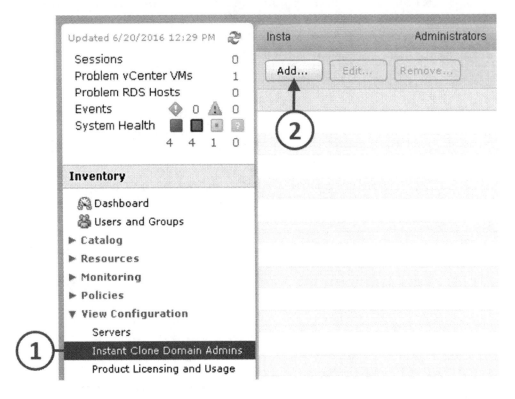

3. You will now see the **Add Domain Admin** box, as shown in the following screenshot:

4. In the **Full domain name** box, click the drop-down menu (**3**), and select the name of the domain in which the account resides. In the example lab, this is **pvolab.com**. Then, in the **User name** box, enter the account name, followed by the password for this account in the **Password** box.

5. Click the **OK** button to continue. You have now successfully configured the domain admin account for Instant Clones.

6. As with the other pools we have created, the process for creating a floating, Instant Clone desktop pool is pretty much the same as we covered in the previous section, with a few changes to reflect this pool being built using Instant Clones. As such, in this section, we will just highlight the main differences in the configuration options.

7. From the Horizon View Administrator screen, click to expand the **Catalog** option, click on **Desktop Pools**, and then, from the **Desktop Pools** pane, click the **Add** button.

8. Then, on the **Add Desktop Pool** screen, click the radio button for **Automated Desktop Pool**, and then click the **Next >** button to continue to the **Assignment** screen.

9. On the **User Assignment** screen, click the radio button for **Floating** and then click the **Next >** button to continue.

10. You will now see the **vCenter Server** configuration screen, as shown in the following screenshot:

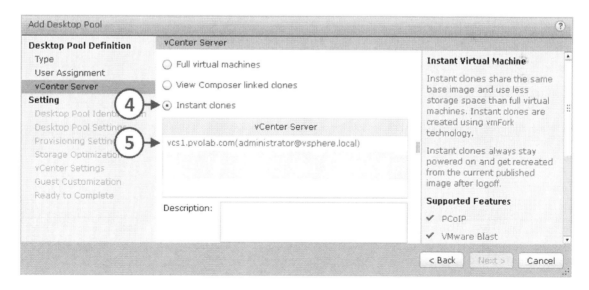

11. Click the radio button for **Instant clones** (4), and then select the vCenter Server from the list of those displayed. In the example lab, this is the vCenter Server called **vcs1.pvolab.com** (5). Click the **Next >** button to continue.

12. Next is the **Desktop Pool Identification** configuration screen. Enter an **ID**, **Display name**, and **Description** for this pool that reflects the fact that it's a Windows 7 floating, Instant Clone desktop pool, and then click the **Next >** button to continue to the **Desktop Pool Settings** screen.

13. Configure your remote settings and remote display protocol and then click the **Next >** button to continue the configuration. Next up is the **Provisioning Settings** screen.

14. Ensure that provisioning is enabled by checking the **Enable provisioning** box, as well as the box below it for **Stop provisioning on error**. Then enter a naming pattern for the newly created virtual desktop machines. Once completed, click the **Next >** button to continue the configuration.

15. The next configuration screen is for **Storage Optimization**. Here you have the option of enabling VMware Virtual SAN. As we don't have a VSAN datastore in the lab environment, this option is not available. The other option is to select different datastores for the OS disk and replica disk.

16. Click the **Next >** button to continue the configuration to the **vCenter Settings** screen.

17. On the **vCenter Settings** configuration screen, in the **Parent VM** box, click the **Browse...** button, as shown in the following screenshot:

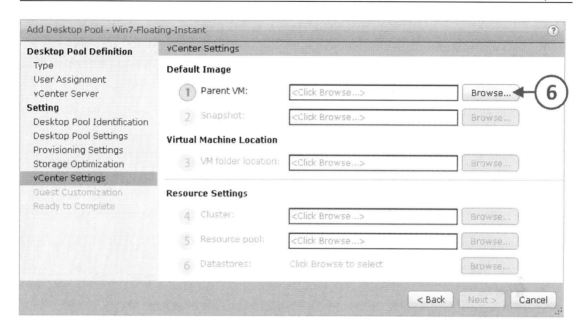

18. You will now see the **Select Parent VM** box, as shown in the following screenshot:

19. Click the virtual machine you want to use as the parent image. In the example lab, this the **Windows 7 Gold Image** machine (7). Click the **OK** button to return to the **vCenter Settings** configuration screen.

20. Next, in the **Snapshot** box, click the **Browse...** button. In the **Select Snapshot** box, click on the snapshot for the parent machine, and then click the **OK** button to return to the **vCenter Settings** configuration screen.

When it comes to configuring the **Resource Settings** section of this configuration, it's worth noting that you need to have a host cluster and resource pool configured. You cannot use standalone hosts for Instant Clone desktop pools.

21. Click the **Next >** button to continue the configuration to the **Guest Customization** screen, as shown in the following screenshot:

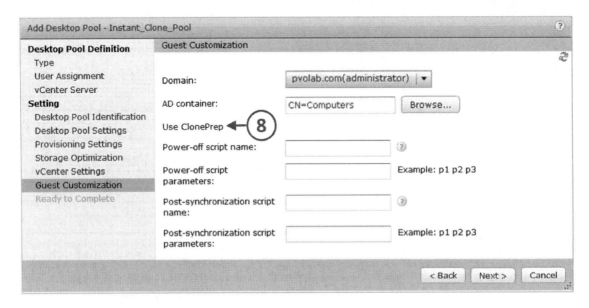

22. In the **Domain** box, from the drop-down menu, select the domain in which the newly created virtual desktop machines will reside.

23. Then, in the **AD container** box, type in the container name of where the desktop accounts should be created. By default, this is set to the **Computers** group in AD.

24. Next you will see the **Use ClonePrep** section. ClonePrep is used to customize Instant Clones during the creation process, similar to how QuickPrep works with Linked Clones. ClonePrep ensures that all the Instant Clone desktops join the Active Directory domain you specified previously.

25. The Instant Clones will have the same SID as the parent VM, as well as keeping the application GUIDs.

26. Under the ClonePrep section, you have the option to add a number of different scripts. When you add an Instant Clone desktop pool, you can specify a script to run immediately after a clone is created and another script to run before the clone is powered off.

ClonePrep scripts must be available on the parent VM and stored in a secure folder so that they are available on each virtual desktop machine that gets created, and so that end users cannot change them. You cannot enter a UNC path to run the scripts from a network share.

27. Now click the **Next >** button to continue to the **Ready to Complete** screen. Review your configuration settings, and then click the **Finish** button to create the desktop pool.

Creating a manual desktop pool

In the previous sections, we have talked about creating automated desktop pools. Horizon View also has the ability to create desktop pools from already existing virtual desktop machines, or even physical desktop machines.

The process for creating manual desktop pools is not too dissimilar to the process we covered previously for automated desktop pools, so in the following section, we will create a manual pool and highlight where the process differs:

1. From the Horizon View Administrator screen, click to expand the **Catalog** option, click on **Desktop Pools**, and then, from the **Desktop Pools** pane, click the **Add** button.

2. Then, on the **Add Desktop Pool** screen, click the radio button for **Manual Desktop Pool**, (1) and then click the **Next >** button, as shown in the following screenshot:

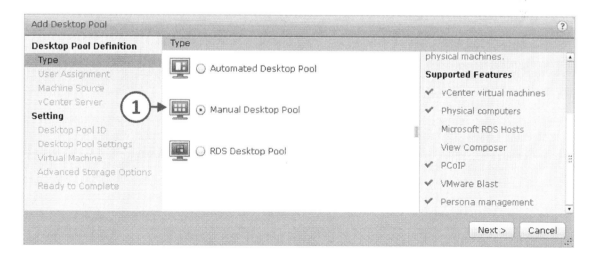

3. You will now see the **User Assignment** screen. Select whether or not you want a dedicated assignment with automatic assignment or a floating assignment, and then click the **Next >** button. Next you will see the **Machine Source** screen, as shown in the following screenshot:

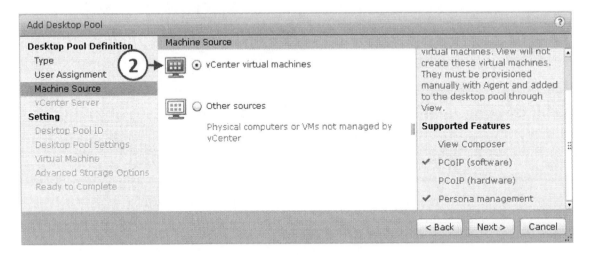

4. On this screen, you can select the type of machine for the pool. In the example lab, click the radio button for **vCenter virtual machines** (2).
5. The other option is to configure physical desktop computers or other virtual machines that are not managed by a vCenter Server as the machines in the pool.

6. Click the **Next>** button to continue the configuration to the **vCenter Server** screen.

7. On the **vCenter Server** configuration screen, click on the relevant vCenter Server to select it, as shown in the following screenshot:

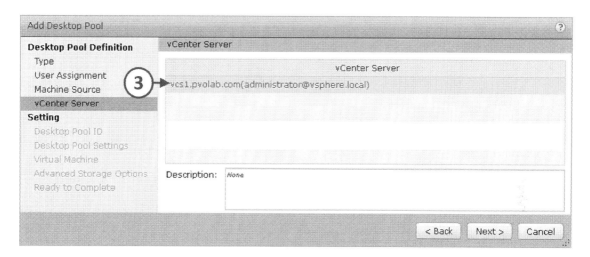

8. Click the **Next>** button to continue the configuration to the **Desktop Pool ID** screen.

9. Enter an **ID**, **Display name**, and **Description** for this pool that reflects the fact that it's a Windows 7 manual desktop pool, and then click the **Next >** button to continue to the **Desktop Pool Settings** screen.

10. Configure your remote settings and remote display protocol, and then click the **Next >** button to continue the configuration. Next is the **Virtual Machine** configuration screen:

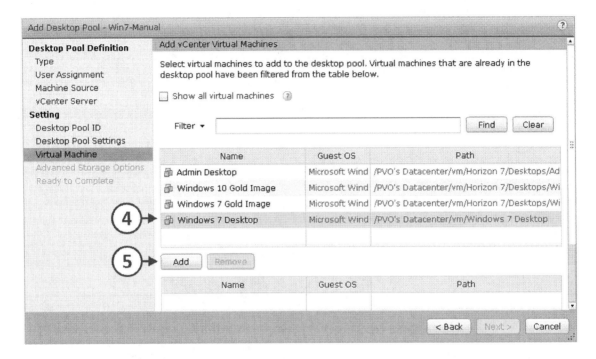

11. Click to highlight the virtual desktop machine you want to add to this manual desktop pool. In the example lab, we are going to add the **Windows 7 Desktop** virtual machine, so highlight it and then click the **Add** button (**5**). You will now see that the virtual desktop machine has been added (**6**), as shown in the following screenshot:

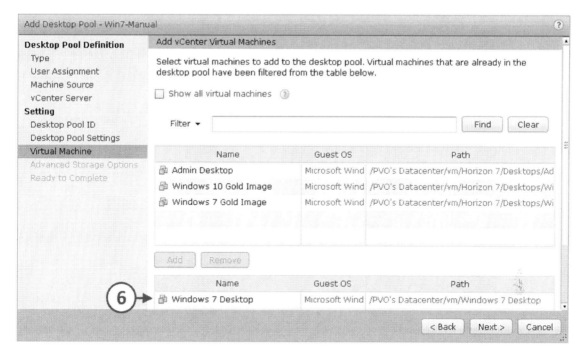

12. Click the **Next >** button to continue the configuration to the **Advanced Storage Options** screen. Check the **Use View Storage Accelerator** box, and then, optionally, configure any blackout times.

13. Now click the **Next >** button to continue to the **Ready to Complete** screen. Review your configuration settings, and then click the **Finish** button to create the desktop pool.

14. Once completed, you will see the pool displayed in the **Desktop Pools** pane in the View Administrator, as shown in the following screenshot:

You will now have created a number of desktop pools, as shown in the following screenshot:

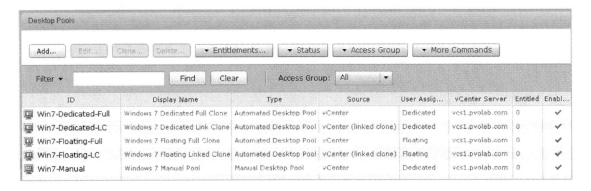

In the following section, we will look at entitling end users to the desktop pools.

Entitling users

Now that you have created a number of desktop pools that contain virtual desktop machines, the next step is to allow the users to have access to the pools and virtual desktop machines:

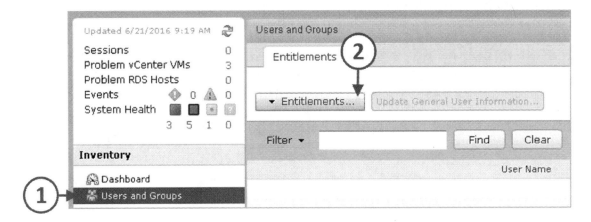

1. From the View Administrator, under the **Inventory** menu in the left-hand pane, click on **Users and Groups** (1). Then, on the **Users and Groups** screen, click the **Entitlements...** button (2). From the menu that pops up, select the option for **Add Desktop Entitlement**.

2. You will now see **Add Desktop Entitlement** the configuration screen, as shown in the following screenshot:

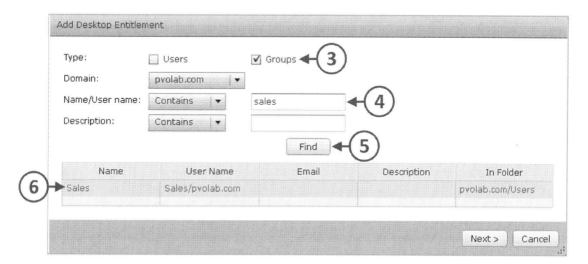

In the example lab, we have an AD group called Sales that we are going to entitle to the Windows 7 floating Full Clone desktop pool.

1. To configure the entitlement for the example lab, first check the box for **Groups** (3). You can also configure individual users.

2. Then, in the **Domain** box, click the down arrow and select the relevant domain. In the example lab, this is configured as **pvolab.com**. Then, in the **Name/User name** box, ensure that the drop-down menu is set to **Contains** and then in the box next to it, type **sales** (4). Now click the **Find** button (5).

3. You will then see the results appear in the following screenshot. In this example, click to select the **Sales** option, and then click the **Next >** button.

4. You will now see the **Select the desktop pools to entitle** box, as shown in the following screenshot:

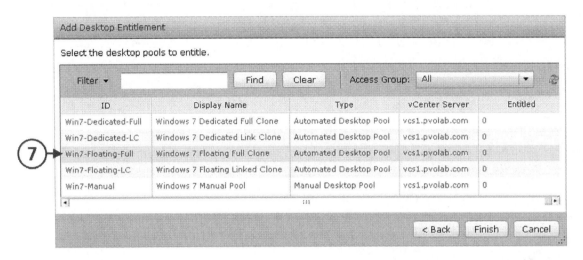

5. Select the relevant desktop pool to entitle the user to. In this example, we are going to entitle the sales group to the Windows 7 floating desktop pool, so click and select **Win7-Floating-Full** pool (7) from the list of available desktop pools.

6. Click the **Finish** button to complete the entitlement process.

You will now return to the **Entitlements** screen, where you will now see the Sales group has been entitled, as shown in the following screenshot:

You have now successfully entitled a desktop pool. If you were now to log in to View as a user that is a member of the sales group, you would now see that the pool is available to select and connect to. We will look at connecting to the virtual desktop machines in more detail in `Chapter 10`, *Horizon View Client Options*.

Managing desktop pools

With an automated desktop pool, once you create and entitle your desktop pool, your desktops will be created, first by creating the replica, and then by creating the Linked Clones. You will be able to see the progress of this process inside the vSphere Client and also from inside the Horizon View Administrator:

1. To do this, from the Horizon View Administrator dashboard screen, under the **Inventory** section in the left-hand pane, select **Catalog**. Now click on **Desktop Pools**. You will see the following screenshot:

2. Select the name of the desktop pool you wish to manage, by double-clicking on it and then selecting the **Inventory** tab (**1**), as shown in the following screenshot:

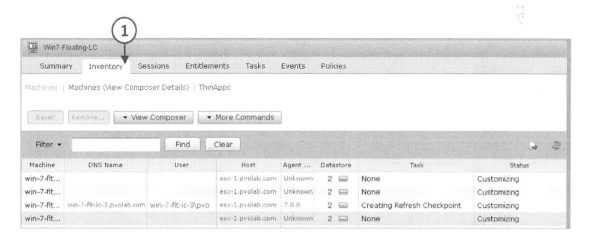

On the **Inventory**, you will see the names of the desktops, including the VM machine name, DNS name, the name of any connected or dedicated users, the hosts on which they reside, the agent version, and the datastore they reside on. You will also see the current status of the virtual desktop machines within the desktop pool.

In total, there are 24 different statuses that get reported on for vCenter-managed virtual machines. You can see a breakdown of all the statuses taken from the Horizon View documentation:

- **Provisioning**: The virtual machine is being provisioned.
- **Customizing**: The virtual machine in an automated pool is being customized.
- **Deleting**: The virtual machine is marked for deletion. View will delete the virtual machine soon.
- **Waiting for Agent**: View Connection Server is waiting to establish communication with View Agent on a virtual machine in a manual pool.
- **Maintenance mode**: The virtual machine is in maintenance mode. Users cannot log in or use the virtual machine.
- **Startup**: View Agent has started on the virtual machine, but other required services, such as the display protocol, are still starting. For example, View Agent cannot establish an RDP connection with client computers until RDP has finished starting. The View Agent startup period allows other processes such as protocol services to start up as well.
- **Agent disabled**: This state can occur in two cases. First, in a desktop pool with the **Delete or refresh machine on logoff** or **Delete machine after logoff** setting enabled, a desktop session is logged out, but the virtual machine is not yet refreshed or deleted. Second, View Connection Server disables View Agent just before sending a request to power off the virtual machine. This state ensures that a new desktop session cannot be started on the virtual machine
- **Agent unreachable**: View Connection Server cannot establish communication with View Agent on a virtual machine.
- **Invalid IP**: The subnet mask registry setting is configured on the virtual machine, and no active network adapters have an IP address within the configured range.
- **Agent needs reboot**: A View component was upgraded, and the virtual machine must be restarted to allow View Agent to operate with the upgraded component.
- **Protocol failure**: A display protocol did not start before the View Agent startup period expired. Note that View Administrator can display machines in a Protocol failure state when one protocol failed but other protocols started successfully. For example, the Protocol failure state might be displayed when HTML access failed but PCoIP and RDP are working. In this case, the machines are available and Horizon Client devices can access them through PCoIP or RDP.

- **Domain failure**: The virtual machine encountered a problem reaching the domain. The domain server was not accessible, or the domain authentication failed.
- **Already used**: In a desktop pool with the **Delete or refresh machine on logoff** or **Delete machine after logoff** setting enabled, there is no session on the virtual machine, but the session was not logged off. This condition might occur if a virtual machine shuts down unexpectedly or the user resets the machine during a session. By default, when a virtual machine is in this state, View prevents any other Horizon Client devices from accessing the desktop.
- **Configuration error**: The display protocol, such as RDP or PCoIP, is not enabled.
- **Provisioning error**: An error occurred during provisioning.
- **Error**: An unknown error occurred in the virtual machine.
- **Unassigned user connected**: A user other than the assigned user is logged in to a virtual machine in a dedicated pool. For example, this state can occur if an administrator starts vSphere Client, opens a console on the virtual machine, and logs in.
- **Unassigned user disconnected**: A user other than the assigned user is logged in and disconnected from a virtual machine in a dedicated assignment pool.
- **Unknown**: The virtual machine is in an unknown state.
- **Provisioned**: The virtual machine is powered off or suspended.
- **Available**: The virtual machine is powered on and ready for a connection. In a dedicated pool, the virtual machine is assigned to a user and will start when the user logs in.
- **Connected**: The virtual machine is in a session and has a remote connection to the Horizon Client device.
- **Disconnected**: The virtual machine is in a session, but it is disconnected from the Horizon Client device.
- **In progress**: The virtual machine is in a transitional state during a maintenance operation.

By right-clicking on any desktop, you are able to undertake any of a number of tasks on that given desktop. You have the following options:

- **Reset**: Will complete a hard reset on the desktop and could be used in the case of a system lockup.
- **Remove**: Will delete the desktop from the pool.

- **Refresh, Recompose, and Rebalance**: These have been described in Chapter 2, *An Overview of Horizon View Architecture and Components,* and can be completed here on an individual desktop basis rather than composing the entire pool.
- **Cancel task**: Cancels any outstanding task on the individual virtual machine.
- **Assign User**: Can be used to allocate a desktop to a specific user.
- **Unassign User**: Removes a user from being entitled to this desktop this allocation.
- **Enter Maintenance Mode**: Places the desktop in a state where users cannot be allocated to the desktop or connect to it while maintenance is carried out.
- **Exit Maintenance Mode**: Returns the desktop to the pool.
- **Disconnect Session**: Disconnects the currently connected user from the pool without logging them off.
- **Logoff Session**: Logs the user off.
- **Send Message**: Sends a message to any given user.

In the following section, we are going to look at a couple of the more common tasks for managing the desktop pools.

Recomposing a desktop pool

One of the more common tasks you are likely to perform is to recompose a desktop pool to update the operating system or applications in the base image, or alternatively, to add new applications. It's always recommended to have test pools available for you to test updates prior to sending them out to your end users.

In this example, we will recompose one of the example desktop pools, but you could also perform a recompose operation on an individual virtual desktop:

1. To recompose the desktop pool, from the Horizon View Administrator dashboard screen, under the **Inventory** section in the left-hand pane, select **Catalog**. Now click on **Desktop Pools**. Double-click on the desktop pool on which you want to perform the recompose operation. You will now see the properties of the chosen desktop pool, as shown in the following screenshot:

2. From the **Summary** tab of your chosen desktop, click the **View Composer** button (**1**), and from the drop-down menu, select the **Recompose** option (**2**).

3. You will now see the **Recompose** screen and the option to select the new snapshot to use as the new image.

4. There is also the option to choose a completely new image by clicking the **Change...** button in the **Parent VM** box. In this example, we have taken our Windows 7 gold image build, powered it on, and made some updates and changes. The virtual desktop machine was then shut down and a new snapshot was created. This is the snapshot that is going to be selected to recompose or rebuild the virtual machines.

5. From the list of snapshots click on the entry for **Windows 7 Update** (**3**), as shown in the following screenshot:

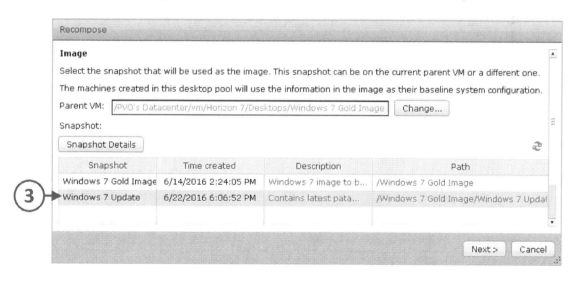

6. Once selected, click the **Next >** button to continue. You will now see the **Scheduling** configuration screen, as shown in the following screenshot:

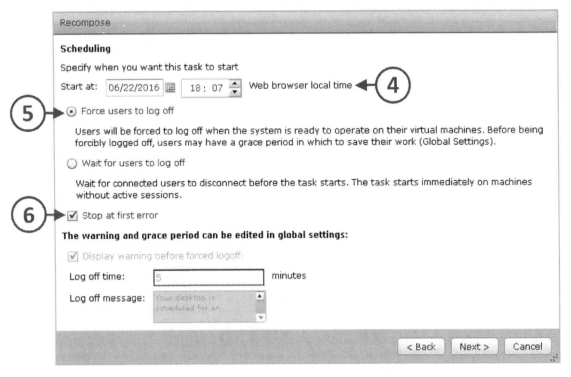

1. The first thing to configure is when you want to start the recompose operation. In the **Start at** box (4), select a date and time.
2. You then have the option to **Force users to log off** or **Wait for users to log off**. In this example, we are going to click the radio button for **Force users to log off** (5).
3. Finally, check the **Stop at first error** box (6).
4. Click the **Next >** button to continue. You will now see the **Ready to Complete** summary screen, as shown in the following screenshot:

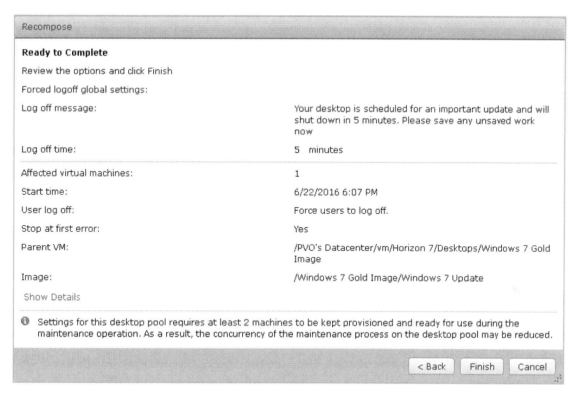

Recompose

Ready to Complete

Review the options and click Finish

Forced logoff global settings:

Log off message:	Your desktop is scheduled for an important update and will shut down in 5 minutes. Please save any unsaved work now
Log off time:	5 minutes
Affected virtual machines:	1
Start time:	6/22/2016 6:07 PM
User log off:	Force users to log off.
Stop at first error:	Yes
Parent VM:	/PVO's Datacenter/vm/Horizon 7/Desktops/Windows 7 Gold Image
Image:	/Windows 7 Gold Image/Windows 7 Update

Show Details

ⓘ Settings for this desktop pool requires at least 2 machines to be kept provisioned and ready for use during the maintenance operation. As a result, the concurrency of the maintenance process on the desktop pool may be reduced.

< Back   Finish   Cancel

7. Check the configuration options, and then click the **Finish** button to start the recompose operation.

Managing persistent disks

One of the other common tasks is to manage the persistent disks.

As previously discussed, a persistent disk can be configured on a dedicated virtual hard disk per user, which will allow you to preserve user data and settings between recompose operations, and more. There are a number of tasks that can be undertaken with regard to persistent disk management.

You are able to detach the virtual disk from a dedicated desktop. The main use case for this could be due to the end user leaving the company, and so the desktop is no longer needed but the data needs to be kept for compliance or audit reasons. It could also be because there is an issue with the desktop and you need to recreate it afresh without losing the user's data. Perform the following steps to detach the persistent disk:

1. From the Horizon View Administrator dashboard screen, under the **Inventory** section in the left-hand pane, select **Catalog**. Now click on **Desktop Pools**. Double-click on the desktop pool from which you want to detach a persistent disk.

2. You will then see the **Summary** page for your chosen desktop pool. Click the **Inventory** tab (**1**) and then, from the list, choose the virtual desktop machine you want to detach the persistent disk from, and then click on **Persistent Disks** (**2**). Here you can see a list of all the persistent disks. Select the disk you wish to detach and then click on the **Detach...** button (**3**), as shown in the following screenshot:

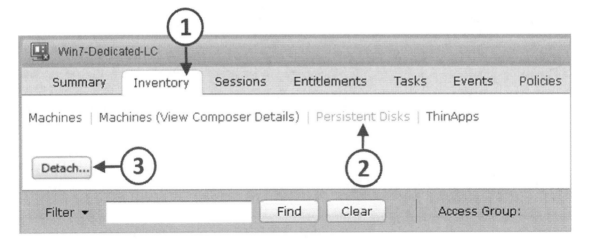

3. Depending on the reason you are detaching the disk, you might wish to keep the detached disk in the current datastore. Alternatively, you can select another datastore just as an archive tier of storage. Finally, click the **OK** button to detach the disk. Assuming the user isn't currently connected to the desktop, the persistent disk will be archived and then the VM will be deleted.

4. Once detached, you can view all the detached disks from the View Administrator screen. You will find this by navigating to the **Resources** section (4) under the **Inventory** list, and then clicking the option for **Persistent Disks** (5). Then, from the top of the screen, select the **Detached** tab (6).

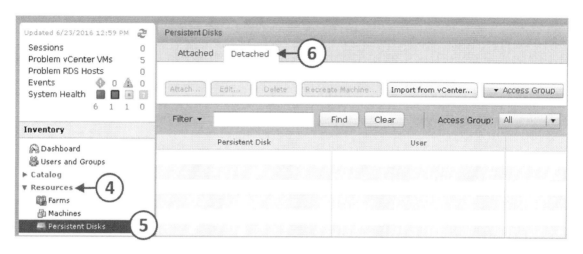

5. Here, you are able to select the disk from the list and reattach the disk to a desktop by clicking the **Attach...** button, assuming the desktop has been reassigned to the user. You can also change who the disk is assigned to by editing the owner, deleting the disk permanently, or recreating a machine with the disk attached to it.

6. The use case for doing this is so that an administrator can reattach a persistent disk in order to access the data on it. As we mentioned before, maybe this is an end user that has left the company and their virtual desktop machine is no longer available.

7. You also have the ability, from the persistent disks management screen, to import existing disks from a vCenter Server. A use case for this is, perhaps, that the user has had an issue with their persistent disk, possibly a corruption or accidental deletion of the whole disk or files held within it.

8. In the example lab, the persistent disks are being stored on a dedicated disk, which in turn is stored on the Tintri Storage Array. One of the features of the Tintri array is the ability to configure regular snapshotting of the persistent disks, as well as any other virtual machines stored on it, providing you with data protection. Using the Tintri tools, you could easily recreate the corrupt disk by restoring from the snapshot.

9. Once you have restored the disk, you can use the View Administrator to import it. To do this, from the View Administrator screen, navigate to the **Resources** section (**4**) under the **Inventory** list, and then click the option for **Persistent Disks** (**5**). Then, from the top of the screen, select the **Detached** tab (**6**).

10. Now click the **Import from vCenter...** button. You will see the **Import Persistent Disk From vCenter** dialog box, as shown in the following screenshot:

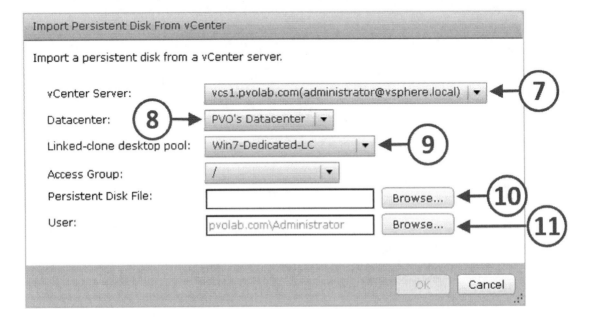

11. In the **vCenter Server** box, from the drop-down menu (**7**), select the vCenter Server that hosts the disk you want to import. Next, in the **Datacenter** box, click the drop-down menu (**8**) and then select the datacenter where the disk resides, and then in the **Linked-clone desktop pool** box, from the drop-down menu (**9**), select the pool where the disk resides.

12. In the **Persistent Disk File** box, click the **Browse...** button (**10**) and navigate to the actual disk file you want to import, and then finally, in the **User** box, click the **Browse...** button (**11**) and select the user who is going to own this disk.

13. Once you have completed the configuration, click the **OK** button. You will now see that the persistent disk has been registered in the **Detached** disks view. From here, you can either recreate the virtual desktop machine by clicking the **Recreate Machine**... button, or click the **Attach...** button to attach it to another virtual machine.

Creating a GPU-enabled desktop pool

In the previous sections, we have covered creating desktop pools using different build options (Linked/full/Instant Clones), and for dedicated and floating assignments, as well as a manual desktop pool. These could have potentially been configured that way based on the end user's requirements.

Another use case for creating a desktop pool is when you have a specific hardware requirement for the virtual desktop machine, such as a high-end graphics cards for taking advantage of either vSGA or vDGA. We have covered previously the building of a virtual desktop machine that is GPU-enabled. In this section, we will build a desktop pool specifically for this virtual desktop machine.

To create the desktop pool, follow the steps as described here:

1. From the **Inventory** section, click **Desktop Pools** (1), and then click the **Add...** button (2).
2. Click the radio button for **Manual Desktop Pool** from the pool type menu and click the **Next >** button to continue.
3. On the **User Assignment** page, click the radio button for **Dedicated** and make sure that the box for **Enable automatic assignment** is **not** checked, and click the **Next >** button to continue.
4. Click the radio button for **vCenter virtual machines** on the **Machine Source** configuration page. This means that the virtual desktop machines will be listed from the vCenter Server. Click the **Next >** button to continue.
5. On the **vCenter Server** page, select the vCenter Server that manages the hosts and virtual desktop machines you want to use.
6. Enter the details for the **Desktop Pool Identification** on the next configuration page. In this example, we will give the pool the **ID** of **vDGA_Desktops** and enter the display name **Windows 7 vDGA**. Click the **Next >** button to continue.
7. You will now see the **Desktop Pool Settings** configuration page, as shown in the following screenshot. Most of the settings are the same as we set for the previous pools, but we need to change some settings in the **Remote Display Protocol** section.

8. Ensure that the **Default display protocol** is set to **PCoIP** (**1**). To allow View to make use of the advanced graphics settings, you need to make sure that the **Allow users to choose protocol** option is set to **No** (**2**). The reason for this is that these features only work with PCoIP. If you leave the option set to **Yes**, then the **3D Renderer** section will remain grayed out and you won't be able to select the option for **Automatic** (**3**):

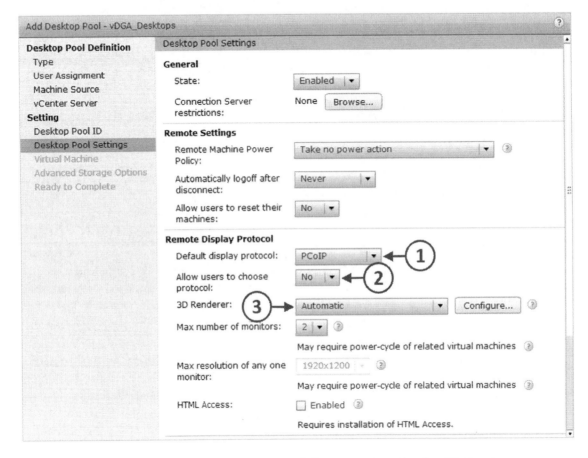

9. As a quick reminder, there are four different options for the 3D Renderer:
   - **Automatic**: ESX reserves GPU resources on a first come, first served basis, and if they can't be fulfilled will revert to software rendering
   - **Software**: ESX uses software rendering only

- **Hardware:** As with **Automatic**, ESX reserves GPU resources on a first come, first served basis, and if they can't be fulfilled, the virtual desktop machine will not power on
- **Disabled:** No 3D rendering configured

10. The other option you have is to configure the amount of video memory allocated to that virtual desktop machine. To configure this option, click the **Configure...** button next to the **3D Renderer** option. You can adjust the slider bar to configure from 64 MB up to 512 MB of VRAM:

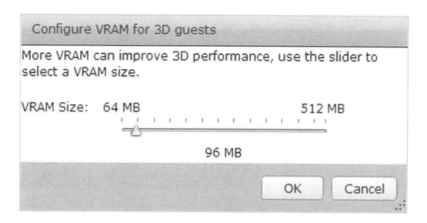

11. On the **Virtual Machine** settings configuration page, under **Add vCenter Virtual Machines**, search for the virtual desktop machines you want to add to this desktop pool. You can either check the box to show all virtual machines or use the **Filter** option to search for specific machines. Select each of the machines you want to add to the pool and then click **Add**.

12. On the **Advanced Storage Options**, check the box for **Use View Storage Accelerator** and click **Next >** to continue.

13. Finally, you will see the **Ready to Complete** page. Check the settings and click **Finish** when you are happy to continue.

You will now have a manual desktop pool created in the View Administrator, which contains your dedicated, GPU-enabled virtual desktop machines. There is one final thing you need to configure, but you can only do that by connecting to the virtual desktop machines using View.

Once you have connected to the virtual desktop machine, open a command prompt window and navigate to the following directory: `C:\program files\common files\VMware\Teradici PCOIP Server\`.

From that directory, run the following command:

```
Montereyenable.exe - enable
```

This enables the NVIDIA APIs. Reboot the virtual desktop machine when complete.

You should now have a working GPU-enabled virtual desktop machine that you can start to entitle to users. To do this, follow the steps that we described in the *Entitling users to a desktop pool* section of this chapter.

If you want to make sure that the virtual desktop machine is using the vDGA and the NVIDIA graphics card, click the **Start** button and then click **Run**. In the **Run** dialog box, type the command dxdiag and click **OK**. The **DirectX Diagnostic Tool** will launch. Click on the **Display** tab at the top. You will see the following screenshot:

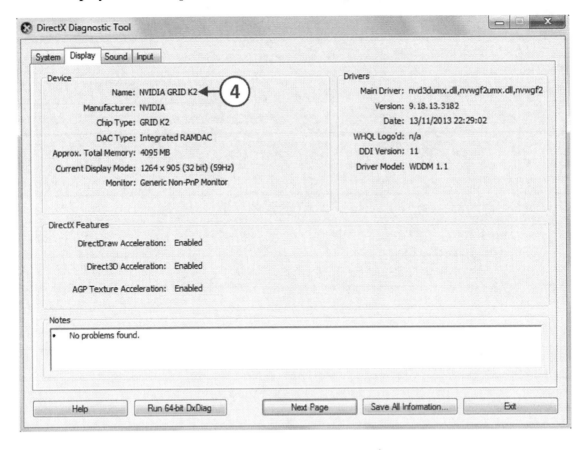

You can see that the graphics card in use is the **NVIDIA GRID K2 (4)**.

One thing to note is that vDGA will not work when opening a console session to the virtual desktop machine from the vSphere Web Client. You won't see anything displayed in the console. You will need to use RDP to connect, or connect to View itself.

Having created the desktop pools and entitled users to be able to connect to virtual desktop machines within the pools, it's a good idea to review your design and check that the infrastructure is performing as expected now that you have virtual desktop machines built. In the following section, we are going to take a look at our environment.

Reviewing the infrastructure post-deployment

So, with pools created and virtual desktop machines built, now is a good time to go back and review the infrastructure to check that everything is running as expected.

Ideally, you should compare the assessment data with the current data from your environment. Back in Chapter 3, *Design and Deployment Considerations*, we looked at Liquidware Labs Stratusphere as a solution for this, as not only will it give us the assessment and the infrastructure performance, it will be useful in the following section when we come to tune the user experience. For the assessment phase we used Stratusphere FIT to provide the assessment data on the current physical environment. We can now use Stratusphere UX to not only monitor the current user experience, but also to compare against the assessment data to show performance improvements.

The following screenshot shows an example of the performance of the host servers:

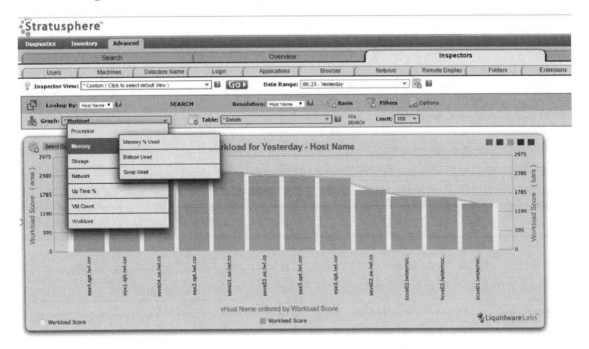

This would allow you to measure CPU, memory, and network performance, allowing you to quickly understand the resources being used and identify any potential bottlenecks.

In the example lab, we have also deployed a Tintri T820 storage array, which has the ability to measure the performance of the virtual desktop machines from a storage and storage performance perspective.

The following screenshot shows an overview of the amount of storage space used, as well as throughput, IOPS, and latency:

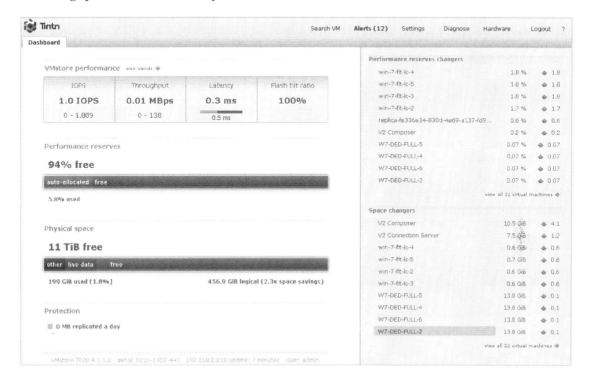

The Tintri solution is VM-aware; this means you can understand the performance for individual virtual desktop machines, as shown in the following screenshot:

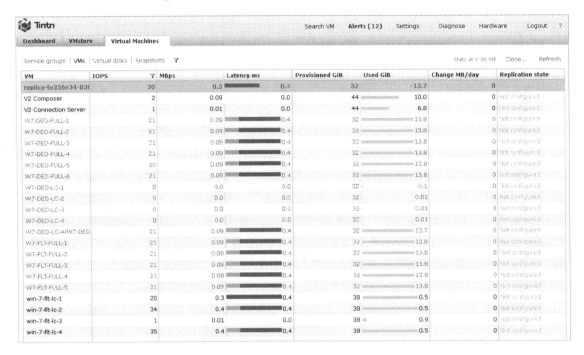

As you can see, each of the virtual desktop machines that were built as part of the desktop pool creations are listed, along with the performance indicators.

Summary

In this chapter, we have configured the Horizon View Administrator to deliver our virtual desktop machines by means of desktop pools. We have built and configured different desktop pools to match our different use cases, creating dedicated and floating-assigned pools, as well as building the virtual desktop machines within the pools using Linked clones, Instant Clones, and Full Clones. We also built and configured a dedicated pool for our high-end graphics users.

We also looked at some of the management tasks you will need to perform on the desktop pools, including recomposing a Linked Clone desktop pool, and managing persistent disks. As part of that, we also stepped back and looked at the infrastructure, now that we had started to build virtual desktop machines, to ensure it was performing as expected.

Further if you want to learn about how to fine tune the user experience of the virtual desktop machines that are delivered to the end users and also want to know about how to have many user profiles in a Horizon View environment using View Persona Management and user environment management. You can go through online chapters:

- For fine tuning the end-user experience, chapter is available at `https://www.pac ktpub.com/sites/default/files/downloads/5657_FineTuningtheEndUserExp erience.pdf`
- For managing user environments in virtual desktop infrastructure, chapter is available at `https://www.packtpub.com/sites/default/files/downloads/565 7_ManagingUserEnvironmentsinVirtualDesktopInfrastructure.pdf`

8
Delivering Remote Applications with View Hosted Apps

So far in this book, we have concentrated on the delivery of virtual desktop machines, but Horizon View also has the ability to deliver remote applications, or published applications, as it's more commonly known, as well as session-based desktops, all from the same platform.

In this chapter, we are going to dive deeper into this feature, which is part of the Horizon Advanced Edition and above, and looks at how Horizon View publishes an application directly into the Horizon View client, without the need for having to launch a full virtual desktop machine.

A use case for this could be a call center worker who uses just a couple of different applications. It's far easier, from a management perspective, to just give them the applications they require rather than a full-blown virtual desktop. Another use case is the ability to launch applications, using the View client running on a device that wouldn't normally be able run that application. For example, you could run the *real* version of Microsoft Word on your iPad using the Horizon View client for iOS.

The infrastructure required for this is based on **Microsoft Remote Desktop Services (RDS)** running at the backend, with **Horizon View** acting as the broker to connect users with the applications or desktop sessions. As it's View-based, it uses View protocols such as PCoIP and Blast as the delivery protocol, taking advantage of all the features the protocols have to offer, as we have discussed previously.

Architectural overview

So what does the architecture look like, and how does the hosted application feature work when compared to the virtual desktop machine brokering? In terms of the architecture, delivering hosted applications is handled in pretty much the same way as virtual desktop machines are managed and brokered.

Horizon View acts as the broker, using the same connection server, but instead of brokering a virtual desktop machine that would be running on the ESXi host server, it is now brokering an application session that is running on a Microsoft Windows server, configured with the RDSH role and the applications installed on it.

The following diagram gives you a high-level outline of the architecture for delivering hosted applications:

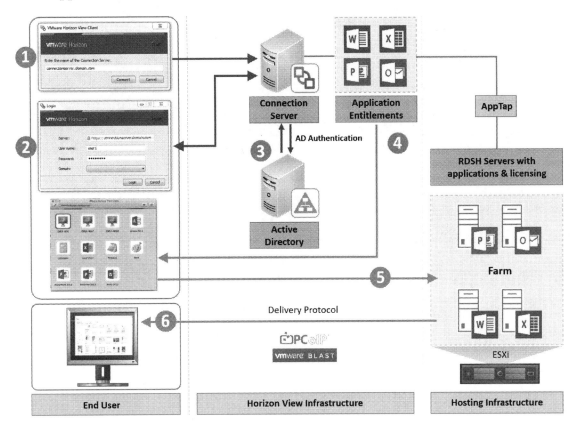

So how does the hosted application feature work?

1. Once authenticated, the client sends a `<get-launch-items>` request to the connection server to request a list of all the entitled application sessions, applications, and desktops for that user. The response contains the following details:
    - `<app-sessions>`, `<desktops>`, `<applications>`
    - Absolute paths to the icons

2. To begin with, as with connecting to a View-delivered virtual desktop machine, you launch the View client and log in to the **connection server**. You enter the details of the View connection server you want to connect to (**1**), enter your username and password (**2**), and then authenticate against AD (**3**).

3. The client fetches any icons it doesn't have already cached through HTTPS using the paths that were provided by the connection server when it sent the response.

4. Access to icon **Uniform Resource Identifiers (URI)** needs to be authenticated. The connection server performs an entitlement check and only returns an icon if that user is entitled to at least one application that has an icon associated with it. For applications that don't have any icons, the client will provide a default icon.

5. A list of entitled desktop and application pools is then displayed to the end user in the View client (**4**).

6. The end user then double-clicks on an application (or desktop) to launch it (**5**), the connection is made, and the application opens in a new window (**6**).

In the following section, we will take a deep dive into what happens during the connection process to connect the user to the application or desktop session they requested.

Application connection sequence

In this section, we are going to break down the connection sequence into three separate parts, showing the process flow of what happens when the user launches an application.

The process starts when the end user double-clicks to launch an application and is illustrated in the following diagram:

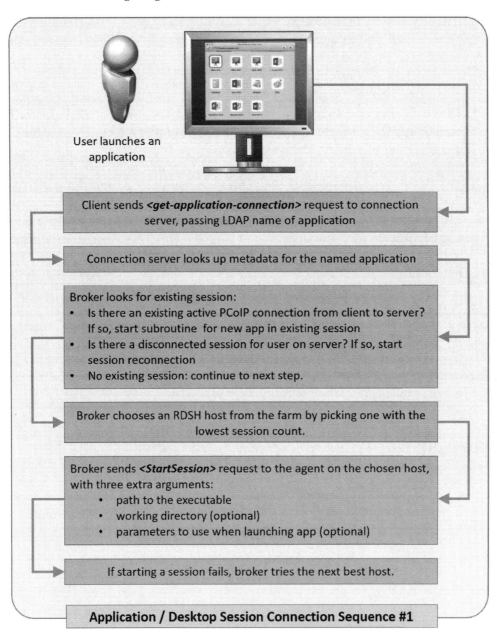

User launches an application

Client sends **<get-application-connection>** request to connection server, passing LDAP name of application

Connection server looks up metadata for the named application

Broker looks for existing session:
- Is there an existing active PCoIP connection from client to server? If so, start subroutine for new app in existing session
- Is there a disconnected session for user on server? If so, start session reconnection
- No existing session: continue to next step.

Broker chooses an RDSH host from the farm by picking one with the lowest session count.

Broker sends **<StartSession>** request to the agent on the chosen host, with three extra arguments:
- path to the executable
- working directory (optional)
- parameters to use when launching app (optional)

If starting a session fails, broker tries the next best host.

Application / Desktop Session Connection Sequence #1

So, now we have a user that has made a request via the View client to the connection server to launch an application.

The next phase of the connection process is for the connection server to talk to the View agent that is installed on the RDS host server.

The following diagram illustrates the next part of the process:

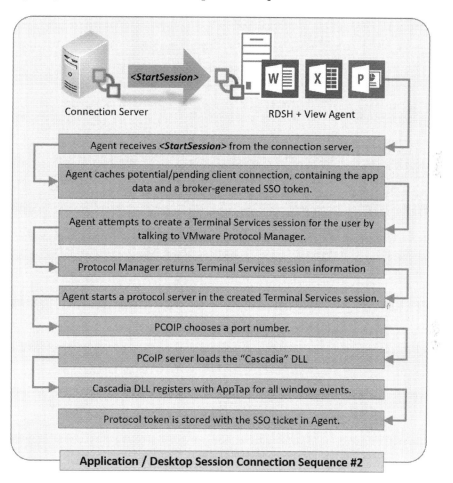

The next step in the connection process is to set up the secure connection to the **PCoIP Secure Gateway server (PSG)**.

A tunnel is set up by the View agent on the RDS server by talking to the PSG. The details of this connection are then forwarded, through the connection server, back to the client. This is pretty much the same way that this process works when connecting to a virtual desktop machine hosted on an ESXi host server.

This process is illustrated in the following diagram, along with the final part of the process, which is to log the end user in and then connect them to the application that they requested.

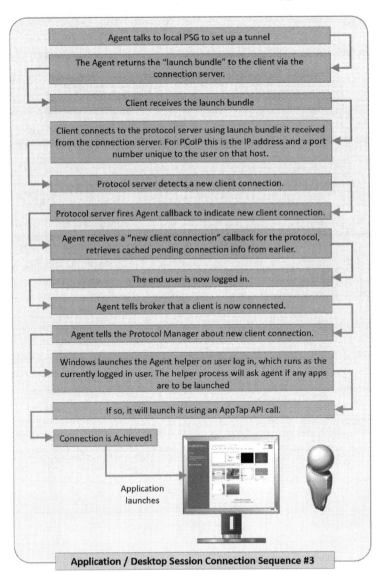

Application / Desktop Session Connection Sequence #3

We have now covered how the process works for connecting the end user to their remote applications. In the following section, we are going to look at some of the specifics around the RDS roles in this environment, starting with some sizing guidelines.

RDSH sizing guidelines

As with the sizing of View for virtual desktop machines, configuring the right specification for the RDSH servers is also key, and in a similar way to how we consider the desktop sizing, we are going to look at different user types.

The VMware recommendation for the user workloads, and the memory requirements is shown in the following table:

User Workload Requirements	Memory	Use Case
Light User	512 MB	Basic application user such as Microsoft Office applications and some web browsing
Medium User	768 MB	Running multiple Microsoft Office applications and light user of multi-media, and more intensive web browsing
Heavy User	1 GB	Advanced application user running 3D-based applications and multi-media, and heavy web-browsing

For the total memory in each RDSH server, VMware recommend that a virtual machine configured as an RDSH server should be provisioned with 64 GB memory, and in terms of CPU requirements, the VMware recommendation is to create virtual servers for the RDSH roles and configure each one with four vCPUs. Make sure that you do not overcommit on the number of cores.

So, for example, if you had a virtual machine running as an RDSH server configured with 64 GB of memory, and had heavy users hosted on it, you would be able to host a maximum of 64 sessions on that server.

For the hardware configuration, let's say you had a physical ESXi host server, configured with a two-socket CPU that had 12 cores, giving you a total of 24 cores.

This would allow a maximum of six RDSH servers, as we are going to provision virtual machines for the RDSH role that each have four cores (24 cores / 4 cores per server). That would mean that the physical server would also need to be configured with 384 GB of memory in total (64 GB x 6 RDSH host servers).

These figures are only guidelines and are based on some of the VMware recommended best practice. It is always best to run an assessment on your environment to work out your optimum configuration.

In the following section, we are going to install and configure the View hosted applications feature.

Installing and configuring View hosted apps

We are now going to start the installation process, starting with configuring the server that is going to be used for hosting the remote applications by adding the RDSH role to it. In the example lab, there is already a Windows Server 2012 server ready-built, called **RDSH-Apps**, to perform this role.

The installation and configuration process is pretty straightforward and can be summarized with the following schematic diagram:

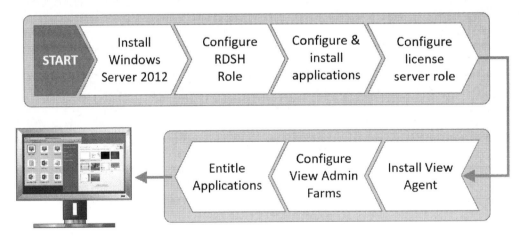

In the following sections, we are going to walk through this process in more detail, starting with configuring the RDSH role.

Configuring the RDS server role

The first thing that we are going to do is to configure the first RDSH server, and then configure this server to deliver the remote applications. The server we are going to configure is RDSH apps:

1. Open a console to the server, and from the **Server Manager Dashboard** page of the server, click on **Add roles and features** (1), as shown in the following screenshot:

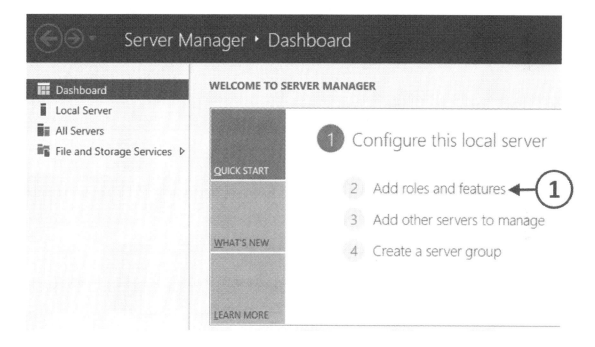

2. The **Add Roles and Features Wizard** will now launch, starting with the **Before you begin** screen, as shown in the following screenshot:

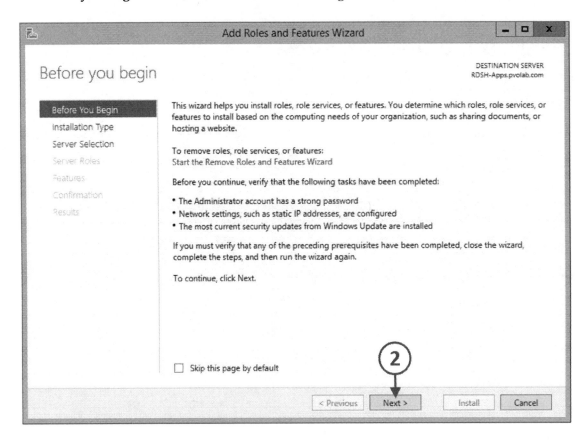

3. Click the **Next >** button (**2**) to continue to the **Installation Type** configuration screen, as shown in the following screenshot:

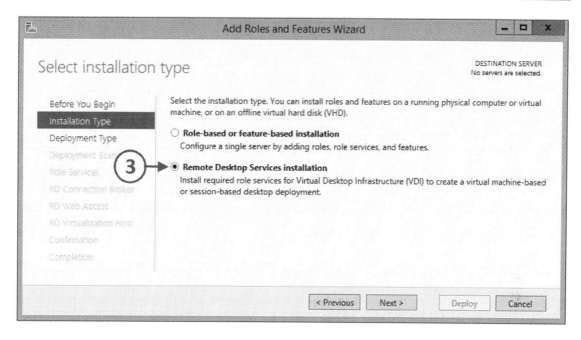

4. Click the radio button for **Remote Desktop Services installation** (3), and then click the **Next >** button to continue.

You will now see the **Deployment Type** configuration screen, as shown in the following screenshot:

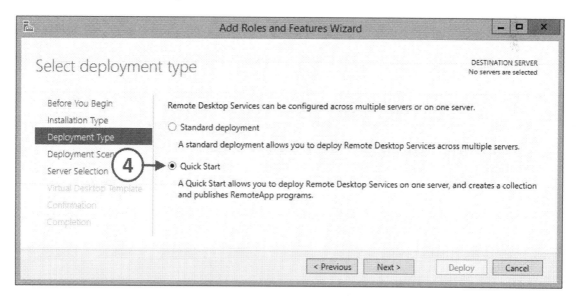

5. Click the radio button for **Quick Start** (4), and then click the **Next >** button to continue.

   Next you will see the **Deployment Scenario** configuration screen, as shown in the following screenshot:

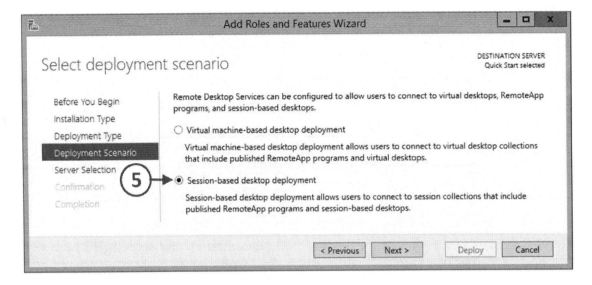

6. Click the radio button for **Session-based desktop deployment** and then click the **Next >** button.

You will now see the **Server Selection** configuration screen, as shown in the following screenshot:

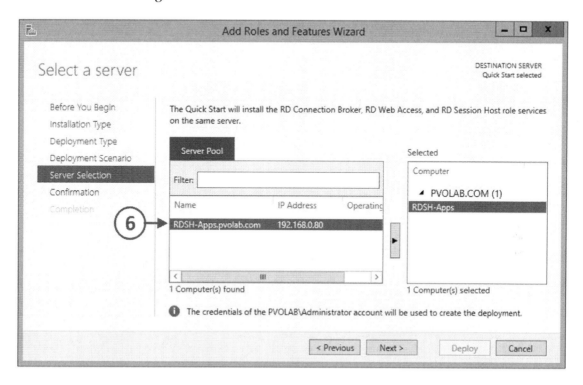

7. From the **Server Pool** list, select the server onto which you want to add the RDSH role.

8. In the example lab, there is only the **RDSH-Apps.pvolab.com** server (6), which has been automatically selected.

9. Click the **Next >** button to continue to the **Confirmation** screen, as shown in the following screenshot:

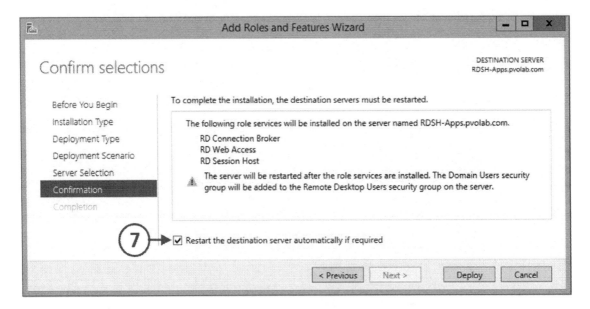

10. Check the role services that will be installed, make sure that you check the **Restart the destination server automatically if required** box, and then click the **Deploy** button.

11. The installation of the feature will now start and the server will reboot. You may have to log back in to check that the installation of the feature completes. Once completed, you will see the following screenshot:

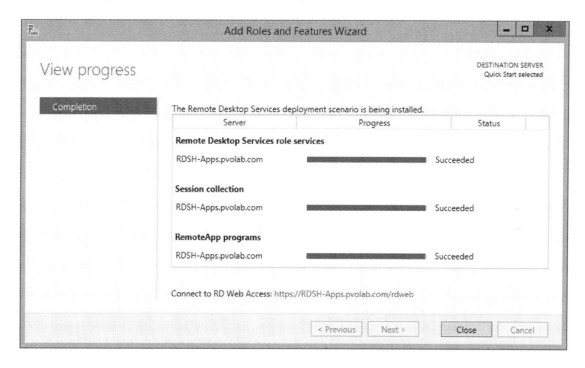

12. Finally, click the **Close** button to complete the installation and close the wizard.

In the following section, we will configure the applications that will be made available as remote applications.

Testing with the standard remote applications

The first applications we are going to configure for session-based remote access are those that are integrated into the Windows operating system and configured by default when you create the RDSH server role-applications, such as Calculator and Notepad.

We are going to test that these applications work as remote applications, by first checking they have been configured, and then whether or not we can access them remotely, before configuring the Horizon View components:

1. From the **Server Manager Dashboard** screen, click on **Remote Desktop Services** (**1**), as shown in the following screenshot:

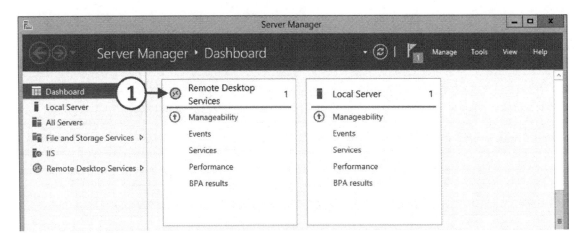

2. You will then see the list of servers that are configured with the RDSH role. In the example lab, this is the **RDSH-APPS** server. Click on this server (**2**), and then click on **QuickSessionCollection…** (**3**), as shown in the following screenshot:

You will now see the **RemoteApp Programs** box, as shown in the following screenshot:

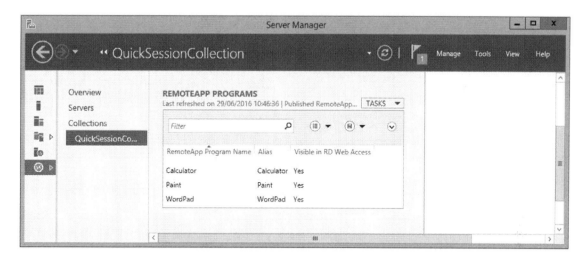

3. This should show **WordPad**, **Paint**, and **Calculator** listed as available applications.

4. Now that the standard applications are available for remote sessions, we are going to try connecting using the RD Web Access web portal.

5. To do this, open a browser from either your desktop or the server itself. It's best to test from a remote desktop rather than the server itself. In the browser, type in the URL of the RDSH server. In the example lab, this address is as follows:
   `https://rdsh-apps.pvolab.com/rdweb`.

6. You will then see the login screen, as shown in the following screenshot:

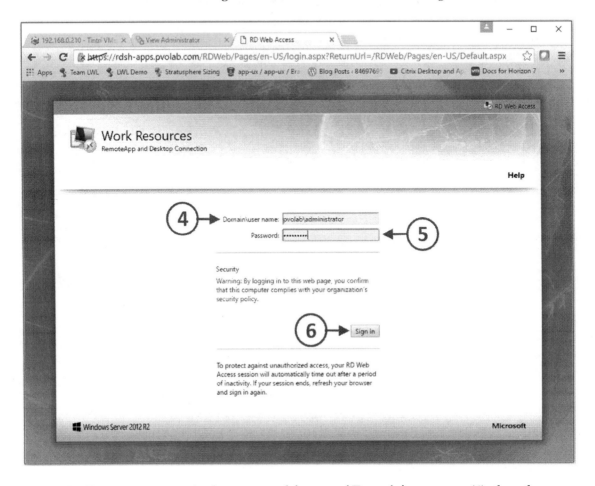

7. Enter a username in the requested format of **Domain\username** (4), then the password (5). Then click the **Sign in** button (6).

You will now see the following web page, which displays the available applications:

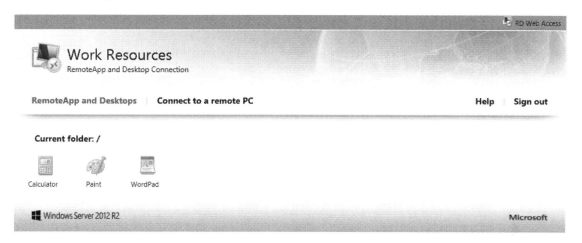

To test an application, double-click on it to launch it. As the application launches, you will see something like the following pop up on your desktop:

The application should then successfully launch.

Now that everything is working and applications can be published, in the following section we are going to add some more applications.

Installing additional applications

In this section, we are going to install some additional applications for remote access, starting with Microsoft Office 2016.

Installing applications is almost identical to installing applications on any other Windows operating system; however, there are a few subtle differences given that this is a remote session host server. We are going to quickly run through the process.

Open a console to the RDSH server on which you want to install the applications and open **Control Panel**, as shown in the following screenshot:

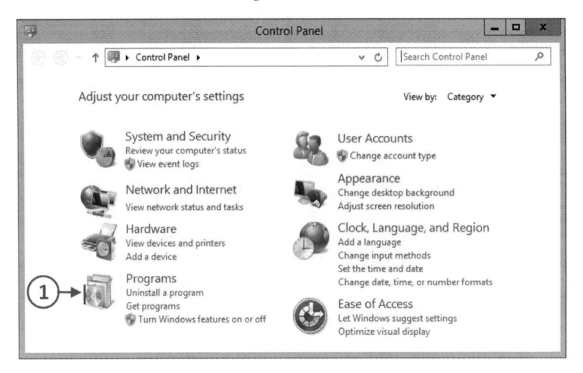

1. Click on **Programs** (**1**). You will now see the **Programs** dialog box, as shown in the following screenshot:

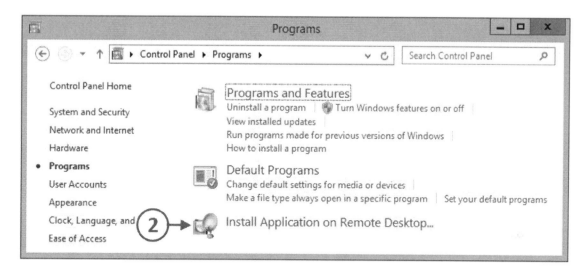

2. Click on **Install Application on Remote Desktop…** (**2**).

   The **Install Program From Floppy Disk or CD-ROM** dialog box appears, as shown in the following screenshot:

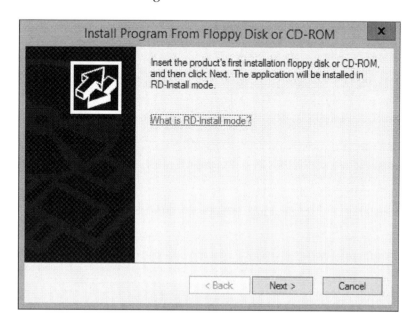

In this dialog box, it highlights something called **RD-Install mode**, so what does that mean?

To install an application on an RDSH host server, it needs to be switched into a special install mode called **RD-Install** to make sure that the applications are able to run in a multi-user environment.

Once you have installed the applications on the RDSH server, the server will then need to be switched back into what is called **execution mode,** or **RD-Execute,** so that users can remotely connect to the server and the applications running on it.

This can also be done at the command line using the following commands:

```
change user /install
change user /execute
```

You can check the current install mode of your RDSH server using the following command:

```
change user /query
```

3. The easiest was to install applications is by doing it from the **Programs** option in the **Control Panel**, which is how we are going to do it in this example. This option takes you through the installation process by automatically switching the server to RD-Install mode, installs the program, and switches the server back to RD-Execute mode once finished.

4. Now click **Next >** to start the installation. The server automatically checks for the installation media and the installation files on the A: drive first, and then the E: drive. If it doesn't locate any media, then the **Run Installation Media** dialog box is displayed, as shown in the following screenshot:

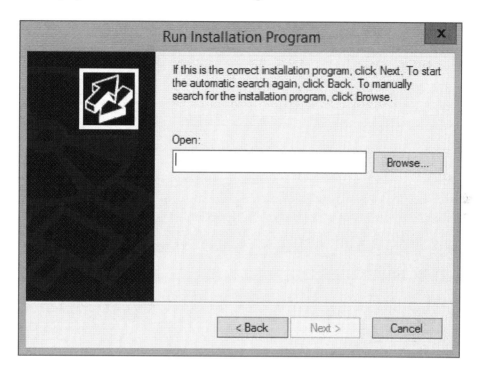

5. In this example, we are going to install Microsoft Office 2016, for which we have copied the .ISO file into the shared folder. It's worth mounting the ISO image first and then browsing to it.

6. To do this, navigate to the shared folder and locate the Office 2016 .ISO file, as shown in the following screenshot:

en_office_professional_plus_2016_x86_x64...	29/10/2015 12:18	Disc Image File	2,365,224 KB
Product Key	29/10/2015 11:34	Text Document	1 KB

7. Double-click the `.ISO` disc image file to mount it, as shown in the following screenshot:

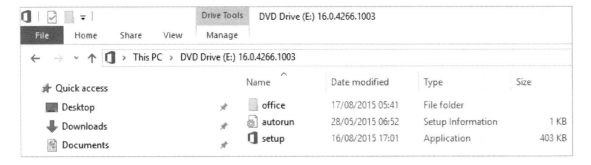

8. With the Office 2016 setup files now available, return to the **Run Installation Media** dialog box and enter the details into the Office installer.

9. In the example lab, this is `e:\setup`, as shown in the following screenshot:

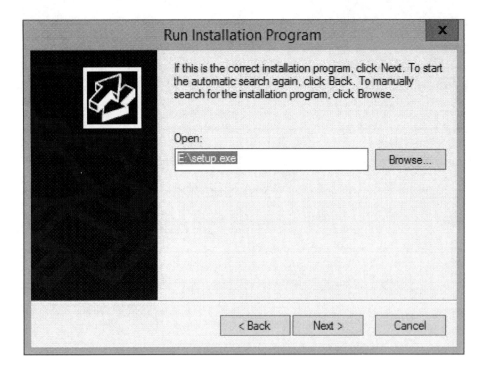

10. Now click the **Next >** button to continue the installation.

11. As the application installer launches, you will also see the following **Finish Admin Install** box, as shown in the following screenshot:

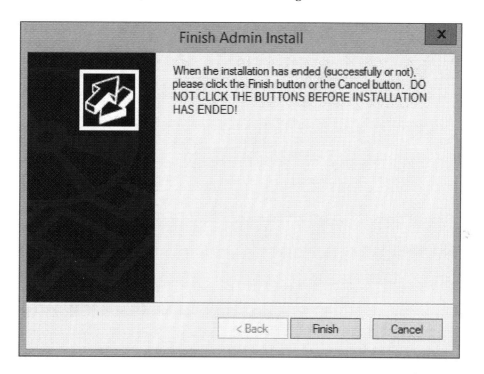

 Ignore this dialog box for now, and make sure that you **DO NOT** click the **Finish** button at this point. You need to complete the application installation first.

12. The installation of Office 2016 will now run, and you should install Office in exactly the same way as you would normally. This is shown in the following screenshot:

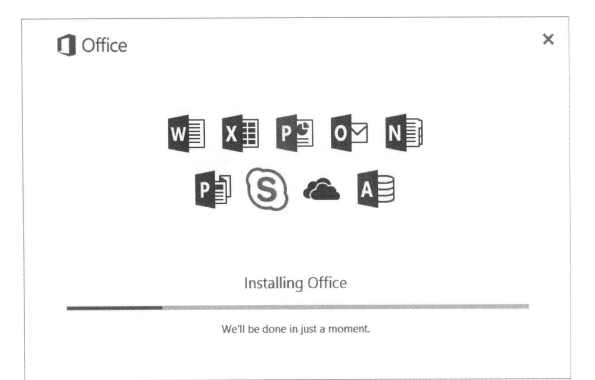

13. Once the installation is complete, return to the **Finish Admin Install** box, as shown in the following screenshot:

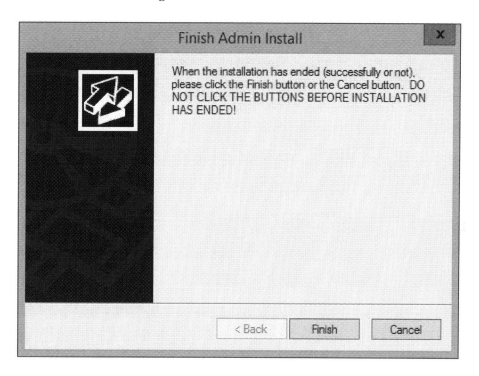

14. Now you can click the **Finish** button.
15. So, now that Microsoft Office 2016 has been installed on the RDSH server, you need to go back and configure which of the individual Office suite applications are going to be made available to the users as remote applications.
16. The first step is to launch the RDS configuration from the **Server ManagerDashboard** screen.

17. Now click to launch the **Remote Desktop Services**, highlight the RDSH server you want to configure, and then click on **QuickSessionCollection (3)**, as shown in the following screenshot:

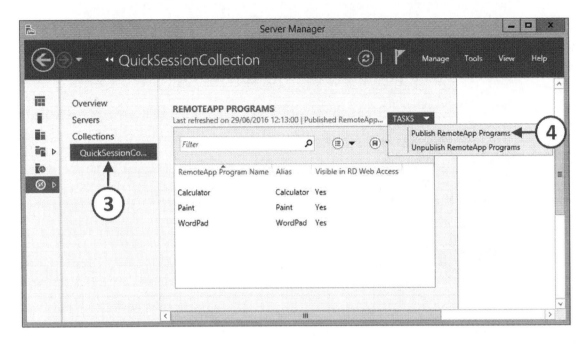

18. Scroll down to the **RemoteApp Programs** dialog box and then click the down arrow on the **TASKS** button in the top right, and then click **Publish RemoteApp Programs (4)**.

19. You will now see the **Publish RemoteApp Programs** configuration screen, as shown in the following screenshot:

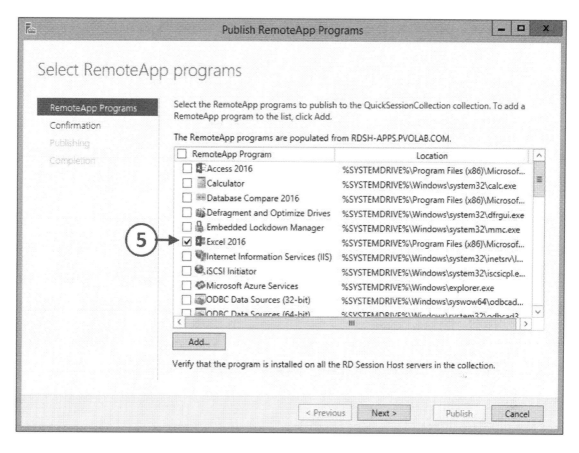

From here, you can select which applications you want to make available to the users.

20. Check the boxes next the applications you want to add (5). In the example lab, we are going to check the boxes for the following applications:
    - Excel 2016
    - OneNote 2016
    - Outlook 2016
    - PowerPoint 2016
    - Publisher 2016
    - Word 2016

21. Once you have selected all the applications you want, click the **Next >** button. You will now see the **Confirmation** box for the applications you selected:

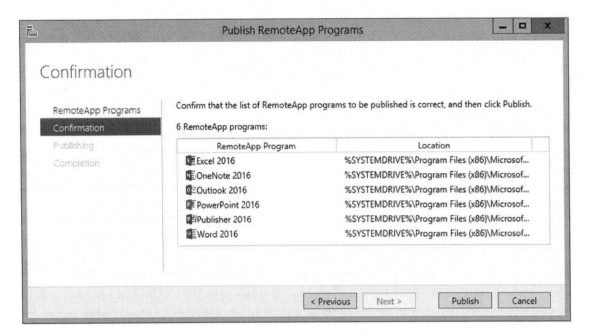

22. Now click the **Publish** button.
23. You will then see a progress bar detailing the progress of the applications being published.

24. Once publishing has completed, you will see the **Completion** screen, as shown in the following screenshot detailing the applications that were successfully published:

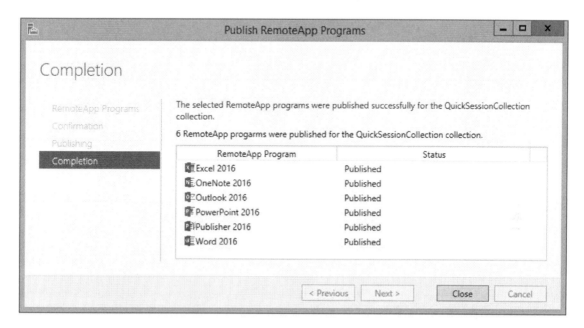

25. Click the **Close** button to complete the publishing process.

As previously, we are going to test that the applications are available from the web access portal. Open a browser and go to the following address: `https://rdsh-apps.pvolab.com/rdweb`

Log in to the portal using the administrator account.

You will see the following screenshot from the RD Web Access portal, showing the newly published applications for Office 2016:

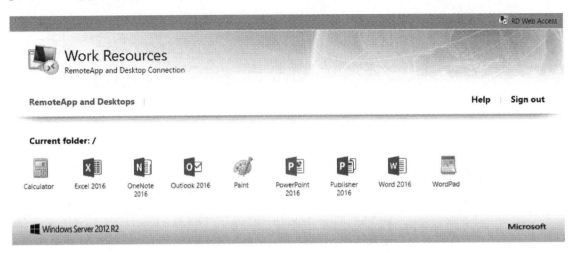

As you can see, the newly published applications are available to the end users. Double-click on one of them to test it launches. Then click on **Sign out** and close the web page.

In the following section, we are going to configure the licensing role.

Configuring the licensing role

The next role we need to configure is the remote desktop licensing role. Unlike a Microsoft RemoteApp deployment, Horizon View only requires the licensing role and the RDSH role, which is very much simpler than a Microsoft full deployment:

1. From the **Server Manager Dashboard** page, click on **Add roles and features (1)**, as shown in the following screenshot:

2. The **Add Roles and Features Wizard** will now launch, as shown in the following screenshot:

3. Click the radio button for **Role-based or feature-based installation** (2), and then click the **Next >** button to continue to the **Server Selection** configuration screen, as shown in the following screenshot:

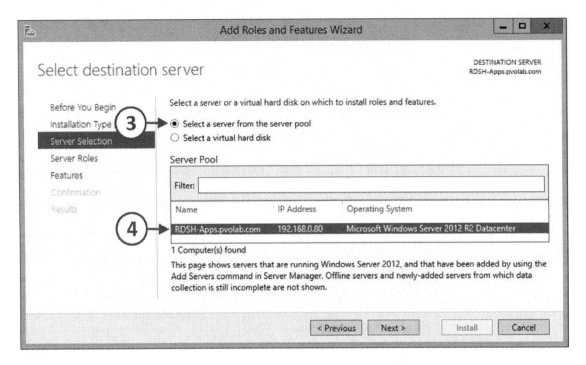

4. Click the radio button for **Select a server from the server pool** (3) and then click the server you want to use. In the example lab, this is the **RDSH-Apps.pvolab.com** server (4).

5. Click the **Next >** button to continue to the **Server Roles** screen:

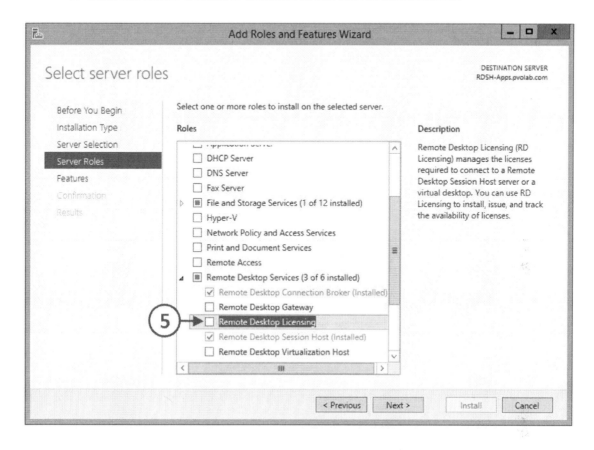

6. Click the box for **Remote Desktop Licensing** (5). You will see the following dialog box:

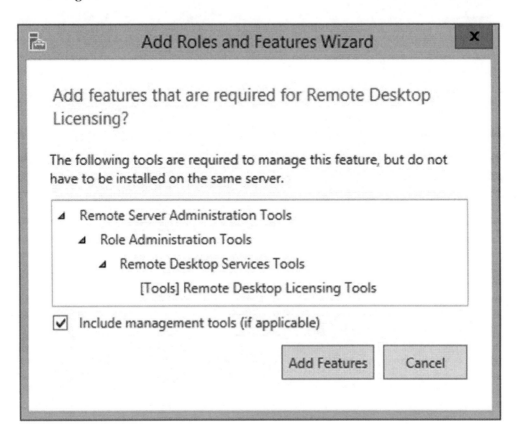

7. Click the **Add Features** button.

You will now see the Features configuration screen, as shown in the following screenshot:

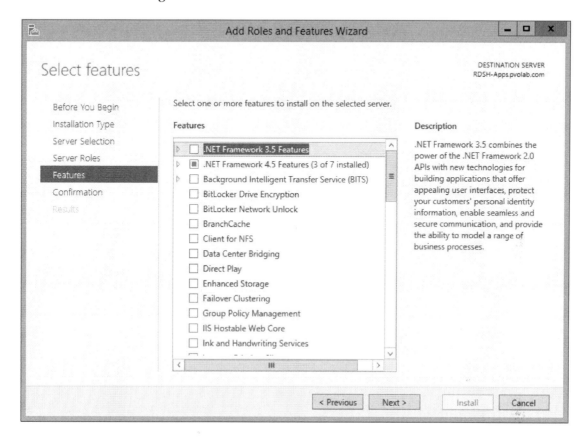

8. Click the **Next >** button to continue.
9. You will now see the **Confirmation** screen.

10. Ensure that the box is checked for **Restart the destination server automatically if required** (6), as shown in the following screenshot:

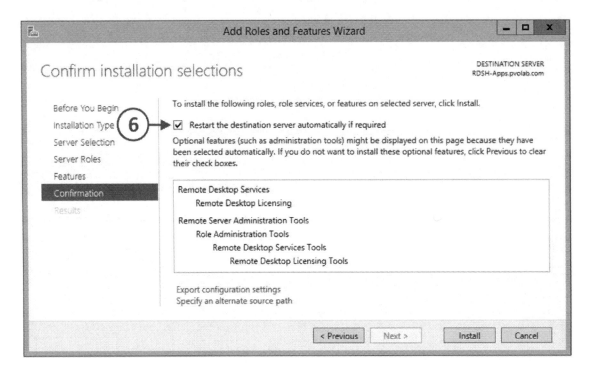

11. Click the **Install** button to install the features. The features will now be installed, as shown in the following screenshot:

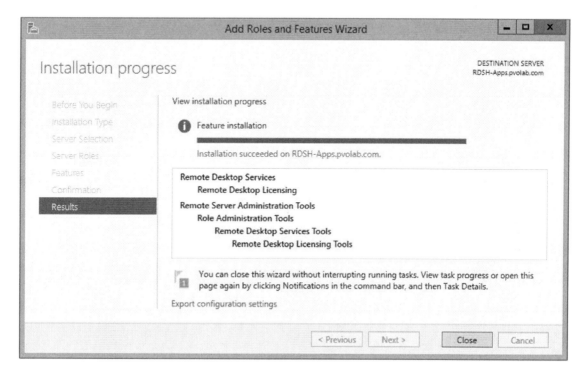

12. Once the features have been installed, click the **Close** button.

The next stage of the installation process is to activate the licensing server.

Activating the licensing role

Now you have added the license server role, the next step is to activate it:

1. From the **Server Manager Dashboard**, click on **Remote Desktop Services**, as shown in the following screenshot:

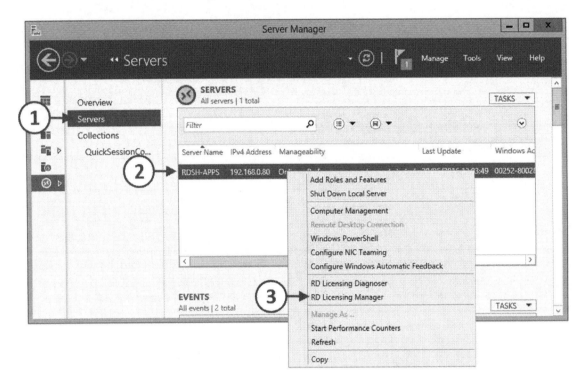

2. Click on **Servers** (**1**), and then select the **RDSH-APPS** server (**2**). Click to highlight the server, right-click, and then from the contextual menu, select the **RD Licensing Manager** option (**3**).

You will now see the **RD Licensing Manager**, as shown in the following screenshot:

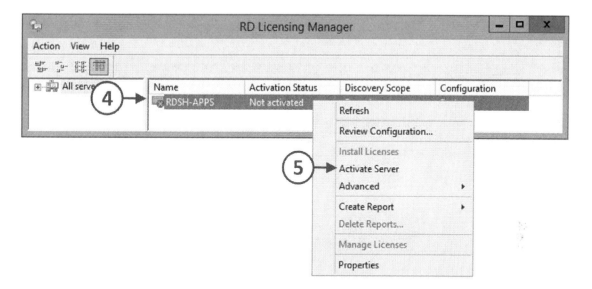

3. Click on the **RDSH-APPS** server (**4**) to highlight it, right-click, and from the contextual menu, select the **Activate Server** (**5**) option.

The **Activate Server Wizard** will now launch, as shown in the following screenshot:

4. Click the **Next >** button to continue.

You will now see the **Connection Method** dialog box, as shown in the following screenshot:

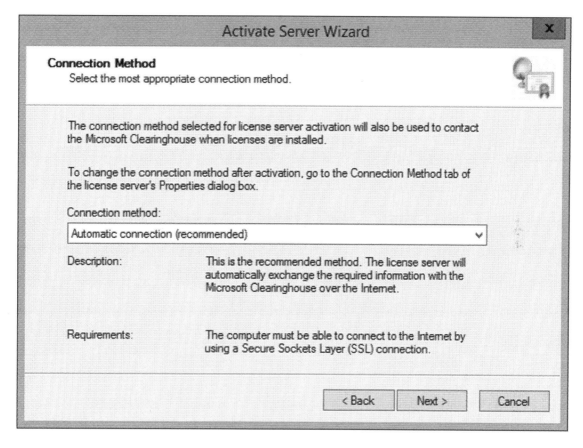

5. In the **Connection method** drop-down box, ensure that you have selected **Automatic connection**, and the click the **Next >** button to continue.

6. You will now see the **Company Information** dialog box, where you can enter your company details. This is shown in the following screenshot:

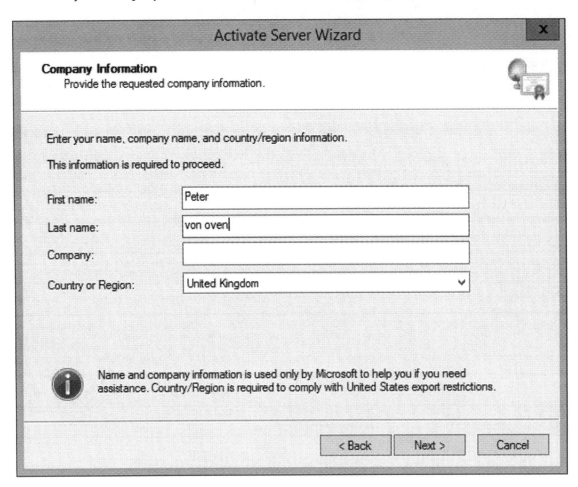

7. Click the **Next >** button to continue. You will now see a second **Company Information** dialog box. The information for this page is optional, so we will leave it blank. Click the **Next >** button to continue.

8. Finally, you will see the **Completing the Activate Server Wizard** screen. Ensure the box is checked for **Start Install Licenses Wizard now** (6), so that you can install licenses:

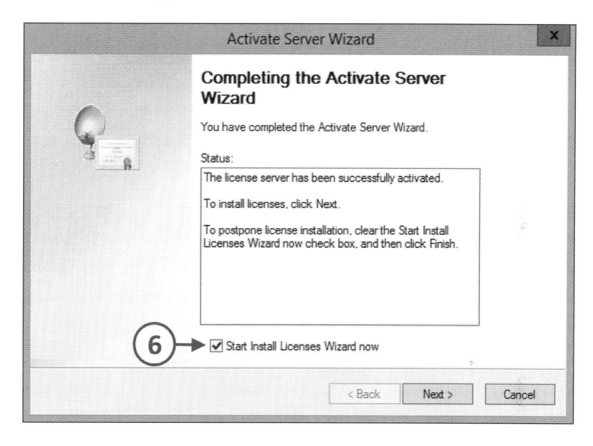

9. Click the **Next >** to continue. The **Install Licenses Wizard** will now launch, as shown in the following screenshot:

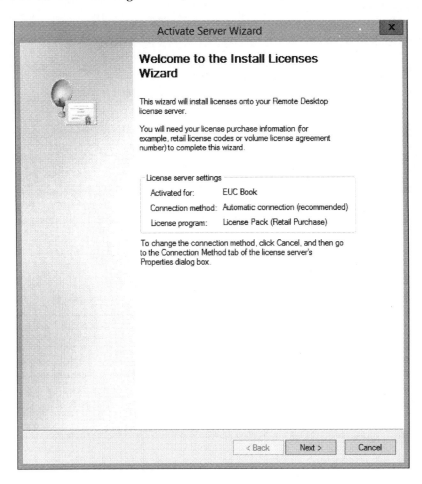

10. You will now see the **License Program** dialog box, where you can choose the licensing model that is appropriate to your environment. In the example lab, the **Other** agreement option has been selected.

11. Click the **Next >** button to continue.

12. In the next dialog box, enter your agreement number and click the **Next >** button to continue to the next dialog box for **Product Version and License Type**, from where you can choose the product type and license type.

13. From the **Product version** box, click the drop-down menu and select the option for **Windows Server 2012 (7)**, and then in the **License type** box, click the drop-down menu and select the option for **RDS Per User CAL (8)**, as shown in the following screenshot:

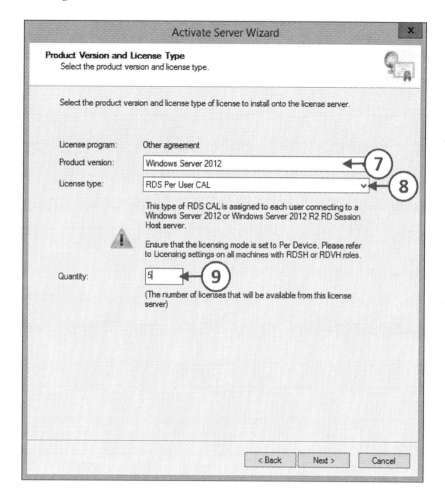

14. Finally, in the **Quantity** box (9), enter the number of licenses that will be made available from this license server.

15. Click the **Next >** button to continue. You will now see the installation progress bar showing the progress of the installation. Once completed, the licenses are then installed on the server and are ready to be used.

In the following section, we are going to install the Horizon View agent onto the RDSH server.

Installing the Horizon View agent for RDSH

In the next part of the process, we are going to install the Horizon View agent onto the RDSH server. The agent is exactly the same agent as the one that you would install on the virtual desktop machines.

Browse to the shared software folder and navigate to the agent installation application, as shown in the following screenshot.

The file you are looking for is VMware-viewagent-x86_64-7.0.0-3618085. The seven-digit number at the end of the filename refers to the build version, and so you may have a different number depending on the build version you are using:

Name	Date modified	Type	Size
VMware-personamanagement-x86_64-7.0.0-3633490	10/04/2016 16:13	Application	17,214 KB
VMware-ThinApp-Enterprise-5.2.1-3655846	10/04/2016 16:18	Application	17,656 KB
VMware-viewagent-x86_64-7.0.0-3618085	10/04/2016 16:13	Application	161,006 KB
VMware-viewcomposer-7.0.0-3613429	10/04/2016 16:14	Application	32,355 KB
VMware-viewconnectionserver-x86_64-7.0.0-3633490	11/04/2016 13:53	Application	182,370 KB
Horizon-v7.01	28/06/2016 15:04	Compressed (zipped)...	363,949 KB
VMware-Horizon-Extras-Bundle-4.0.0-3616726	10/04/2016 16:14	Compressed (zipped)...	2,739 KB
VMware-UEM-9.0	29/06/2016 20:13	Compressed (zipped)...	28,819 KB
VMware-horizonagent-linux-x86_64-7.0.0-3617131.tar.gz	10/04/2016 16:15	GZ File	76,580 KB

Double-click to launch the View Agent installer to install the Horizon View agent onto the RDSH server:

1. You will now see the **Welcome to the Installation Wizard for VMware Horizon View Agent** dialog box, as shown in the following screenshot:

2. Click the **Next >** button to start the installation.

    You will now see the **License Agreement** dialog box.

3. Click the radio button for **I accept the terms in the license agreement**, as shown in the following screenshot:

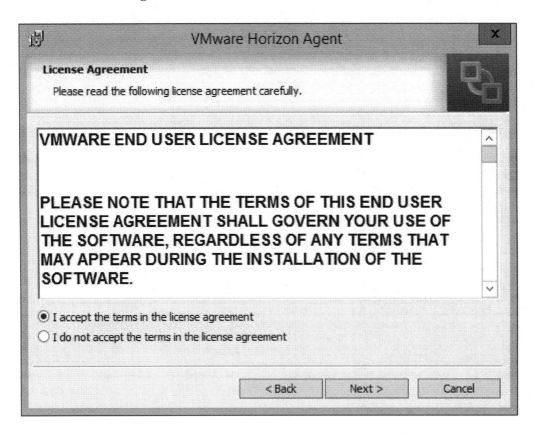

4. Click the **Next >** button to continue the installation.

You will now see the **Network protocol configuration** dialog box, as shown in the following screenshot:

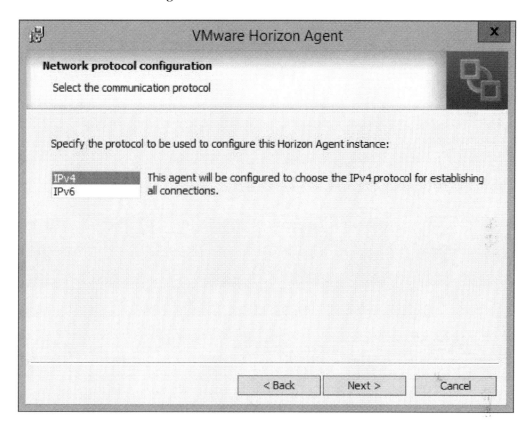

5. Click on **IPv4** and then click on the **Next >** button to continue the installation.

You will now see the **Custom Setup** dialog, which allows you to select which components and features of the View agent you want to install. This is shown in the following screenshot:

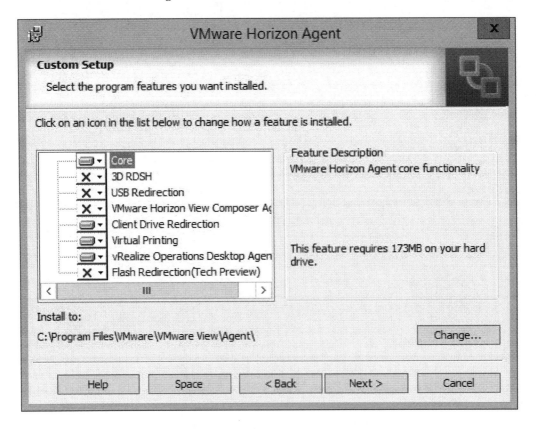

6. In the example lab, we are going to accept the default options; however, you can choose to install the **3D RDSH**, **USB Redirection**, **View Composer**, and **Flash Redirection** options should you want to.

7. As you can see, there are a number of features that can be installed as part of the View Agent installation. These are listed as follows:
    - **Core**: Installs the core features required for RDSH
    - **3D RDSH**: Enabled 3D acceleration in RDSH sessions
    - **USB Redirection**: Redirects USB devices from the client to the RDSH session
    - **VMware Horizon View Composer Agent**: This allows RDS host servers to be built from a single parent image using the linked clone technology, to easily deploy an RDS server farm
    - **Client Redirection**: Allows clients to share local drives with the RDS sessions (not supported when using IPv6)
    - **Virtual Printing**: Allows printing from RDS sessions
    - **vRealize Operations Desktop Agent**: Allows the management agent to be deployed for monitoring RDS sessions with vRealize
    - **Flash Redirection (Tech Preview)**: Enables the Flash redirection feature with RDS sessions (note that this is currently a tech preview in this version of Horizon View)

8. Click the **Next >** button to continue the installation.

9. In the next dialog box, the **Register with Horizon 7 Connection Server** configuration screen, we are going to configure the agent to talk to the connection server. This allows the connection server to read the published applications list from the RemoteApp catalog, and allows you to create pools within View.

10. In the **hostname or IP address** box (**1**), enter the name of the connection server. In the example lab, we are using the connection server called **hzn7-cs1**. In the **Authentication** section, click the radio button for **Specify administrator credentials** (**2**), and then in the **Username** box (**3**), enter the user account you want to use to connect to the connection server, followed by the password in the **Password** box (**4**), as shown in the following screenshot:

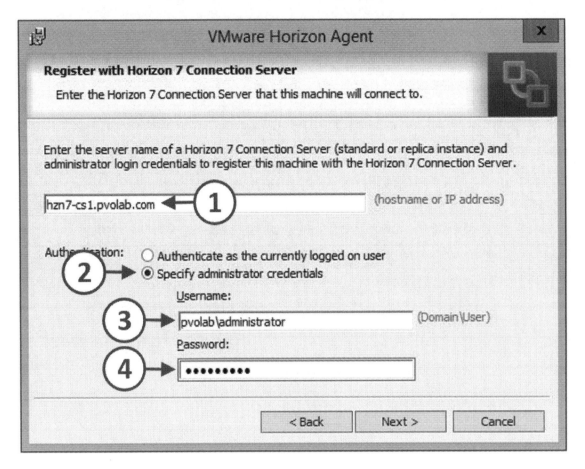

 Make sure you use the format **domain\user** to enter the username, and also that the account has the correct privileges to access the connection server. You would typically use a service account for this.

11. Click the **Next >** button to continue the installation.

12. You will now see the **Ready to Install the Program** screen. Click the **Install** button to start the installation process.

13. Once the agent is successfully installed, you will see the **Installer Complete** screen. Click **Finish** to quit the installation.

> One of the most common reasons that the installation of the view agent fails is down to the configuration of the RDSH server. More often than not, there are no sound drivers loaded on the Windows server running the RDSH role. If this is the case, then the installation of the agent will fail and automatically roll back. If that happens, it's worth checking this first.

You will now be prompted to reboot the server once installation has completed. Click the **Yes** button in the dialog box to reboot.

We have now completed the first part of the Horizon View configuration. In the next step of the process, we will turn our attention to View Administrator and configure the application pools.

Configuring hosted apps in the View Administrator

The next stage in the installation and configuration process is performed using the View Administrator console and, like a standard View setup, involves creating pools and entitlements. However, rather than creating pools for virtual desktop machines, this time we are going to configure application pools.

Before you do that, you first of all need to set up a farm, which contains the newly built RDSH server:

1. Open a browser and connect to View Administrator. In our example lab, the address for View Administrator is `https://hzn7-cs1.pvolab.com/admin/`.

2. Log in to View Administrator using the administrator account and password, as shown in the following screenshot:

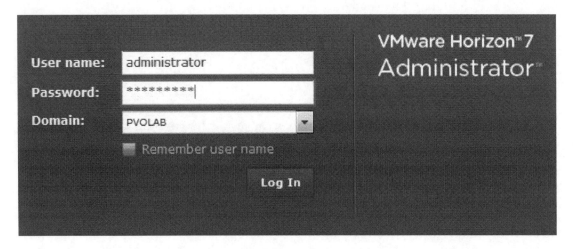

3. You will now see the View Administrator dashboard.
4. From here, expand the arrow for **Resources** from the **Inventory** pane on the left, and then click on **Farms** (**1**). Now click the **Add...** button (**2**), as shown in the following screenshot:

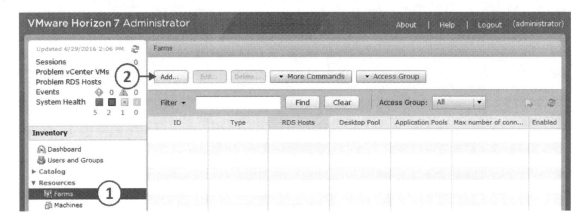

5. You will now see the **Add Farm** configuration screen.

In the **Type** section, click the radio button for **Manual Farm** (3), as shown in the following screenshot:

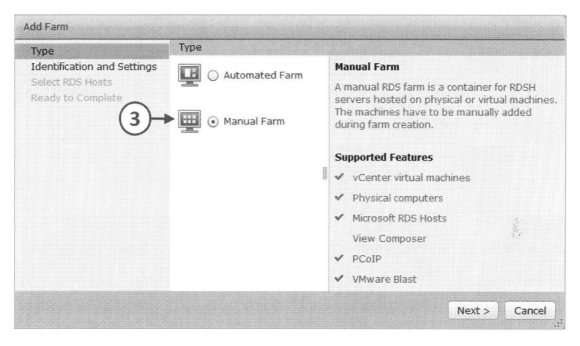

6. Click the **Next >** button to continue the configuration.
7. You will now see the **Indentation and Settings** configuration section.
8. In the **ID** box (4) enter an ID for the farm that will be used by View to identify it. In the example lab, this is called **View-Hosted-Apps**.

> You cannot use spaces for the ID, only letters (upper and lower case), numbers (0-9), and – (minus) or _ (underscore) characters.

9. In the **Description** box (5), enter an optional description for the farm, and then from the **Access Group** dropdown, select an access group, if you have one.
10. Next, under **Farm Settings**, set the **Default display protocol** to PCoIP (6) and from the **Allow users to choose protocol** dropdown (7), select **No**.
11. In the **Empty session timeout** (8) enter a time after which the session should timeout when not being used, and then in the **When timeout occurs** box (9), from the drop-down menu, select what happens at timeout. In the example lab, this is set to disconnect the user from the session.

12. The next option is whether or not to **Log off disconnected sessions (10)**. This option will log off any disconnected sessions. In the example lab, this is set to **Never**.

13. Finally, check the **Enabled** box **(11)** to allow HTML access to hosted applications, as shown in the following screenshot:

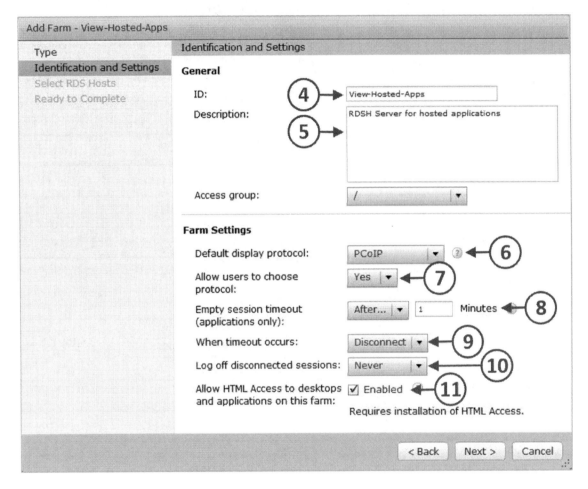

14. Once you have completed the configuration options on this screen, click the **Next >** button to continue.

15. You will now see the **Select RDS Hosts** configuration screen from where you select which hosts are going to participate in this farm.

16. Click and highlight the **rdsh-apps.pvolab.com** entry from the table, as shown in the following screenshot:

17. Click the **Next >** button to continue to the **Ready to Complete** screen, as shown in the following screenshot:

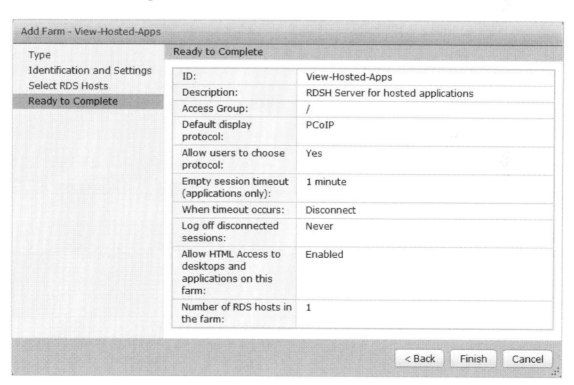

18. Check that the settings you have entered are correct, and click the **Finish** button.

You have now successfully created a new farm configuration for the hosted applications, as shown in the following screenshot:

You will also see the **RDS Farm** listed in the **System Health** box on the View Administrator dashboard. You will see the farm name and server name listed in the box, along with a green box to show they are working correctly, as shown in the following:

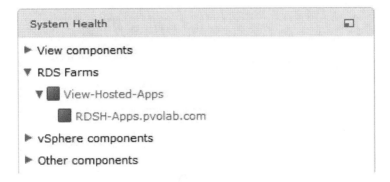

In the following section, we are going to create an application pool.

Creating an application pool for hosted apps

In this section, we are going to create an application pool. This allows you to create a pool that contains a number of different applications. You may want to create application pools to reflect different departments, for example:

1. From View Administrator, expand the arrow for **Catalog** from the **Inventory** pane on the left, and then click on **Application Pools (1)**.

2. Now click the **Add...** button (**2**), as shown in the following screenshot:

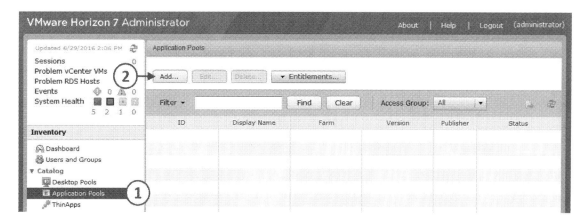

3. You will now see the **Add Application Pools** configuration screen.
4. From the **Select an RDS farm** drop-down menu (**3**), select the farm that we created previously for our published applications. In the example lab, select the farm called **View-Hosted-Apps** from the menu.
5. Next, click the radio button for **Select installed applications** (**4**). This will automatically list all the applications that are installed on that particular RDSH server. There is also the option to add an application pool manually.
6. From the list of applications displayed, check the box next to each application you want to add to the application pool. In the example lab, we are going to add the following applications:
    - Calculator
    - Paint
    - Excel 2016
    - PowerPoint 2016
    - Word 2016
    - Publisher 2016
    - Outlook 2016

This is shown in the following screenshot:

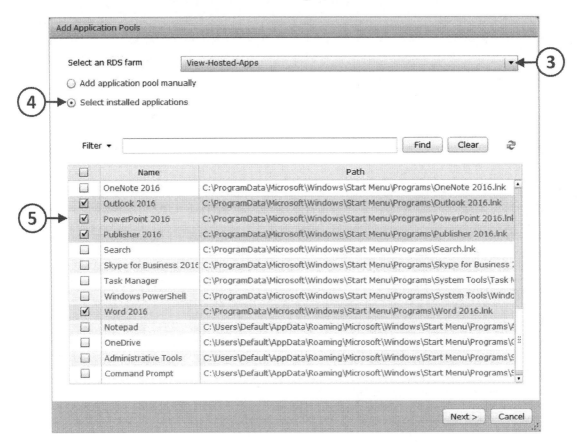

7. When you have selected all the required applications, click the **Next >** button to continue.

8. You will now see the **Edit ID and Display Name** screen. Here you can choose to edit the **ID** and the display name for the applications if you want to. This is shown in the following screenshot:

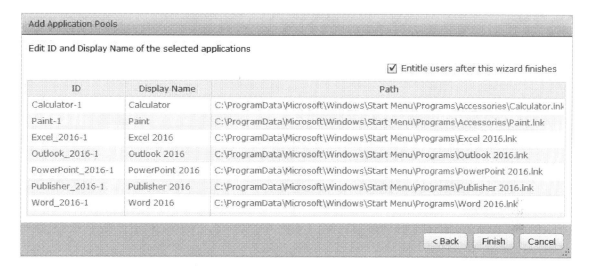

9. Click the **Finish** button to complete the configuration. You will see that the application pool has been created.

Now that you have your application pool all set up and ready to go, the next step is to entitle end users to the pool and allow them to launch applications.

Entitling users to application pools

Perform the following steps to entitle users to the application pools:

1. We are now going to entitle a user to be able to access desktop sessions. From the View Administrator dashboard screen, click on **Users and Groups (1)** under the **Inventory** section on the left-hand side.

2. Then, click the **Entitlements** button (**2**), and from the displayed options, click the **Add Application Entitlement** option (**3**), as shown in the following screenshot:

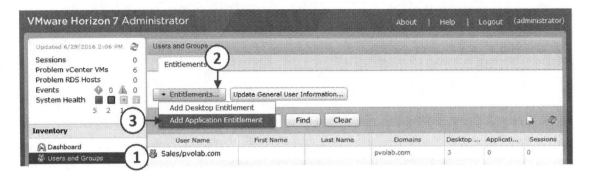

3. You will now see the **Find User or Group** configuration screen.

4. Check the **Users** box (**4**), and then from the **Domain** drop-down menu, select the domain for the user you want to entitle. In our example, we are going to use `pvolab.com` domain.

5. In the **Name/User name** box (**5**), enter the user details you want to entitle. In the example lab, we are going to entitle the user called **jsmith**, so type this into the box and click **Find** (**6**) to search for the user in the domain.

   When the user has been found, their details will be displayed in the table. Select the user by clicking on the entry in the table to highlight them, as shown in the following screenshot:

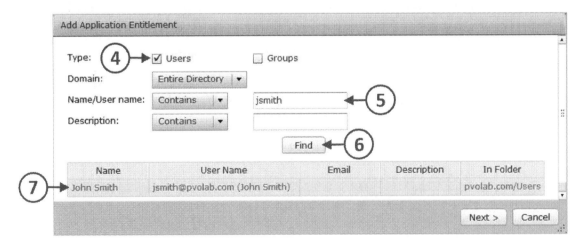

6. Now click the **Next >** button. You will see the **Select the Application pools to entitle** configuration screen, as shown in the following screenshot:

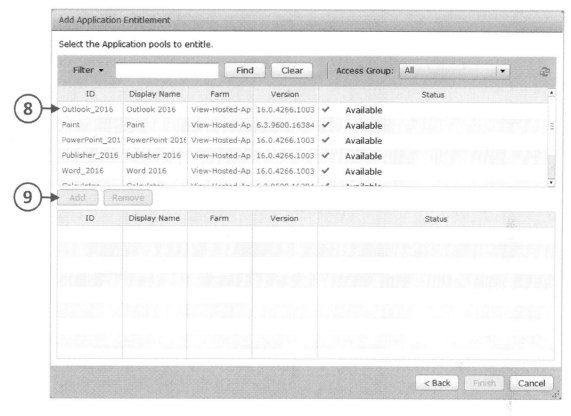

7. Click on each application you want to entitle to the user by highlighting it (**8**), and then clicking the **Add** button (**9**).

In this example, we are going to add all the applications, so you end up with something like the following screenshot:

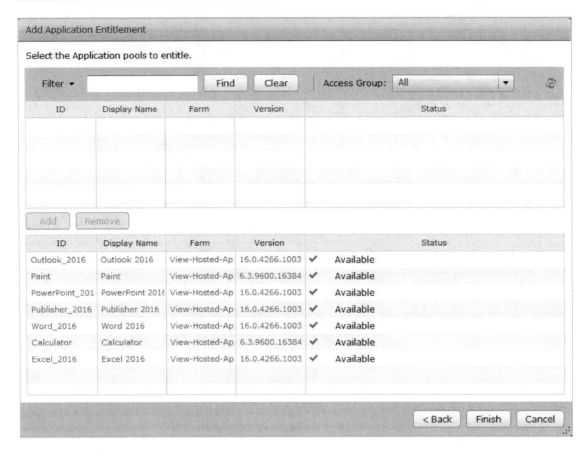

8. Once you have added the applications, click the **Finish** button.
9. You will now return to the **Users and Groups** screen showing the entitlements, as shown in the following screenshot:

10. You can see that the user **jsmith** has been entitled to seven applications.

As a final check, we are going to launch the Horizon View client, log in as the test user, and then launch one of the applications.

 Make sure you are using the latest version of the Horizon View client, version 3.0 and above. Older versions will still work with VDI desktops, but will not show any View hosted applications.

Launch the VMware Horizon client and make sure that the address of the connection server has been added.

We will cover the Horizon View client in `Chapter 10`, *Horizon View Client Options*.

11. In the example lab, we are connecting to the **hzn7-cs1.pvolab.com** connection server, as shown in the following screenshot:

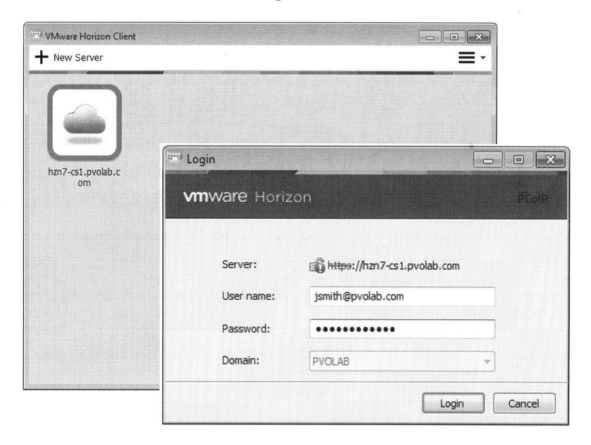

12. Double-click on the **hzn7-cs1.pvolab.com** entry in the VMware Horizon client. You will then see the user login box.

13. Enter the **User name** and **Password** for the example user jsmith, and then click the **Login** button.

> Once authenticated, the Horizon client will connect to the application pool and display the available applications, as shown in the following screenshot:

Double-click on any of the applications to ensure that they launch correctly.

You have now successfully installed, configured, and delivered a View hosted applications environment. In this example, we have deployed a single RDSH server to host our remote applications; however, in a production environment, you are more likely to have multiple servers in a farm. In the final section of this chapter, we are going to look at how you load balance the session connections across multiple servers in a farm.

Load balancing hosted apps in View

The next thing we are going to cover is how the connection broker decides which of the RDS host servers in the farm that is running the requested application is actually going to deliver the application. There are two options for configuring load balancing.

For the first option, there is no real complicated science behind the load balancing from a View perspective. It is purely based on how many sessions are available on any given RDSH server. That means when a user logs in and launches a remote application, the application is delivered from the server that has the highest amount of free sessions available, that is, the one that is least busy.

This is shown in the following diagram:

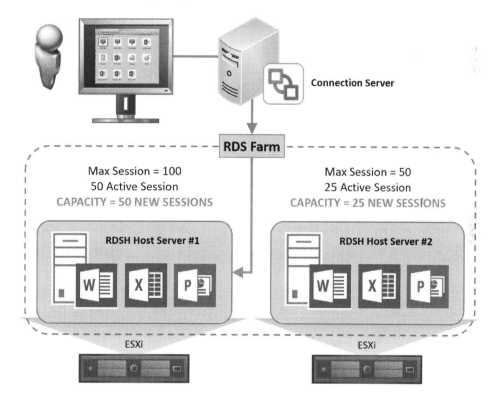

This first option works fine, but how does it know what each session is consuming in terms of resources? A particular host may well have enough capacity for additional sessions based on the number of sessions it has free, but what if those sessions it's already hosting are consuming vast amounts of resources?

This is where the second option comes in, as it uses more in-depth information to place sessions, which is based on measuring the CPU and memory utilization of each host, rather than the number of free sessions.

To enable this load balancing method, there are a number of manual steps you need to complete, as we will now describe.

First of all, this method is based on executing scripts, and therefore, you need to ensure that those scripts are stored on each RDS host server in the farm. You can create your own scripts; however, there are a couple of example scripts that ship as part of the View Agent installation. You will find them in the following folder once the View agent has been installed (the View Agent installation is covered earlier on in this chapter): `C:\Program Files\VMware\VMware View\Agent\scripts`.

You will then see the two example scripts, as shown in the following screenshot:

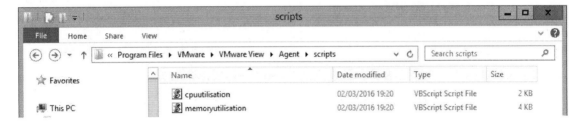

As the names suggest, one script monitors CPU, and the other monitors memory utilization. Each script monitors its respective component and returns the following values to make the decision on placing sessions:

- *0 – for utilization > 90%*
- *1 – for utilization > 75%*
- *2 – for utilization > 25%*
- *3 – for utilization > 25%*

Let's now configure the CPU script for use in the example lab by completing the following tasks. The first of these is to enable the View Script Host service:

1. Open a console to the RDSH host server RDSH-Apps, and from the desktop of the server, launch a **RUN** command box by pressing the Windows key and *R*. You will see the following screenshot:

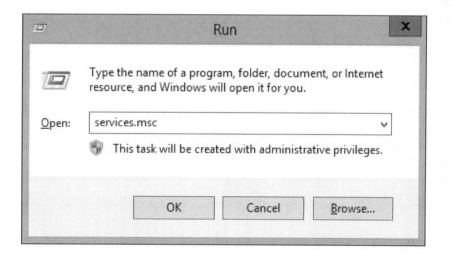

2. In the **Open** box, type `services.msc` to launch the **Services** management screen.
3. Scroll down until you find the entry for **VMware Horizon View Script Host (1)**. Click on it to highlight it, and then right-click.

4. From the contextual menu, select the **Properties** option (2), as shown in the following screenshot:

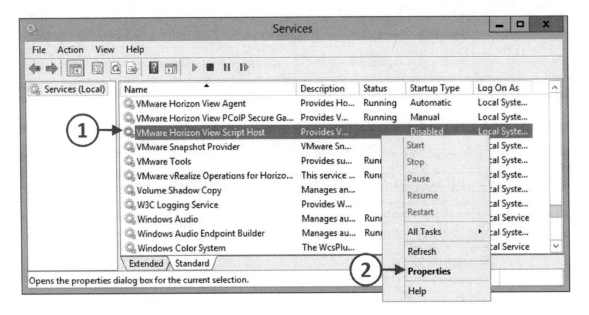

5. You will now see the **VMware Horizon View Script Host Properties** screen, as shown in the following screenshot:

6. First of all, in the **Startup type** box, from the drop-down menu (**3**), select the option for **Automatic** so that this service starts when the server boots. Next, click the **Apply** button (**4**), and finally, click the **Start** button to load the service now. You should now see the following, showing the service running:

VMware Horizon View PCoIP Secure Ga...	Provides VMwa...	Running	Manual	Local Syste...
VMware Horizon View Script Host	Provides VMwa...	Running	Automatic	Local Syste...
VMware Snapshot Provider	VMware Snaps...		Manual	Local Syste...

7. Once completed, close the Services management screen. The next step is to add the script details to the registry of the server.
8. Launch a **RUN** command box again, and in the **Open** box, type `regedit` to launch the registry editor. Once in the registry editor, navigate to the following section:

HKLM | Software | VMwareInc. | VMware VDM

9. Then from the **VMware VDM** section (**6**), expand **ScriptEvents** (**7**) and then click on **RdshLoad** (**8**), as shown in the following screenshot:

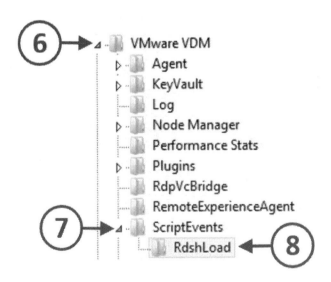

10. Now right-click in the right-hand side pane and from the menu, click on **New** (**9**), and then select the option for **String Value** (**10**), as shown in the following screenshot:

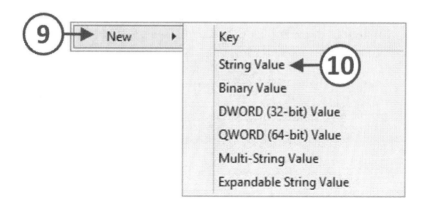

11. You will now be able to enter a new string value. In the example lab, this is called **cpuutilisation** (**11**) to reflect the script that will be run, as shown in the following screenshot:

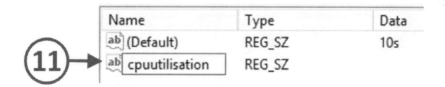

12. Next, you need to edit the newly created string value, and enter a value.
13. Highlight the **cpuutilisation** entry (**12**), right-click, and from the contextual menu, click the option for **Modify...** (**13**):

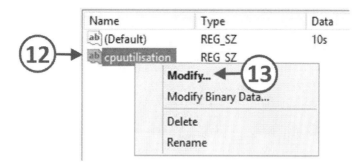

14. You will now see the **Edit String** box. In the **Value data** box (**14**), enter the path to the script. In the example lab, this is as follows: `C:\Program Files\VMware\VMware View\Agent\scripts\cpuutilisation.vbs`.

This is shown in the following screenshot:

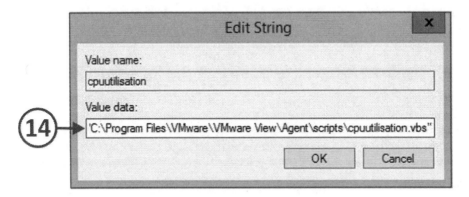

15. Click the **OK** button the save the changes, and then exit the registry editor.

As you have changed the properties of the VMware Horizon View agent, you will need to restart this service for the changes to be applied.

16. Launch a **RUN** command box by pressing the Windows key and *R*.

17. In the **Open** box, type `services.msc` to launch the **Services** management screen.

18. Scroll down until you find the entry for **VMware Horizon View Agent** (**15**). Click on it to highlight it, and then right-click.

19. From the contextual menu, select the **Restart** option (**16**) to restart the service, as shown in the following screenshot:

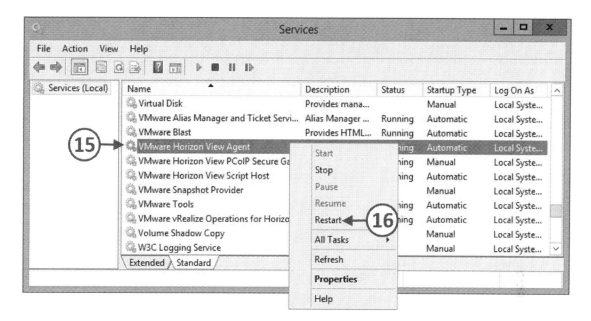

20. Once the service has restarted, you can close the **Services** management screen.

You have now completed the configuration steps, and the load balancing will be calculated based on CPU utilization. You can check that this is working by following these steps:

21. From the **View Administrator Dashboard**, navigate to the **System Health** box. Then, expand the options for **RDS Farms** and the farm for **View-Hosted-Apps**. Now click on the **RDSH-Apps.pvolab.com** server. You will see the following screenshot:

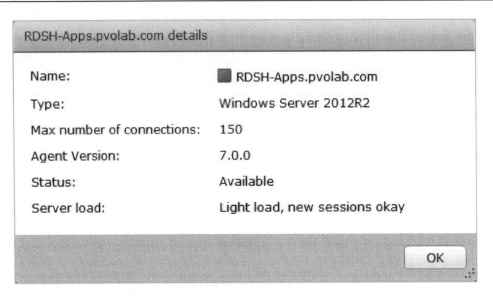

22. You will see that, at the bottom of the box, there is a **Server load** option. This is being measured from the script, and as you can see, currently the CPU load is light and new sessions are able to be resourced by this particular server.

23. Click **OK** to close the box. You have now successfully configured the optional load balancing feature.

Summary

In this chapter, we have discussed how to deliver remote/published applications with the Horizon View hosted applications feature. We started off by looking at the architecture and a deep dive into how it works, before walking through the installation and configuration process of both the Microsoft RDSH components and the Horizon View components needed to make it work.

We then configured an RDS farm and an application pool, and then entitled a test user to the pool. Finally, to check that everything was working, we logged in as the user and tested the environment by launching a remote application.

In the final section, we looked at how to configure load balancing in a View hosted application environment.

In the next chapter, we are going to look at how we apply the same methodology to deliver session-based desktops.

9
Delivering Session-Based Desktops with Horizon View

Following on from the previous chapter, where we configured Horizon View to deliver hosted applications using a Microsoft RDSH environment, in this chapter, we will cover the other half of View's hosting functionality and take a look at the ability of View to deliver session-based desktops, again, using a Microsoft RDSH host server. The key advantage of this feature is that you don't need to deploy a full VDI-based desktop to an end user, they just use a session from the host.

As with the hosted applications feature we covered in `Chapter 8`, *Delivering Remote Applications with View Hosted Apps*, the desktop sessions will be delivered to the end user's device using the Horizon View Client. We will cover the installation of the RDSH role and the configuration of the desktop sessions.

Architectural overview

So, let's take a look at the architecture and how session-based desktops work when compared to the standard View virtual desktop machine brokering. In terms of architecture, delivering desktop sessions is pretty much the same as delivering remote applications.

Horizon View acts as the broker, but instead of brokering a virtual desktop machine that is running on the ESXi host server or an RDSH published application, it is now brokering a desktop session that is running on a Microsoft Windows Server. This server is configured with the RDS role and a number of customizations and policies to make the Windows Server GUI interface look more like that of the Windows 8 desktop operating system.

The following diagram gives you an outline of the architecture:

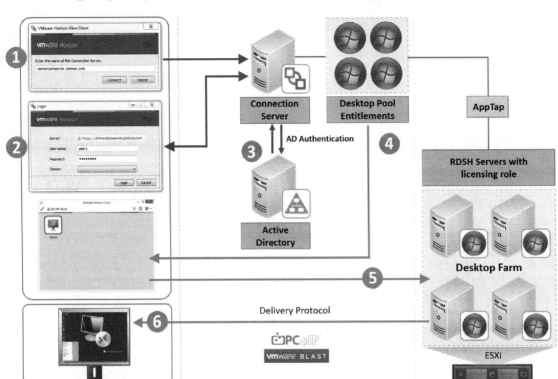

So, how does the architecture work? Basically, in exactly the same way as we have already discussed in Chapter 8, *Delivering Remote Applications with View Hosted Apps*, but now we are delivering remote desktop sessions rather than applications.

Rather than covering the same ground again by describing in detail how this solution works and the system requirements, please refer back to that chapter, and in particular the application connection sequence section.

RDSH sizing guidelines

As with the sizing of View for virtual desktop machines, configuring the right specification for the RDSH servers is also key, and in a similar way to how we consider desktop sizing, we are going to look at different user types.

The VMware recommendation for the user workloads and the memory requirements is shown in the following table:

User Workload Requirements		
	Memory	**Use Case**
Light User	512 MB	Basic application user such as Microsoft Office applications and some web browsing
Medium User	768 MB	Running multiple Microsoft Office applications and light user of multi-media, and more intensive web browsing
Heavy User	1 GB	Advanced application user running 3D-based applications and multi-media, and heavy web-browsing

For the total memory in each RDSH server, VMware recommends that a virtual machine configured as an RDSH server should be provisioned with 64 GB memory, and in terms of CPU requirements, the VMware recommendation is to create virtual servers for the RDSH roles and configure each one with four vCPUs. Make sure that you do not overcommit on the number of cores.

So for example, if you had a virtual machine running as an RDSH server configured with 64 GB of memory and had heavy users hosted on it, you would be able to host a maximum of 64 sessions on that server.

For the hardware configuration, let's say you had a physical ESXi host server configured with a two-socket CPU that had 12-cores giving you a total of 24 cores.

This would allow a maximum of six RDSH servers, as we are going to provision virtual machines for the RDSH role, each with four cores (24 cores / 4 cores per server). That would mean that the physical server would also need to be configured with 384 GB of memory in total (64 GB x 6 RDSH host servers).

These figures are only guidelines and based on some of the VMware-recommended best practices. It is always best to run an assessment on your environment to work out your optimum configuration and what is required.

In the next section, we are going to install and configure the View hosted applications feature.

Load balancing desktop sessions in View

At the end of the previous chapter, we looked at how you would configure load balancing, and how the Connection Server decides which server in the farm is going to be used to resource the session.

This also applies to the hosting of desktop sessions as well, and as you would expect, delivering remote desktop sessions is no different in the way it works with View.

By default, which server resources the session is purely based on how many sessions are available on any given RDSH server at the time of the request. So that means when a user logs in and launches a desktop session, that session is delivered from the server that has the highest amount of free sessions available, that is to say, the one that isn't the busiest.

This is shown in the following diagram:

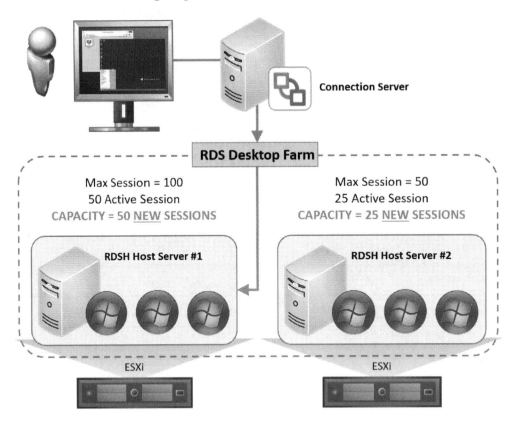

However, if you remember, in the previous chapter we looked at an optional feature whereby you could deploy scripts that would monitor the CPU and memory utilization of the RDS host servers.

When delivering desktop sessions, this might be a better option to more accurately load balance the desktop sessions across all the hosts on the farm. Please refer back to the Load Balancing hosted apps in View section of that chapter to configure this feature.

With the load balancing and architecture now covered, in the next section, we are going to start the installation and get the example lab environment up and running ready to deliver the desktop sessions to the end users.

Installing and configuring desktop sessions in View

We are now going to start the installation process, starting with configuring the server that is going to be used for delivering the session-based desktops, and adding the RDSH role to it.

The installation process is relatively straightforward and is illustrated in the following schematic diagram:

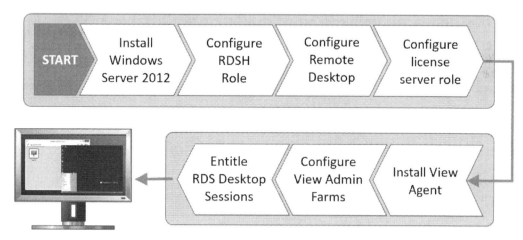

In the example lab, there is already a Windows Server 2012 server ready built, called **RDSH Desktops**, to perform this role.

 You can only have either desktop sessions or a published application per session collection on an RDSH host server. There is a workaround to have both; however, it is not supported. For our example lab, we are going to configure a separate RDSH host for each session type just to make it easier.

In the following sections, we are going to walk through the installation and configuration process in more detail.

Configuring the RDSH role

In this section, we will cover the installation of the RDSH role to host our desktop sessions. We will assume that you already have a new server built for this purpose. In the example lab, the server named `rdsh-desktops.pvolab.com` is going to be used for this role.

1. Open a console to the server, and from the **Server Manager Dashboard** page of the server, click on **Add roles and features (1)** as shown in the following screenshot:

2. The **Add Roles and Features Wizard** will now launch, starting with the **Before You Begin** screen, as shown in the following screenshot:

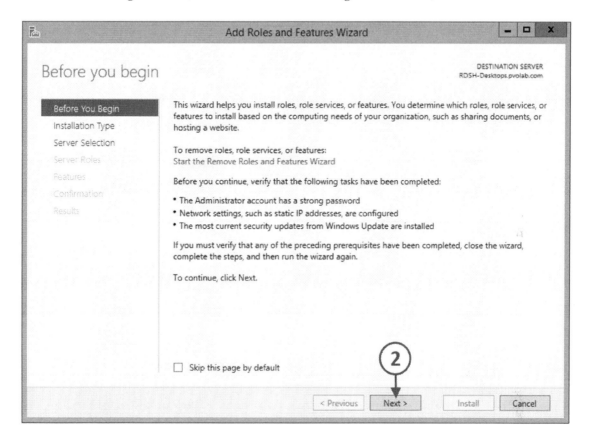

3. Click the **Next >** button (**2**) to continue to the **Installation Type** configuration screen as shown in the following screenshot:

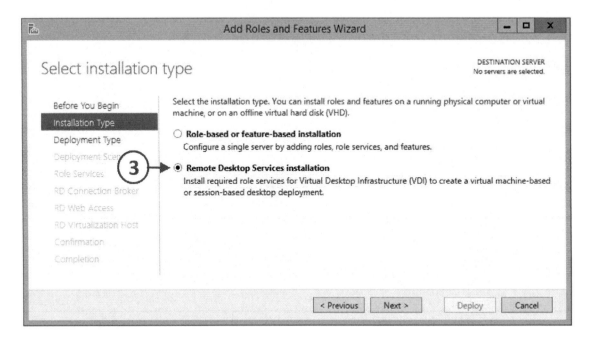

4. Click the radio button for **Remote Desktop Services installation** (**3**), and then click the **Next >** button to continue.

   You will now see the **Deployment Type** configuration screen, as shown in the following screenshot:

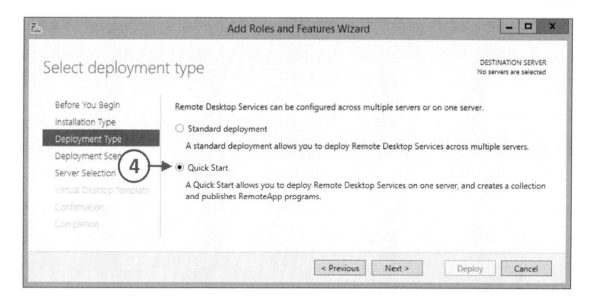

5. Click the radio button for **Quick Start** (4), and then click the **Next >** button to continue.

    Next, you will see the **Deployment Scenario** configuration screen, as shown in the following screenshot:

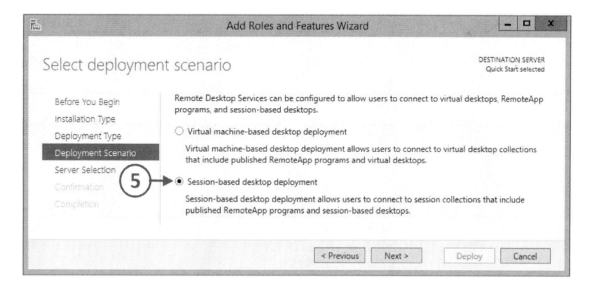

6. Click the radio button for **Session-based desktop deployment** and then click the **Next >** button.

You will now see the **Server Selection** configuration screen, as shown in the following:

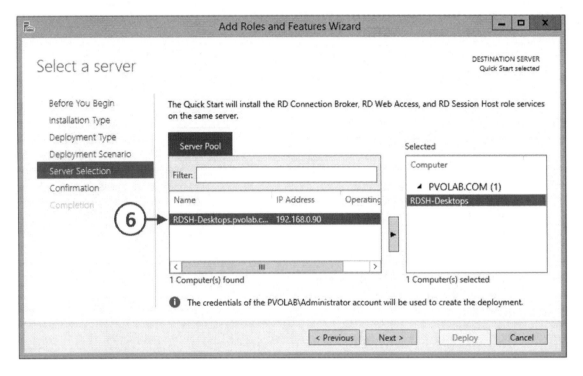

7. From the **Server Pool** list, select the server onto which you want to add the RDSH role.

8. In the example lab, this is the **RDSH-Desktops.pvolab.com** server (6), which has been automatically selected.

9. Click the **Next >** button to continue to the **Confirmation** screen, as shown in the following screenshot:

10. Check the role services that will be installed, make sure that you tick the **Restart the destination server automatically if required** box (7), and then click the **Deploy** button.

11. The installation of the feature will now start and the server will reboot. You may have to log back in to check that the installation of the feature completes. Once completed, you will see the following screenshot:

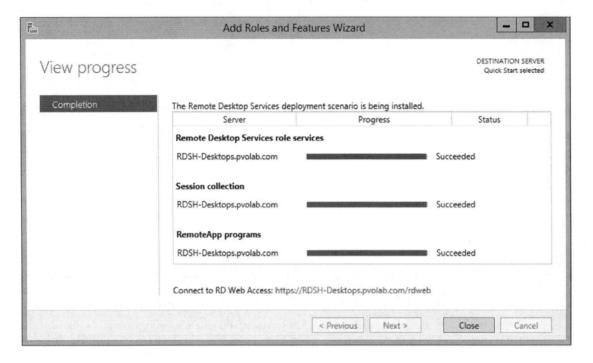

12. Finally, click the **Close** button to complete the installation and close the wizard.

In the next section, we will configure the newly created RDSH server in preparation for delivery of desktop sessions to the end users.

Configuring RDSH to deliver desktop sessions

We used the QuickStart installation method for setting up our RDSH role, and it also included some configured, published applications. As we are going to use this RDSH host server for only desktop sessions, the first thing we are going to do is unpublish those applications.

1. To unpublish the applications, from the **Server Manager Dashboard** screen, click on **Remote Desktop Services (1)**, as shown in the following screenshot:

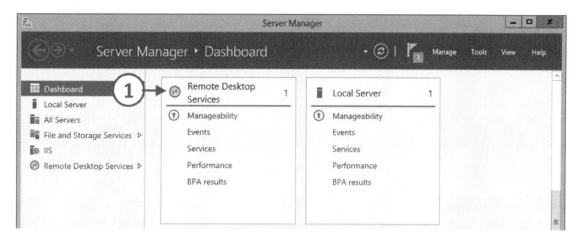

2. You will then see the list of servers that are configured with the RDSH role. In the example lab, this is the **RDSH Desktop** server. Click on this server, and then click on **QuickSessionCollection...** (2), as shown in the following screenshot:

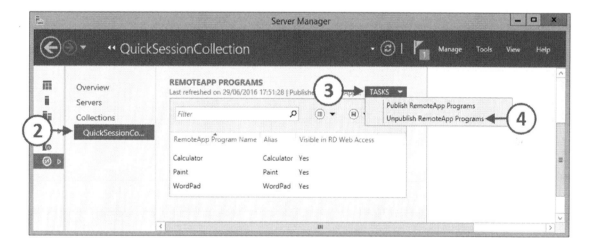

3. Scroll down to the **RemoteApp Programs** box, and then click on the **Tasks** box (**3**). Then from the menu options, click on **Unpublish RemoteApp Programs** (**4**).

You will now see the **Select RemoteApp programs** dialog box, as shown in the following screenshot:

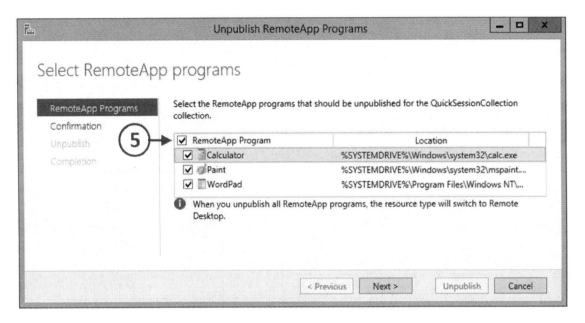

4. Tick the box for **RemoteApp Program** (**5**), to select all the currently published RemoteApps.

5. Now click the **Next >** button. You will now see the **Confirmation** screen, as shown in the following screenshot:

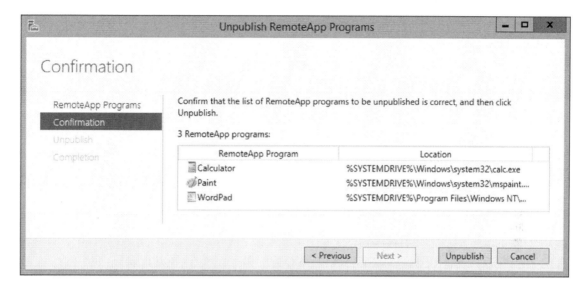

6. Click the **Unpublish** button to unpublish the selected RemoteApps.

You will now see the **Completion** screen, as shown in the following screenshot:

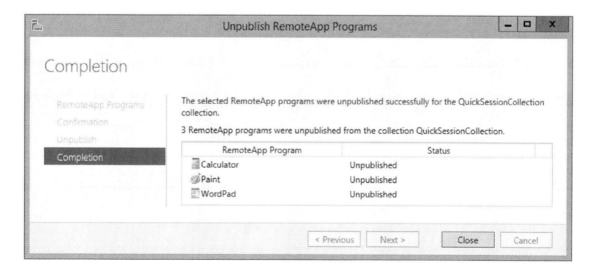

Now, that you have unpublished the applications that were configured as part of the default installation process, you can now move on and add collections for the desktop sessions, as well as installing and configuring the license server role.

The license server installation was covered in the previous chapter, so refer back to that chapter for installation and configuration details.

In the example lab, we are going to skip the collection configuration and use the default settings, and continue the configuration of the RDSH host with the installation of the Horizon Agent.

Installing the Horizon View Agent for RDSH

In the next part of the process, we are going to install the Horizon View Agent onto the RDSH server. The agent is exactly the same agent as the one that you would install on the virtual desktop machines.

Browse to the shared software folder and navigate to the agent installation application as shown in the following screenshot:

The file you are looking for is `VMware-viewagent-x86_64-7.0.0-3618085`. The seven-digit number at the end of the filename refers to the build version and so you may have a different number depending on the build version you are using, as shown in the following screenshot:

Name	Date modified	Type	Size
VMware-personamanagement-x86_64-7.0.0-3633490	10/04/2016 16:13	Application	17,214 KB
VMware-ThinApp-Enterprise-5.2.1-3655846	10/04/2016 16:18	Application	17,656 KB
VMware-viewagent-x86_64-7.0.0-3618085	10/04/2016 16:13	Application	161,006 KB
VMware-viewcomposer-7.0.0-3613429	10/04/2016 16:14	Application	32,355 KB
VMware-viewconnectionserver-x86_64-7.0.0-3633490	11/04/2016 13:53	Application	182,370 KB
Horizon-v7.01	28/06/2016 15:04	Compressed (zipped)...	363,949 KB
VMware-Horizon-Extras-Bundle-4.0.0-3616726	10/04/2016 16:14	Compressed (zipped)...	2,739 KB
VMware-UEM-9.0	29/06/2016 20:13	Compressed (zipped)...	28,819 KB
VMware-horizonagent-linux-x86_64-7.0.0-3617131.tar.gz	10/04/2016 16:15	GZ File	76,580 KB

1. Double-click to launch the View Agent installer.

2. You will now see the **Welcome to the Installation Wizard for VMware Horizon View Agent** dialog box, as shown in the following screenshot:

3. Click the **Next >** button to start the installation.
4. You will now see the License Agreement dialog box.

5. Click the radio button for **I accept the terms in the license agreement,** as shown in the following screenshot:

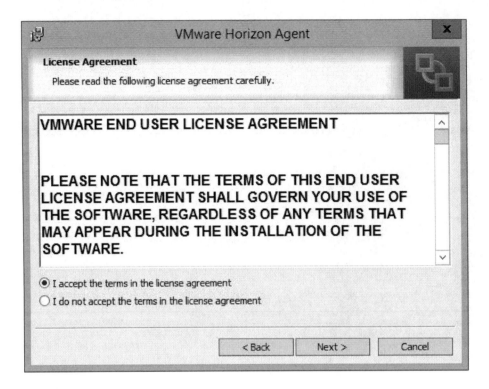

6. Click the **Next >** button to continue the installation.

   You will now see the **Network protocol configuration** dialog box, as shown in the following screenshot:

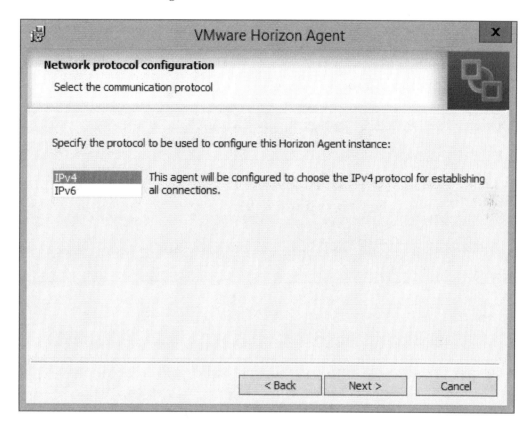

7. Click on **IPv4** and then click the **Next >** button to continue the installation.

8. You will now see the **Custom Setup** dialog, which allows you to select which components and features of the View Agent you want to install.

This is shown in the following screenshot:

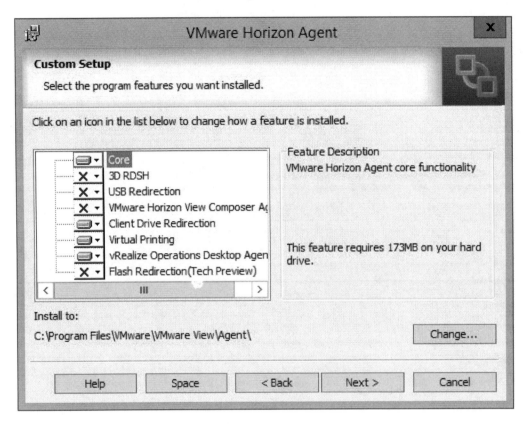

9. In the example lab, we are going to accept the default options, however, you can choose to install the **3D RDSH**, **USB Redirection**, **View Composer**, and **Flash Redirection** options should you want to.

10. As you can see, there are a number of features that can be installed as part of the View Agent installation. These are listed as follows:

- **Core**: Installs the core features required for RDSH.
- **3D RDSH**: Enables 3D acceleration in RDSH sessions.
- **USB Redirection**: Redirects USB devices from the client to the RDSH session
- **VMware Horizon View Composer Agent**: This allows RDS host servers to be built from a single parent image using the linked clone technology to easily deploy an RDS server farm
- **Client Redirection**: Allows clients to share local drives with the RDS sessions (not supported when using IPv6)
- **Virtual Printing**: Allows printing from RDS sessions
- **vRealize Operations Desktop Agent**: Allows the management agent to be deployed for monitoring RDS sessions with vRealize
- **Flash Redirection (Tech Preview)**: enables the Flash redirection feature with RDS sessions (note that this is currently a tech preview in this version of Horizon View)

11. Click the **Next >** button to continue the installation.

12. In the next dialog box, the **Register with Horizon 7 Connection Server** configuration screen, we are going to configure the agent to talk to the Connection Server. This allows the Connection Server to read the published applications list from the RemoteApp catalog and allow you to create pools within View.

13. In the **hostname or IP address** box (**1**), enter the name of the connection server. In the example, we are using the Connection Server called **hzn7-cs1**. In the **Authentication** section, click the radio button for **Specify administrator credentials** (**2**), and then in the **Username** box (**3**) enter the user account you want to use to connect to the Connection Server, followed by the password in the **Password** box (**4**), as shown in the following screenshot:

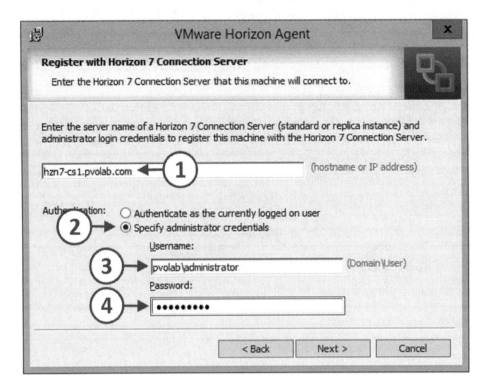

 Make sure you use the format **domain\user** to enter the username, and also that the account has the correct privileges to access the Connection Server. You would typically use a service account for this.

14. Click the **Next >** button to continue the installation.

15. You will now see the **Ready to Install the Program** screen. Click the **Install** button to start the installation process.

16. Once successfully installed, you will see the **Installer Complete** screen. Click **Finish** to quit the installation.

 One of the most common reasons that the installation of the View Agent fails is down to the configuration of the RDSH server. More often than not, there are no sound drivers loaded on the Windows Server running the RDSH role. If this is the case, then the installation of the agent will fail and automatically roll back. If that happens, it's worth checking this first.

17. You will now be prompted to reboot the server once installation has completed. Click the **Yes** button in the dialog box to reboot.

We have now completed the first part of the Horizon View configuration. In the next step of the process, we will turn our attention to the View Administrator and configure the desktop pools for session-based desktops.

Configuring View to deliver desktop sessions

With the configuration of the RDSH server completed, the next stage in the installation and configuration process is performed from within the View Administrator console and, like a standard View, setup involves creating pools and entitlements.

Before you do that, you first need to set up a farm that contains the newly-built RDSH Desktop session server.

Creating a farm for desktop sessions

To create a farm for desktop sessions, perform the following steps:

1. Open a browser and connect to the View Administrator. In the example lab, the address for the View Administrator is
`https://hzn7-cs1.pvolab.com/admin/`.

2. Log in to the View Administrator using the administrator account and password, as shown in the following screenshot:

3. You will now see the View Administrator Dashboard.

   From here, expand the arrow for **Resources** from the **Inventory** pane on the left, and then click on **Farms (1)**. Now click the **Add...** button **(2)**, as shown in the following screenshot:

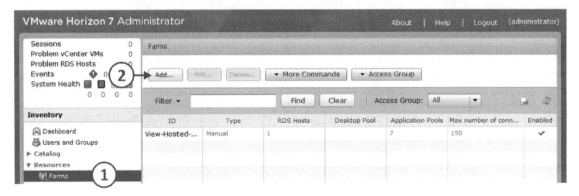

4. You will now see the **Add Farm** configuration screen.

5. In the **Type** section, click the radio button for **Manual Farm** (3), as shown in the following screenshot:

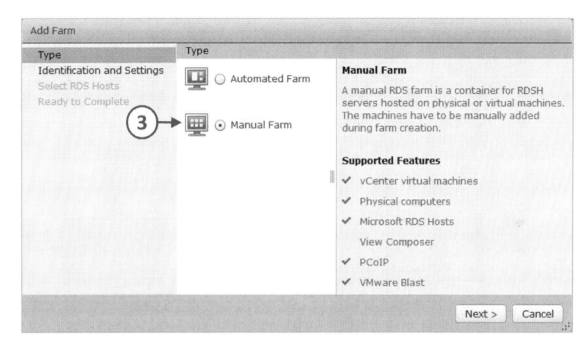

6. Click the **Next >** button to continue the configuration.
7. You will now see the **Indentation and Settings** configuration screen.
8. In the **ID** box (4), enter an ID for the farm that will be used by View to identify it. In the example lab, this is called **RDSH-Desktop-Sessions**.

> You cannot use spaces for the ID, only letters (upper and lower case), numbers (0-9), and – (minus) or _ (underscore) characters.

9. In the **Description** box (5), enter an optional description for the farm and then from the **Access Group** drop-down menu, select an access group if you have one.
10. Next, under **Farm Settings**, set the **Default display protocol** to **PCoIP** (6) and from the **Allow users to choose protocol** drop-down menu (7), select **No**.
11. In the **Empty session timeout** (8), enter a time after which the session should time out when not being used, and then in the **When timeout occurs** box (9), from the drop-down menu, select what happens at the timeout. In the example lab, this is set to disconnect the user from the session.

12. The next option is whether or not to **Log off disconnected sessions (10)**. This option will log off any disconnected sessions. In the example lab, this is set to **Never** happen.

13. Finally, tick the **Enabled** box **(11)** to allow HTML access to hosted applications, as shown in the following screenshot:

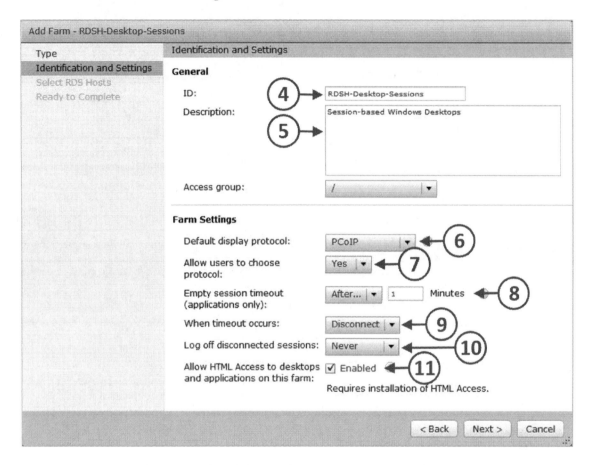

14. Once you have completed the configuration options on this screen, click the **Next > button to continue.

15. You will now see the **Select RDS Hosts** configuration screen from where you select which hosts are going to participate in this farm.

16. Click and highlight the **rdsh-desktops.pvolab.com** entry from the table, as shown in the following screenshot:

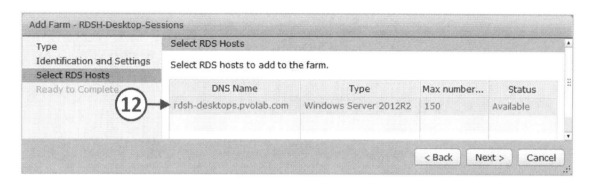

17. Click the **Next >** button to continue to the **Ready to Complete** screen, as shown in the following screenshot:

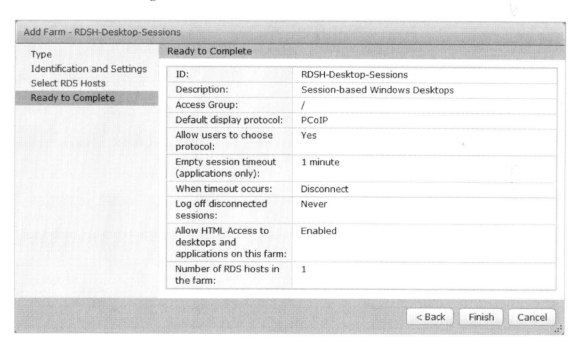

18. Check that the settings you have entered are correct, and click the **Finish** button.

19. You have now successfully created a new farm configuration for the desktop sessions (13), as shown in the following screenshot:

20. You will also see **RDS Farm** listed in the **System Health** box on the View Administrator Dashboard. You will see the farm name and server name listed in the box, along with a green box to show they are working correctly as shown in the following:

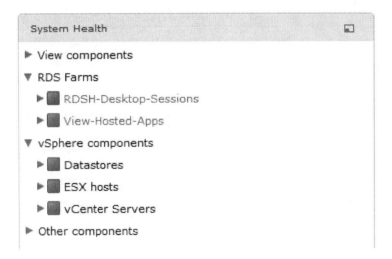

In the next section, we are going to create a desktop pool.

Creating a desktop pool for session-based desktops

In this section, we are going to create a desktop pool. This allows you to create a pool that contains the hosted desktop sessions. You may want to create different pools using different farms to reflect different departments, desktop requirements, for example.

1. From the View Administrator, expand the arrow for **Catalog** from the **Inventory** pane on the left, and then click on **Desktop Pools** (**1**).
2. Now click the **Add...** button (**2**), as shown in the following screenshot:

3. You will now see the Add Desktop Pool configuration screen, and the first option to select is to define the type of pool you want to create.
4. Click on the radio button for **RDS Desktop Pool**(**3**), as shown in the following screenshot:

5. Click the **Next >** button to continue to the next configuration screen.

6. You will now see the **Desktop Pool Identification** screen, as shown in the following screenshot:

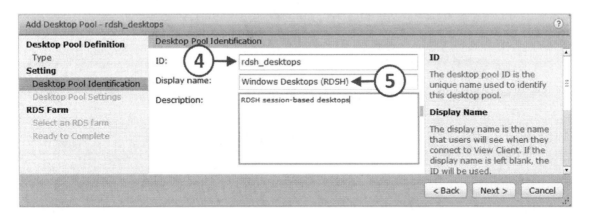

7. In the **ID** box (**4**), enter an ID for the pool. In the example lab, we are going to call it the **rdsh_desktops** pool.

 As with the Farm ID, you cannot use spaces for the ID, only letters (upper and lower case), numbers (0-9), and – (minus) or _ (underscore) characters.

8. In the **Display name** box (5), enter a name that will be displayed to the end users.

9. Click the **Next >** button to continue the configuration.

10. You will now see the Desktop Pool Settings screen.

11. In the **State** box (**6**), from the drop-down menu, select **Enabled** to enable this pool.

12. Next, configure the **Adobe Flash Settings for Sessions** section. On the **Adobe Flash Quality** drop-down (**7**), select **Do not control**. The other options available are:

   • **Do not control**: It allows the web page to determine the best setting
   • **Low (default):** Low quality means less bandwidth consumption
   • **Medium**: Medium quality means average bandwidth consumption
   • **High**: High quality means more bandwidth consumption

13. Then, from the Adobe Flash throttling drop-down menu (8), select Disabled. The other options available are:

- **Disabled**: Throttling is turned off
- **Conservative**: Update interval set to 100 milliseconds
- **Moderate**: Update interval set to 500 milliseconds
- **Aggressive**: Update interval set to 2500 milliseconds

Adobe Flash updates the screen by default using a timer service to determine the update interval. By changing this time interval setting, you can control the frame rate of the screen updates and, therefore, reduce the bandwidth requirements.

These settings are shown in the following screenshot:

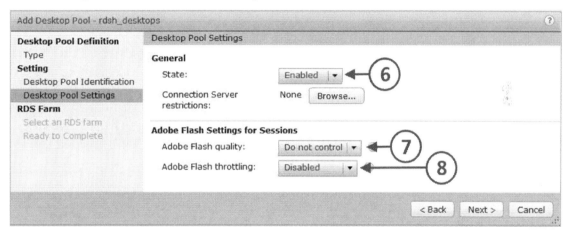

14. Click the **Next >** button to continue the configuration. You will now see the **Select an RDS farm** configuration screen, as shown in the following screenshot:

15. Click on the radio button for **Select an RDS farm for this desktop pool** (9), and then from the farms that are listed, select the Farm ID for the farm that will resource the desktop sessions. In the example lab, this is the **RDSH-Desktop-Sessions** farm (**10**).

16. Click the **Next >** button to continue the configuration.

17. You will now see the **Ready to Complete** screen as shown in the following screenshot:

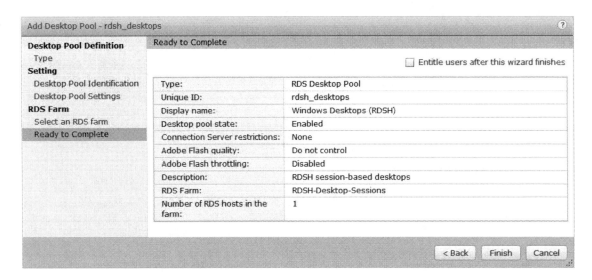

18. Check that the settings you have entered are correct, and click the **Finish** button.

You have now successfully created a new farm configuration for the desktop sessions as shown in the following screenshot:

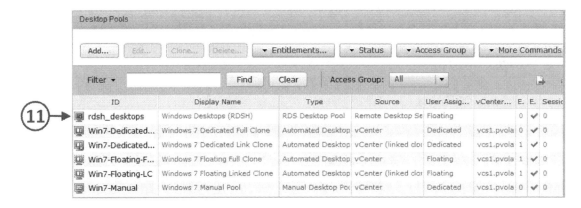

In the next section, we are going to entitle an end user to the desktop pool which will then enable them to connect to a hosted desktop session.

Entitling users to desktop sessions

Now we have created the desktop pool for the desktop sessions, next we are going to entitle a user to be able to access desktop sessions:

1. To do this, from the View Administrator **Dashboard** screen, click on **Users and Groups** (**1**) under the **Inventory** section on the left-hand side.

2. Then click the **Entitlements** button (**2**), and from the displayed options, click the **Add Desktop Entitlement** option (**3**) as shown in the following screenshot:

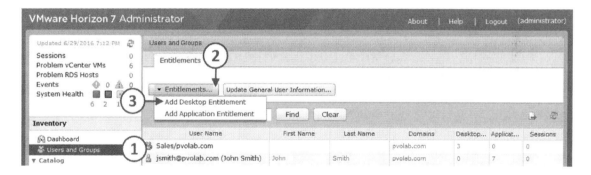

3. You will now see the **Find User or Group** configuration screen.

4. Tick the **Users** box (**4**), and then from the **Domain** drop-down menu, select the domain for the user you want to entitle. In our example, we are going to use the **pvolab.com** domain.

5. In the **Name/User name** box (**5**), enter the user details you want to entitle. In the example, we are going to entitle the user called `powens`, so type this into the box and click **Find** (**6**) to search for the user in the domain.

6. When the user is found, their details will be displayed in the table. Select the user by clicking on the entry in the table to highlight them, as shown in the following screenshot:

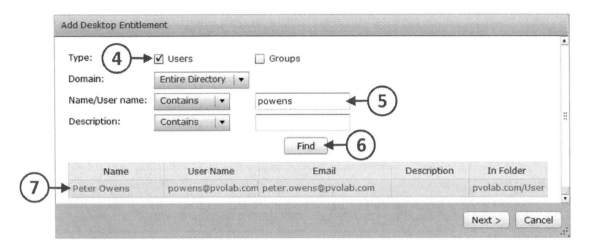

7. Now click the **Next >** button to continue the configuration.
8. You will now see the **Select the Desktop pools to entitle** configuration screen, as shown in the following screenshot:

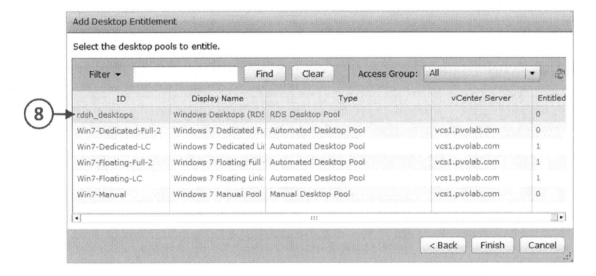

9. Click on the desktop pool that you want to entitle the user to by highlighting it (8). In this example, we are entitling the end user to the **rdsh_desktops** pool.

10. Once you have selected the desktop pool, click the **Finish** button to complete the configuration. You will now return to the **Users and Groups** screen showing the entitlements, as shown in the following screenshot:

11. You can see that the user **powens** has been entitled to one desktop.

12. Now that you have your desktop pool set up, and a user entitlement configured, the next step is to test that the user can log in and access a desktop session.

13. To do this, we are going to launch the Horizon View Client, log in as the test user, and then launch a desktop session, so now launch the VMware Horizon Client making sure that you have the address of the Connection Server added.

> We will cover the Horizon View Client options in the next chapter, `Chapter 10`, *Horizon View Client Options*.

14. In the example lab, we are connecting to the **hzn7-cs1.pvolab.com** Connection Server, as shown in the following screenshot:

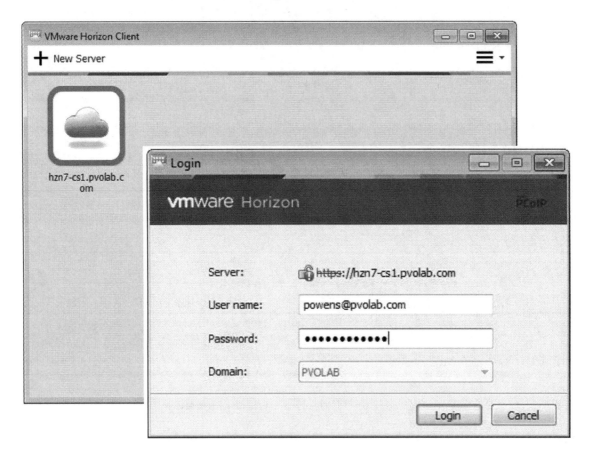

15. Double-click on the **hzn7-cs1.pvolab.com** entry in the VMware Horizon Client. You will then see the user login box.
16. Enter the **User name** and **Password** for the example user jsmith, and then click the **Login** button.

Once authenticated, the Horizon Client will connect to the Connection Server and display the pools that the user is entitled to, as shown in the following screenshot:

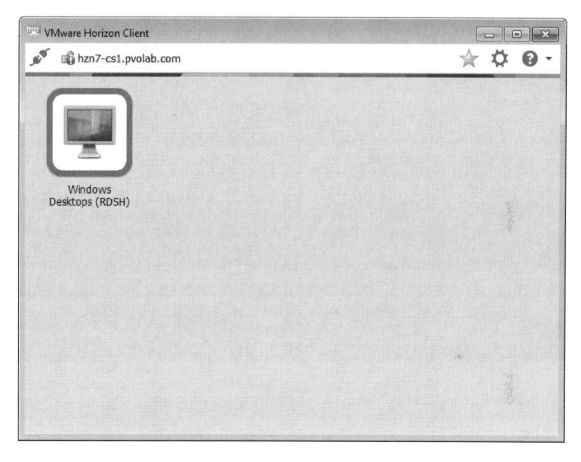

In this example, you can see that the **Windows Desktops (RDSH)** pool is available to the end user.

17. To test that the user can connect to a session, double-click on the icon for **Windows Desktops (RDSH)**. You will then see a desktop session launch, as shown in the following screenshot:

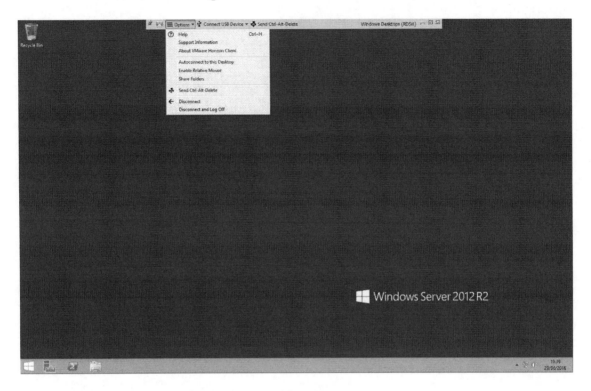

You have now successfully delivered a remote desktop session to an end user from an RDSH server, brokered using Horizon View.

As you will have just seen, the desktop session that you were connected to looks and feels like Windows Server 2012, basically because that's exactly what it is! There are some additional configuration tasks that you can perform to make it look more like a Windows desktop rather than a server. We will cover a couple of these in the next section.

Enhancing the end-user experience

In Windows Server 2012, there are some configuration steps you can take to make the desktop GUI look and behave more like a Windows desktop environment, which is much better for the end-user experience and stops them having access to server-based tools.

We are only going to cover a couple of the basics as examples, as configuring Windows Servers is out of scope for this book, and given that there are so many options when it comes to configuring things such as policies, that could end up being a whole book in its own right.

Configuring the Desktop Experience feature

The first thing we can configure is to add the **Desktop Experience** feature to the Windows Server hosting the remote desktop sessions.

To do this, perform the following steps:

1. Open a console to the RDSH Desktops server in the example lab, and launch the Server Manager. From the **Server Manager Dashboard,** click on **Add roles and features (1),** as shown in the following screenshot:

2. You will now see, **Add Role and Features Wizard**.
3. On the **Before you begin** screen, click the **Next >** button to continue.
4. You will now see the **Installation Type** screen. Click on the radio button for **Role-based or feature-based installation**, and then click the **Next >** button to continue.

5. On the **Server Selection** screen, click on the radio button for **Select a server from the server pool**, and then click on the server you want to add this feature too. In the example lab, this is the **rdsh-desktops.pvolab.com** server.

6. Click the **Next >** button to continue to the **Server Roles** screen, and click the **Next >** button to continue.

7. You will now see the **Features** screen. Scroll down to **User Interface and Infrastructure (2 of 3 installed)** section (**2**), and then tick the box for **Desktop Experience** (**3**), as shown in the following screenshot:

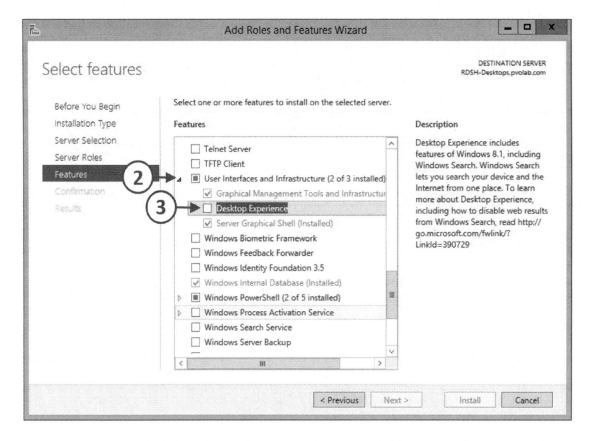

8. As you tick the box for **Desktop Experience**, the **Add Roles and Features Wizard** that is required for **Desktop Experience** will pop up, as shown in the following screenshot:

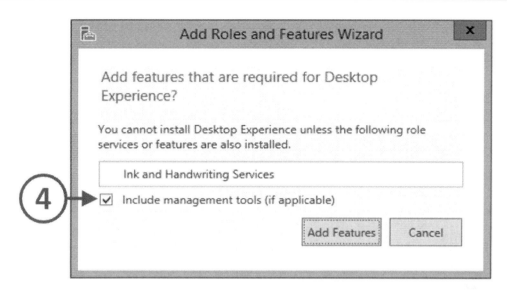

9. Check the box for **Include management tools (4)**, and then click the **Add Features** button.

10. You will now return to the **Features** screen. Click the **Next >** button to continue to the **Confirmation** screen, as shown in the following screenshot:

11. Check the box for **Restart the destination server automatically if required (5)**, and then click the **Install** button.

12. Once the installation has successfully completed, you will see the **Results** screen, as shown in the following screenshot:

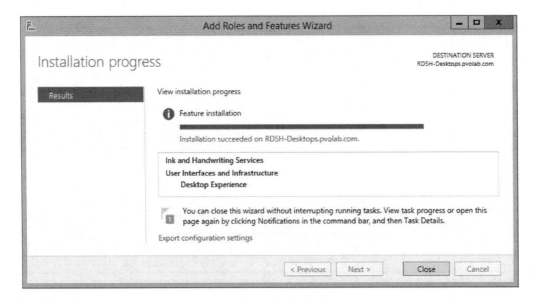

13. Click the **Close** button to complete the installation and close the wizard.

You have now installed the **Desktop Experience** feature. Restart the server to invoke this feature. When the server reboots, you should be able to configure the appearance of the desktop interface, by adding background themes and so on.

The final thing we are going to cover is how to turn off the **Server Manager**.

Configuring the Server Manager

As we are using a server to host a desktop session, you want to prevent the **Server Manager** from launching on an end user's desktop session.

1. To do this, launch the **Server Manager** on the RDSH Desktops server. Then, from the menu in the top-right of the screen, click on **Manage (1)**, and then from the drop-down menu, click the **Server Manager Properties** option **(2)**, as shown in the following screenshot:

2. You will then see the Server Manager Properties dialog box as shown in the following screenshot:

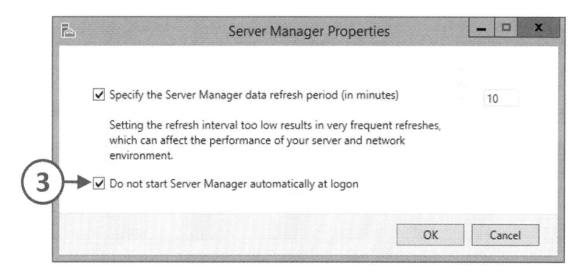

3. Click the box for **Do not start Server Manager automatically at logon** (3), click the **OK** button, and then close the Server Manager.

Summary

In this chapter, we have configured the RDSH server role in preparation for delivering a session-based desktop to the end users in your environment.

Once we built and configured the RDSH role, we then went on to configure the View Administrator and created a farm for the desktop sessions, as well as creating a desktop pool. The next step was to entitle an end user to be able to log in and connect to a desktop session.

Finally, we touched upon a couple of things to start you off on configuring the RDSH session to look and feel more like a desktop operating system, rather than a server operating system.

In the next chapter, we will take a closer look at the different View Client options.

10
Horizon View Client Options

In this chapter, we will discuss the options for how end users connect to their virtual desktops and hosted applications using the various **View Client** options available, both hardware and software options. View Client is how the end user interacts with their virtual desktops and hosted applications. Its main job is to receive and display virtual desktops and applications on the end users' devices, and send the keystrokes and mouse movements back to the virtual desktop and applications.

We will discuss each of the various different client options available and why you would choose one over the other based on the use case. So, let's start by looking at the software-based client options.

Software clients

To get the best user experience, a user connects to their virtual desktop machine from their client device using a piece of software called *Horizon View Client*. Horizon View Client is a piece of software that is installed on the local client device and allows users to communicate with the View connection server, allowing them to authenticate, select a desktop or application from a desktop pool they are entitled to, and then establish the connection between the client and the virtual desktop machine.

In the more recent versions of Horizon, the software client has been unbundled from the major View releases, which means that the client downloads are updated more often and without having to wait for the next release of View. This reflects the fast pace at which new devices come to the market.

There are a number of different platform versions available, depending on the choice of the endpoint device. In this section, we are going to give you a high-level overview of each of the available versions, along with any specific requirements.

You can download Horizon View clients by visiting the following link: `http://www.vmware`
`.com/go/viewclients`.

Horizon Client for Windows

The Horizon View client for Linux allows you to access your Windows virtual desktops and View-hosted applications from a Windows-based device and delivers the best possible user experience over either a LAN or a WAN connection.

The following screenshot shows Horizon Client for Windows connecting to the example lab. Here you can see that there are three virtual desktop pools available, along with a number of hosted and published applications:

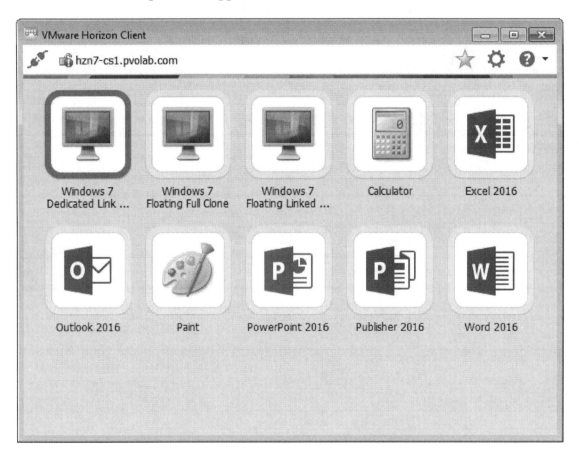

With the latest client and the latest versions of View, USB 3.0 redirection is supported from the guest to the VDI desktop, among other improvements in performance, printing, and ease of use. Some of these new features are listed as follows:

- **Full support of Flash Redirection**: Flash content in an IE browser is sent directly to the Windows-based endpoint device, running Horizon Agent 7.0 or later, and played in a Flash container window. Refer to `Online Chapter`, *Fine Tuning the End-User Experience* available at `https://www.packtpub.com/sites/default/files/downloads/5657_FineTuningtheEndUserExperience.pdf`, on how to configure the policy for this feature.
- **Automatic upgrade**: The Horizon client can be upgraded through the user interface.
- **Client device authentication**: The device that Horizon Client runs on can be authenticated.
- **Support for login as current user in a nested environment**: In a nested environment (Horizon Client running on a Horizon desktop and accessing another Horizon application or desktop), users can log in as the current user.

The latest Horizon client, version 4.1, requires the following Windows operating systems:

- 32-bit or 64-bit Windows 10, Home, Pro, Enterprise, or **Internet of Things (IoT)** Enterprise
- 32-bit or 64-bit Windows 8, 8.1, or 8.1 Pro, Enterprise, or Industry Embedded
- 32-bit or 64-bit Windows 7 SP1, Home, Enterprise, Ultimate, or Professional edition
- Windows 2012 Server SP2

The Horizon client is supported with the latest releases of Horizon View 5.3.x, VMware Horizon 6.0.x, VMware Horizon 6 version 6.1.x or 6.2.x, and VMware Horizon 7.

The Horizon View client requires SSL for connections to the View connection server. Therefore, you must enter a fully qualified domain name for the View connection server, rather than just its IP address, in the View Server field of the Horizon View client.

In the following section, we will take a look at the Android client.

VMware Horizon Client for Android

The Horizon View client for Android-based devices, like the Windows client, allows you to access your Windows virtual desktops and hosted applications from an Android tablet or smartphone device.

The client software can be downloaded as an app from the Google Play Store.

In the following screenshot, you can see an example of the Horizon client for Android. Here you can see that the user is entitled to two virtual desktop machines, two RDS-hosted desktop sessions, as well as a number of View-hosted applications.

The Horizon View client supports native Android gestures for quick and easy navigation around the desktop. When working on a Windows desktop, the full-screen touchpad feature lets you touch anywhere on the screen to move the mouse pointer around the Windows virtual desktop.

The Unity Touch sidebar makes it easy to browse, search, open, and close Windows applications and files, as well as switch between running applications, all without using the Windows Start menu or taskbar.

In the following example screenshot, you can see Microsoft PowerPoint and Adobe Reader running as View-hosted applications alongside the Unity Touch feature being used, allowing you to easily run applications from the slide-in menu on the left:

The latest Horizon client, version 4.1, requires the following Android versions:

- Android 4 (Ice Cream Sandwich)
- Android 4.1, 4.2, and 4.3 (Jelly Bean)
- Android 4.4 (KitKat)
- Android 5 (Lollipop)
- Android 6 (Marshmallow)

For more information on Horizon View Client for Android, visit the following link: `http://tinyurl.com/jmxyo7a`.

In the following section, we will look at the iOS client.

VMware Horizon Client for iOS

The Horizon client for iOS allows you to access your Windows virtual desktop from an iOS-based device such as an iPhone or iPad.

With the latest version of the client (version 4.1), there are a number of new features, listed as follows:

- **iOS 9.3 support**: Supports devices running iOS 9.3.
- **IPv6 DNS64/NAT64 network support**: Supports iPv6 when installing on a device running iOS 9.2 or later.
- **Linux remote desktop support**: Log in to a Linux remote desktop from Horizon Client for iOS.
- **Enhanced Horizon Client user interface for in-session settings**: In-session settings user interface is redesigned to enhance the user experience.
- **Network recovery for VMware Blast sessions**: If you lose network connection during a VMware Blast session, the client will attempt to reconnect to the network. The network recovery feature also supports IP roaming, allowing you to resume your VMware Blast session even when switching to a Wi-Fi network.

In the following screenshot, you can see three screens taken from the iOS Horizon Client:

On the first screen, you can see the login to the Horizon connection servers, the second screen shows the entitled desktop pools available to the end user, and the final screen shows the end user connected to a Windows desktop. You can also see on-screen the input options menu open, allowing us to change settings and change the mouse mode, as well as display the keyboard and more.

The Horizon View client for the iPad and iPhone supports native iPad and iPhone gestures for quick and easy navigation around your desktop. As with the Android client, when working on a Windows desktop, the full-screen touchpad feature lets you touch anywhere on the screen to move the mouse pointer around the Windows virtual desktop.

The Unity Touch sidebar makes it easy to browse, search, open, and close Windows applications and files, and switch between running applications, all without using the Windows Start menu or taskbar. Unity Touch (iOS 5 or later), supports full-screen mode, iOS dictation, better language, localization support, and an enhanced presentation mode, that allows you to use an external monitor or AirPlay in order to show your View desktop while your iPad or iPhone turns into a keyboard and touchpad.

The Horizon View client for iOS requires iOS 8.4.1 or later, including iOS 9.x, and supports the following devices:

- iPhone 4, 4S, 5, 5s, 5c, 6, 6 Plus, 6s, 6s Plus, and SE
- iPad 2, iPad (third generation), iPad (forth generation), iPad mini, iPad mini 3, iPad mini 4, iPad mini with Retina display, iPad Air, iPad Air 2, and iPad Pro

The Horizon View client for iOS is supported with VMware View 5.3.x or later, and can be downloaded from either the VMware client download page or from the Apple store.

For more information on Horizon View Client for iOS, visit the following link: `http://tiny url.com/jewt5vh`.

In the following section, we will look at the Linux client.

Horizon View Client for Linux

The Horizon View client for Windows allows you to access your Windows virtual desktops and View-hosted applications from a Windows-based device and delivers the best possible user experience over either a LAN or a WAN connection. It supports the following features:

- Support for Windows Media MMR
- H.264 support for Intel-based Linux devices
- GUI for USB redirection
- Clipboard size is configurable up to a maximum of 16 MB
- OpenSSL 1.0.2h support

Horizon Client for Linux 4.1 is supported on the following operating systems when you use the VMware provided installer:

- Ubuntu 12.04 and 14.04 (32-bit and 64-bit)
- Red Hat Enterprise Linux 6.7 (32-bit and 64-bit)
- Red Hat Enterprise Linux 7.2 (64-bit)
- SUSE Linux Enterprise Desktop (SLED) 11 SP4 (32-bit)
- CentOS 6.7 (32-bit)

In terms of the supported Horizon View versions, the Horizon client for Linux is supported with the latest maintenance release of Horizon View 5.3.x, VMware Horizon 6.0.x, VMware Horizon 6 version 6.1.x, VMware Horizon 6 version 6.2.x, and Horizon 7 version 7.0.x. The following screenshot show, an example of the Linux client:

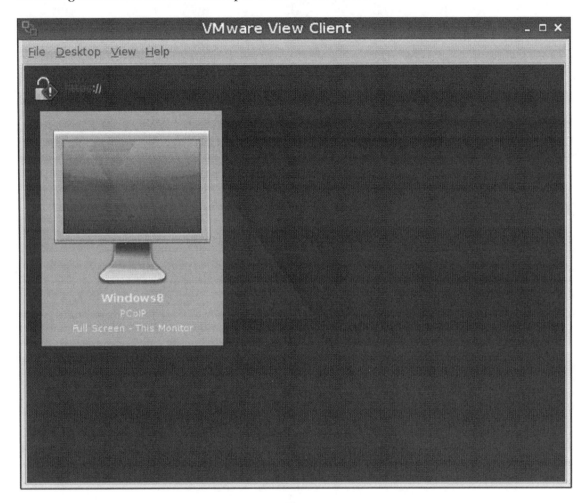

For more information on the Horizon View client for Linux, visit the following link: http://tinyurl.com/hthvogd.

In the following section, we will look at the Mac OS X client.

Horizon View Client for Mac OS X

The Horizon View Client for Mac OS X allows you to access your Windows virtual desktop machines and View-hosted applications from an Apple Mac.

With the latest version of the Mac OS X client (version 4.1) there are a number of new features, listed as follows:

- **Mouse shortcut mappings**: Allows you to configure a single-button Apple mouse to send a right-click and middle-click to virtual desktops and applications.
- **Language-specific key mappings**: Allows you to select or deselect the **Enable Language Specific Key Mappings** checkbox when configuring keyboard shortcut mappings to configure language-specific key mappings.
- **Configurable clipboard memory size for cut-and-paste operations**: Allows you to configure the client clipboard memory size for cut-and-paste operations between the client endpoint device, and the virtual desktops and hosted applications. With Horizon 7 version 7.0.1 and later, you can use GPOs to configure the server clipboard memory size. This policy setting was covered in `Online Chapter`, *Fine Tuning the End-User Experience* available at `https://www.pa cktpub.com/sites/default/files/downloads/5657_FineTuningtheEndUserEx perience.pdf`.
- **Network recovery for VMware Blast sessions**: If you lose network connection during a VMware Blast session, the client will attempt to reconnect to the network. The network recovery feature also supports IP roaming, allowing you to resume your VMware Blast session even when switching to a Wi-Fi network.

- **Remember this password checkbox:** Selecting the **Remember this password** checkbox when you log in will save your credentials if this feature is enabled by the desktop admins. When selected, your credentials are added to the login fields in the Horizon Client on subsequent connections.

As well as the preceding list of latest features, the Mac OS X client also supports the features listed in the following screenshot:

Client Feature	OS X Client Support
RSA SecurID	☑
Single sign-on	☑
PCoIP display protocol	☑
VMware Blast display protocol	☑
RDP display protocol	☑
USB redirection	☑
Client drive redirection	☑
Real-Time Audio-Video (RTAV)	☑
Virtual printing	☑
Location-based printing	☑
Smart cards	☑
Multiple monitors	☑

An example of the Mac OS X client is shown in the following screenshot:

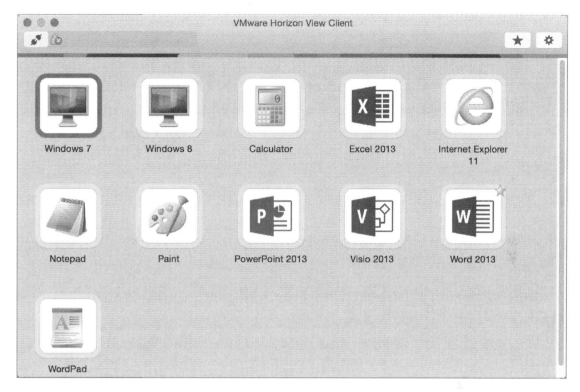

In terms of support, the latest 4.1 release of the Mac OS X client supports the following operating systems:

- Mac OS X Mavericks (10.9)
- Mac OS X Yosemite (10.10)
- Mac OS X El Capitan (10.11)

When it comes to the supported Horizon View versions, the Horizon client for Mac OS X is supported with the latest maintenance release of Horizon View 5.3.x and later, and can be downloaded from the Apple store or the VMware client download page.

For more information on the Horizon View Client for Mac OS X, visit the following link: `http://tinyurl.com/h2zob47`.

In the following section, we will look at the Chrome OS client.

Horizon View Client for Chrome OS

The Horizon View client for Chrome OS allows you to access your Windows virtual desktop machines and View-hosted applications from a device running the Chrome OS, such as a Chromebook.

To run the Horizon client for Chrome OS, you will need a Chromebook with Chrome OS, stable channel, and ARC version 41.4410.244.13 or later.

When it comes to the supported Horizon View versions, the Horizon client for Chrome OS is supported with the latest maintenance release of Horizon View 5.3.x and later, and can be downloaded from the Google Play Store or the VMware client download page.

For more information on the Horizon View client for Chrome OS, visit the following link: `http://tinyurl.com/hpfqdzy`.

Now that we have looked at the software client options that are available, in the following section, we will look at some of the hardware-based options.

Hardware clients

One of the things we hear a lot from speaking with customers is that the endpoint device is irrelevant when connecting to a virtual desktop machine, as, "It's just a dumb device to access the infrastructure and display my desktop screen, so that means I can buy the cheapest device possible and that will be fine, right?"

The correct answer is that it depends on the use case for the users and what their requirements around features and functionality are. Then, you can choose the most suitable endpoint device for them to connect from.

The other confusion that seems to be out there is what the difference between a thin client and a Zero client is, and whether there is actually a difference at all.

In this section, we are going to cover the different types of hardware clients available, explaining what each one is and the use case for which one is best to choose.

Thin clients

A **thin client** is a hardware endpoint device that's used to connect to the network and deliver a remote desktop and application session. Unlike a typical PC or **fat client** that has the memory, storage, and computing power to run applications on its own, a thin client relies on the computing power of the servers running in the data center to do all the processing.

Typically, a client device will have just enough processing power and resources to access and use the computing resources of the server. They have little or no storage (just enough to host their own internal OS), and more importantly, no moving parts, which means they don't go wrong very often. Due to the reduced CPU and memory capacity, a thin client will draw a fraction of the power that a PC would normally need, meaning that thin clients should be cheaper to run and manage, as well as have longer life cycles.

One thing they do have in common with a PC is an operating system. A thin client will have its own local operating system installed, typically embedded on a flash card, and would be running the vendor's own cut-down version of Linux distribution such as Dell Wyse ThinOS or Microsoft Windows Embedded. In addition, it would be running the appropriate client software to connect to the appropriate virtual desktop infrastructure, such as a Horizon client with PCoIP to connect to VMware View-based virtual desktops and hosted apps, and the Citrix receiver to connect to a Citrix-based infrastructure, and so on. Usually, a thin client will have all the connection options installed, giving you the choice and flexibility to connect to different infrastructures.

Now, this is where you need to make the right choice of device, as the operating system will be embedded on the device. As mentioned previously, the use case for the user will typically dictate the type of device. For example, if you are going to deploy unified communications with Microsoft Skype for Business, then you will need a Windows Embedded operating system, as it will more than likely require some of the Windows multimedia functionality. Always check before going off and buying the cheapest device.

There are also a couple of other points to bear in mind with thin clients. If the device is running on a local operating system, this will still need to be managed and maintained. The other consideration is around licensing and the fact that you will need a Windows VDA license if you are connecting from a non-Windows device. This needs to be taken into account when looking at cost models and looking at TCO and ROI.

Zero clients

A **zero client** performs the same functionality as a thin client; however, instead of an operating system, a Zero client will have a highly tuned on-board processor specifically designed for one of the VDI protocols (PCoIP, HDX, or RemoteFX). For example, the VMware View-based zero clients would use the on-board Tera2 hardware chipset such as a Dell Wyse 5030/7030, or a 10ZiG V1200-P. These devices are still small, light, have no moving parts, and consume minimal power, just like a thin client.

Most of the decoding and display processes take place on dedicated hardware and are therefore more efficient and deliver better performance than using a software client and a standard CPU and GPU setup as with a thin client.

Zero clients have boot up speeds of just a few seconds and are immune to viruses, decreasing the overall downtime of the device and increasing the productivity to the end user. The Zero client device requires very little maintenance and rarely needs an update unless there is a significant change or enhancement to the VDI protocol or the occasional BIOS-related update.

There are a couple of things to watch out for. First is the licensing: as these devices are not running an operating system, you need to look at VDA licensing for using a non-Windows device. The final thing is that if you change your VDI infrastructure from PCoIP to a new protocol, then the device is not able to be used with a different protocol, so you lose the flexibility that you get with a thin client. However, you will get much better performance.

Repurposed PCs (thick clients)

It is also possible to repurpose existing physical PCs to be used as **thick clients**. There are a number of ways to achieve this, but you must ensure it is simple for the user to use and does not confuse the usage between a virtual desktop machine and the physical desktop machine that is sitting in front of them.

The two most popular ways of creating a thick client would be, first, to use local policy or Group Policy to lock down the Windows PC and to change the shell to the Horizon client only, and, second, to use third-party software such as Devon IT's VDI Blaster technology; this allows a simple thin client operating system to be deployed and configured on the users' machines.

Don't forget, if you opt for the first option and keep Windows installed on the thick client, you still may need to consider anti-virus software and security policies—more so than you would with a cut-down and restricted Linux-based thin client operating system.

HTML5 browser desktop access

In the previous sections, we have talked about either using a software-based or hardware-based client to access our virtual desktop from, but there is also a third method, which is to use an HTML5-enabled browser on any device. The key use case for using this method is when installing client software on an endpoint device is not possible. For example, you might have a bring-your-own-device policy, where end users don't want to install client software, or you might want to use a public-facing endpoint in a hotel lobby, for example, where the device is locked down and you cannot install the client software.

This is where this use case comes in, allowing you to access your virtual desktop machine using an HTML5-enabled web browser, which also requires no additional plugins or software to be downloaded and installed. The HTML desktop access is what is referred to as the VMware Blast protocol.

To connect to your virtual desktop machine or View-hosted application using the browser, open the browser, and in the address bar, type the address of your connection server.

In the example lab, the address is `https://hzn7-cs1.pvolab.com`.

Before you access your virtual desktop machine, you will first see a web page that displays two different options. You have the choice of downloading the full version of the Horizon client, or you can continue and connect via HTML.

This is shown in the following screenshot:

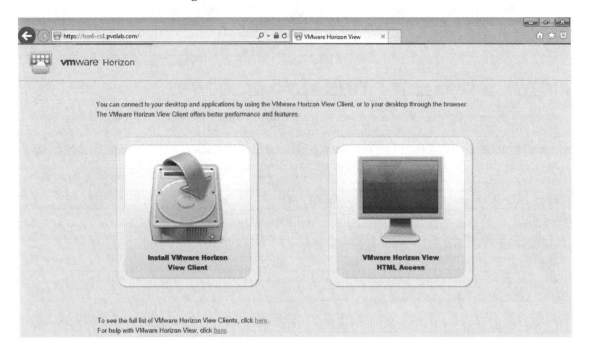

This web page is configurable, allowing you to personalize it to your own specific environment. You can configure the following options:

- Hide the HTML Access icon
- Hide the View Client icon
- Change the URL of the web page for downloading the View client
- Create links for specific View Client installers
- Configure other links on the page

In this example, we are going to use the HTML access method, so you would click on the **VMware Horizon View HTML Access** button. You will then be prompted to log in using the credentials you would normally use for logging in to the network. This is shown in the following screenshot:

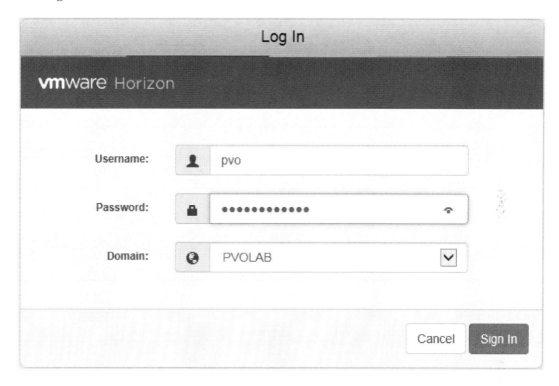

Enter your login credentials and click the **Sign In** button.

In this example, the end user has been entitled to a **Windows 8.1 Desktop** pool, as shown in the following screenshot:

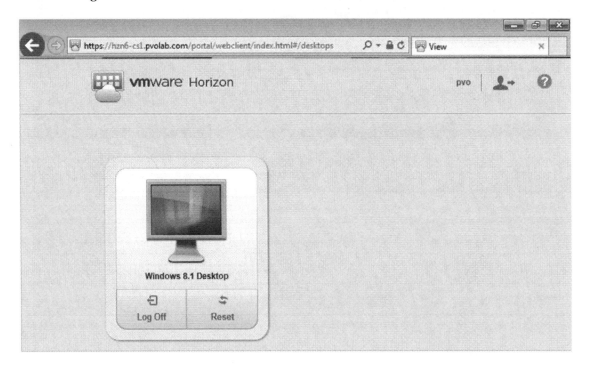

If you click on the **Windows 8.1 Desktop** option, you will now see another browser tab open. In this tab, you will see that your virtual desktop machine is being displayed in the browser, as shown in the following screenshot:

To use the HTML access feature, you need to run a supported browser. The browsers currently supported are as follows:

- Chrome 50, 51
- Internet Explorer 11
- Safari 8 and 9
- Mobile Safari on iOS devices running iOS 8 or iOS 9
- Firefox 45 and 46
- Microsoft Edge 20 and 25

You also need to make sure that you have enabled the desktop pool for HTML access, as well as having the remote experience agent installed on the virtual desktop.

For more information on the Horizon View HTML access feature, visit the following link: h ttp://tinyurl.com/z55j8o4.

We have now explored the various different options for how an end user connects to their virtual desktops and View-hosted applications.

Summary

In this chapter, we have taken a closer look at the available options for connecting to a virtual desktop machine or View-hosted application from an endpoint device.

We discussed software-based clients, hardware-based clients, and the HTML access feature, looking at the pros and cons of each type of access method and why you might choose one over the other.

In the following chapter, we will discuss how to upgrade from a previous version of Horizon View to the latest version.

11

Upgrading to a New Version of Horizon View

In this chapter, we are going to cover the upgrade process and recommendations for upgrading your VMware View environment to the latest version, and in this example, we will upgrade from Horizon 6 to Horizon 7. We will start by discussing the elements that need to be considered before undertaking the upgrade, how we undertake the upgrade to ensure there is minimum disruption to our users and finally the step-by-step process of completing the upgrade.

Upgrade compatibility

Before undertaking any upgrades, you should start off by reading the release notes and the upgrade guide for Horizon View. With a number of interdependent components, not only do you need to check the compatibility between the different versions of these components, but also ensure that you undertake the upgrade in the correct order, to minimize the risk of failure and disruption to our users.

In this section, we are going to look at the compatibility, starting with which versions you are able to upgrade to Horizon 7. The following list shows the different versions:

- Latest maintenance release of Horizon View 5.3
- Latest maintenance release of VMware Horizon 6.0 (with View)
- Latest maintenance release of VMware Horizon 6 version 6.1
- Latest maintenance release of VMware Horizon 6 version 6.2

You also need to check the compatibility between the different View components and whether Horizon 7 works with earlier versions of these components. By components, we mean the connection server, the security server, and so on.

The following screenshot shows the version compatibility:

Horizon 7 Component	Earlier Versions of				
	Connection Server	Security Server	View Composer	View Agent	Horizon Client
Connection Server	Only during upgrade	Pair before upgrade	☒	Only during upgrade	☑
Security Server	☒	N/A	☒	Only during upgrade	☑
View Composer	Only during upgrade	Only during upgrade	N/A	Only during upgrade	N/A
Horizon Agent	Only during upgrade	☒	☒	N/A	Only during upgrade
Horizon Client 4.0	☑	☑	☑	☑	N/A

As such, the process by which the upgrade needs to take place is as follows:

1. View Composer upgrade
2. View connection server upgrade
3. View security server upgrade
4. Upgrading Group Policies
5. Upgrading vCenter (if required)
6. Upgrading ESXi Hosts and Virtual Machine Hardware/Tools (if required)
7. Upgrading View agents
8. Recomposing desktop pools

You will also need to think about the impact of any upgrade that may need to be undertaken on your end users. For example, you wouldn't want to upgrade a View Connection Server in the middle of a working day, with potentially 2,000 users connected to it. You would normally schedule any upgrades to take place out of hours, or at least ensure that each View connection server is removed from the load balancer the night before the planned upgrade.

You could also decide to build new View Connection Servers with the latest Horizon version rather than upgrading the existing connection servers, and then simply point the users at the new servers and remove the old connection servers, once completed.

Upgrading View Composer

In the first part of the process, we are going to upgrade the View Composer server.

Before you begin the upgrade

There are a couple pf prerequisites you need to have completed before starting the upgrade of View Composer. You need to perform the following steps prior to commencing with the upgrade:

1. Check the prerequisites with the VMware Horizon View installation guide to ensure all components to be upgraded meet the minimum requirements for resources, operating system, and applicable database versions.
2. If your View Composer server is installed on a virtual machine, snapshot the virtual machine before starting.
3. Backup your vCenter and View Composer databases.
4. Backup the folder containing the SSL certificates on your View Composer server. Certificates can be found in the following folder:
   `%ALLUSERSPROFILE%\Application Data\VMware\VMware VirtualCenter.`
5. Document the IP address and hostname of your vCenter server.
6. Ensure the user names and passwords are documented for the accounts used to access your composer database.

With the prerequisite tasks completed, the next step is to disable provisioning:

1. Log in to View Administrator, expand the **Catalog** option and click on **Desktop Pools** (1). Then click and highlight the desktop pool you want to disable (2), right-click, and from the contextual menu, select **Disable Provisioning…** (3), as shown in the following screenshot:

You will see the following message:

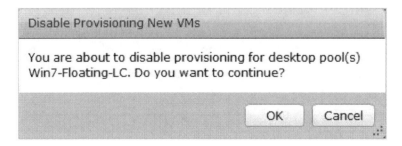

2. Click the **OK** button to disable provisioning.

3. You will need to disable provisioning for all desktop pools that are going to be affected by the View Composer upgrade. This prevents any new desktops from being provisioned.

4. Next, you need to modify any desktop pools that are set to refresh on logoff, to ensure they are set to never refresh. From the **Catalog** option, click on **Desktop Pools** (4), and then click and highlight the desktop pool you want to edit (5), right-click, and from the contextual menu, select **Edit...** (6), as shown in the following screenshot:

You will now see the **Edit Win7-Floating-LC** dialog box, as shown in the following screenshot:

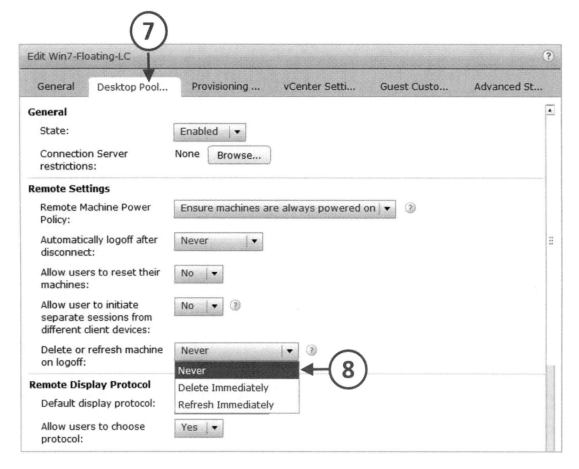

5. Click the **Desktop Pool...** tab (7), and then, in the **Delete or refresh machine on logoff** section, from the drop-down menu, select the option **Never** (8).

6. Click the **OK** button to save the changes and close the dialog box.

Completing the View Composer upgrade

Once you have completed all the prerequisites and have planned the upgrades so as to have a minimal effect on your end users, you are able to start the upgrade.

The next stage is to install the new version of the View Composer software.

We are not going to cover this, as it's exactly the same process as we covered in Chapter 4, *Installing and Configuring Horizon View*, and the *View Composer installation process* section, with the slight difference that the old version gets uninstalled first. Follow the instructions in that section, remembering that you have already set up the database details, so all you need to do is enter the DSN details when requested.

Verifying the upgrade

Now that the upgrade has completed, the next stage is to check that everything is back up and running:

1. First, from the View Composer server, launch the **Services** console by opening a **Run** dialog box and typing services.msc. On the **Services** screen, scroll down and check that the **VMware Horizon View Composer** service is running, as shown in the following screenshot:

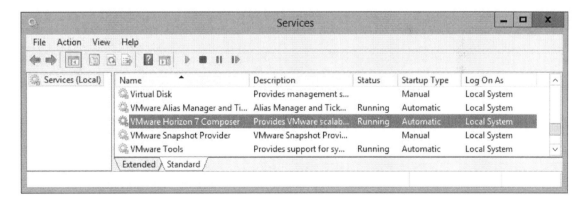

2. We are also going to run through the View Composer verification process. From View Administrator, click on **Servers** (**9**), as shown in the following screenshot:

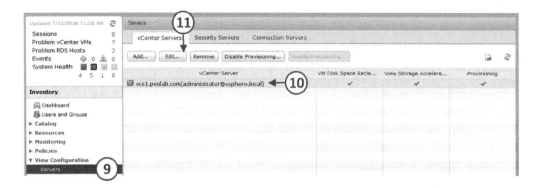

3. Highlight the relevant **vCenter Server** (**10**) and then click the **Edit...** button (**11**). You will now see the **Edit vCenter Server** dialog box, as shown in the following screenshot:

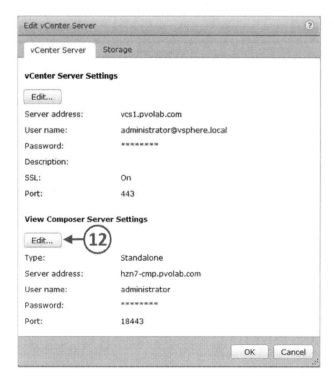

4. In the **View Composer Server Settings** section, click the **Edit...** button (**12**). You will now see the following screenshot:

5. Click the **Verify Server Information** button (**13**).

6. You will now see the **Domains** section populated, along with the desktop pool information, as shown in the following screenshot:

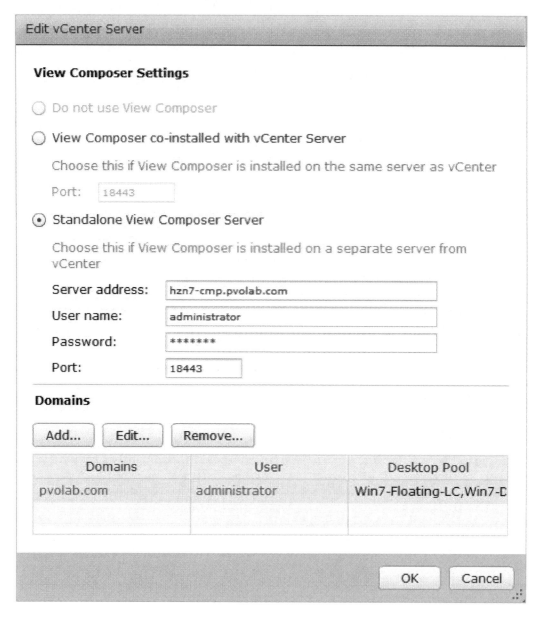

7. Click the **OK** button to close the dialog box.

You have now successfully completed the upgrade procedure for the View Composer server. Obviously, if you are using multiple Composer servers, you will need to repeat these steps on all your View Composer servers.

Upgrading the View Connection Server

You are now in a position to upgrade all the View connection servers within your infrastructure.

Before you begin the upgrade

There are a couple of prerequisites you need to have completed before starting the upgrade of the View connection server:

1. Check the prerequisites with the VMware Horizon View installation guide to ensure all components to be upgraded meet the minimum requirements for resources, operating system, and so on.
2. If your View connection server is installed on a virtual machine, snapshot the virtual machine. Please note, if you need to recover this snapshot, you will first need to uninstall any replicated connection servers before reverting the master to the snapshot.
3. Ensure your documentation is up to date, including pool configuration, global configuration settings, IP addresses, batch files, SQL credentials for the event database, and load balancer configuration.
4. Use the vdmexport.exe command line utility to back up the existing configuration help within the LDAP database. From the command line, run the following command:

   ```
   vdmexport > {backup location\filename.ldf}
   ```

Completing the Connection Server upgrade

Once you have completed all the prerequisites and have planned the upgrades so as to have a minimal effect on your end users, you are able to start the upgrade.

The next stage is to install the new version of the View connection server software.

We are not going to cover this, as it's exactly the same process as we covered in `Chapter 4,` *Installing and Configuring Horizon View,* in the *View Connection Server installation process* section, with the slight difference that the old version gets uninstalled first. Follow the instructions in that section to install the connection server software.

Once the installation has finished and the server has rebooted, you should be able to see that the upgrade has completed successfully by accessing View Administrator, as shown in the following screenshot:

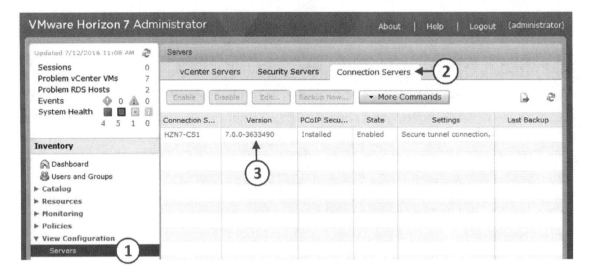

Click on **Servers** (**1**) and then click the **Connection Servers** tab (**2**). You can then check the version number for the associated connection server (**3**).

You have now successfully completed the upgrade procedure for the View Connection Server. Obviously, if you are using multiple connection servers, you will need to repeat these steps on all your View connection servers.

Alternative View Connection Server upgrade method

There may be a situation where you decide to upgrade View Connection Servers by adding new Horizon 7 connection servers to your existing Horizon connection servers, and then remove the old connection servers from the configuration when you are ready to do so. We aren't going to cover the procedure for the installation of the new replica View connection servers here, as this is extensively covered in `Chapter 4`, *Installing and Configuring Horizon View*, but it is important to understand how to remove the old View connection servers correctly, by performing the following steps:

Once you have installed the new version of the connection server and are ready to remove your first old-version connection server, you will need to ensure that the View Connection Server to be removed has been removed from any load balancers and is no longer in use by the users, that is, nobody is connected to it.

You will then need to uninstall the **AD LDS Instance VMwareVDMS(1)** and then the **VMware Horizon Connection Server** (2) from the View connection server you want to remove, as shown in the following screenshot:

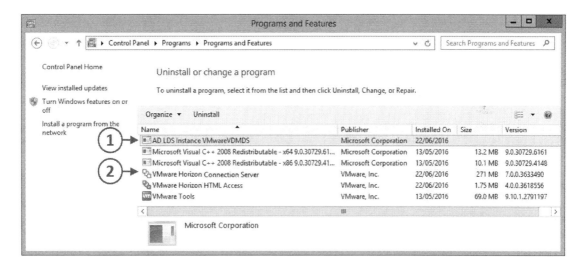

Once completed, you will need to connect to all of your remaining connection servers, open a command line, and run the following command:

```
"C:\Program Files\VMware\VMware View\Server\tools\bin\vdmadmin.exe" -S -r -
s server_name
```

This removes this connection server from the other connection servers. You will then get confirmation of the scheduled removal of the server from the configuration, and the server will no longer be displayed on the View Administrator screen.

Upgrading the View Security Server

The next step in upgrading your Horizon View environment is to upgrade the security servers that are used for the external users to connect to their desktops. Keep in mind, this won't be added to your domain, so you will need to log in using local credentials.

Before you begin the upgrade

There are a couple of prerequisites you need to have completed before starting the upgrade of the View security server.

By default, since View 5.3, traffic between the security server and connection server is governed by IPSEC rules. When you complete an upgrade of a View security server, these rules will need to be recreated, and if the existing rules still exist, this will fail.

As such, VMware has built-in functionality to clear the IPSEC rules prior to the upgrade being started. To do this, from the View Administrator screen, click on **Servers** (1) and then the **Security Servers** tab (2). Now highlight the security server, click on **More Commands** (3), and then select the **Prepare for Upgrade or Reinstallation...** option (4), as shown in the following screenshot:

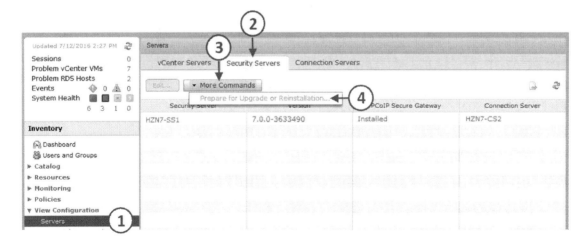

Once you have completed this action, the security server is no longer able to communicate with the connection server, so ensure this is only completed as part of planned maintenance to the security server, to avoid disruption, as external users may now be unable to log in and connect to a virtual desktop machine.

Completing the View Security Server upgrade

Once you have completed all the prerequisites and have planned the upgrades so as to have the minimal effect on your end users, you are able to start the upgrade.

Before you actually install the new version of the security server, you first need to set the pairing password. To do this, from the View Administrator console, select **Servers** (**1**), and then click on the **Connection Servers** tab (**2**). Select your View connection server, and then click on the **More Commands** button (**3**). Select the option for **Specify Security Server Pairing Password…** (**4**), as shown in the following screenshot:

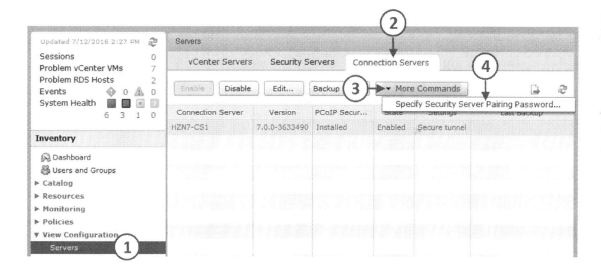

You will now see the **Specify Security Server Pairing Password** dialog box, as shown in the following screenshot:

Enter your chosen password, and then confirm it. If you need to extend the time to live for the password, enter a new time. Click the **OK** button.

The next stage is to install the new version of the View security server software.

We are not going to cover this, as it's exactly the same process as we covered in Chapter 4, *Installing and Configuring Horizon View*, in the *View Security Server installation process* section, with the slight difference that the old version gets uninstalled first. Follow the instructions in that section to install the security server software.

Once the installation has completed and the server has rebooted, you should be able to see that the upgrade has completed successfully by logging into the View Administrator console, navigating to the **Servers** section, and then clicking on the **Security Servers** tab, and checking the version number for the security server you just upgraded.

Upgrading Group Policy templates

As part of new Horizon versions, there will be a number of new features, some of which will be controlled via group policy. Therefore, you will need to upgrade the Group Policy administrative templates to the latest version when upgrading to a new version of Horizon View. This is easily achieved through the Group Policy Object Editor on your domain controllers.

We are not going to cover the process on how to do this, as it has been extensively covered in `Online Chapter`, *Fine Tuning the End-User Experience* available at `https://www.packtpub` `.com/sites/default/files/downloads/5657_FineTuningtheEndUserExperience.pdf`.

 One thing to be aware of is that any policy changes can affect the end users, and some policies may have been deprecated and other new ones added. It's worth creating a new GPO for any new versions so that you can roll back to the previous one if the users start to report any issues.

In the following section, we are going to look at upgrading the Horizon agent.

Upgrading the VMware Horizon agent

Upgrading the Horizon agent is probably one of the simplest tasks of the upgrade process. You are going to need to upgrade the agents in all of your golden images and then recompose the desktop pools.

With non-persistent desktops, this is a relatively simple task of upgrading the agent, taking a new snapshot, and recomposing all the pools. With persistent desktops, you may need to take further consideration into the effect of recomposing the pool, or alternatively, look at manually upgrading the agent on each virtual desktop machine, or deploying an applications deployment tool.

You also need to consider that the Horizon agent may be installed on an RDSH host server used for delivering desktop sessions and View-hosted applications. For this, you will need to schedule the time where you can take host machines out of the farm in order to perform the upgrade.

We are not going to go through the Horizon Agent installation process, as this has been covered previously in `Chapter 6`, *Building and Optimizing the Virtual Desktop OS*.

Upgrading the Horizon client

There is no built-in method to upgrade Horizon clients automatically, and you also need to bear in mind that Horizon clients are on a different release cycle to the main Horizon infrastructure solution.

If you are running thin clients as end-user devices for your users, the upgrade procedure is usually easily managed with the management software that comes with the thin clients.

If you are using re-provisioned PCs, or maybe laptops, to connect to the Horizon View environment, you are going to need to either manually update the client, direct your users to do so, or use a third-party software deployment tool to complete the upgrade.

Summary

In this chapter, we have covered the process of upgrading your VMware View environment to a newer version, walking through what you need to do for each of the individual infrastructure components. The actual upgrade process itself is relatively easy, but you must take the time to check and complete the prerequisites first.

You also need to keep in mind the importance of planning the update to minimize the effect on your end users.

12
Troubleshooting Tips

As you have learned throughout this book, a successful VDI or end-user computing project is made up of multiple components, and its success comes down to delivering a good user experience and not just simply whether it is working or not. As such, it is important to have a well-defined methodology and the tools to be able to adequately diagnose and fix issues within your environment. In this chapter, we are going to cover some of the troubleshooting techniques and other methods for monitoring the end-user experience within Horizon View.

General troubleshooting tips

In this first section, we are going to briefly look at some of the more general things to look at around the end users, and then the supporting infrastructure components, such as a disk, networking, and connectivity.

Looking at the bigger picture

The common issue when introducing any VDI technology is that it can quickly become the point of blame when an issue occurs within your environment. You need to remember that the Horizon View technology is just one component of the overall infrastructure, along with the desktop that the user is utilizing. Just because the desktop is sitting within a VDI environment doesn't always mean it's a View issue. It could well be a desktop, network, or application issue that would have occurred in a physical environment too.

When a user reports an issue, or you notice an issue within the infrastructure, you will need to think logically as to which component within the infrastructure is the likely cause and where you will start your troubleshooting journey. Maybe it is a storage issue, or maybe it's a Windows issue and not anything to do with VDI at all!

Is the issue affecting more than one user?

A good place to start examining any issues within your environment is by understanding who is experiencing the issue and whether more than one user has reported the same issue. If you try and recreate the issue, do you get the same results? Can another user with the same permissions and the same resources recreate the issue?

If you find that the issue is really only related to a single user, then consider the type of issue they are having. The following lists some examples:

- What device are they connecting from?
- What connection are they connecting over, and have they tried with PCoIP, RDP, or Blast?
- Could it be a bandwidth or connection reliability issue?
- Could a port be blocked?
- Do they have a specific application or permission requirements?
- Are they entitled to the correct pools?

If you believe the issue relates to something to do with their desktop, then maybe consider refreshing it; this is the beauty of VDI, you could simply rebuild a new desktop and not spend hours trying to troubleshoot and fix application or OS issues if a simple refresh could resolve it.

If the issue is affecting more than one user, consider seeing if a fix could be applied to the base image and then rolled out to your desktop pools to simplify the process of resolving the issue.

Performance issues

This is probably one of the widest subject areas to look at when troubleshooting your View environment. Performance issues could relate to so many areas and aspects, and in some cases, could also be down to personal opinions.

User-reported performance issues

If your users are reporting poor performance, then ask them to try and be more specific, rather than just saying, "It's slow." Is it taking a long time to log in, or is it an application that is taking longer than expected to load? Keep a log of the issue, along with the time and date the issue occurred or whether it's an ongoing issue.

Ask the users the following when the issue occurs:

- How are they measuring the performance?
- At what time of day do they experience the problem?
- Are they doing something specific when they experience the problem?
- Are they connecting from somewhere specific or from a specific device when they have the issue?

Wherever possible, try to visit the end user and understand their issue first-hand. This will enable you to the get to the bottom of the issue with ease. Hopefully, as we discussed in Chapter 3, *Design and Deployment Considerations*, you will have engaged the end users early and they will be positive, on-board with the overall solution, and willing to help.

Non-VDI-related issues

Performance issues on a desktop can be caused by many factors, regardless of whether or not they are virtual or physical desktops. Common areas for consideration include the following:

- Extended logon times
- Application crashes
- Long application load times
- Operating system crashes
- Poor application performance
- Permission errors

As previously mentioned, many of these issues can and will occur whether the desktop is virtualized or not, but in the virtualized environment, they may be easier to resolve. For example, if you find you are getting OS or application crashes, consider patching these elements to the latest updates and recomposing the image for all users. This could take a lot longer and be a lot more difficult with a physical desktop estate.

Maybe login times or application load times are suffering due to a CPU performance issue; with physical desktops, you would be stuck with the hardware unless you replace or upgrade the constrained components, but in a VDI environment, you can consider tweaking the spec at the push of a button, as long as you have the underlying resources.

The important point to understand is that generic desktop issues will still exist regardless, so use the VDI platform to your advantage to help resolve these. We have worked with so many organizations that have deployed, that once the solution is implemented, they tend to forget about generic desktop support and spend far too much time digging deep into the VDI architecture infrastructure looking for faults when the answer may be a simple Windows OS or application issue.

Bandwidth, connectivity, and networking

Networking-related issues can often be the most difficult to get to the bottom of. Where possible, ensure that you work closely with your networking team to ensure there is suitable end-to-end monitoring in place.

While your users are connecting on a LAN, you would hope there would be plenty of bandwidths, and latency would be low enough, and therefore, connectivity would be reliable. If you are struggling on a LAN consider the following:

- Has anything on the network changed?
- Is the user connecting via a wired or wireless network?
- Have you configured PCoIP for QoS on your switches?
- Is the network currently reliable?
- Are you seeing any dropped packets between any of the following:
    - Clients to the core switching
    - Clients to servers
    - Clients to VDI desktops

- Is the latency as expected?
- Even on the LAN, in larger environments, bandwidth could be an issue; have you considered the sum of the bandwidth required for your client devices to VDI desktops?
- Are you routing between networks? Do the routers work at a suitable performance level?
- Are the load balancers sized correctly for your environment?

When your users are connecting over a WAN, it can sometimes be more difficult to troubleshoot or guarantee connection quality.

For remote or branch offices, ensure that the Internet connection is suitably sized, where possible, ensure that you have configured QoS for the PCoIP protocol end-to-end, and ensure that you have suitably configured the PCoIP policy to cope with the reduced bandwidth availability.

When troubleshooting issues, investigate the relevant logs on the client and on the View connection servers, as well as any intermediary components such as the load balancers and routers.

The following list contains some of the more common faults that a user will report:

- **Black Screens**: This is commonly caused by ports blocking the PCoIP protocol somewhere in the chain. Check that the PCoIP port is open, such as port 4172.
- **Disconnections**: High latency and dropped packets will cause the users to be disconnected from their desktops. Ensure that you allow enough time for users to reconnect before refreshing desktops.
- **Poor Resolution Images**: Due to the nature of the protocol, if there is low bandwidth, users may complain about low-quality images. Consider limiting the image build options in the user policy.

Compute

CPU and memory issues on your host servers can have a large knock-on effect on the experience for your users. As with most technical solutions, we would recommend that while you are going through your initial testing and roll out, you document your baseline for key performance characteristics, such CPU and memory utilization, and deeper metrics such as CPU ready times.

With these baselines in your toolkit, it makes it easier to compare when you have issues to find out what could be causing the problem. Likewise, using technology such as vRealize Operations for Horizon will help you understand performance utilization over time, or maybe a third-party product such as Liquidware Labs Stratusphere, which can provide both the baseline metrics (measured during the assessment phase) and the ongoing management of the entire user experience.

Within your VDI infrastructure, you don't want to be experiencing any memory overcommit; consider how much memory is allocated to your virtual desktops and the total memory within your hosts. Ideally, you want to ensure that your total allocated memory is less than the total in your hosts minus one host, in the case of failure or maintenance. If you are experiencing performance issues related to memory or CPU, check if memory is being swapped for any of the VMs. Is there any ballooning within the environment? Understand what your CPU Ready characteristics are. The acceptable CPU Ready figures within your VDI environment will vary based on the environment and users. Generally speaking, you are going to want to keep CPU Ready below 5% per allocated CPU, with 10% at peak.

It can be very easy when growing your VDI solution from the initial design to forget to sanity check these metrics and keep an eye on them as you grow, and all of a sudden you may find you have a compute performance-related issue.

Disk

As we have previously mentioned, the disk solution deployed is a key component for a successful VDI deployment. You need to be able to keep an eye on the disk performance, which is key to avoiding issues in the future.

In the example lab environment, we are using a *Tintri storage* array, which is ideal for deploying in a VDI environment. As well as providing the capacity and performance required, being *VM-aware* storage, it also allows you to review the performance statistics over time. Tools like this are invaluable to you to avoid performance issues, or when the worst does happen, to be able to quickly identify where the issue lies. Ensure you understand the tools that are available to you with your storage vendor.

How much latency is acceptable within your environment is going to very much depend on the users; also, consider what will happen as you scale up the solution. While we may say that disk latency of less than 25 ms is generally acceptable, it doesn't mean that a user that has been using a desktop with sub-25 ms latency would be happy or not even notice that all of a sudden they were experiencing 25ms latency or more. Likewise, if a user is completing disk-intensive processes, 25 ms may be simply be too much for the user to start with.

The following screenshot shows the Tintri management console and disk measuring operations:

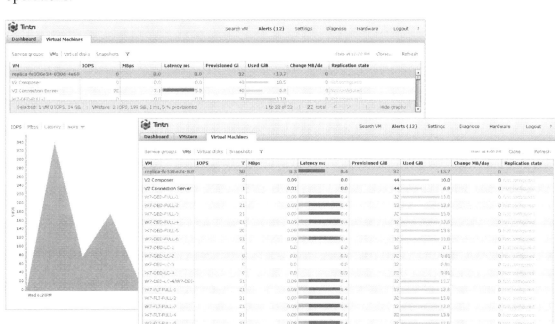

Having covered some of the more general troubleshooting tips around the infrastructure components, in the following section, we are going to look at Horizon View-specific issues.

Troubleshooting Horizon View issues

There are a number of components that we have discussed throughout this book, which makes up your Horizon View infrastructure, and while they are generally very reliable, they can, of course, fail at some point, with serious knock-on effects. Wherever possible, you should be ensuring that your solution is highly available, and where not possible, ensure that the components are sufficiently monitored, using components such as vRealize Operations for Horizon.

View general infrastructure issues

The first port of call when troubleshooting your Horizon View infrastructure should be the event log within the Horizon View Administrator console. You can quickly and easily access the event log by clicking alerts in the top left-hand corner of the screen:

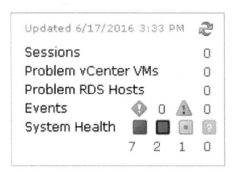

You should also utilize the dashboard view in View Administrator to get a quick overview of the health of your environment. This screen will show you the health of all the key components within your infrastructure, such as vCenter, hosts, View connection servers, View security servers, desktops, RDS hosts, datastores, and more.

This is a great resource to start troubleshooting infrastructure issues within your Horizon View environment.

Also, you should not forget the simplest of troubleshooting steps when experiencing issues with your Horizon View infrastructure, such as the following:

- Are all the servers, desktops, hosts, and so on contactable on the network?
- Are all the required services started?
- Is there sufficient free space on all servers?
- Are the memory and CPU maxed out?
- Have you checked all the events logs?

Consideration also needs to be given to the backend database systems and the effect that would be felt if they were to go offline. Ensure your SQL solution is reliant and the same as all other components if you are having issues with your vCenter or View Composer. Ensure you check the SQL server for the following:

- Sufficient resources
- Are the services started?
- Are the correct ports open?
- Is there enough free disk space for the database and logs?

View infrastructure component issues

Of course, there may be issues that arise, which are outside of those that we have discussed so far. Where Horizon View is very good in these situations is with error reporting, which quickly allows you to easily pinpoint the issue. Unfortunately, though, sometimes the corrective actions can be quite cumbersome and manual to implement.

Issues you may see that require specific corrective actions are as follows:

- Manual removal of a View connection server or security server after loss of a component or OS corruptions
- Manual removal of VDI desktops or whole pools
- Recovery of Horizon View from a backup
- Recovery of a persistent disk from a backup
- Persistent disks running out of space for users

We aren't going to cover all the specific corrective actions for all of these processes here, as we could write an entire book to do them justice, but there are some great knowledge-base articles already available on VMware's KB site at the following address: http://kb.vmware.com/.

One issue that we will cover briefly, and one that does come up fairly often, is with View Composer and inconsistencies in the database that lead to provisioning errors. VMware has a tool to address this called the **ViewDBChk** tool, which we will cover in the following section.

Fixing View Composer issues with the ViewDBChk tool

Provisioning errors can occur when there are inconsistencies between the LDAP, vCenter server, and View Composer databases, and are often caused by editing a virtual desktop machine directly in the vCenter server inventory, or restoring a virtual desktop machine from a backup.

The **ViewDBChk** tool allows View administrators to scan for machines that cannot be provisioned and also allows you to remove invalid database entries. This then allows the connection server to re-provision desktops without any errors.

You will find the ViewDBChk tool in the View folder that gets created at install time. The folder can be found by navigating to `C:\Program Files\VMware\VMware View\Server\Tools\bin`.

The tool is command-line driven and has a number of parameters for each of the functions you can perform. These are listed in the following screenshot:

Command Parameter	Output / Result
`--findDesktop`	Finds a desktop pool
`--enableDesktop`	Enables a desktop pool
`--disableDesktop`	Disables a desktop pool
`--findMachine`	Finds a machine
`--removeMachine`	Removes a machine from a desktop pool. Before removing a machine, ViewDbChk prompts the user to disable the desktop pool. After removing the machine, ViewDbChk prompts the user to re-enable the desktop pool.
`--scanMachines`	Searches for machines that are in an error or cloneerror state or have missing virtual machines, lists the problem machines grouped by desktop pool, and gives the option to remove the machines. Before removing a machine, ViewDbChk prompts the user to disable the desktop pool. After removing all erroneous machines in a desktop pool, ViewDbChk prompts the user to re-enable the desktop pool.
`--help`	Displays the syntax of ViewDbChk
`--desktopName desktop_name`	Specifies the desktop pool name
`--machineName machine_name`	Specifies the machine name
`--limit maximum_deletes`	Limits the number of machines that ViewDbChk can remove. The default is 1.
`--force`	Forces machine removal without user confirmation
`--noErrorCheck`	Forces the removal of machines that have no errors
`--verbose`	Enables verbose logging

For example, to run the command to remove a machine from a desktop pool, at the command prompt, type the following command:

```
ViewDbChk --removeMachine --desktopName
```

In the following section, we are going to look at some of the additional tools available for monitoring and managing the environment.

vRealize Operations for Horizon

vRealize Operations for Horizon is available as part of Horizon Enterprise or as a separate product. Where vRealize Operations differs from most monitoring tools is in its analytics engine. Most monitoring tools are based around setting thresholds for key values, such as CPU or memory consumed. The issue with these kinds of alarms is that by simply stumbling over a threshold value, it doesn't necessarily mean there is an issue. Sometimes, it is within the normal parameters of the applications in use, or potentially, the problem could be one of the resources not being consumed when it should be.

With the analytics engine included within vRealize Operations, it is able to learn and understand what the normal working parameters of your environment are; from this, it is then able to alert you when an error occurs that falls outside these parameters. It is also able to track growth and consumption over time to pre-empt an issue prior to it occurring.

vRealize Operations for Horizon should be installed, where possible, at the beginning of your project. vRealize Operations is deployed simply via a single virtual appliance or vApp, and when deployed and configured, it starts listening and learning about your environment.

There are three key metrics tracked with vRealize Operations; these are, Health, Risk, and Efficiency:

- **Health** reports on the current health status of your environment. Items that could affect health would be high packet loss, component failure, disk capacity at a critical level, and more.
- **Risk** indicates an issue within your environment, which, if left unintended, could very well become an issue to the health of your environment.

- **Efficiency** reports on considerations such as overprovision, which, if rectified, could help you get more out of your environment to maximize the investment. An example of this would be VMs with overprovisioned CPU or memory:

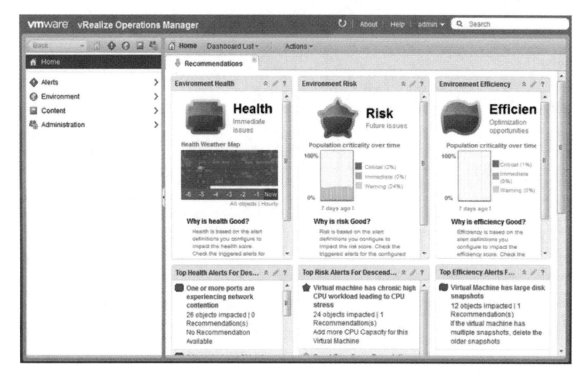

vRealize Operations for Horizon also includes specific features to ensure you fully understand the health of your Horizon View environment, including the full visibility of the PCoIP protocol, as well as integration for health monitoring with the View connection server, View Security, and more.

The analytics engine of vRealize Operations will learn about your environment and understand what is normal, raising alarms based on dynamic thresholds for your environment rather than meaningless static thresholds.

Within vRealize Operations, a smart alerts feature is also incorporated, which allows you to quickly understand the root cause of an issue within your infrastructure and the recommended remediation actions to resolve the issue.

Third-party management tools

As well as the VMware monitoring solutions, there are other solutions available. One that is worth mentioning is Liquidware Labs Stratusphere UX, as this is designed more with the end users in mind and monitors the entire end-user experience:

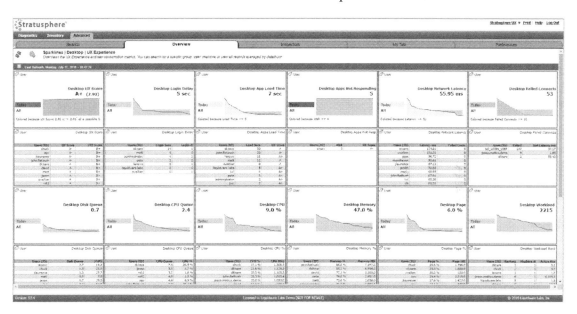

It also provides the assessment features that are essential in planning and designing an environment.

Getting further help

There are a number of resources available if you are struggling to get to the bottom of an issue with Horizon View. First and foremost, we would recommend logging a call as early as possible with VMware Support to get the best assistance possible to resolve your issue.

There are also a large amount of resources online, such as blogs. Google *VMware Planet V12N* for a list of VMware bloggers that may have suitable resources.

There is also the VMware Community, which has a wealth of resources available at `https:/ /communities.vmware.com`.

Finally, and possibly the most useful resource, is the VMware knowledge base, as we have mentioned previously in this chapter. At the time of writing this, there are 300 specific support topics related to Horizon View, including video how-to guides, alongside step-by-step resolution guides.

Summary

In this chapter, we have covered some of the methods and areas to consider when troubleshooting issues within your Horizon View environment. Consideration should be given to the bigger picture to ensure that you fully understand the issues the user is facing and which area of the user's desktop experience could be causing these issues. Where possible, use monitoring tools such as vRealize Operations for Horizon to find the root cause of the problem. There are a number of areas within Horizon View you should check if you believe you have infrastructure problems; these include the dashboard, and the event log, within Horizon View Administrator.

Finally, we covered getting further help from VMware Knowledge Base.

We have now reached the end of this book, and upon reaching this point, you should now have a greater understanding of the architecture of the Horizon suite and how to design your end-user computing solution. You should also understand the stages and details involved with rolling out Horizon View for your users, including installing the various components, and configuring, designing, and building the desktop images and pools. You will have learned about the various methods to layer your applications to your desktops using technology such as ThinApp, RDSH-published applications, and App Layers.

Designing and rolling out any end-user computing solution to any organization is a task that must be taken with care and understanding for the users, and we hope the elements that we have covered within this book will better equip you for the tasks ahead.

Index

Z

Made in the USA
San Bernardino, CA
15 February 2018